Now Playing

Roleplaying in Every TV Genre

Writing and Game Design
Bradford Younie

Proofing & Editing
Ralph Mack, Carol Pandolph, Joe Pandolph, Derek "Malcus" Belanger

Cover Art
Thomas Denmark

Art Concepts
Ralph Mack (Cover), Bradford Younie

Interior Art
Thomas Denmark, Ben Van Dyken, Cartography by Anna M. Dobritt, Ralph Mack

Playtesting
Derek "Malcus" Belanger, Carl Bobo, Peter Daigle, Ralph Mack, Thomas Martin, Scott Mazzaro, Mark McShane, Matthew Papajohn, Mike Pento, Michael Rhys, Bill Schreiber, John Sussenberger, Lisa Sussenberger, Matt Woodard.

Carnivore Games
PO Box 846
Londonderry, NH 03053-0846

Now Playing, some specific game terms, icons and personalities are copyright © 2003 Carnivore Games.

No part of this book may be reproduced without written permission from the publisher, except for review purposes. Any similarity to characters, situations, corporations, organizations, etc. is strictly fictional or coincidental. This book uses some adult settings, characters and themes, are fictional and intended for entertainment purposes.

Comments and questions can be submitted via the Internet at support@carnivoregames.com or via a letter with a self-addressed, stamped envelope.

For product updates and releases, visit the Carnivore Games web site at www.carnivoregames.com

First Printing. February 2004

Stock CAR1000

ISBN 0-9749150-0-9

Printed in Canada

About Fudge

Fudge is a role-playing game written by Steffan O'Sullivan, with extensive input from the Usenet community of rec.games.design. The basic rules of Fudge are available on the internet at http://www.fudgerpg.com and in book form from Grey Ghost Games, P.O. Box 838, Randolph, MA 02368. They may be used with any gaming genre. While an individual work derived from Fudge may specify certain attributes and skills, many more are possible with Fudge. Every Game Master using Fudge is encouraged to add or ignore any character traits. Anyone who wishes to distribute such material for free may do so; merely include this ABOUT FUDGE notice and disclaimer (complete with Fudge copyright notice). If you wish to charge a fee for such material, other than as an article in a magazine or other periodical, you must first obtain a royalty-free license from the author of Fudge, Steffan O'Sullivan, P.O. Box 465, Plymouth, NH 03264.

Disclaimer

The following materials based on Fudge, entitled *Now Playing*, are created by, made available by, and Copyright (C) 2003 by Carnivore Games, and are not necessarily endorsed in any way by Steffan O'Sullivan or any publisher of other Fudge materials. Neither Steffan O'Sullivan nor any publisher of other Fudge materials is in any way responsible for the content of these materials unless specifically credited. Original Fudge materials Copyright (C)1992-1995 by Steffan O'Sullivan, All Rights Reserved.

Table of Contents

Chapter One: Introduction — 1
- This is Roleplaying — 2
- This is Now Playing — 2
- What is Roleplaying? — 4
- How Roleplaying Works — 4
- Roleplaying TV — 6

Casting

Chapter Two: Creating Characters — 13
- Creating A Star — 14
- Character Traits — 16
- Scale — 20
- Powers — 22
- Non-Human Species — 22
- Advancing Characters — 24

Chapter Three: Skills — 25
- Skill Descriptions — 28

Chapter Four: Gifts & Faults — 45
- Gifts — 46
- Gift Descriptions — 47
- Fault Descriptions — 52

Chapter Five: Props — 63
- Standard of Living — 64
- Weapons — 67
- Explosives — 73
- Armor — 75
- Vehicles — 76
- The Zoo — 81

Acting

Chapter Six: Filming — 89
- Performing Tasks — 90
- The Use of Luck — 92
- Combat — 94
- Healing — 103
- Vehicles — 104
- Magic — 106
- Converting Systems — 108

Chapter Seven: Directing — 109
- The Job of Directing — 110
- Prepare for the Session — 110
- The Scenes — 117
- Acting — 118
- Challenges of Directing — 121

Screenwriting

Chapter Eight: Shows — 127
- The Show — 128
- The Formats — 128
- Adapting a Real Show — 129
- Creating Your Own Show — 131
- Powers and Technology — 131
- The Cast — 134
- Choosing a Genre — 135
- Action & Adventure — 136
- Cop Shows — 137
- The Drama — 138
- Situation Comedy — 139
- Mysteries & Thrillers — 140
- Cartoons — 142

Chapter Nine: Writing Episodes — 143
- Anatomy of an Episode — 144
- Planning the Season — 145
- Goal of the Episode — 146
- Episode Formats — 146
- Planning the Episode — 147

FPI: The Show

Chapter Ten: FPI — 155
- The Foundation — 156
- Organization — 157
- Art of Ghost Hunting — 160
- Show Plotlines — 161
- The Cast — 161
- Episode Guide — 169

Chapter Eleven: The Paranormal — 171
- What is Paranormal? — 172
- Psychic Powers — 172
- Ritual Magic — 175
- The Spirit World — 176
- Strange Creatures — 178
- Extra-Terrestrials — 180

Episode: The Big Dig — 201

Episode: Haunted Holiday — 195

List of Tables

Cost for Specific Skill Levels	19
Scale Multipliers	20
Table 3-1: Mental Skills	26
Skill Level Costs Based on Defaults	26
Table 3-3: Social Skills	27
Table 3-2: Physical Skills	27
Example Autopsy Relative Degrees	29
Example Computer Task Difficulty Levels	30
Example Hypnosis Will Test Levels	34
Example Animal Training Difficulty Levels	44
Table 4-2: Faults	52
Example Symptoms of Manic-Depressive	57
Example Pain Threshold Difficulty Levels	58
Table 5-1: Standard of Living Resource Tickets	64
Table 5-2: Prop Bins and Resource Ticket Costs	65
Table 5-3: Guns	66
Table 5-5: Melee Weapons	67
Table 5-4: Strength Modifiers for Melee Weapons	67
Table 5-6: Explosives	72
Table 5-7: Armor	73
Table 5-8: Example Vehicles	74
Table 6-1: Trait Levels and Modifiers	90
Item Sizes and Concealment Modifiers	94
Shield Penalties	97
Table 6-2: Burst Success	99
Stamina Test Results for Endurance	100
3-18 Level	108
FUDGE Level	108
Percentile Level	108
FUDGE Level	108
Experience Point Awards	124
Table 4-2: Faults	213
Misc Default Values	213
Free Traits & Levels	213
Attributes	213
Cost for Shifting Traits	213
Cost for Specific Skill Levels	213
Table 5-1: Standard of Living Resource Tickets	214
Table 3-3: Social Skills	214
Table 3-2: Physical Skills	214
Table 3-1: Mental Skills	214

suspense...

comedy

Soap Opera

Action!

Drama

SCI-FI

HORROR

Introduction

Chapter 1

Now Playing

Introduction

This is Television

Two police detectives track down a serial killer. The crew of a starship encounters a derelict ship adrift in space. A team of superheroes matches wits and brawn with a new villain. A reporter from a local tabloid investigates the story of people being bitten by vampires, only to find out that it may be true!

What do all these story ideas have in common? They all sound like episodes of some TV shows. The fact is that all television shows have a lot in common. They have to; it's the nature of television. They all must be shown on the same networks during a very rigid schedule. All shows must fit in either a half-hour or a full hour time slot. One episode must air every week. Each episode must take a certain number of commercial breaks. They must be episodic, which means that every episode must be a complete story in itself, but must also maintain continuity with every other episode that has aired. There are other standards that shows typically follow, but you get the idea.

This is Roleplaying

"'Freeze! Police!' I shout then charge after the suspect, and try to tackle him." Both the Director and the actor roll some dice, then the Director says, "You both run hard, and eventually you begin to catch up on him." They both roll some more dice, then the Director says, "You leap at him, and land square in the middle of his back. As the two of you tumble to the ground, he squirms and you fall off him. He now jumps to his feet and runs. What do you do?" I grimace, then say "I draw my pistol and fire it into the air. 'I said *freeze!*' I shout at the suspect, then aim the gun at his back. If he runs, I'll shoot him!"

A roleplaying game is much like the old "cops and robbers" game that we used to play as children. However, instead of running around outside with toy guns, we take the game inside and sit around a table. One person is chosen to describe the setting to everyone, and to act out all the roles that no one else is playing. I'll call this person the Director, although she has had many other labels, like Game Master and Referee. Everyone else acts out the role of one of the leading characters. The acting is done verbally and with what body language can be used while sitting at a table. The actor simply tells the Director about any physical action that his character wants to make. Of course, to avoid all the senseless squabbling over who shot whom, we must introduce a system or rules. These rules govern how a character can perform physical actions while his player is sitting at a table. This often involves rolling dice.

As you can see, roleplaying games have their own set of commonalities and standards, just like television shows have. The details may differ from game to game, but the basic structure always remains the same.

This is Now Playing

Now Playing is a game that blends the rules and structure of both television and roleplaying into a game that plays like a roleplaying game, but feels like a TV show. It has the same basic structure as all roleplaying games. It also follows the same formats and standards that all TV shows adhere to. When you have finished reading this book, you will be able to take the setting of any television show that you already know a lot about, and create and run your own episodes of the show as a roleplaying game. As you play your games, you will feel as though you are in a TV show.

Summary of Chapters

The chapters of this book have been split into four major sections. These sections divide the content of the book into logical categories. These categories are as follows:

Casting: Contains everything you need to know to create characters for the game.

Acting: Contains everything you need to know to play the game.

Screenwriting: Contains everything you need to adapt an existing show into a roleplaying game, create your own "shows," and create episodes of a show that you can run. This chapter is designed specifically for Directors. Anyone who plans to just play a role does not need to read this section.

FPI: The Show: Contains a fully defined TV show, created specifically for *Now Playing*. This includes a full description of the show's setting, as well as one complete episode. Once you know how to play the game, you can read and run this episode right away. The first two chapters are open to both Director and actors. The last is not.

Casting

Chapter Two: Creating Characters covers all of the rules for creating characters. All of your traits are explained here, such as attributes, skills, gifts, faults and powers. The rules for purchasing traits is described here in detail, as is the means for advancing your characters through Experience Points.

Chapter Three: Skills lists and defines all of the skills that are available to your characters.

Chapter Four: Gifts & Faults lists and defines all of the gifts and faults that are available to your characters.

Chapter Five: Props lists and defines all of the equipment that you can outfit your characters with. It also includes definitions of a variety of animals and other creatures that you can use in your games.

Now Playing

Acting

Chapter Six: Filming describes all of the rules for playing the game. This includes using FUDGE dice, performing tests, handling combat, healing, luck, vehicles, and magic.

Chapter Seven: Directing teaches the art of directing, or game mastering, a roleplaying game. The advice it offers will help you direct your game as a television show.

Screenwriting

Chapter Eight: Shows instructs you on how to adapt an existing TV show into a *Now Playing* game. It also explains how to create your own TV show as a roleplaying game. It discusses how to help the actors create characters that fit well in your show. Finally, it describes all of the most common genres of TV shows, and offers tips on how to deal with them in *Now Playing*.

Chapter Nine: Writing Episodes gives you all the tools you need to know to create episodes for your shows that will have the feel of TV. This chapter takes many of the methods and tools used in crafting real television shows and applies them to creating roleplaying scenarios your can run for your friends.

The Show: FPI

Chapter Ten: The Foundation describes the setting of the show FPI. It explains how the Foundation for Paranormal Investigation was founded, how it is organized, and what responsibilities its members have.

Chapter Eleven: The Paranormal describes how paranormal phenomena exist in the world of FPI, and how it can be handled within the game.

Chapter Twelve: Haunted Holiday is a complete, ready to run episode of FPI. It includes both the leading and supporting cast, as well as a setting and story. Once you know how to play *Now Playing*, you can simply read this chapter and run the game.

Conventions

Text Conventions

There are a number of different types of information being presented in this book. Each type of information is presented with a different graphical look. The text you are reading here represents the standard text of the book.

Boldfaced italics are used to represent works of fiction designed to add flavor and atmosphere to the content being discussed in the chapter or section.

Normal italics are used to denote examples that are scattered throughout the text of the book. These examples are meant to add clarity to a rule or concept being presented.

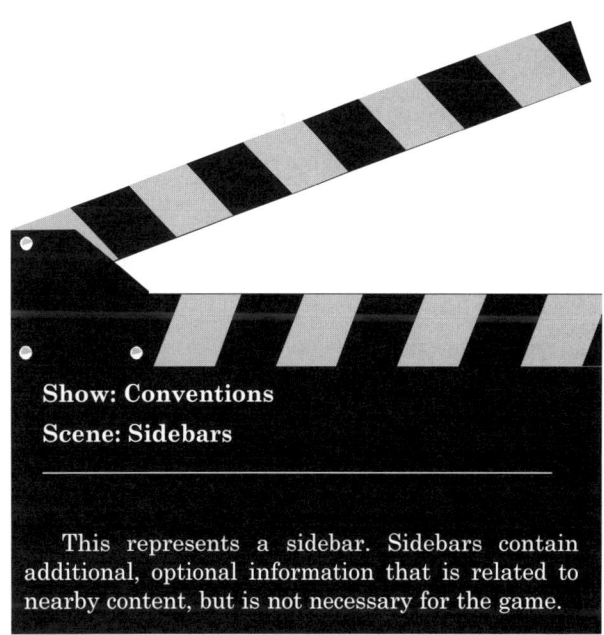

Show: Conventions
Scene: Sidebars

This represents a sidebar. Sidebars contain additional, optional information that is related to nearby content, but is not necessary for the game.

This represents a full-page example or sidebar. In most cases, it is used to illustrate how a specific rule or concept in the text can be used during roleplaying. This means that you will see examples of actual roleplaying sessions within these boxes.

Gender

Every roleplaying game struggles to find the best way to handle gender balancing in the examples and text of their books. Some omit gender altogether in exchange for the term "the character." Others switch back and forth between gender for every chapter or major section.

In *Now Playing*, gender balancing is handled very simply. All references to the Director will be female. All references to actors or characters will be male. In cases where two or more actors or characters are being referenced in the same section, both genders may be used to avoid confusion.

About the Author

Bradford Younie was born in Weymouth, Massachusetts and has spent most of his life in southern New Hampshire. He has worked most of his adult life as a software engineer, but his passion has always been for fiction writing and roleplaying games.

Now Playing

Introduction

When not writing roleplaying games, he spends lots of time with his wife Andrea and his three children, Edward, Heather and Kayleigh. He also reads novels, dabbles with the computers, and watches lots of television.

What is Roleplaying?

Simply put, roleplaying is acting. It is a special type of acting that is not designed to entertain an audience, but instead to entertain the actors themselves. In a roleplaying game, you create a character and you learn that character. You get to know as much about that character as you can and you get into your role. This is because your role is all you have! There is no script. There is no physical set, and no actual props. All you have is a sheet of paper that describes your character, some dice, and your own imagination and desire to act.

How Roleplaying Works

Before you can understand how a roleplaying game works, you have to learn what makes up a roleplaying game. The following are the necessary elements of a roleplaying game:

The Actors

These are the people who are playing the game. Well, that is, all except for one. One lucky person is the Director, and we'll discuss her next.

Each actor plays a leading role in the game. He has a character, which he either created himself or was given by the Director. He learns the character. He gets into the role, just as a TV star would with his role. However, the actor of a roleplaying game must understand the role in a more complete way. This is because he will not only need to emulate the character in speech and body language alone, as a TV actor would. He must learn to think like the character and to make all of the decisions for that character. There is no script in a roleplaying game, so anything that the character says or does is completely up to the actor. This is an improvisational acting experience!

The Director

The Director has the hardest job of all. A roleplaying game is played with everyone sitting at a table. There are no sets. There is no stage. There are no costumes or props. Lastly, there are no scripts. So, what do you have? Well, you have the Director. The Director is your set. She is all of your props. She plays every supporting character in the show. She is the show, and she is the episode. The Director is the hardest working person in the game, and has many jobs to do. I'll explain each one in turn, and that should make things pretty clear.

Storyteller

This is how the Director is the set, the props, the show and the episode. Whenever the cast (that is, the actors' characters) enters a new place, the Director must describe that place in detail. Every time something happens, the Director must describe it in full, in the cast's perspective.

Example: *The cast members are part of the crew of a futuristic starship. They have just docked a shuttle to a derelict Earth spaceship. They know the atmosphere is breathable, but do not know if there are life forms on board. They are about to open the hatch door and get their first glimpse of the ship's interior. The Director clears her throat, and begins talking...*

"The hatch door slides open with a hiss and an loud scraping noise. Before you is the small airlock, and the sight of it fills you with dread. Most of the lights have been shot out, and the one that remains is flickering haphazardly. The smell of smoke hangs heavy in the air. The walls are heavily scorched by laser fire. The ceiling has fallen in places and wires and conduits are dangling before you. Dried blood stains the floor, but there are no bodies. The single door to the ship, a reinforced airlock door, is hanging askew in its tracks. If you wanted to go through the door, you would have duck down and climb through one corner. The lighting from the hallway does not look any different from this room, and you cannot yet see any details beyond the door. Aside from a slight buzz from the lights, you are all met with a deathly silence."

After the Director describes the scene, the actors can ask questions about any aspect of the scene. The Director must decide if his character would know the information he's asking for, and then describe it if he would.

Actor

The Director must play the entire supporting cast. Essentially, the Director must play any character that is not being played by an actor. So, the Director does get to act as well. And the roles she plays are not limited by race. She must play each and every animal, creature, monster or robot that the cast encounters during the course of the episode.

Referee

The Director is in control of the game system. She must resolve any disputes regarding the rules to the game, and she is free to adapt any of the rules to fit the setting of her show. When it comes to the rules, what she says goes.

Mother Nature

She controls all outside forces. This includes the weather, the behavior of animals, and any other natural occurrence. Again, the results of these outside forces must be described in story form.

Now Playing

The Cast

The cast represents all of the characters that are portrayed by both the actors and the Director. The cast is broken down into two categories: the leading cast and the supporting cast. The leading cast represents the characters that the actors play. All of the Director's characters are supporting cast members.

These are represented in two ways: by a high-level description of their personality, physical appearance, and background; and by game system data that is written down on a character sheet for easy reference. This data is used when making dice rolls to determine the outcome of actions and events.

The Show

The show is the setting of the show. For instance, with a science fiction show, the show would include the time period, the level of technology, the history of the world between now and then, information on any alien civilizations and cultures, the political situations of the setting, etc. In essence, the show is the world in which the episodes take place.

The Episodes

The episodes are the actual stories that the cast will play in. This is what gets acted out. The relationship between the show and episodes are the same for *Now Playing* as they are in television. The Director or some other person will create each episode, and then the Director will run the episodes.

Just like with television, once the show has been defined, you can create and play a potentially infinite number of episodes. Although you may be able to buy some published episodes, you are encouraged to create your own episodes. Of course, the actors should not be involved in the creation of the episodes, since they are the ones who will be playing in them.

The Game System

The game system is nothing more than the rules of play. I have mentioned that you need to roll dice to determine the results of random events. These rules are part of the game system.

There are two major parts to the game system: creating characters, and playing the game.

Let's say that you want your character to shoot a gun at a target. In real life, no matter how good you are at shooting guns, you will sometimes hit the target and sometimes miss. There is definitely a certain randomness to this task. This randomness is caused by many things, such as wind, the gun's recoil, imperfections in the bullet, and so on. However, that is not the only factor to determine if you hit the target. Your skill with the gun is another. Therefore, your skill with the gun combined with the random factor will determine if you are going to hit.

In the game, it will work the same way. When you create your character, you get to choose skills that your character knows, and specify how good he is with each. These levels are represented in some form that can be kept track of. When your character shoots the gun, you roll dice to represent the random factor, and then add the result to your gun skill. The Director compares that result to a level of difficulty that she decided on ahead of time to find out if you hit.

This is just one example of a game system mechanic. Some roleplaying games have a great many rules. *Now Playing* only has a few, and is therefore quite easy to learn and play. You will find that after you have created characters and are playing the game, you will rarely need to refer to the book.

The Flow of the Game

Once the actors have created their characters, the game can begin. The way the game works is as follows:

The Director describes the first scene. Once she has described it, the actors may ask her questions regarding the scene that perhaps she did not explain well enough or neglected to explain. She will answer the questions as best she can, as long as she believes that the characters should know the answer.

Once the actors understand where they are and what's going on, they can decide what they will do and do it. They should always do it "in character," meaning by speaking as their characters and acting as their characters. Of course, since they are sitting at a table, they cannot, for instance, hop in a car and start a chase. Instead, they tell the Director what they will do. The Director will decide if it's technically possible for the characters to do the things they want, and will then resolve the actions. The actors and Director will roll dice as needed to determine the results, and the Director will describe them.

That's basically it. The game continues like this until the episode is over. Now, you may read the above description and think you understand it, or you may just scratch your head and say "huh?" The fact is, there is only one sure-fire way to explain how a roleplaying game flows, and that's by having you either play one or watch one. Well, obviously, a book can't be interactive enough to have you play with it, so instead, we'll give you an example to read. At the end of this chapter, there is an example of a scene as roleplayed by hypothetical characters and Director. Read it through. It will give you a good idea of how the game flows. When you read it, keep in mind that the dialog would not be scripted. What they say are all things that come to the top of their heads. They are just acting like those characters and will talk and behave as them.

Now Playing

Roleplaying TV

Now that you know what roleplaying is, and how it works, we can talk about how TV works into the game.

Some roleplaying games simulate the tactics of combat and reconnaissance in great detail. Game play focuses on making coordinated tactical decisions in defeating enemies. Their game systems are quite complex because they cover all the details regarding the tactics of combat. There are other games, however, that do not focus much on the tactics, but instead put their emphasis on the acting. In these games, whole sessions can go by without a single combat scene. The interplay between the characters is what is important in these games, and therefore requires fully developed characters, but not a lot of game system rules.

Tactics or Interaction?

Television shows are perfectly suited to the latter of these two types of roleplaying games. That is because in a TV show, the focus is always on the characters. Very few shows focus on the details of the action. The gunfights are brief, and are meant only to add some climax to the episode. The majority of the episode is focused on the leading characters and their interaction among themselves and with the supporting cast. In a murder mystery or crime drama, the cast will be spending a lot of time speaking with witnesses and suspects, and discussing the details of the case with each other. There will occasionally be scenes where the cast searches for clues and chases the suspects, but they tend to be brief.

Because television focuses on the characters, so does *Now Playing*. The game system is simple and very few rules. Creating characters can be as quick as ten minutes, once you know what your character's concept is. Game play is even easier. After you have played it once, you will rarely need to refer back to the book.

Terminology

Now Playing is all about television. The games that you will create and play are fashioned after TV shows and movies, and so it seems fitting to use TV production lingo when referring to parts of the game.

The following are the special terms that are used in this book, followed by a description of what they mean to both new and experienced gamers alike.

Series

A series is a collection of episodes that chronicle something over time. This is usually about the cast of characters, or a certain place or perhaps the adventures of a

Now Playing

Example Roleplaying Scene

SHOW: Mean Streets. EPISODE: On the Run SCENE: Visiting Kathy

The two leading characters are police detectives who are hunting down a drug store robber who shot and killed the clerk. They are visiting the suspect's girlfriend Kathy McDunn to try to get information on his whereabouts.

Director: Ms. McDunn's apartment is on the second floor of the tenement. Her door is halfway down the hall on the left. Like the rest of the building, the hallway is dirty and dingy; with week-old pizza boxes and other refuse littering the floor. The number on her door is crooked. You think you might hear a TV set coming from inside the apartment.

Jake: We'll stand on either side of the door, and I'll knock.

Director: <Rolls dice to see if they hear movement inside. They don't.> There is a pause. A woman's voice calls "Who is it?" She sounds cautious.

Jake: "Police officers, Ma'am. We'd like to have a few words with you."

Director: <Rolls again. They still don't hear.> Another pause. "Okay, just a minute." There's the sound of someone walking to the door. You can hear the dead-bolt click aside, and the door opens a crack. The chain lock is in place. You can see a woman's face through the crack in the door. She's a blonde, and her hair looks a mess. "What can I do for ya?"

Jake: "It's about Robert Porter. We'd like to talk to you about him. May we come in?"

Director: "Bob? What's he done now?"

Craig: Is she bluffing? <Rolls a Sense Motive test and tells the Director the result.>

Director: Yeah, she responded too quickly. It sounded rehearsed.

Craig: "We just need to ask him some questions. May we come inside?"

Director: "He's not here. I don't know where he is."

Jake: "We're not saying he is. But we have some questions about him that we think you might be able to answer. Will you please let us in?"

Director: She sighs. "Sure. Of course. Come in." She closes the door, undoes the chain lock, then opens the door again. She takes her time doing it.

Jake: "Thank you." I walk inside, giving the place a quick once-over. "This shouldn't take long."

Craig: I come in too. I'm going to let Jake ask most of the questions. I'll poke around a bit. I'll try to look like I'm just killing time, but I'm really looking for Bob and anything that might lead us to him.

Director: Great. You're inside. She closes the door. The apartment is only a little cleaner than the hallway. You are in the kitchen, which has a table with some letters on it. The living room, which is the only room in your line of sight, has an old, beat-up couch, a coffee table and an old recliner. You doubt it would actually recline at this point. The TV is against the far wall. It's playing the news. There is a doorway next to the TV that goes into a little hallway. On one side of the hallway is the bedroom; on the other side is the bathroom. She goes into the living room and sits down on the recliner. "So, what do you want to know?"

Jake: I'll follow her in, and sit down near her, facing her. I want to be able to look at her face while we talk.

Director: The couch is not very close to her chair.

Jake: I'll grab a kitchen chair and bring it in.

Director: Okay. She looks at you strangely, but says nothing about it. "You know, I haven't seen him for days now."

Jake: "So, you haven't seen him in days? You're his girlfriend, right? Weren't you worried?"

Director: She shrugs. "Nah, he comes and goes. He's always disappearing. I'm done worrying about him."

Craig: I'm going to walk around the living room absently, looking at pictures or anything that might clue me in. I want to peek into the bedroom, but I know I don't have the right to just barge in, so I'll just wander over so I can peek in without being too obvious.

Jake: "Do you know of any place he might go if here were in trouble?"

Introduction

Now Playing

Director: Craig, you see a pack of cigarettes on the coffee table. They're half empty. "He visits his folks now and then, but I don't know where they live. They're outside the city; I know that. I think he said it's an hour's drive." <Roll to see if she notices him peeking into the bedroom. She does> "Hey, what are you doing? That's my bedroom! Don't you need a warrant or something for that?"

Craig: "Sorry." I move away, and go to the coffee table. I pick up the pack of cigarettes and offer one to Ms. McDuff. "Here. Want one?"

Director: She waves her hand in dismissal. "No thanks."

Craig: Ah, she doesn't smoke. These must be his then. "Do you live alone here?"

Director: "Yeah, I do."

Craig: "Interesting. Then if you don't smoke, whose are these?"

Director: "Um, well, I didn't say they weren't mine. I, uh, just don't want one now." As she babbles, you suddenly hear a noise coming from the bedroom. It sounded like something falling off a table.

Craig: I run into the bathroom, drawing my revolver as I do.

Director: She stands up shouting, "Hey! You can't go in there!"

Jake: I stand up, and put my hand up to stop her from moving. I draw my gun and rush to help. "Probable cause, ma'am."

Director: The bedroom is pretty standard for a slum. But the queen-sized bed is not made. The window is open, and you can see a fire escape just outside the window. A penny jar is on the floor in by the window. It had apparently fallen off the bureau that's beside the window.

Craig: I run to the window and look out.

Director: You can see Bob Porter climbing down the fire escape as fast as he can. He looks scared.

Craig: "He's getting away!" I motion with my gun for Jake to cut him off, and I climb out onto the fire escape. I'll climb down after him.

Jake: I'll book out the door and head to the back door. I want to cut him off.

Director: Okay, make a Climb skill test. <Rolls Bob's climb test.> <Craig's roll is less than Bob's> He's climbing faster than you, and he has a head start. He'll be at the bottom of the stairs long before you.

Craig: Can I get a clear shot from here?

Director: Not right now. If he were to try to run from the alley, then yes, you could.

Craig: Good. I'll keep climbing, but be ready to shoot him if he makes a break for it. "Police! Freeze or I'll shoot!"

Director: He gets to the bottom of the fire escape. He hops down and books for the back of the building.

Craig: I'll shoot. <Rolls his gun skill test.>

Director: <Compares the test result to his predetermined difficulty level.> You missed.

Craig: I'll take one more shot, and then keep climbing. <Rolls his gun skill test again.>

Director: <This time it's a hit. He calculates damage.> You nicked him in the left arm. He grabs his arm as he runs around the corner. Kathy is shouting hysterics.

Jake: I'm running as fast as I can to the back door. I'll burst out and look around for him.

Director: Just as you burst out, he comes running around the corner. He's holding his left arm with his hand. He skids to a stop when he sees you, and makes to turn.

Jake: I am my gun at him. "Freeze! You're surrounded Bob!"

Director: He tries to run around the corner.

Jake: I shoot. <Rolls his gun skill test.>

Director: <Compares the results.> Wow! You hit him square in the back. He drops, falling on his chest. He's not moving. Craig, you manage to get down from the fire escape. You heard the shot and saw Bob drop.

Jake: I come over to Bob, keeping a safe distance, and leveling the gun on him. I try to see if he's conscious.

Craig: "I'll get an ambulance!" I run back to our car to call for assistance.

Director: He's out cold. He may even be dead. Looks like you've got him.

Now Playing

ship or spaceship. Most of the episodes are not directly connected to each other and can be watched or played out in any order.

Serial

A serial is very much like a series, except that it is designed to tell one big, complete story throughout the course of its episodes. Each episode tells part of the story, and although the episodes all must have a beginning, middle and end, each one is completely dependent upon the episodes that have come before it and those that will come after.

The advantage to a serial is that you can tell a much more detailed and grandiose story that spans seasons. The disadvantage is that if someone starts watching in the middle of a season, he will most likely feel lost and confused.

Miniseries

Like a serial, a miniseries is a collection of episodes that tell one complete story. They are always short-lived shows, however, running a span of usually five or less episodes. Unlike a serial, each episode of a miniseries does not need to have an ending of its own. Instead it could end right after some climactic event, leaving the viewer to wait anxiously for the next episode.

Season

A season is a collection of episodes in a show. Most seasons contain twenty-four episodes, but that is not necessary. It is important to choose a logical point to break each season at, usually breaking between two major sections of a story.

Leading Cast

This refers to all of the characters that are played by the actors.

Supporting Cast

The Supporting Cast includes all of the Supporting Characters, which are played by the Director. They make up the incidental characters, bad guys and other people that the Cast encounters during an episode.

Cast

This is used to refer to all characters in the show, both starring and supporting.

Show

Last, but not least, we have the Show. The Show is an entire campaign. It is a collection of related episodes. The entire show may tell one story, but that is not necessary.

The show contains the setting, Cast (both lead and supporting) and a series or serial of episodes.

Where to Begin?

If you are already an experienced roleplayer, you can skip this section altogether. This is geared for people who have never played a roleplaying game before.

If you have gotten this far, then you are ready to start playing. The rest of the book has all the information you need to know to play *Now Playing*. Each topic is broken down into convenient chapters, to make playing and in-game references as easy as possible. But right now, what you need is a breakdown of exactly what to do to begin playing. This section will tell you just that. The complete process for playing the game is laid out in the following sub-sections. Each one fully describes what to do to complete each step.

Roleplaying games are not quick games to prepare and play. They usually require a fair amount of planning, and playing normally takes several hours at least, and most often even spans several sessions. Most of the sections describe what you must do to prepare for the game. Each section will point you to the chapters in the book that will help you with the step it's describing.

Choose a Show

This is the first step. You all have to agree on a show that you want to play. In most cases, you will have already made this decision before you even pick up the book, but it is still the first step nonetheless.

Think of a TV show that you and your friends would all enjoy playing. It does not matter what genre it is, as long as you all want to play it. This is probably the easiest decision to make in this step.

Exact Show or a Spin-Off?

Do you all want to play the same characters that are on the show, or do you want to create your own characters that will star in the same setting? This will determine your method for creating characters. Chapter Two: Creating Characters will describe two methods for building your characters, one that assumes that the characters are brand new, and the other that assumes you are using characters that already exist in the show. Discuss this with your group, and make sure you get a consensus.

Keep in mind that this is your game, so if you want to mix and match characters, where some are ones from the series, while others are brand new, then that is up to you. Just be careful to make sure they are all balance well (that they are all about equally "powerful").

If you do choose to run a spin-off, then that also means that you have the opportunity to change anything you want about the plot of the show. This is your chance

Now Playing

to add your own creativity and make the show the way you think it should have been!

Choose a Director

One person in the group must be the Director. She will be the one who controls the setting and plays all the supporting roles. Everyone else will be an actor and will play a starring role in the show.

The new Director should read Chapter Seven: Directing to learn tricks and advice on how to direct a show.

Define or Adapt the Show

Now that you know what show you are playing and you know who is directing it, the Director must now figure out how to run it as a roleplaying game. *Now Playing* makes this easy.

First, you must make sure you know the setting of the show. Follow the rules put down in Chapter Eight: Shows to help you adapt the show. The most time-consuming effort would be if the show has any fancy technology or non-human races that need to be defined. These are still not tough, but will need a little attention before you can start playing.

Also, some shows have a storyline that runs throughout the show. If this one does, you must figure out how to introduce your own episodes and characters without causing havoc with the continuity of the show. For this reason, it may be a good idea to change the story to fit your own storyline. This way, you can treat it as though it is a spin-off and not worry about maintaining continuity. This is a decision that you should discuss with the actors, because with a real show, the actors may be very picky about how you handle it and you want everyone to be happy with your decisions.

Create Character Concepts

At this point, each actor must come up with a concept for his character. If an actor will be playing an existing character from the real show, he must tell the Director. He should also learn as much about that character as possible. If possible, he should watch several episodes of the show with a notebook and pen, and take notes on the character's personality, background and abilities. He must learn the character as much as possible so that he can do a good job playing him.

If he chooses to create a new character, he must fully decide what he wants to play. Discuss the character with the Director. She may already have an idea of how the show will play out, and will therefore have an idea of what types of characters would work out well. For instance, if the show is about the adventures of a particular starship, the actors should be careful not to create a character that is not closely associated with that ship, or he may have little use in the show.

You must know as much about the character's personality as possible, so flesh out the details as much as you can.

Refer to Chapter Two: Creating Characters for tips on creating a character concept.

Once you have come up with your concept, show it or describe it to the Director. She has to approve it because only she knows if the character will fit into the setting and plot of her episodes.

Create the Characters

This is different than creating the concepts. Now, you must deal with the game system rules for creating the character. This includes figuring out physical and mental details of the character, what skills he knows, and how good he is with them. It also covers any special abilities that he may have, as well as any faults that may cause a challenge during the game. The entire Casting section of the book (Chapters Two through Five) contains everything you need to create and outfit your characters.

Write the Episode

When I say "write," I mean to create it. It is recommended to write the details down, at least in notes, but you probably do not need to write it all down.

Follow the rules and advice set down in Chapter Nine: Writing Episodes for help in creating episodes of your show.

Always make sure you tailor the episode specifically for the cast of characters that the actors have created.

Play!

Finally, you are ready to play. The process to get to this point really does not take that long, and once you have defined your show, and the cast is made, all that needs to be done for each episode is for the Director to create the next episode, and then you can all play.

This chapter has already described the flow of the game, and the rules governing how to play are detailed in Chapter Six: Filming.

The Director should read Chapter Seven: Directing for good advice and rules for directing a show.

Create the Next Episode and Play Again

Once the Director finishes running one episode, she can then begin the task of creating the next. At this point, the work is easy because you already have the show defined, and you already have your characters. In fact, you have now already played your roles, and so you should be more comfortable playing them. You may want to tweak your characters a little before the next episode. This is okay, because it is important that you are happy with the roles you will play.

Casting

Scene 1   Creating Characters

Scene 2   Skills

Scene 3   Gifts and Faults

Scene 4   Props

I stood outside the door to my office, looking around, still not sure what to do. The director was watching me expectantly. "I wish I had a script." I said.

"You've got a character," she replied confidently. "You've got everything you need. Just do what Sam Diamond would do."

All right, I thought, get into character. You're Sam Diamond, private dick. Well, here goes. I took a deep breath, and opened the door. A woman sat at a desk beside the door to my office. She looked up. "Hi Boss, got mail for ya", she said in the heaviest Bronx accent I have ever heard.

"What is it?" I replied.

"Bills. The electric company wants to get paid. For that matter, I do too."

I rolled my eyes. I can see my work is cut out for me. "Don't worry. You'll get paid soon."

"Yeah, right," she replied derisively, "You always say that." Her tone then changed, but only a little. "Ya know there's a better way to pay me. A little wining and dining goes a long way with a lady." Her voice had the hint of hope masked heavily with humor.

I wasn't interested, but I bet she wouldn't be bad if she'd just let her hair down and took off those horned-rims. "Yeah, yeah," I replied, trying to remember her name. Christ, they had just told me before the scene began, but then, this whole thing was tough. "Keep dreaming. Maybe I'll take you up on it some day."

She chuckled, "I ain't countin' on it anymore."

I went into my office and closed the door. The office was dark, dingy and sparsely decorated. I walked behind my desk, tossing my wet trench coat on the couch as I walked by, and looked out the window. It had a great view of a brick wall. A neon sign hung directly beside the window. It read "Joe's Bar" with a big red arrow pointing down. The "o" was flickering. I hadn't been here a minute yet and it already annoyed me.

I sat down in my chair, picked up the newspaper sitting on the desk and leaned back, setting my feet on the desk. No sooner had I done this, than a knock came at the door. Sally stuck her head in...Sally! That's her name. Anyway, she stuck her head in and said "Boss, there's a lady here to see ya. Says it's important."

"Sure," I said, not moving from my spot. "Send her in."

"Sure thing, Boss," she said and her head disappeared.

Then she walked in. Wow! What a lady! I practically fell over as I scrambled to stand up. She was tall and leggy, with big painted lips and lots of blonde hair. She was dressed to kill, too. Her dress clung to every curve of her body like skin, and a slit up the side showed a hint of leg as she stood there watching me.

When the door closed, she spoke in a deep husky voice that I felt all the way to my toes. "Mr. Diamond," she said, "I need your help."

"Um, sure." I stumbled over the words. Christ, this improv thing is tough! As it is, I have no idea if she's just gonna talk or tear my clothes off! I hope the latter. "Here, have a seat." I gestured the chair that sat in front of the desk.

She sauntered over with a swing I ain't never seen in my back yard, and sat down. She crossed her legs, showing lots of creamy skin through the slit in her dress. She saw where my eyes were and smiled. I blushed. "How can I help you?" I asked, forcing myself to sit down.

"My husband's been arrested." She didn't sound too upset, but then again, my mind was elsewhere.

"So," I replied, trying to keep my cool. "I ain't a lawyer."

"No, you don't understand. He's innocent. He's been framed."

"Oh..." Light dawns over Marblehead. "And you want me to catch the guys who did it and prove his innocence."

"That's right. I can pay you. My husband is rich."

"Okay, so who is he," I asked. I had a feeling there was a catch to it.

She put a newspaper down on the table, folded open to one page. The headline read "Restaurateur Arrested for Murder". There's the catch. I just read that article before she came in. The cops thought it was a Mob killing before they caught him. If he's been framed, then the Mob's behind it. "Whoa, honey!" I said, holding up my hands as though the paper were toxic. "That's too rich for my blood. It's outta my league."

"Please, Mr. Diamond. He won't last long in jail." She looked at me, and for the first time I saw the helplessness in her eyes. I began to melt.

"Look, we're talking about the Mob, here. You know that. It's too much for me."

She stood up. She straightened the wrinkles on her dress slowly and carefully; so that I could watch her hands touch every curve. Then she walked around to stand over me. She leaned over and whispered in my ear. The smell of her perfume and the sight of her voluminous breasts so close were almost impossible to bear. "Mr. Diamond," she whispered. I knew she was just acting, like me, but right now, she could've talked me into buying a bridge. "I can't bear to be alone. I'm too young to be alone. I need to be touched; to be held." As she said this, she cupped my cheek with the palm of her hand. "Please, Mr. Diamond. I will do anything to get my husband back. Anything."

Aw, that did it. I caved. I shook my head like I was going to say "no". Perhaps that's what I meant to say; I'm not sure anymore. "All right. I'll poke around a bit, and see what I can find. But I can't promise anything."

She hugged me then, long and hard. She didn't need to, but I was glad she did.

Creating Characters

Chapter 2

Casting

Creating A Star

Hello there, and welcome to *Now Playing*. Just take a seat here on the stage and we'll get started. Here's where it all begins: the Casting Department. The Director has a show ready to film, er, play, and she now has her actors: you. However, the last thing we need to get under way is a leading cast. Here at *Now Playing*, we have learned that the actors get into their roles better if they create them rather than if they have them handed out. And since there's no script to worry about, we won't have any trouble doing this.

Now, you're probably wondering how you're going to create your own role. Well, it's really not hard. It all boils down to a handful of simple steps. I'll be teaching you those steps and before you know it, you'll have your character all made.

Concept vs. Game Mechanics

There are two phases for creating a character. First, there is the character concept, and second, there are the game mechanics. Both parts are important, and are usually handled separately. However, some elements of one phase may help flesh out the details of another.

Character Concept

This covers the majority of the character creation process. This defines who the character is, what he does for a living, what his personality is like, what motivations and goals he has, and so on. The more detailed the character's background and personality is, the easier the he will be to roleplay.

It is easy for players of roleplaying games to gloss over this part and dive straight into the mechanics. Many a game has been played with cardboard characters that have great statistics, but none of them feels like TV characters. If you want the show to really feel like television and if you want your character to be fun to play, you *must* put most of your effort here. After all, you are all actors who do not have a script. All you have is your character. If you don't have a richly developed character, then the game is not much better than a board game!

Game Mechanics

This is what defines the character in game terms. When things happen in the game that has a chance of failure, dice are rolled to determine the result. These dice rolls must be compared with something in order to decide success or failure. You must also know what you're rolling against. This is where the mechanics come in. The wonderful character that you have created must be transposed into a set of statistics that can be used either to modify a dice roll or to set a target value for the roll.

Although there are parts of the game mechanics that can help you figure out what your character will be like, such as the gifts and faults, the majority of the mechanics will be worked out after you have figured out the concept of the character.

The Character Concept

Each actor in a *Now Playing* game plays a starring role in the show. The sections that follow are meant to help each actor create his character concept and to flesh out most of the details about his personality and background.

Know the Show

Watch Some Episodes

Before you can really start to create your character, you must understand the show. If the show is based on an existing TV show, then watch some episodes to hopefully spark an inspiration.

Example: The show is about the crew of a starship that has crashed on a remote and harsh planet and their struggle for survival. One episode centers around the first child born on the planet. In the episode, the child develops some kind of psychic power that links him with all of the native life on the planet. The planet considers the crew to be a threat, and he therefore practically destroys the colony before the stars manage to sever the psychic link. When they do, the child becomes normal. If the game's show takes place many years later, that character could be an excellent idea for a starring role. Just think of the emotional baggage he would carry with him, knowing that he practically destroyed everyone, not to mention how people would treat him!

Discuss With the Director

Whether the show really existed or if the Director created it, you should still discuss your character concept with the Director. Only the Director knows the details of the storyline and the direction she wants it to go in. It is quite possible that a perfectly good character will not make a good starring role.

Work the Cast Dynamics

One unavoidable difference between real TV shows and a roleplaying game is that most shows have only a few starring characters, where an RPG can have many. When working up your character, you must keep in mind the concepts of the other starring characters, and make sure your character will be able to work well with the others.

Here's a good rule of thumb when picking personality traits for your character: if the trait adds to the story and

Creating Characters

14

Casting

helps the dynamics of the cast interaction, then it's good; if it draws too much attention away from the story, then don't take that trait. For example, making your character obsessive compulsive may work fine, as long as you give him the means to function in the show, but a heavily chauvinistic man with some female cast members would cause so much distraction that it would destroy the momentum of the show.

Find One Defining Trait

Most starring roles have one special trait that makes him stand out from the rest. This trait will define who he is and why he is a star of this particular show. For instance, having the character's brother abducted by aliens when they were kids would make him ideal for a show about aliens and the paranormal.

The key trait, however, does not have to be directly linked to the storyline of the show. For example, one show features a main character who is a detective that suffers from Obsessive Compulsive Disorder. He can't stand anything that is not neat and tidy, and can't resist straightening crooked pictures, washing his hands, and so forth. Believe it or not, the show is a murder mystery, and he's a private detective. His disorder works to his advantage, as he is extraordinarily sensitive to anything that is not "in order". Therefore, he'll notice every tiny detail that doesn't make sense, like scuffed shoes on a paraplegic, or a two-day-old cup of coffee on the desk of someone who claimed to be out of the office all week. From a first glance, the character's trait seems completely unrelated, but it really works out nicely.

Personality & Background

Television, more so than most other medium, focuses more heavily on the characters and their interactions and development than on any other aspect of the show. Because of this fact, it is extremely important to have well developed characters that have a lot of personality. Figuring out his background and personality is key to a good starring character.

Inspiration Is the Key

Chances are, you probably already have a good idea of what your character will be like. Quite often, you get an inspiration when the Director describes the concept of the show. If this is true, then you're halfway there! If not, you must find other means for being inspired. The following are some ideas of where to look:

Browse through the lists of gifts and faults in Chapter Four: Gifts & Faults. These are designed specifically to add spice to your roleplaying and individuality to your character.

Someone you know may have a trait that would be both fun to play and fitting for the show. Since imitation *is* the highest form of flattery, you shouldn't feel awkward about doing this.

Watch some TV Either watch the same show you plan to play, or if the show is made up for the game, watch a similar type of show. One of the characters on the show may inspire you.

Ask Yourself "Why"

Whenever you decide on a personality trait, ask yourself "why does he have it?" and "how did he get it?" This will help develop that trait and to custom tailor it to your character. When you can answer that question, it will be so much easier to roleplay the trait.

Sometimes you'll find that the answer to your questions won't make sense or will tell you that the trait just isn't right. If you can't come up with an answer to why you have chosen a particular trait or history, then it's a good sign that you shouldn't take it.

The Character Questionnaire

The questionnaire included in the back of the book can help force you to define the character. If you fill out the questionnaire for your character, you can feel confident that the character is pretty well defined. Feel free to photocopy it and fill it out for each character you design. You can even use it for characters in all the games you play, not just with *Now Playing*!

The questionnaire is written in the perspective that assumes you are the character. This may help you get into character.

When you have finished creating your character, it may be good to keep this questionnaire with your character sheet. It has lots of great information about your character, so it could help as a resource when you're playing him.

Don't Over-Develop

Tape one random episode of your favorite TV series from somewhere in the middle of a later season. Then, go rent the pilot episode of your favorite TV series. Finally, sit down in front of the television one evening and watch them both back-to-back, starting with the later episode. Pay close attention to the main character. When you watch the pilot, you may be very surprised at how thin his personality is compared to what he has become.

In TV, they don't develop the main characters too much at first for two reasons: they don't know exactly where the character will go from season to season, and, more importantly, they don't know what the actor is going to do with him. It's vitally important that the actor puts some of himself and his passion into the character, and the writers cannot predict how that will affect the character. So, they keep the character light to begin with, then wait and see how the actor fits into the role. Once the character has gotten comfortable, then they can begin playing with more details and development.

Casting

This is true with any character you make. No matter how much thought and effort you put into creating your role, you will not fully be able to predict how you will handle the character once you start playing him.

So, do yourself a favor and follow the lead that television offers. Take the one or two key inspiration points of your character and flesh out the details of them, then work out a basic personality concept and leave the rest open to development. You'll find yourself feeling less restricted, and looking forward to how he will grow as the seasons go by.

Draw a Picture

Some actors who are artistically inclined like to draw a picture of their characters, so that they can get a good idea of who they're playing. It makes a great way to round-out the character concept.

Character Traits

A trait is something about your character that defines who he is. A trait could represent how strong or intelligent he is, or what things he is good at. They are used to determine what skills he has and how good he is at them. When creating your character, you must assign traits to your character.

All of the different traits that make up your character are described below:

Attributes

Attributes are physical and mental abilities that help define who you are. They are not skills that are learned through study and practice, but are features of your body and personality that can grow and develop as you mature.

Attributes can boost your chances when using untrained skills, and can help you salvage a little from a spectacularly failed skill test.

Every character has six basic attributes:

Brawn
Agility
Stamina
Reasoning
Perception
Will

Brawn

Your Brawn determines your physical prowess, and governs how well you can lift or push heavy objects. It can also make a difference in a brawl or melee combat.

Agility

Agility represents how nimble you are, how fast you can run, and how well you dodge, balance and so forth. Agility also represents your hand-eye coordination, which is vital when firing a ranged weapon, such as a gun or bow. Thieves and spies need excellent agility for picking pockets, sneaking, hiding and shadowing suspects.

Stamina

Stamina represents your toughness and physical endurance. This is your pain threshold and can be used to represent how much physical torture you can take before you give in. Whenever you are pushing yourself physically, you are testing your stamina. Climbing a mountain, marching non-stop for a long time could require stamina tests to see when you drop from fatigue.

Reasoning

Reasoning represents the ability to think, to reason, and to remember. An intelligent person can think logically and can make decisions based on facts and analysis.

Perception

Perception represents your awareness. A very perceptive person will notice that rat scurrying in the shadows and notice the discrete exchange of glances between two people. This attribute covers all perceptive senses, such as touch, smell, hearing and sight.

You can use Perception to notice the differences in things. For instance, a successful Perception roll will let you tell that the birdcall you just heard was really a man imitating a bird.

Will

Will represents mental stamina. It determines how well your character can handle mental and emotional stress, fear, shock, and even psychic attacks.

Most Will tests are used to prevent some form of mental anguish or damage, and are rarely used to perform a task.

Skills

Unlike attributes, skills are more variable. Virtually anything that you can learn through study or schooling and improve upon through practice is a skill.

Now Playing includes many skills, complete with descriptions, but there really can be any number of skills. There will be times when you feel your character should have a certain skill that is not defined in this book. Discuss it with your Director and then by all means, create it.

Casting

The list of available skills and their descriptions can be found in Chapter Three: Skills.

Gifts

A gift is something special and positive about you that you just have. It helps to define who you are, but it is not something that will change over time. Some gifts have a direct effect on the mechanics of the game, either by modifying a skill or attribute roll or by enabling a specific ability. Some gifts, however, may simply be a roleplaying element, and have no direct effect to any dice rolls or action results.

Gifts are always beneficial and are befitting of the term "gift".

The list of available gifts and their descriptions can be found in Chapter Four: Gifts and Faults

Since most gifts do not have any direct game-system rules associated with them, it would be easy to add more gifts as needed.

Faults

Like gifts, faults are just something you have. They are not something that you can roll against, and they do not change over time: either you have it or you don't. In many cases, you are born with it, but sometimes you gain it later in life.

Unlike gifts, however, faults are usually bad. These are things that have a negative impact on your character, either by placing a penalty on certain rolls or simply by making your character challenging to roleplay. A birth defect or disease could be a fault, but phobias and other such physical and psychological problems could be as well.

Obligations are another form of fault. They are not necessarily negative traits, but they constrain the character's actions, making certain situations very difficult. Code of Honor is a prime example of this. It is in no way a bad trait, but it does restrict the character's actions. This can cause some great problems in times of crisis.

The list of available faults and their descriptions can be found in Chapter Four: Gifts and Faults. Like gifts, you can always create your own faults if the one you want is not available. Just run it past your Director to see if she approves.

Powers

These represent any special powers or abilities that extend beyond the human norm. Psychic powers, photographic memory, cybernetics and superpowers are all examples of Powers.

Powers are not available in all shows, and how they are handled is up to the Director. If you want to give your character a power, ask your Director and work it out with her.

Powers vs. Gifts

Sometimes it can be hard to decide if a certain trait should be a gift or a power, since they can be very similar. They both are abilities or traits that give the character some form of advantage. The key difference, though, is that a power gives an advantage that is *beyond the human norm*. For instance, having very quick reflexes is humanly possible, where the ability to read people's thoughts is not normally possible for a human. Sometimes you can tell if the trait is a power if the advantage it gives is too powerful to have the cost of only one gift.

Example: Originally, the power Photographic Memory was going to be a gift because there are people who have photographic memory, so it is technically not beyond human capability. However, the ability to be able study a scene that you saw hours and even days after it took place as though looking at an extremely detailed picture is way too powerful for one gift. So, now it is included in Now Playing *as a Power.*

Trait Levels

Since attributes and skills can differ from person to person, and can be improved upon over time, there must be a way to track your progress with them. You need to know how good you are at the trait any time, so each skill and attribute has a competency level that describes how good you are with it. Dice rolls can be made against these levels to determine success or failure. See Chapter Six: Filming for details on performing these rolls.

Each level describes how good you are with the trait. The following levels, listed from best to worse, are as follows:

Superb
Great
Good
Fair
Mediocre
Poor
Terrible

Once a skill or attribute reaches Superb, it cannot be raised any higher; that's as good as you can be at it. The only exception is if the Director allows Legendary traits.

Casting

Creating Characters

Legendary Traits

Sometimes a show may call for a character that has a higher trait than that of the human norm. The Legendary level is one level higher than Superb.

Legendary traits should be used with caution, as it could easily cause the characters to be too powerful for the show. It is intended for characters with literally "legendary" traits, such as a Hercules or other god-like heroes.

Referring to Traits and Their Levels

It may make sense to refer to a trait by putting its level in front, such as "Great Brawn" or "Fair Reasoning".

Creating The Character

By now, you should have your character concept defined. Perhaps you even selected some gifts and faults while defining his concept. Now it's time to define the character's game system statistics. The following sections cover the process. Take a character sheet (either photocopied from this book or downloaded from the *Now Playing* web site) and begin.

Determining Your Attributes

Each character has the same six attributes that determine his physical and mental makeup. The only thing that you need to define is the level of each one.

Free Levels

All attributes are set to Fair by default. You can then raise one or more of them by spending your free levels.

Each character starts with three "free levels" with which you can spend to increase any combination of attributes. For instance, you can spend 2 of your free levels on your Brawn, raising it up from the default of Fair to Great. Then you can spend the last one on your Perception to raise it to Good. Since you just used up your free levels, all the other attributes remain at Fair.

Normally, when creating a character, you cannot set any attribute to a level higher than Great. this gives you something to aspire to. There are times, however, when the Director may choose to change this restriction. A good example is in a show where Powers are in play. A superhero show would expect characters to have their Brawn even greater than Superb. Shows like this would most likely benefit from the Legendary attribute, described below.

Shifting Levels

Once you have spent your free levels, you can now shift your levels by subtracting levels from one attribute to add them to another. In essence, when you subtract a level from an attribute, the level that you took away becomes a free level that you can now spend to increase another attribute.

You can continue to shift your attributes until you are satisfied. If you lower a trait below Terrible, then it is non-existent. This means that you cannot even attempt to use the trait.

Legendary Attributes

There is one level for an attribute or skill that has not yet been discussed. It is called Legendary, and it sits one level higher than Superb.

Superb is the maximum for normal humans. Legendary is allowed only by the Director's decision and is

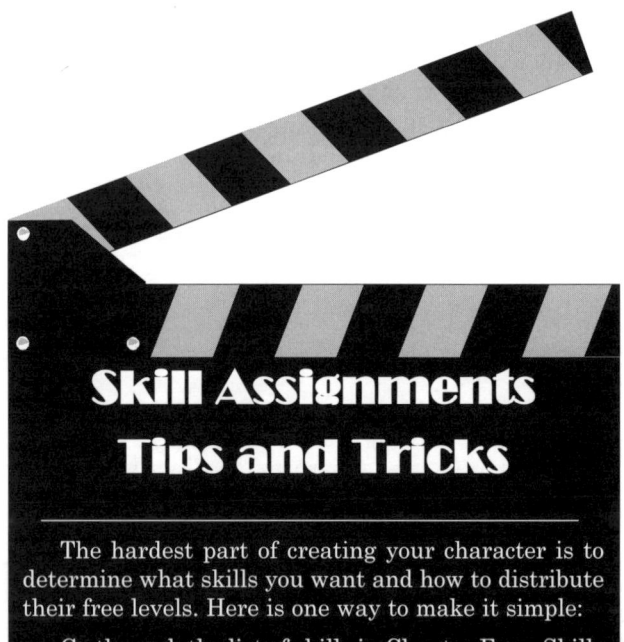

Skill Assignments Tips and Tricks

The hardest part of creating your character is to determine what skills you want and how to distribute their free levels. Here is one way to make it simple:

Go through the list of skills in Chapter Four: Skills and write down on a piece of scrap paper all of the skills that you think will fit your character. In a column beside each skill, jot down an abbreviation of the skill's default level (i.e., T, P, M, F, G, R, S, and blank for non-existent).

Then, in a new column, increment all of the skills you want to increment by one only. When you're done, you will have most of your skills at Fair and a few at Terrible (for those that were non-existent). Count the number of levels you applied in that new column to find out how many free levels you have spent, and write it down in a "Total" line below the list of skills. Subtract that number from 30 and that tells you how many free levels you have left (or if you have gone over).

Continue making columns to increment your skills until you have spent all 30 of your free levels. You may find that you will need to remove some skills in order to get the levels you want in the more important

Casting

reserved for those characters that really need to have a super-human attribute. This should be used with extreme caution, as it can easily overbalance the game. However, there are times when the show warrants such a character. Hercules, being the son of a god, was known to have super-human strength. In this case, it may be appropriate for Hercules to have Legendary Brawn. To help balance him out, you can shrink one or more of his other attributes.

A character cannot start out with any traits set to Legendary without permission from the Director.

Determining Your Skills

Your character begins with 30 free levels that can be used to distribute among your skills. Like with attributes, you can spend your free levels among any of available skills. With attributes, it was easy because there are only six to distribute. However, there are a great number of skills.

Unlike attributes, you are allowed to purchase a Superb skill when creating your character.

The following table breaks down the cost of specific skill levels to help you decide what levels of each skill you can afford. The table illustrates how many free levels you must spend to achieve the desired level for any one skill. The cost will differ between skills that default to Poor and those that default to Non-existent.

You will notice that when dropping a skill whose default is Poor down to Terrible, the cost is -1. This means that you would actually gain an additional free level that you can spend on another skill.

Cost for Specific Skill Levels		
Desired Level	**Non-Existent**	**Poor**
Superb	7	5
Great	6	4
Good	5	3
Fair	4	2
Mediocre	3	1
Poor	2	0
Terrible	1	-1

Default Levels

The default level for skills is either Poor or Non-Existent. Most skills can be used without any formal training. Those skills will default to Poor. There are skills, however, that must be learned before they can be used. Pilot is a prime example. These have non-existent levels as default, which means that you cannot use the skill at all until you purchase a level in it. When you purchase a skill level for a non-existent skill, the first level you buy is Terrible, and you must increase it from there.

While shifting, it is possible to lower a skill to a level that is below its default. This represents ineptitude, and is worse than being untrained.

You cannot lower the level of any trait below Terrible.

Determining Your Gifts And Faults

All characters start out with one free gift and no faults. If you would like another gift, you can choose to take a fault. For every fault you take, you can take a new gift. You may also spend attribute and/or skill levels in order to gain more gifts as discussed below.

Although there is no limit to the number of gifts and faults you purchase, you should be careful. Having too many of either can make your character hard to play. Faults are especially dangerous in this way. Faults are debilitating, and by adding several faults, you can easily make an unplayable character.

Shifting Between Trait Types

There are more shifting options available. You can pay skill levels to buy attribute levels and visa-versa. You can also trade in gifts for skill or attribute levels. However, this is not a one-to-one transition. A level of an attribute is more valuable than a skill level, and therefore it will cost more than one skill level to increase an attribute.

The cost breakdown is as follows:

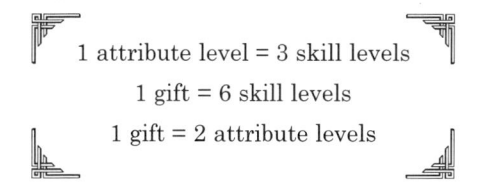

1 attribute level = 3 skill levels

1 gift = 6 skill levels

1 gift = 2 attribute levels

For example, Jack can trade one gift for 6 skill levels, or since an attribute level costs 3 skill levels, he could trade in the gift for 2 levels of an attribute.

Once the levels have been subtracted and the conversion cost paid, they can be applied any way you want. For example, the 2 attribute levels that Jack gets from trading in his gift does not have to be applied to just one attribute. He could choose to apply one level to Brawn and the other to Agility.

Shifting With Faults

Normally taking a fault will automatically give you a gift. If you would rather it give you skill or attribute levels instead, then you can take the fault to gain an unnamed gift, then immediately trade that gift in for skill or attribute levels as described above.

Luck

Sometimes a character lives through situations where no one could be expected to survive. Either by fate or by

Casting

pure luck, the character has managed to pull off an almost impossible task.

At the beginning of every game session, each character is given 3 luck points. Additional luck points can be gained by taking the Lucky gift.

Experienced Characters

Sometimes the Director will want to run a show that requires a cast that is more experienced and capable than a normal beginning character would be. This is easy to do, but does require a little extra work when creating the character.

First, create the character like normal as a starting character.

Then, the Director must decide how experienced the character should be. She will decide on a number of Experience Points (EP) that all of the main characters will start out with. For instance, 20 EP would be good for moderately experienced characters.

Once the characters have experience points, they can spend them to increase their traits as described in the Advancing Characters section below.

Scale

What is Scale?

Scale is meant to represent how large and massive a creature is compared to the human norm. For instance, a Tyrannosaurus Rex with Fair Brawn is not as strong as a T-Rex with a Great Brawn, but it could swallow a human in one bite! In this case, it would not matter how strong the human is. Even if he had Legendary Brawn, he would still be no match for the dinosaur.

Scale is recorded using numbers. Humans have a Scale of zero. Any creature whose mass is significantly greater than that of humans has a Scale of one or more. Any creature whose mass is significantly smaller than that of humans has a Scale of -1 or lower.

Scale affects both the Brawn attribute and combat damage. A character's Scale is applied as a modifier to all Brawn-based trait tests, such as Brawn tests, the Brawl skill, and so on. It is also applied as a modifier to a character's Defensive Factor in regards to damage only. The effects of Scale on tests and combat are described in detail in Chapter Six: Filming.

Determining Scale

This is the only tricky rule in *Now Playing*, and luckily only happens when you are defining a new species. However, it is not really as tough as it looks. Here are some simple steps to determining the Scale of your new species:

How Big is It?

You must first decide how much bigger and massive it is compared to a human. Do this in the form of a multiplier. For instance, a grizzly bear is about three times bigger than a human. You do not have to be precise, as long as it's close enough for your game.

Do not consider just height and width, but its whole mass as well. A creature can be very tall, but not very heavy or massive.

You can consult the chart below to find a well-known

Scale Multipliers

Scale	Size	Speed
-11	0.01	0.13
-10	0.02	0.16
-9	0.03	0.19
-8	0.04	0.23
-7	0.06	0.28
-6	0.1	0.3
-5	0.15	0.4
-4	0.2	0.5
-3	0.3	0.6
-2	0.5	0.7
-1	0.7	0.8
0	1	1
1	1.5	1.2
2	2.3	1.4
3	3.5	1.7
4	5	2
5	7.5	2.5
6	10	3
7	15	3.5
8	25	4
9	40	5
10	60	6
11	90	7.5
12	130	9
13	200	11
14	300	13
15	450	15
16	650	18
17	1000	22
18	1500	27
19	2500	32
20	4000	38

Casting

animal that has a similar Scale to the creature you are creating.

Find the Appropriate Scale

The nearby table *Scale Multipliers* lists all the multipliers from near 0, all the way to 4000. This should cover any Scale you would want to assign. Simply find the multiplier that most closely fits the one you chose for your creature, and use the Scale that it corresponds to.

This is not rocket science, and therefore does not need to be exact. Just use whatever feels right for your show.

Purchasing Scale

Scale is purchased as a Power. The price of the Power must be set by the Director, and will represent the amount of Scale being purchased. The lowest cost of a Power is two gifts, so a good rule of thumb is to start with a cost of two gifts, and then increment from there.

Partial Scales

There may be rare occasions when you would want Scale to apply only to a certain type of physical ability. For instance, a superhero with super speed would have an Agility that's on a much higher Scale than any normal human. However, he is no stronger or massive than anyone else. Only his speed and agility is affected.

In these cases, you can either apply the Scale directly to an attribute, causing it to only modify that one attribute, or you can tie it to a specific type of task. In the case of the super-fast superhero, his Scale will have no effect on his Offensive Factor, but will have a tremendous effect on his Defensive Factor, as he is exceeding tough to hit.

Defined Species

The section Non-Human Species of this chapter discusses how to create new species of creatures that can be used for creating cast members. These species will have checks and balances defined in so that a character of that species will not be out of balance from the others. In that

Casting

case, you will follow the rules for creating a character of that species.

Powers

From psychics to mutants to super heroes, there are many types of characters that exhibit special abilities that are beyond the capability of human beings, as we know them. This section will describe the different types of Powers and how to add them to your character.

Availability of Powers

Powers are very setting-oriented, and will not work in some shows. For instance, a normal police drama or romance show would have no place for any super-human powers or magic. However, shows about super heroes, the occult and the paranormal would.

The bottom line here is that the use of Powers is strictly up to the Director. If you decide that you want your character to have a power, you will need to discuss it with her and work out a plan that you both like. It may be that she would allow certain types of Powers, like psi or magic, but would disallow cyber or mutant powers. There's a possibility that she might allow the power you want, but would require certain restrictions to help balance the power out.

Example: You are creating a character for FPI and you want a power that allows you to communicate with spirits of the dead. You discuss it with the Director, and she says that it is too powerful for the game as it is. You talk about it some more and you both decide that instead, you can communicate with them non-verbally, but only if they contact you. This would give the Director more control over the power to make sure it does not get abused.

Purchasing A Power

Each power is gained as an expensive gift. You purchase the power by spending free gifts for it, or by spending experience points. However, the cost will vary. The Director must decide on a suitable cost for the power, based on the availability of Powers in the show and the details of the power itself. Once she decides on the cost, you must pay it in order to take the power.

Standard Cost: Generally, all Powers should begin with a cost twice that of a gift. So to take the Photographic Memory power, you would pay two free gifts, and may therefore have to take a fault just to cover the cost. The Director, however, may increase the cost as she sees fit, since Powers are so very linked with the nature of the show.

Associated Skills

Some Powers just work and require no skill to use. For instance, X-Ray vision would just always work and its effectiveness would simply depend on what is being looked through. Those details would be defined up front when the power is created, like not being able to see through lead.

Some Powers, however, require a certain amount of skill to control its use. These come with a related skill, defaulting to Terrible, which is used to control it. You advance this skill as normal, and if you take the power at character creation, you can apply your free skill levels to boost it.

Example: Having angel-like wings as a power would automatically give you the ability to fly, but that's it. When you gain the power, you would also gain the default level of Terrible with the Flying skill.

Some associated skills already exist, but others exist only for your power. This depends on the power and would need to be defined along with it. In any case, once you have the skill, you can advance it as though it were a normal skill. You should not have to do much to define a Power's skill. Skills, generally, should be simple to define and use. For instance, if you choose the Flight Power, the obvious associated skill would by Fly. Defining the Fly skill is really a matter of common sense. To fly, the character must make a Fly test. If it fails, he either cannot take off or falls. You can modify this depending on the specifics of the character.

Combat Powers

Some Powers can be wielded like a weapon. Any power like these must have their own Strength defined for damage purposes. In addition, you must define a combat skill or attribute to accompany it. For instance, if the power allows you to make your fist as hard as iron, then you would link it with your Brawl or Martial Art skill in regards to combat.

Likewise, if a power emulates armor, all statistics for handling armor must be determined for it.

Non-Human Species

Most TV shows takes place on the earth that we all know, and there are no alien species or bizarre creatures. But there are some shows that are not like that. There is an increasing number of science fiction shows and shows on the paranormal that introduce a wide assortment of creatures and non-human people. For these shows, you will need to do some work up front to create the new species and allow the actors to create characters of these species.

Not all non-human species are extra-terrestrial or even fictional. We are surrounded by a wide variety of creatures that are not human: animals. Animals are also treated as non-human species in *Now Playing*.

This section will describe how to create species, and will include a sample species as an example.

Casting

Starring Species or Supporting Species

The Director must decide if the starring characters can be of this species, or if it is reserved only for supporting characters. For instance, for a modern-day sci-fi show about an alien invasion, the Director would most likely not allow an actor to play one of the aliens, but would keep them only as supporting characters.

Describe the Species

This step may seem obvious, but it is very important. You must define in your own mind exactly what makes the species different from humans. Are they larger and stronger? Do they have any special Powers or abilities? Do they have special physical features, such as natural weapons (claws, etc.) or natural body armor? Once you have this list of differences, you can begin working the species out.

Defining Special Abilities

Each special ability can be defined as either a Power, a gift, or perhaps a fault as the case may be. If a species has a powerful ability then you should try to give it some kind of fault that can help to balance it out. A well-made TV show should have done that for you. If your show is based on an existing show, then watch that show and study the species. There may be a species described in a show that is quite definitely unbalanced, being grossly more powerful than the others. In those rare cases, the Director can balance the character by adjusting gift, fault and skill level requirements.

If a special ability is a natural weapon, then you or the Director must decide what the weapon's strength is. Chapter Five: Props describes how to determine a weapon's strength.

If the species has some form of natural body armor, you must determine its Defensive Factor and all other armor stats.

Also, keep Scale in mind. If the species is exceedingly large or small compared to humans, then consider increasing or decreasing its scale.

Attributes

It is possible that a species will normally have higher or lower levels of certain attributes for its norm. In this case, adjust the default levels for those attributes. For instance, if the species is normally very weak, but very fast, you can default its Brawn to Mediocre and its Agility to Good instead of Fair for all attributes.

Free Levels, Gifts & Faults

Some species may be more or less skillful than others are, or perhaps gain automatic gifts or faults. For instance, you can specify that all characters of the species gain +5 free skill levels.

Defining the Species' Culture

How fully you define the culture depends on both the show and the species. If the species is meant to be available for starring characters, then it should be fully defined. If it is meant to be just for supporting roles, then it depends fully on the show. If the species plays a major role in the show, then it may need to be fully defined. If they are meant just as an occasional antagonist, then you need define only the parts of the species that are required for the show. You could start a show with a species only partially defined and then define it over time as the seasons play out.

Animals, Beasts & Monsters

All non-human species, whether they are aliens or just animals, are treated this way. When it comes down to it, every creature is just a character. It's just that some are not human and others are even not intelligent. You would simply use the rules stated in this section to create your creature.

To help, Chapter Five: Props includes a zoo that is full of the stats and descriptions of a variety of animals and creatures. You can use them as defined, or modify them to suit your needs. You can also use them as templates for additional creatures.

Animals as Stars

Believe it or not, you really can make a show that centers on animals as the starring characters. For instance, you can run a show about the adventures of a pack of wolves in the Alaskan tundra.

Since all creatures are characters, you can use the same rules for creating characters that are wolves, as you would use to create human characters. You would also need to apply all of the racial differences described for that species.

Adjusting Scale: One thing you would want to do when focusing the starring cast on a species that's different from humans is to adjust the scale. A scale of zero usually represents the "human norm", but really it represents the "starring characters' norm". This is done so that for all combat between the starring characters won't need to deal with scale. Therefore, if all of the characters were of a species whose scale is different from that of humans, you would set their scale to zero and adjust the scales of all other creatures appropriately.

For example, if you are playing a show that stars a warren of bunnies, then you would want to reset the Scale to favor the bunnies. Let us say that bunnies normally have a Scale of -7 because of their size in relation to humans. You would set the Scale for creatures to be +7 larger than their scale indicates. This would mean that humans are now at a Scale of 7 and the bunnies (our

Casting

stars) have a scale of 0.

NOTE: When adjusting scale to center on a particular species, you must be sure to adjust the Scale accordingly for weapons as well. Any weapon that has its own Strength must be adjusted as well. Otherwise, if the Strength of a shotgun remains as is, it would hurt a rabbit the same way it would normally hurt a human. A shotgun remaining at Scale 0 would have hardly any effect on a human with a Scale of 7.

Advancing Characters

After a character has been in a show for a while, it makes sense that he will improve his skills and attributes, and perhaps even gain a new gift or fault.

This section describes the process for applying the effects of experience on a character.

Experience Points

Throughout the course of a show, the Director will award experience points (EP) to each of the main and recurring characters. At certain stages of the show, determined by the Director, the actors can spend these experience points to increase attributes and skills and to gain new gifts and faults. The number of experience points awarded and the frequency that it occurs is strictly up to the Director. Usually, she will award experience at the end of every session, but it really depends on the situation. Experience is always awarded for excellent use of skills and attributes, for heroic actions and outstanding roleplaying.

For more details regarding awarding of experience, refer to Chapter Seven: Directing.

Spending Experience Points

You can spend Experience Points to purchase levels in any attribute or skill, as well as to buy new gifts or to remove a fault. However, the cost will differ according to what you are trying to improve. For instance, attributes are very difficult to improve, and therefore cost more EP to increase a level.

The experience point cost for each advancement is described below:

When to Advance

In most cases, the Director will let you spend experience points to increase your traits between episodes, and often between sessions. This allows you to improve your character gradually over time, rather than in big occasional leaps. You should always ask the Director for permission, though, as she has the last word.

It is recommended that the Director only lets you increase skills and attributes that you have used in the sessions since your last advancement. The idea here is the increases in your skills become closely linked to the actions that you take in the game. This adds realism, as well as giving you an incentive to use skills that you may not be very good at.

Example: You have no levels of the Throw skill. However, you now own a knife and would like to become proficient at throwing it. You do not want to try throwing during the game with such bad skill in it. However, the Director will not let you spend any Experience Points on Throw unless you use the skill in game. Therefore, when you're chasing an enemy, you decide to grab a rock and throw it at him. Whether you hit or miss is irrelevant. Either way it makes the scene more fun. The bonus is that you can now spend some EP on the skill.

Raising a skill from:	To:	Costs:
Terrible	Poor	1 EP
Poor	Mediocre	1 EP
Mediocre	Fair	1 EP
Fair	Good	2 EP
Good	Great	4 EP
Great	Superb	8 EP
Superb	Legendary	16 EP*
Legendary	Legendary 2nd	30 EP*
Each add'l level of Legendary:		50 EP*

Raising an attribute:

Triple the cost for skills of the same level.

Adding a gift:

6 EP (or more)*

Removing a fault:

6 EP (or more)*

* These all require the Director's approval.

Skills

Chapter 3

Casting

Choosing Skills

Purchasing the skills that your character has can be the most tedious part of creating your character. The fact that *Now Playing* includes so many skills adds to that tedium. However, since you can run shows of virtually any genre, it's important that all the skills your character may need are included in the game.

This chapter lists and describes all of the skills that are available in *Now Playing*. Choose wisely; taking many skills that are of little use to your character can take precious free levels away from the more useful skills.

Anatomy of a Skill

In *Now Playing*, skills are designed to be very simple in regards to the game system. You will find that the skill descriptions do not go into much (if any) system details, but instead focus only on the skill itself. The following is a breakdown of the rules regarding how skills are defined.

Description

In most cases, the description of the skill is very story related and does not have much in the way of game system rules. There will be suggested limits, target levels, penalties or bonuses in some skill descriptions, while others will be very simplistic and leave much up to your own interpretation.

Default Level

You can use most skills without any kind of training in them at all. For instance, you don't need to have training or experience in swimming to be able to tread water. Some skills, however, are useless without some form of training. You cannot perform surgery, for example, without having some form of training.

All skills that can be used "untrained" default to a skill level of Poor. This means that you do not need to purchase any levels of this skill in order to be Poor at it. The first level you would buy for one of these skills will be Mediocre.

All skills that require training default to "non-existent" ("NE" on the skill tables). You cannot even attempt these skills without having purchased at least one level in that skill. Since the skill doesn't even exist without buying levels, you would start at Terrible with the first level you buy.

Skill Level Costs Based on Defaults		
Desired Level	**Non-existent**	**Poor**
Superb	7	5
Great	6	4
Good	5	3
Fair	4	2
Mediocre	3	1
Poor	2	0
Terrible	1	-1

Table 3-1: Mental Skills

Skill	Default	Skill	Default	Skill	Default
Animal Care	NE	Engineering (pick a type)	NE	Profile	NE
Appraise	Poor	First Aid	Poor	Psychology	NE
Area Knowledge	Poor	Forgery	Poor	Read Lips	Poor
Autopsy	NE	Hypnosis	NE	Religion (pick one)	Poor
Business Sense	Poor	Interpret Language	NE	Repair Device (pick one)	Poor
Computer Use	NE	Knowledge (pick one)	Poor	Research	Poor
Concentrate	Poor	Language (pick one)	NE	Ritual (pick one)	NE
Cryptozoology	Poor	Nature Lore	Poor	Science (pick one)	NE
Culture (pick one)	Poor	Navigate	Poor	Streetsmarts	Poor
Decipher Script	NE	Notice	Poor	Surgery	NE
Demolitions	NE	Occult Knowledge	Poor	Surveillance	Poor
Diagnose	NE	Pantomime	Poor	Train Animal	NE
Direction Sense	Poor	Parapsychology	NE	Treat Injury	NE
Disable Device (pick one)	NE	Photography (pick type)	Poor	UFOlogy	Poor
Disguise	Poor	Primitive Tools	Poor	Write	Poor

Casting

Meta Skills

Some skills actually represent a group of related skills. These are denoted by the use of a general name and instructions in the skill table on how to choose the skill. For example, "Drive (pick vehicle)" in Table 3-2: Physical Skills

When you buy a level in a meta skill, you must choose a sub-skill for it. For instance, when you buy a rank in Drive, you must specify the type of vehicle you have the skill to drive. You would then use the meta skill name as a prefix for the sub-skill. For instance, if you pick the Drive skill and the Car sub-skill, you would write "Drive Car" in the character sheet.

Skill Categories

Because of the large number of skills, they have been sorted into categories for easy reference. The categories themselves have no relevance in the game system.

These categories include: Mental Skills, Physical Skills, and Social Skills.

Mental Skills

This includes all skills that require mental concentration and thought. Some of these skills, such as Computer Use, perform some action based on thought or concentration. Other skills, such as Archaeology, simply represent the character's knowledge of a specific topic.

Physical Skills

These skills are physical in nature. All physical activities, such as climbing, running, acrobatics, shooting a gun, and even driving a car are included in this category.

Social Skills

From sales to carousing to even performing on stage, these skills all require social interaction for their success. Salespersons, actors, con-men and leaders all pick skills from this category.

Adding & Changing Skills

Certainly, with such a diverse range of settings, it is quite likely that an actor or the Director may want to include some skills that are not already included. The Director is encouraged to modify the skill lists as needed to support the show she is running.

Adding Skills

All you need to do to add a skill is to think up a name, description and default level. You should consider the two suggestions when adding your own skills:

Simplicity: It is highly recommended that you do not tie many game system rules to the definition of your skills. This will usually only complicate game play, and would make the skill feel out of place when compared

Table 3-2: Physical Skills

Skill	Default	Skill	Default	Skill	Default
Acrobatics	Poor	Hide Traces	Poor	Shadow	Poor
Balance	Poor	Jump	Poor	Sleight of Hand	Poor
Brawl	Poor	Martial Art (pick one)	NE	Stealth	Poor
Breaking & Entering	Poor	Mimic Animal Noises	Poor	Swim	Poor
Climb	Poor	Pick Lock	Poor	Throw	Poor
Craft (pick type of item)	Poor	Pick Pocket	Poor	Track	Poor
Dodge	Poor	Pilot (pick craft)	NE	Weapon (pick one)	Poor
Drive (pick vehicle)	Poor	Ride Animal (pick one)	NE	Zero-G Maneuver	Poor
Escape Artist	Poor	Run	Poor		
Fish	Poor	Sail	Poor		

Table 3-3: Social Skills

Skill	Default	Skill	Default	Skill	Default
Bluff	Poor	Haggle	Poor	Perform	Poor
Camaraderie	Poor	Hold Your Liquor	Poor	Persuade	Poor
Diplomacy	Poor	Innuendo	Poor	Seduce	Poor
Etiquette	Poor	Interrogate	Poor	Sense Motive	Poor
Gamble	Poor	Intimidate	Poor	Tall Tales	Poor
Gather Information	Poor	Oratory	Poor	Uplift Spirits	Poor

with the rest of the skills.

Standard Defaults: You should always use one of the two standard default levels of Non-Existent and Poor whenever possible. This will make the skill easy to learn and memorize. If you start varying the default levels, you add complexity, which can detract from the game. Remember, game play should always be smooth and with little emphasis on the system. When you vary the default levels, you force the actors to be constantly looking up skills in the book each time they use an untrained skill just to know what the default level is.

Deleting Skills

Some shows may actually make certain skills unavailable. For instance, the Computer Use skill will not be available in a show that takes place in a Victorian era setting.

Changing Skills

Sometimes the setting may require that you change the definition of a skill to fit the show you are running better. This is perfectly acceptable, as long as you are careful to keep it simple.

Example: The Computer Use skill gives a character with the level of Terrible enough experience with computers to be able to do most forms of computer use without making a skill test. In a 1960's setting, your show might not make that assumption, and would require a test for doing any kind of operation. After all, back then there was no such thing as an easy to learn operating system!

Skill Descriptions

This section will describe each of the skills included in *Now Playing*. You can change the definition of each skill when you need to make it fit better to the show you are running.

Mental Skills

Acrobatics (Poor)

You are skilled at leaping, swinging and tumbling. It is a good idea to choose a type of acrobatics, such as gymnastics or skating, but you do not have to. If you do not, then the Director may choose to give you a penalty for generalizing.

You can make Acrobatics skill tests to perform an act of acrobatics. If you try to perform an acrobatic act that is outside of the specialization you chose, then the Director may apply a penalty.

Animal Care (Non-existent)

You know how to take care of animals.

If the Director deems it appropriate, you may need to choose a specific type of animal, but by default, this is not necessary.

You know how to feed, groom, and otherwise care for the animal on a regular basis. You can identify normal animal problems, such as worms, and can keep them healthy under normal circumstances. You understand the animal's diet and what must be done to keep it healthy and happy.

This skill does not give you any knowledge of veterinarian medicine, nor does it allow you to train an animal.

Appraise (Poor)

You can determine the worth of an item by inspecting it. The worth of the item may not necessarily be in monetary terms, but can include inspecting the item for quality, authenticity, etc.

The Director must set a suitable target level and the Relative Degree of the roll will determine how much information you will learn.

The Director may choose not to tell you what the target level is so that if you fail, you may not know it. An almost successful roll may mean that you appraise the item and are quite off, but do not know it.

Area Knowledge (Poor)

You are very familiar with the area, and can find your way around without difficulty.

When you take this skill, you must choose a specific area. This area can be the city or town you live in, or it can be your favorite vacation spot. You know that area so well, that you can always find the quickest shortcut to wherever you are going. You know the businesses in the area, and understand how they operate. That is, you know that old man Willard opens up his coffee shop every day at 4:00 AM, and that Mack's Paper Stand gets their morning delivery at 5:30 AM. You also may know the routines of some of those who live in the area. For instance, you may know that Mrs. Maynard walks her Scotty dog every evening at 6:00 PM sharp.

Whenever something breaks in the rhythm of your area, you may make an Area Knowledge test to tell what is not right. Of course, you have to be in a position to have noticed the change. If the break in rhythm is subtle, like if Mrs. Maynard suddenly misses her evening walk, the Director may call for a Notice skill test just to realize that something is not right. Then, you can make the Area Knowledge test to figure out exactly what it is.

When in chase, you can use your Area Knowledge to find the best shortcuts or tricky maneuvers that can shake your pursuers, or to cut off your quarry if you're

Casting

doing the chasing.

If a certain clue points to a specific type of place, then you can come up with accurate suggestions of places in the area that fit that description. Again, make an Area Knowledge test. How well you make the test and how many matches there are will determine how many suggestions you can think of.

Autopsy (Non-existent)

You are trained in examining and dissecting a corpse with the intent of determining the cause of death.

This use of skill does not produce a simple success or failure, but is instead measured by degree. Since this skill represents the gathering of facts, of which there are always many, the result of the test will determine what clues or facts are found. The Director will set a base target level that must be met in order to uncover any information about the patient. The amount by which the test succeeds (the test's Relative Degree) will then determine how successful the autopsy was. The Director must know how many facts can be found in order to determine how many of them were found in the autopsy.

This skill assumes that you are performing the autopsy in a proper environment with proper equipment. If the autopsy is not taking place in a hospital or other well-equipped facility, then the Director may raise the Difficulty Level of the skill test.

| Example Autopsy Relative Degrees ||
Relative Degree	Facts Found
0	One third
1	One half
2	Two thirds
3	All

Balance (Poor)

You are good at staying on your feet on slippery surfaces, narrow ledges, and on thrashing surfaces. Sailors need great balance when trying to walk or even stand on deck during a storm.

You must make Balance tests whenever you are on unsteady ground or a narrow ledge. If you are trying to perform a delicate act on an unsteady surface, you may need to make a Balance test before making the other skill test. For instance, if you are in a swordfight on the deck of a ship, the Director may have you make a Balance test first.

Bluff (Poor)

You can lie very successfully. With not only your words, but also your gestures and expressions, you can make people believe you are telling the truth when you are actually telling a falsehood. Sometimes no words need to be spoken to make a bluff. In gambling, you can bluff a "poker face" to make your opponents think you have an excellent hand when you do not.

This is always an opposed action against the other person's Reasoning test or Sense Motive skill test. If you fail your Bluff skill test, you have not duped the other party.

Brawl (Poor)

Use this skill whenever you are in unarmed combat. This includes punching, kicking, biting, and other forms of hand-to-hand fighting. This does not include any style of Martial Arts, but does include boxing and wrestling.

When in a brawl, use this skill as your attack roll. When brawling, your Brawn modifies your Offensive Factor.

Breaking & Entering (Poor)

You are skilled at forcibly entering a building or room without detection. You can find the easiest way to enter the building and jimmy windows.

When trying to force entry, make a Breaking & Entry test. How well you succeed will determine how quickly and quietly you managed to do it. You must have the right equipment to break in.

You can use this skill to find the best likely mode of entry. The Director must make the roll herself so that if you fail, you might be led to think you found the best place to enter. Then, when it is too late, you find out that you failed.

Business Sense (Poor)

You have learned how to handle business situations and to make sound financial and corporate decisions. You can use this skill to determine if a proposition that is being offered makes good sense.

Camaraderie (Poor)

You have this way of instilling a sense of companionship with others.

You can make Camaraderie skill tests when trying to convince supporting cast to work together to help a fellow comrade or to motivate your team to work harder at a worthwhile task.

Computer Use (Non-existent)

You are skilled in the use of computers and computer-controlled devices.

A successful Computer Use test would indicate that the task was completed successfully. In a modern day setting, most people who have had at least a little computer experience or training (purchased one level) can perform most common tasks on a personal computer without having to make a skill test, because computers nowadays are much easier to learn and use than they used to be. Any challenging tasks, however, would require a skill test.

There are many types of tasks that can be performed with Computer Use, and each one has a different difficulty level. The following table lists some of these tasks and suggests difficulty levels for them.

Example Computer Task Difficulty Levels	
Task	Level
Sending email on a personal computer.	Automatic
Operating an unfamiliar program.	Mediocre
Using a complex piece of software you have never used before.	Good
Configuring a computer operating system.	Good
Hacking into a small company with normal user privileges.	Great
Hacking into a small company with power user privileges.	Superb

It is important to note that Computer Use does not include the ability to create computer software. That can be done by either the Craft Software or Software Engineering skills.

Climb (Poor)

You are good at climbing up and down surfaces. You can find footholds in nearly sheer surfaces and through force of will an perseverance, you can climb difficult surfaces for great distances.

Concentrate (Poor)

You can keep your focus on a specific task amid much distraction.

When performing a task that requires focus, such as performing a magical ritual, you must make Concentrate tests at regular intervals to be able to continue with the task if there is anything happening that can distract you. The interval in which you must make your Concentrate tests depends on the amount of time required to perform the task, and the amount of distraction. Therefore, the Director must decide on an appropriate interval.

Example: Jelena is attempting a ritual to banish an evil spirit. The ritual takes 5 minutes to perform and any interruptions will not only cause failure, but could free the

Casting

spirit from the house in which it is trapped. The spirit is howling, causing wind and hurling objects about the room. The Director decides that in order to succeed in the ritual, she must make a Concentrate test every minute at a difficulty of Good. She rolls three Concentrate tests, resulting in Great, Good and Superb, respectively. She was able to maintain her concentration. Now she can make her Ritual test to find out if she successfully banishes the spirit.

Craft (Poor)

You are skilled at creating something that you can sell for money.

When you take this skill, you must pick a type of craft. Examples of some common crafts are as follows: sculpture, painting, pottery, woodwork, etc. It is possible to create computer software with this skill, although Software Engineering may be more appropriate.

A successful Craft test means that you created the item well, and it is of at least good quality. The Relative Degree will specify how well made the item is. The amount of time required to make the item depends on both the type of item being made and the Relative Degree of the Craft test.

Crafting an item assumes that you have all of the materials and tools necessary for the job. Some items may require multiple Craft tests to complete the item, and is decided by the Director.

Once made, you can either keep and use the item, or sell it. If you created the item successfully, then it is fully usable. Selling the item and determining the price depends on the Relative Degree of the Craft skill test. The more successful the test, the more money you can make from selling it. Exactly how much money you can sell or barter the item for is up to the Director.

Cryptozoology (Poor)

From vampires and werewolves to the Loch Ness monster and Bigfoot, you are an expert on all bizarre creatures of myth and legend.

You can make a Cryptozoology test to remember any known fact about a specific legendary creature. The fact must be either documented somewhere or told as a folk tale in order for you to know it. The Difficulty Level of the test depends on the obscurity of the fact and the creature in question.

Culture (Poor)

When you take this skill, pick a specific culture.

You have studied this culture to some length, and have an understanding of its people and way of life. You know some of its history and its influences. You can identify a member of that culture from a quick meeting.

Decipher Script (Non-existent)

You can take a written document or artifact and by studying the symbol patterns, determine its meaning. The difficulty of this kind of task can vary greatly depending on your knowledge of language used and the history of the artifact.

Demolitions (Non-existent)

Use this skill to create and set explosive devices.

Creating an explosive device will require a Demolitions test to make sure it is done right. A failed test could mean either that you just couldn't manage to do it and you know that it won't work, or that you think it's right, but it simply won't detonate when it's supposed to. This result is up to the Director, and can be based on how badly you failed your test.

Simply setting an explosive device is not difficult, and will always succeed, but setting it in a position that will be most effective can be. If you failed to properly set the explosive, the amount by which you failed is added as a bonus to the Dodge tests of all those within the blast radius.

Example: Jack sets some dynamite near the entrance to a cave that his enemies are in. He controls the dynamite by a plunger device from a distance. The Difficulty Level of the Demolitions test to set the dynamite is Fair. He rolled a Poor, which is two below the level he needed. He accidentally left part of the blast area blocked with rock. When the enemies come out of the cave, and Jack detonates the dynamite, the brunt of the blast goes away from the targets. Each of the men leaving the cave gets a +2 (because Jack failed by 2) to their Dodge tests to avoid injury.

Diagnose (Non-existent)

You are skilled at diagnosing an illness or injury. You can examine the symptoms that the patient is experiencing and figure out a cause of the illness. Not all people in the medical profession can accurately diagnose an illness. In addition, some doctors are excellent at treating injuries and illnesses once they are made known to them, but are not as skilled at detecting the illness.

The Director should either roll the test for the character or not tell the actor what the Difficulty Level is. This is because a mis-diagnosis can be very important. If the Diagnose test almost succeeded, then the you did well enough not to have made a mistake. You simply cannot figure out what is wrong with the patient. If, however, you failed your test by a high margin, then you may have messed up badly, and mis-diagnosed the illness.

Diplomacy (Poor)

You are good at negotiating deals, and speaking with "political correctness".

Casting

Use Diplomacy when trying to lead a group of supporting cast in a specific task. You can use this to perform most forms of negotiations between yourself and others, as well as between third parties.

Direction Sense (Poor)

You have the ability to figure out your direction wherever you are. If you were blindfolded and dumped in the middle of nowhere in the middle cloudy night, you may still be able to figure out in what direction north lies.

The Difficulty Level will depend upon the availability of the various tell-tales signs. For instance, if the sun is out, no test may be necessary. If it's exactly noon, then the test might still be easy. A cloudy night with sign of stars or moon would be difficult, but still possible for someone with this skill.

Disable Device (Non-existent)

You are good at examining a device and figuring out how to disable it. The more complicated the device, the more difficult it will be to disable. When you take this skill, you must choose a type of device. For instance, you can choose electronic devices, computers, explosives, or alarms.

If you are computer illiterate (have no levels in Computer Use), then you cannot disable a computer short of smashing it or unplugging it.

You must have the proper tools for disabling the device. You cannot remove a car's tire without a lug wrench or some other tool that will do the job.

Disguise (Poor)

You know how to dress, apply make-up and create "special effects" to change your appearance. You know how to use foam "fat-suits" to make you look larger. You can apply make-up to change facial features, add scars, on so on. You are good at deciding what is needed to do the job, because sometimes just a haircut or change of dress is enough!

There are two good ways of handling disguises, and either way is good. The Director must decide which is the best way to handle it in her show:

1. You can make the Disguise test once when you put it on and mark it down. Then, anyone who might recognize you makes a Notice test against your original Disguise test results.
2. Do not make the Disguise test when you put it on. Instead, make an opposed Disguise test against the other person's Notice each time someone might recognize you. The idea here is that wearing a disguise includes how you act while wearing it.

You can also use this skill to recognize a disguise on someone else. Because you know all about disguises, you have a unique perspective on the subject, and are therefore more likely to notice one on someone else.

Dodge (Poor)

You can attempt to avoid being hit by thrown objects or other hazards.

Similar Skills

There are several skills described in *Now Playing* that are very similar, but have subtle differences. These skills are Diplomacy, Oratory, Persuade, Seduce and Uplift Spirits. Each one focuses on influencing the actions of others. The big difference lies in they types and goals of that influence. The best way to understand their differences is to compare them:

Diplomacy deals with professional or political situations. It involves mediating disputes between others, and finding a way to get your point across without insulting anyone's intelligence.

Oratory works through speech. It involves getting up in front of others and speaking about the issues you are concerned with in order to make people agree with you. It is not an interactive skill. You present your case clearly and concisely in speech, and then hope that people see things your way.

Seduce is the art of using your body language and sexual innuendo to achieve a specific goal: make others sexually attracted to you. Seduce can be used in conjunction with Persuade to get the other person to do as you wish, but it does not do the persuading by itself.

Uplift Spirits is another specific application of enforcing one's will on others. In this case, you are simply trying to make people feel better. You are not trying to get them to do something, just to feel a certain way.

Persuade works for all situations where none of the other skills apply. Persuade can take the form of pleading, begging, asking, and arguing and is simply a general way of trying to get what you want.

Casting

By ducking, hopping, swerving and twisting your body, you can try to avoid being hit by anything that is coming your way.

Dodging bullets is, of course, impossible. However, you can run, swerve, duck and bob to make yourself a harder target. Remember, it's not the bullet that you're trying to dodge—it's the shooter's aim!

Drive (Poor)

Use this skill to operate a specific type of land vehicle, including cars, large trucks, tanks, construction vehicles, etc. It also includes motorboats as well. You must choose which type of vehicle you a trained with when you take this skill.

Skill tests are not required for most normal driving tasks. Tests are required when the task becomes challenging. This includes combat, driving faster than the vehicle's cruise speed, poor driving conditions, chases, tailing, etc.

For each Drive test, apply the vehicle's Handling modifier to the roll. The Difficulty Level for the test depends upon the type of maneuver you are doing and the conditions that you are doing it in.

In a modern day show, it is assumed that every character has a driver's license and knows how to drive a car. This means that driving a car under normal conditions should not require a skill check. The exception to this rule is if the character has chosen the Can't Drive fault.

Engineering (Non-existent)

You are trained to use science to design and construct something. This includes creating structures, machines, and even less tangible things such as computer programs.

There are many different forms of engineering and you must pick one. In all cases, engineering involves both designing and creating some kind of item. Some engineers only focus on the design, while others just implement the designs. There are those, however, that do both. The most common modern-day forms of engineering are described below.

Escape Artist (Poor)

You are skilled at escaping from bonds. Whether you are tied up, in a straight jacket or even wearing handcuffs, you are skilled at getting out of them. You can even manage to get out of locked crates and other such traps.

Any kind of escape requires a successful Escape Artist test. The Director must decide on a Difficulty Level that is appropriate for each attempt. For instance, if you're hands are simply tied behind your back, a Good test may be all that's needed. But if you were trying not to be noticed by guards sitting in the room, it would require at least a Great test to get out without being caught.

Etiquette (Poor)

You can behave with proper manners even in the strictest situations.

When choosing this skill, pick a culture. If you do not, it will imply your own culture. You are well versed in the rules of politeness in that society.

When in a social situation where manners count, make an Etiquette test whenever you make an action to insure that you are following the proper rules behavior.

First Aid (Poor)

You can treat small injuries and perform some emergency treatment on injured people. This includes such temporary or minor treatments, such as CPR, cleaning and bandaging wounds, tourniquets, etc.

This skill cannot be used to do more formal treatments that a paramedic or doctor can do. Therefore, First Aid can only be used to treat Light & Severe Wounds, and cannot be used on Incapacitated or worse. The only exception is that First Aid can be used to stabilize a Near Death.

Fish (Poor)

You are good at catching fish. You need all the appropriate tools, such as a fishing rod, line and hook, or perhaps a net. This skill covers all forms of fishing, including lobster fishing and fly fishing.

Forgery (Poor)

You can sign or write a document to make it look like someone else' writing. It requires all the tools necessary, including pens, ink, paper, and lighting. Forging a document can be a very time-consuming task and requires total concentration.

Like with Disguise, you can make the test once and then oppose that one result against every attempt to identify the forged document, or you can not make the Forgery test until someone tries to read it.

Gamble (Poor)

You are skilled at playing games of chance.

Gambling is really a combination of luck, knowledge of the game itself and the use of the Bluff skill. If the scene requires heavy focus on the act of gambling, then the Director may want to require two tests for each round of the game (i.e., each hand of cards). One will be a Gamble test, which determines if you make the right strategic choices in the game. The second will be a Bluff test to make sure that you don't give away the value of your hand with your gestures and facial expression. In most cases, though, this level of complexity is unnecessary and may even bog down the scene. In these cases, a simple Gamble test will suffice.

Casting

Gather Information (Poor)

You are good at collecting information from a variety of sources.

You can hang out unobtrusively in a bar and take careful note of the conversations, and extract all of the useful information from the chatter. You can browse the newspapers and listen to the radio to pick out useful information. You can have casual conversations with people in such a subtle way that you can pull the information from them without letting them know you are.

Gathering information in this manner takes time and effort. Expect to spend an entire day or more frequenting bars, clubs and various other places trying to pick up snatches of information. Most likely you would jot down some notes after leaving each place, and then go somewhere to sort through it.

Haggle (Poor)

You are good at arguing a deal in order to convince the other party to go with a deal that is more to your liking.

Haggling is most often used to talk a salesman into a lower price for an item, but could really be used when working out most deals.

It is very difficult to make a skill like this work against another leading cast member. Instead, this skill should only be used when haggling with supporting cast.

Hide Traces (Poor)

You can hide all traces of your presence in a place. You are good at covering your tracks and making sure that no one will know that you were ever here.

The result of your Hide Traces test will be the Difficulty Level of any attempts to track or notice your trail.

There are some places that may be impossible to hide your traces, so the Director must use care with this skill. This skill only deals with hiding physical evidence, and does not include removing your record from cameras and other electronic devices.

Hold Your Liquor (Poor)

You can drink to excess with little physical or mental effect. You can drink most people under the table and still manage to walk out of the bar.

Use this skill when doing large amounts of drinking. Make a test after each few drinks to see how much it affects you. Keep in mind that you will not be untouched by the liquor's effects completely even if you make every single test. This skill merely minimizes the effects of the liquor.

Hypnosis (Non-existent)

You can put another person into a trance-like state. While the subject is in this state, you may give commands to retrieve hidden or suppressed memories, or to even implant a post-hypnotic suggestion.

Hypnotizing is an opposed action. The Difficulty Level of the test is equal to the subject's Will.

Normally, only a willing subject can be hypnotized, but that rule can be adjusted to fit the particular show.

Once hypnotized, each command or post-hypnotic suggestion requires a Will test from the subject. The subject will involuntarily resist each command or suggestion. Since the roll is made to *resist* the command, the Difficulty Level will be higher for the easier commands. The following table lists some example commands, and their suggested Difficulty Levels.

| Example Hypnosis Will Test Levels ||
Command	Level
Retrieving a memory that has not been suppressed	Good
Retrieving a suppressed memory from a traumatic event	Great
Retrieving a memory suppressed by drugs or by a very traumatic event	Superb

Post-Hypnotic Suggestions: If you are under a post-hypnotic suggestion and the trigger occurs, you must make a Will test. If you fail the test, then the suggestion kicks in and you must do whatever it instructs. If you make the test, nothing will happen. If you make 3 successful tests in a row for the same suggestion, then the suggestion will be gone and no more tests will be necessary. The Difficulty Level of the Will test depends on how much the suggestion goes against your nature. For instance, a suggestion to hit anyone who says a certain word would be easier for a pacifist to resist than a hothead. The Director must decide on a Difficulty Level that is appropriate. As with commands, it is important to note that the easier the suggestion is to resist, the *lower* the Difficulty Level.

If you are under a post-hypnotic suggestion to have no memory of a slice of time and you are exposed to something directly related to it (i.e., if the memory was of a stabbing and you see a butcher chopping up a bloody slab of meat), you must make a Will test. If you succeed, then your mind has broken through part of the suggestion, and you remember a part that pertains to the triggering event. If you successfully make 3 such tests for the same memory, then the entire suggestion is broken and you remember everything. The extent of your recovered memory (until you remember all) is up to the Director.

Innuendo (Poor)

You can hide a hidden message in a statement or conversation.

You can say something out loud to a group of people that makes perfect sense to them and seems quite ordinary, but only those few people that you aim the message

Casting

at can understand the hidden meaning in your words.

This skill is opposed by the Innuendo skills or Notice skill of the entire audience. Of course, anyone who is expecting a hidden message will get a bonus to his rolls. The size of the bonus depends on the situation and is up to the Director.

Interpret Language (Non-existent)

You are skilled at learning a new language by listening and studying it. You can pick out patterns in the words in a spoken conversation, and by studying these patterns and they way they are spoken, you can begin to translate.

This can be a very time-consuming job, taking many hours. The use of computers and other such tools can help cut down the amount of time required.

There are two ways that this skill can be used:

Translate speech on the fly: This requires two Interpret Language tests. The first one is to figure out bits of what the person who is speaking the language is saying, and the second is to properly word your reply. Failure in the first test may mean that you're simply baffled, or it could mean that you misunderstand it. The Director should actually say what is being said, using gibberish for the words the character could not understand and real words for those he can. The second roll determines how well you respond. This should be roleplayed out! See the example below to get an idea of how to do this.

This is exceedingly difficult, and can only be done with a language that has similarities to one that you already know. Any results, no matter how successful you are, will only be partial. Your speech will be broken at best, and the listener's understanding of what you say will be based on your Interpret Language skill test.

Learn The Language: You can gain free skill levels in any language that you manage to translate on the fly (see above). At the end of any session where you have roleplayed out the activity of translating a language on the fly, you gain a free level in that language. This will work until you are proficient in that language. Therefore, you cannot gain any levels above Fair in this manner. It is important to note that you must earn these levels, not just by rolling dice, but also by actually roleplaying out the scenes.

Casting

Interrogate (Poor)

You are good at grilling a person for information. You are good at asking the right questions with the right blend of threat and intimidation to cause the target to talk.

Use this skill when trying to pry information from someone. It is an opposed action against the target's Will attribute. It is assumed that each use of this skill takes some time and much questioning. You can retry the skill test as often as the situation will allow. Generally, you would get one Interrogate skill test per hour of interrogation.

Intimidate (Poor)

You can force a person into doing as you bid by instilling fear in him. This is often done by threats, both literal and implied. A very huge and hulking character can intimidate someone simply by looking dangerous. Cops have the law on their side when intimidating a suspect; the thought of prison has a tendency to instill fear into the toughest of crooks.

You can generally only try this once on any one person. Once you fail an attempt at intimidation, you usually cannot hope to succeed with the same person unless the situation changes. For instance, if you try to intimidate a stranger by your looks and bearing alone and fail, it is seriously doubtful that you could scare him again, since he knows you have already tried and failed. However, if you change the playing field by flashing him your police badge, you should then be able to make a second attempt.

Jump (Poor)

You are good at jumping distances without injury.

Use this skill to jump and leap, like jumping across a chasm, or leaping up to grab the landing strut of a rising helicopter. A failed test means that you failed to achieve the goal you were jumping to make.

Knowledge (Poor)

When you take this skill, pick a specific type of knowledge.

This skill includes all general knowledge skills that are not covered by their own skills. Some examples would be Astrology, Astronomy, Marketing, Fashion Design, etc.

Language (Non-existent)

You have studied a foreign language and can speak, read and write it without much trouble.

When you take this skill, you must choose a language. The languages include any that are available in your show. This could include those for all nationalities and even special languages, such as Braille and sign language.

It is assumed that everyone is fluent in their native language, and thus will never need to make any skill tests when using that language.

Unlike all other skills, you normally do not need to make any skill tests in order to have simple conversational speech with the language. The only time you need to make a Language skill test is when you are writing or reading a challenging document or book, or when trying to appear more fluent in the language than you really are.

Since this skill represents all languages you learn after your primary language, it is assumed that you will speak it with an obvious accent.

Braille: This is a written language for the blind. Each letter is made up of raised dots on a surface. It is up to the Director to decide if skill tests are needed for this language.

Sign Language: This is a language made for deaf people. You speak by using special hand signals to represent letters and words. As with Braille, the Director must decide whether skill tests are necessary for using or understanding sign language.

Literature (Poor)

You are an avid reader and are well versed in literature. You can recite poetry and call up all kinds of tidbits of knowledge from the books you have read. Of course, the books are all fictional, but there is much useful information buried in those books, as most provide insight on life in one way or another.

In an adventure show, this skill can be rather obscure, but not always useless. Consider a serial killer is imitating something that takes place in some famous novel or play, or is at least influenced by it. This can help you predict his next move.

Martial Art (Non-existent)

You have training in one style of Martial Art. You can choose a style when you take this skill, but it's not really necessary unless the Director has developed a martial arts system that requires it.

The Martial Art skill can be used both offensively and defensively, as described below:

Offensive: When using the Martial Art skill in combat, your skill test is your attack roll. Because your limbs are like weapons, you also get an automatic "weapon strength" of +1 to add to your Offensive Factor. This means you do an extra point of damage when you hit your target.

Your weapon strength bonus is only applied when damaging targets that are vulnerable to Martial Art attacks. This would include most unarmored living beings, and wooden doors and boards. Any other targets are up to the Director to decide upon. Certainly, there are other things that would be vulnerable to a skilled Martial Artist, so ask your Director when considering using this skill on it.

Defensive: You can use your Martial Art skill as your opposed roll when defending against certain forms of attack. The attack must be something that the martial art can be used against, which is ultimately up to the Director.

Martial Art System: It is possible to expand this skill into a whole Martial Arts system that can even show differences in Martial Art styles, such as Karate, Kung Fu, Aikido, Judo and others. This can be very useful in a Martial Arts related show. This book does not discuss this, but instead leaves it up to the Director to work out the details.

Mimic Animal Noises (Poor)

You are very skilled at making convincing animal sounds.

Using this skill will always be an opposed action. The result of your Mimic Animal Noises test will be the Difficulty Level of the listeners' Notice tests. Anyone making his Notice tests will realize that the noise was faked.

Your character must have decent knowledge of the animal being mimicked. For instance, you can always attempt to mimic a dog or cat, but to mimic a screech owl means that you must know what screech owls sound like. For an uncommon animal, the Director may require an Animal Lore skill test to make sure you know the animal well enough.

Nature Lore (Poor)

You know all about nature and can literally live off the land. When stranded in the wild, you can forage for food, find shelter and survive. You know about the various plants and wildlife, and will know which berries are good to eat and which are poisonous. You know what side of trees moss grows on and you know to always go to the bathroom away from camp.

Navigate (Poor)

You know how to read charts and maps and to chart the course of a ship or other craft. You can look at the stars to get your bearings, and to tell if you're on course or not.

This skill does not include the ability to pilot a craft, but is simply to handle setting and maintaining a course and to prevent getting lost.

Notice (Poor)

You are skilled at using your senses to notice things that are hard to detect.

When you are actively seeking something, you can make a Notice test to try and find it. The Director may choose to make Notice tests for you in secret when you happen to be near something important.

Occult Knowledge (Poor)

You have studied many forms of the occult in the world, including the Celtic Druids, witchcraft, Satanism, ritual magic traditions, western shamanism, and so on.

This does not mean that you know how to do magic, or that you're a practicing witch, but you would have levels in this skill if you were a witch or magician.

Oratory (Poor)

You are good at speaking to an audience. You have a way of keeping everyone's attention and getting your point across.

This is very useful when trying to sway an audience of supporting cast to agree with you. This skill may be used to impress leading cast, but can only directly effect supporting characters. A prime example of using this skill is to sway a jury in a courtroom.

Pantomime (Poor)

By using your body without speech, you can communicate and get your point across by emulating actions and emotions.

This can take time, and requires room to move. The result of your Pantomime test will determine how well your message will be interpreted.

You can also use this skill to make money, in which case, it will behave like the Perform skill. The important distinction between Pantomime and Perform is that although pantomiming is often used as a form of entertainment, it has the additional ability to silently communicate information. You can consider the Pantomime skill to be a specialized form of the Perform skill. This way, if you want to use this skill for making money, follow the rules for Perform. If you are trying to make certain people understand a specific message, then treat the skill as described above.

Parapsychology (Non-existent)

Parapsychology is the study of the evidence of psychic phenomena. You are familiar with cases involving Clairvoyance, Telepathy, Psychokinesis, Telekinesis and other extraordinary mind powers.

You can make a Parapsychology test to perform tests on a subject to determine if he has any psychic ability, and to measure the extent of that power.

Casting

Perform (Poor)

You can able to perform in public.

When you take this skill, you must choose a type of performance. This can include, but is not limited to, singing, a musical instrument, stand-up comedy, acting, and dancing.

This is usually an opposed action against the Will of the audience, but for an entire audience of many people, the Director can just set one Difficulty Level and let the actor roll against that.

A successful Perform test means that the audience enjoys the performance at least to the point of paying attention to it, and possibly even to pay to see it. For a long performance, multiple tests may be required to keep the audience's attention.

When performing for money, like as a street performer, the Relative Degree of the test result will determine how much money the audience gives. The Director must determine the actual amount of money earned. This can be handled an award of Resource Tickets.

You can use Perform to do pantomime, but it would only be for entertainment purposes. To be able to use the skill to silently convey a message is a much more detailed task, and requires the Pantomime skill.

Persuade (Poor)

You are good at convincing people to do as you say. This can be done through begging, pleading or just simply reasoning with the person.

This can be an opposed action if the person being persuaded is resisting it. In this case, the other's Will attribute will oppose it. Otherwise, the Director will just choose a Difficulty Level.

This skill cannot be used on a leading cast member.

Photography (Poor)

You are skilled in the art of taking pictures.

This skill can represent both still cameras and movie filming, but since they are treated quite differently, you must pick one of these when you take the skill. If you want to have skill with both, you must take the skill twice and treat them as separate skills.

You can use this skill to take quality photographs that can be sold for money. This skill can also be crucial to an investigation by ensuring that the crime scene was photographed in such a way that it will contain all the pertinent clues in good quality.

Pick Lock (Poor)

You know how to open locks with a minimal amount of tools.

You must have the proper equipment. For some locks, it could just be a credit card. Others may require special lock picking tools. This skill does not include disarming electronic or computer controlled locks.

Pick Pocket (Poor)

You are adept at taking things from people's pockets without being caught. This skill really extends to any act where you are trying to take something with your hands so gently that nothing becomes aware of your actions.

As well as for pickpocketing, you can use this skill for other dexterous tasks, such as to carefully pull a small item out of a container that is surrounded by bomb triggers or alarms.

Pilot (Non-existent)

You are trained in the operation of a flying vehicle.

When taking this skill, you must choose a specific type of air or spacecraft. How specific you must be depends on how detailed the Director wants. Generally, you would pick a type of craft that works in one specific way. For instance, you can pick Pilot Single Engine Airplane to be able to fly all small, single-engine aircraft. You could also pick Pilot Lear Jet for all jet aircraft that are similar in design to a Lear jet. Pilot Fighter Jet would be another good one, and so on.

Unlike the vehicles that require the Drive skill, all crafts that you pilot are much more complicated. If you have no levels in Pilot, you might be able to keep it flying once it's in the air, but not much other than that. For theatrical effect, the Director might let you use this skill at Terrible to keep it flying and to try to land, but normally, this would not work.

Primitive Tools (Poor)

You know how to make simple tools and shelters from materials that you scavenge from your surroundings.

Like primitive cultures, you can make stone axes, lean-tos and other simple tools that you can use to help you survive in the wild.

Once you decide on a tool to make, you can make a Primitive Tools test to determine if you succeed in making it. The Relative Degree of the test will show how well the tool was made. The quality of the tool will affect how well it will do its job, and how long it will last.

Before you can make the tool, you must gather all the materials and tools required to construct it. This will require successful Nature Lore skill tests or Notice tests to find adequate materials.

Profile (Non-existent)

By studying a person's actions and behavior, you can work up a personality profile on her. This profile can be used to understand her motives and intentions, and can even help to predict her next actions. The most common use of this skill is for tracking down and catching serial killers.

Working up a profile of a subject requires a successful Profiling test. This will give you some insight into the psyche of the subject. The Director will set the Difficulty Level based on the amount of information you already have on the subject. A successful test will not give you a complete profile, but will only produce a piece of it. In this way, you can continue to make tests as more clues surface.

A failed test means one of two things: that you simply cannot determine anything about the subject, or that you work up a piece of a profile that is not accurate. The details of a failed test are up to the Director.

The Director must take care as to how much of the profile to reveal to you with each successful test. Any details revealed must coincide with the clues that you have already found.

Psychology (Non-existent)

You are skilled at studying how people think and behave. This scholarly skill means that you have studied this subject, most likely at a school or university, and that you have done much research on it.

You can make Psychology tests to match a person's behavior with one of the known case studies or documented patterns. This is not the same as the Profiling skill, as it only matches a person's behavior with currently documented patterns. With Profiling, you get into the person's head and learn about his behavior by studying the subject's behavior and fully immersing yourself in his actions.

You can use the Psychology skill to help a person recover from some kind of traumatic experience or other mental or behavioral problem. This will take a long time and will require many successful Psychology skill tests spread out over many weeks or months. Any failed tests during the patient's treatment may cause a relapse or a setback that would require more therapy than was originally called for. How long the therapy will take and how difficult it will be depends on the problem being worked out and is up to the Director.

Read Lips (Poor)

You can tell what a person is saying by watching his lips move. You must know the language in which he is speaking. You must also be within at least 30 feet in clear line of sight and with good lighting in order to make out any words.

A successful test means that you were able to make out at least some of what the subject was saying. The Relative Degree will determine just how many words you were able to catch. If the Difficulty Level was Good, for instance, and you made a Good Read Lips test, then you probably were only able to catch hints of what was being said, by catching only a few key words. If your roll was higher than the Difficulty Level, you will catch more of the conversation, perhaps even all of it.

The Director should make this test. A failed test means that either you didn't catch any of the words, or you misinterpreted the words. The latter is always the worse, because you believe that you were successful, but are now being led astray. This will only work if the Director makes the roll and only roleplays out the result without telling the actors what she rolled.

Religion (Poor)

You have studied a specific religion and understand its basic beliefs, structure and history. When you take this skill, you must choose a specific religion.

This is a scholarly skill that deals with information only. You cannot perform an exorcism with this skill, nor can you do anything that would require intimate knowledge and experience in the subject. However, you can use this skill to pose as a priest or other member of religious office. This is not the same as the Disguise skill. You can use Disguise to dress like a priest, but that alone will not work if you are forced to interact with other clergy. You must have a good understanding of the nuances of the religion and its organization in order to play the role of a priest convincingly.

Repair Device (Poor)

You are skilled at repairing a specific type of device. You must specify the type of device or item when choosing this skill. For instance, the character could choose Repair Cars, Repair Computers or Repair Electronics. Generic or broad names for a device like "electronics" applies only to common devices, such as radios, televisions, VCR's, etc., but do not include special or complicated devices like computers.

Determining the Difficulty Level for a specific repair can be tricky. You have to take into account the difficulty of the device you are repairing, as well as the tools and resources available.

The amount of time required for each repair can vary greatly from task to task, and therefore must be determined by the Director.

Jury-Rigging: You can choose to attempt temporary or jury-rigged repairs. This makes the skill test easier by lowering the Difficulty Level by one, and cuts the required time in half. However, each time the equipment is used there is an ever-increasing chance it will break again. While in use, the Director must make a roll at regular intervals to see if the device breaks again. A successful roll means that the device breaks. The Difficulty Level of the roll will start as the result of Repair test, but will decrease by 1 for each subsequent roll. The size of the interval can vary with the type of device repaired and the kind of jury-rig made. For instance, a car in use would put a lot of strain on a jury-rigged engine, and would require a test every minute or two in game time. A jury-rigged radio may require a test only once every hour.

Research (Poor)

This skill represents the act of searching for information from a variety of sources, including books, the Internet, scientific journals, and other sources of information. Research takes time and concentration and is usually better done by a team.

A successful Research test means that some useful information on the topic has been gathered. One test may not produce all of the information available on the topic, but will always produce something useful.

Generally, there is no restriction on repeated attempts, but there are a couple things to keep in mind: research takes time, and it also takes resources. If the research requires studying books, then in order to retry the attempt, there must be a new source of reading materials. This will be up to the Director.

Research In Teams: If a team is conducting the research, then each team member will make separate Research tests. Each successful character will produce different information, that is, none will gather the duplicate data.

Ride Animal (Non-existent)

You have learned how to ride a specific type of animal.

You must choose a specific type of animal when you take this skill. Some examples would be horse, camel, and elephant.

Riding an animal takes more than just being able to stay on its back. You must be able to control the animal and make it do as you instruct. This requires much training. Therefore, you cannot use this skill untrained unless someone is there to control the animal for you. In this case, you are not riding, but are merely a passenger.

Ritual (Non-existent)

The Ritual skill represents knowledge and instruction in a particular occult ritual.

A successful test means that the Ritual was completed successfully. It is recommended that the Director either make the test for you, or that she keep the Difficulty Level a secret. Even if the ritual is a failure, the energy was still released and the spell cast. The problem is that if the ritual failed, the results of the spell will take an unpredictable form and could be quite dangerous.

See Magic in Chapter Six: Filming for more details on performing rituals and casting spells.

Run (Poor)

You can run quickly.

How fast you can run is determined by the result of you skill test. If you are racing another person, or are in a chase, the test is contested against your opponent's Run test.

When trying to run for long periods, your endurance will be tested and you will be subject to fatigue. Refer to Chapter Six: Filming for rules on Fatigue.

Sail (Poor)

You have learned how to rig and sail a sailboat. You know how to set the rigging, which includes attaching and putting up the sails, connecting all of the removable parts and preparing the boat for sailing.

The waves and ripples on the water will tell an experienced sailor which way the wind is blowing and what its strength is. You can look ahead in the water and pick out lulls and pockets of strong wind. You can find the best route based on where the best wind is ahead of you.

The Sail skill only applies to wind powered boats. Use the Drive skill to operate motorboats.

Science (Non-existent)

You have studied and worked in a particular field of science. When you take this skill, you must choose a specific scientific field.

Unlike Engineering, this skill does not teach you how to build or create things. Through study, research and experimentation, you learn facts, and prove theories about the intricacies of the world.

There are a wide variety of scientific fields of study, and you must pick one when you take this skill. Some examples are Biology, Rocket Science, Genetics, and Physics.

Seduce (Poor)

You can cause a person you desire to agree to a sexu-

Casting

Example Sub Skills

There are four generic skills that you must pick a specialization in when you take levels in it. This page lists several examples of sub skills that you can choose for each of these skills.

Craft

Sculpting: You are skilled at creating works of art with clay or stone.

Painting: You are a skilled painter, either as an art form or in a more constructive way.

Carpentry: You are skilled at working with wood.

Pottery: You can create pots, vases and other such items out of clay.

Construction: You are skilled at building structures.

Culinary Arts: You are a skilled cook, and can impress people with the food you make.

Knowledge

Art: You have studied art in all its forms. You can use this to identify forged art.

Astrology: You know how to create horoscopes by interpreting dates and times and the locations of the planets.

Criminology: You are trained in the study of crime. You have studied criminals and their behavior.

Geography: You have studied the earth and its features, as well as the distribution of life on the earth.

History: You have studied the history of the world. You know about the events of civilization and how they affected the civilizations that exist today.

Law: You are well versed in laws of your country, and on the detailed process for practicing law in that country..

Literature: You are an avid reader and are well versed in literature.

Mythology: You have studied the mythology of a variety of cultures.

Politics: You know how your country's government works including all of the laws, procedures and "red tape" involved.

Tactics: You are skilled at deploying and maneuvering troops in combat.

Zoology: You understand facts about animals and their behavior.

Engineering

Architectural: This covers the design and construction of buildings and other structures such as parks, parking lots, plazas and shopping malls.

Software: This involves the design and writing of computer software, whether it is an application like a word processor, a computer virus, or even an operating system.

Electronic: This involves designing, creating and repairing electronic devices, such as audio/video equipment, computers, telephones, microwaves, and so on.

Mechanical: This focuses on the design and creation of machines.

Science

Archaeology: The study of ancient civilizations. You have a broad knowledge of ancient people and civilizations.

Astronomy: You study the science of space and the stars.

Biology: You study the science of life and the living organism. You may choose a specialty of this type of science, such as marine biology.

Chemistry: You have been trained to handle chemicals and to mix them to create drugs and other solutions.

Paleontology: You are knowledgeable about prehistoric animals and the techniques for finding and digging up fossils.

Forensics: You are trained in the use of science and technology to investigate and determine facts in a criminal case.

Geology: You have studied the science of the earth and how it functions.

Genetics: You study the science dealing with heredity and with the transmission of inherited characteristics. A geneticist is an expert with DNA.

Herbology: You can identify all types of herbs and their properties.

Physics: You study matter and energy and the interaction between the two.

Rocket Science: You have studied the art of designing fasions.

al encounter with you. You have this way of turning a person on and making her want you sexually.

Seduction is an opposed action against the other's Will. A successful Seduce test means that the seduced person will desire you, but will not necessarily give in to a sexual situation. The Relative Degree of the test, coupled with how badly the person wanted to resist the seduction, will determine just how successful you are.

This skill can be used on any character, including leading cast, as long as the he is vulnerable to your charms. For instance, a man probably could not seduce a heterosexual male, although in TV anything is possible!

Sexual Dominance: It is possible to use your sexuality to get a person to do what you want. This requires more than just seduction. You first make a Seduce test. Then you make your Persuade test. The Director can lower the Persuade test's Difficulty Level by the amount of the Seduce test's Relative Degree.

Example: Jessica wants robber to put down the gun that he's waving at her. She takes a deep breath, arching her back to make the most of her chest. She adjusts her weight on her hips, allowing her skirt to fall away from one of her legs. She then looks at him with her big beautiful eyes, wets her lips, and says in the sultriest voice she could muster, "Oh please put down the gun. You have me at your mercy. I won't struggle. Honest." She first makes a Seduce test for all of the sexy things she did. It succeeds with a Relative Degree of 3. She then makes a Persuade test to see if her pleading works. The Director decides that the man is pretty edgy, so the Difficulty Level would be Great. However, she did manage to seduce him. He really wants her bad, and is now thinking that he might have a willing and beautiful sex partner. She subtracts the 3 from the DL, bringing it down from Great to Mediocre. The Persuade test succeeds and the robber puts the gun under his belt. Now all Jessica has to do is disable the robber and prevent his advances—but at least the gun is away!

Sense Motive (Poor)

You are good at reading a person's body language and speech to gain insight on his motives. This can be used to tell if a person is lying or is affected by something someone said or did.

When someone is using the Bluff skill, you can oppose his test with Sense Motive. You can also use the skill to notice if something else is up with him. Perhaps he twitched a bit when someone nearby said something or he looked a bit nervous when you gave him some information.

Shadow (Poor)

You are skilled at following someone without detection. This is much more difficult than simply hiding. You need to keep track of the person you're shadowing and following him without losing him, yet at the same time, you need to do it without looking obvious and without him noticing you.

When shadowing someone, you must make Shadow tests at regular intervals. This is an opposed action against the subject's Notice skill. The result of your Shadow test is the Difficulty Level of the subject's Notice test.

One failed Shadowing attempt will mean that the subject has noticed you and is at least suspicious. However, unless the subject recognizes you as someone he should be suspicious of, you may need to fail two or more Shadow tests before he knows for certain that you are following him.

Sleight of Hand (Poor)

You are able to make things appear to disappear in front of peoples' eyes by performing tricks with your hands.

The tricks of making a coin disappear from your hand then reappear behind a person's ear is a typical example of this. A useful example would be to make a floppy disk with vital information appear to your enemies to fall from hand into a river, when in reality, it slipped into your sleeve.

Because you are trying to trick another's senses, this is an opposed action against the audience's Notice tests.

Stealth (Poor)

You can move without a sound, and hide from others.

This is always an opposed action against the other's Notice test. Anyone making his Notice test will hear or see you. How completely you are found depends on the Relative Degree of the test and is up to the Director. If the Relative Degree is 1 or 2, then perhaps the person heard something, but is not sure what it was. A Relative Degree of 3 or higher could mean that he saw you quite clearly and knows where you are.

Streetsmarts (Poor)

You are shrewd and adept at surviving in a hostile urban environment. If anyone is able to walk through the rough parts of the city and survive, it is you! You know how street gangs operate and how to make yourself be an undesirable target.

Make Streetsmarts tests to walk through rough neighborhoods while presenting as small an opportunity to criminals as possible. How well this can be done depends both on the Relative Degree of the test and the situation. The Director must decide just how well this can be done.

You can make Streetsmarts tests to use your knowledge of criminal elements to help solve a mystery or answer a question. For instance, you can make a test to realize that a crime that a street gang is being blamed for is not something that a gang would do.

Casting

You can sometimes make Streetsmarts tests when having dealings with criminals.

Surgery (Non-existent)

You can perform surgery on a patient. This is different from Treat Injury, which only handles less serious medical care. Surgery involves cutting the patient open and working directly on his internal organs.

You can make Surgery tests to perform a surgical routine, as well as to decide whether surgery is needed for the patient. The Diagnose skill is required for deciding if surgery is required.

Surveillance (Poor)

You are trained in the placement and use of sophisticated surveillance devices, such as wiretaps, hidden cameras, laser eavesdroppers and the like. This skill can be used untrained (using the default level), but only for installing simple recording devices, such as a hidden tape recorder.

This skill covers only the electronics side of espionage. Following someone requires the Shadow skill. You must use the Drive skill to tail someone. Use the Stealth skill to sneak up on someone, and the Track skill to follow someone's trail.

Setting A Surveillance Device: A successful test means that the device is set in a good location, and its presence will be difficult to detect. The Director should make this test for you. A failed test means that the device is not placed for good reception. You will not know that it was badly set until the device is used. All Surveillance tests to use the device will fail, no matter what the roll is.

The result of the placement roll determines the Difficulty Level for all Notice tests made to notice the device and all Surveillance tests made to use it.

Every hour that a person is within sight of the device, the Director should make a Notice test for him to see if he notices the device.

Using a Surveillance Device: When using the device, a successful test means that you manage to gather useful information. Keep in mind that just because a device was installed properly, you may not have configured it properly on the receiving end. A failed Surveillance test when using the device could mean that you just did not catch the information, or it could mean that you did not tune the device properly and are not getting adequate reception.

Swim (Poor)

You are able to swim in water.

When used untrained, you can attempt to tread water, and possibly dog paddle your way to shore, but even that will be difficult. When untrained, you must always make Swim tests to perform any act of swimming, no matter how simple.

When you have purchased at least one level in Swim, you will not need to make a Swim test to swim in calm water under good conditions. Any attempts to swim in challenging conditions will require a Swim test.

Tall Tales (Poor)

You can weave false stories with such skill that you can even get people to believe that they are true.

The Director can choose to allow a bonus if the actor drums up the tale himself.

Throw (Poor)

You can throw things at a distance and with accuracy.

Use this skill for all thrown weapons, such as knives, axes and shuriken.

Hurling a very heavy object with accuracy would require two tests: first a Brawn test to heft and hurl the object, and then a Throw test to determine the accuracy of the throw.

Track (Poor)

You are skilled at picking out the telltale signs of the passage of a particular quarry and then following that trail to find it.

The Difficulty Level of the test depends on many factors. The older the trail, the harder it will be to find. The environment may also make the trail more difficult. For instance, following the trail of someone on a city street could be nearly impossible, while following a trail made by a large animal trudging through three feet of snow would be easy. Rain and other types of weather could obscure the trail, or wash away the scent, adding to the difficulty.

You can use the Hide Traces skill to make a trail more difficult to track. See that skill for details on the modifier to the Difficulty Level if the target of your search is actively trying to hide its tracks.

Train Animal (Non-existent)

You know how to train animals. The difficulty of this skill will vary with the type of animal that you are trying to train. Training any kind of animal requires much time and effort, taking anywhere from a full day to months. Training a domestic animal will take a relatively short amount of time, where training a wild animal will take much longer and will have a higher Difficulty Level.

The following table lists some examples and suggested difficulty levels:

The difficulty levels below assume that you are only going to make one skill roll to determine ultimate success. If the training process will occur over time, such as

Casting

two to three times as long, then the Director may decrease the difficulty some and require multiple rolls. For instance, you could make one test per week of game time.

Example Animal Training Difficulty Levels		
Animal	Difficulty	Time Req.
Dog, cat, or farm animal	Fair	2 days
Horse	Good	1 week
Wolf	Great	3 weeks
Predatory cat (jaguar, etc.)	Superb	1 month +

In any event, the Relative Degree of the skill roll should determine how well you trained the animal. In this way, the animal may not be fully trained and could turn on its master. A good rule of thumb is that if the Train Animal test succeeded by three or more levels, then the animal has been fully trained, and will not turn. If it succeeded only by two or less levels, then there is a chance that it could turn on its master.

Whenever the animal is not fully trained and is told to do something that is against its nature, it may break from its training. How it behaves when this happens depends on the animal. To determine if it does as it is told or not, make a Will test for the animal against the last Train Animal test. Success means that it will not do what it was told, and will follow its natural instincts. Failure means that its willpower just isn't strong enough to go against its master.

Treat Injury (Non-existent)

You are skilled at treating and caring for injuries. From tending wounds and breaks to treating colds, viruses and other illnesses, you can give extended care to an ill person.

This skill does not include quick stabilization of injuries, which are covered by the First Aid skill, nor performing surgery, which is handled by the Surgery skill. However, this does cover all other forms of treating injuries and illnesses. Nursing a sick person back to health, treating poisons, and caring for a diseased patient are all examples of this skill.

How to use this skill depends on the injury being treated and how long the treatment must last. If the injury requires regular or constant care over a period of time, then Treat Injury tests should be made periodically to insure that the injury is treated properly throughout the course of recovery. A failure may mean a relapse!

Some injuries require only a quick fix, such as the proper prescription of a medicine, or applying stitches. In these cases, only one test is required.

UFOlogy (Poor)

You have studied Unidentified Flying Objects and are familiar with many of the reported cases. If you are using this skill untrained, you are only aware of what is known in pop culture, such as what you would see on television. If you have purchased any levels of this skill, then you have done some more extensive research on the subject (or have had some experience in it) and are more knowledgeable.

This is a knowledge skill, which means that a successful UFOlogy test will mean that you know something of value. When confronted with a clue, the Director may make the test secretly for you in the event that the clue sparks a memory of something you already know.

If you are actively trying to remember something or make some kind of connection, you can make the roll yourself.

Uplift Spirits (Poor)

You can make sad people feel better or raise a person's outlook from hopeless to hopeful.

This is usually only done on supporting cast, but can really be used on anyone. The Director may allow a bonus to the test if the actor does a good job of roleplaying it out.

Weapon (Poor)

You are skilled in the use of a specific type of weapon.

You must choose a specific weapon skill. In most shows, it is not necessary to be too specific. Some good types of weapon skills are archery, artillery, broadsword, club, fencing, gun, knife, laser, and whip.

Do not use this skill for thrown weapons. Thrown weapons use the Throw skill.

Write (Poor)

You are skilled at expressing your thoughts and emotions into written words. You can use this skill to write a book, a set of instructions, a technical document or any other written document. The level of success (Relative Degree) you have in the test indicates how well written the document is.

When writing instructions or a technical document, the result of the test will determine the Difficulty Level of the Notice tests required to understand the instructions.

Zero-G Maneuver (Poor)

You are good at moving around in a zero gravity environment. This includes flipping around, stabilizing yourself and using handholds and footholds to get around.

You need to have handholds and footholds in order to maneuver. If there is nothing to grab, you are helpless.

Gifts & Faults

Chapter 4

Casting

Gifts

A gift is something special and positive about you that you have. It helps to define who you are, but does not improve over time as skills and Attributes do. Because of this, they do not have the levels (Terrible through Superb) that the other traits have. Instead, either you have the gift or you don't.

Some gifts have a direct effect on the mechanics of the game, either by modifying a skill or attribute roll or by enabling a specific ability. Some gifts, however, may simply be a role-playing element, and have no direct effect to any dice rolls or action results.

Stacking Gifts

It is possible, in some rare cases, to improve upon a gift. You can do this by stacking them. To stack a gift, you simply purchase the same gift more than once. This can add benefits that the gift did not have by itself.

Not all gifts can be stacked. In fact, the vast majority of them cannot. To know if a gift can be stacked, refer to its description in this chapter. Only those gifts that say they can stack actually can, all others cannot.

The benefits that stacking a gift can give depend completely on the gift in question. The description of the gift will explain how it stacks and what the benefits are.

Meta Gifts

Like skills, there are some gifts that are too general to stand by themselves. Each one represents a category of gifts. These are called meta gifts. When you take a meta gift, you must choose a specific sub-gift. An example would be the Keen Sense gift. When you pick it, you must choose a specific sense, such as Hearing, Sight, Smell, etc.

With a meta gift, you can take the gift several times without stacking them, each time choosing a new sub-gift. For instance, you can take Contact Law Enforcement and Contact Government.

Two meta gifts that apply to different sub-gifts do not stack on each other. If they apply to the same sub-gift, then you can stack them if the gift's description allows it.

Losing Gifts

It is possible that you will lose a gift. For instance, if you have the Contact gift, and you abuse it, the Director may choose to have the contact either die or choose not to help you anymore. Sometimes, the loss of the gift simply makes sense in the episode, based on the events that take place.

When you lose a gift, it is gone. Period. This means that your character will be potentially unbalanced, which is not desirable. The Director must work out a way to help bring some balance to the character. This could be by awarding Experience Points to the character for the event that caused the loss of the gift. After all, losing a gift is a major life experience! Sometimes it may make sense to trade one gift for another. For instance, you could lose the Presumed Dead gift because you just saved the world, but also gain the Famous gift for the notoriety you get for your deeds.

Director Controlled Faults

Sometimes the Director may choose to force you to activate a fault. She should only do this when she feels it

Table 4-1: Gifts		
Adrenaline Rush	Foreign Tech	Quick Reflexes*
Always Keep Your Cool	Grapevine (pick type)*	Rapid Reload
Ambidexterity	High Pain Threshold*	Refuge*
Animal Empathy	Increased Income*	Savoir-Faire
Artful Dodger	Inheritance *	Shot on the Run
Attractive*	Keen Sense (pick one)*	Single minded
Beautiful speaking voice	Lucky*	Skill Specialization
Blind-Fight	Never forget a feature (pick one)	Stunning Fist
Born to Money	No Identity	Sucker Punch*
Contact (pick one)*	Offensive Driver	Tough Hide*
Danger Sense*	Passionate (pick one)	Trustworthy
Defensive Driver	Patron (pick one person)	Two-Weapon Fighting
Diplomatic Immunity	Perfect Timing	Well-Traveled
Famous	Presumed Dead	
Favor (pick one person)	Quick Draw	
* These gifts can stack.		

Casting

is necessary or if she feels that you have been neglecting the fault. Taking a fault gives you obvious benefits in the form of additional gifts. Therefore, you cannot take a fault without behaving in the manner that the fault describes, or your character will be unbalanced.

When the Director feels it necessary, she can make a Will test for your character secretly. If it succeeds, then she says nothing and lets you continue to act normally. If the test fails, then you must succumb to your fault and change your behavior accordingly.

Gift Descriptions

Adrenaline Rush

You enter a frenzied state where you can perform feats that are beyond normal human limits.

In both movies and TV, there are always those heroes who can occasionally outrun an explosion, be hit by many bullets or arrows without slowing down, or perform other feats of tremendous stamina. This is caused by an incredible rush of adrenaline.

For one round, you can ignore all effects of damage and gain a +2 to all skill and Attribute tests.

Afterwards, you will be terribly exhausted for 5 minutes, suffering a -2 penalty to all skill and Attribute tests.

You can only use this gift once per game session.

Note: The use of this gift is strictly up to the Director. She may choose to not allow this gift at all if it does not fit with the realism of the show.

Always Keep Your Cool

You can always manage to stay calm and focused in the worst of situations. Your body language almost never betrays you when you bluff, so anyone trying to use Sense Motive on you gets a -1 penalty. In addition, you gain a +1 bonus to all tests made to avoid panicking or succumbing to fear or other emotional outburst.

Ambidexterity

You are equally skilled with either hand. You can use your off hand without any penalties, as though it were your primary hand. In essence, you are both right handed and left handed.

Without this gift, you suffer a -1 penalty to any test made when using your off hand. For instance, if you are Good with a handgun, firing it with your off hand reduces your skill to only Fair.

Animal Empathy

You have a special bond with animals.

Animals have a natural tendency to like you. This adds a +1 bonus to all tests when trying to befriend or handle an animal.

Artful Dodger

You are phenomenally adept at dodging attacks. You astound others and frustrate your enemies by running through a hail of bullets without taking a single hit.

You gain a +2 to your Defensive Factor. This bonus does not apply at any time when you cannot physically dodge.

Attractive

You are very good looking. People tend to treat you more favorably than others.

You gain a +1 to all Seduction tests.

You can stack one additional gift onto Attractive. This will change the gift to Gorgeous. Your bonus will increase to +2, but you will have the added disadvantage of being extremely noticeable. Anyone looking at you will be favorably inclined toward you and is likely to gawk. In a bar or other social gathering, you must expect people of the opposite sex to approach you almost constantly. You may conceal your good looks to counteract this effect, but it will also remove your bonus during that time as well.

Beautiful Speaking Voice

Your voice is so beautiful that people cannot help but listen when you speak.

This gives you a +1 to all Oratory skill tests, and to all Perform skill tests that involve speaking.

Blind-Fight

You can fight in pitch darkness or without your sight with only a -1 penalty instead of the normal -2.

Contact

You know someone that can help you from time to time. When you choose this gift, you must pick a specific type of contact. Some examples are Law Enforcement, Government, Hollywood, Mafia, Street Gang, etc.

The contact is only one person and must be someone with only low to moderate power in the organization. For instance, picking a contact in law enforcement would give you a detective or street cop. He can be useful and can give you some good information and help, but his aid would be limited to one precinct.

This gift can stack. Each time, the contact gains more access. Your detective friend is promoted to Lieutenant, or your FBI agent contact becomes assistant director. If that would not make sense for this specific contact, then you could lose the contact you already have and gain a new one with greater reach.

Gifts & Faults

Casting

Danger Sense

You get a strange feeling when danger is near. Call it intuition if you will, but when danger is near, you sometimes get a strange sensation. The feeling is different for each person, but some common ones are goose bumps, the hairs rising on the back of the neck, or an unexplained shiver.

The Director must always make this test for you, because only she knows when danger is really around. The Director will secretly make a Notice test for you. The Difficulty Level will depend on the level of danger. The more dangerous it is to you, the easier it is to sense, so the lower the Difficulty Level.

Danger Sense will never explain the cause or type of danger. All it will do is give you the ominous feeling that something is just not right. The Director should describe it in a way that will heighten the tension in the scene.

Danger Sense is not always accurate. This is why it is not a Supernormal Power. In potentially dangerous situations, the Director should occasionally make the test whether there is real danger or not. Sometimes, when the test is successful and there is no real danger, she could describe the feeling.

If the Director allows it, you can stack one additional Danger Sense gift onto it. When this happens, it becomes a Power and is now always accurate.

Defensive Driver

You have a knack for avoiding accidents while driving.

You gain a +1 bonus to all opposed Drive tests that you make to avoid some kind of conflict, such as when someone tries to run you off the road or to avoid a collision.

The Defensive Driver gift applies to all Drive skill tests for all vehicles. It does not apply to any Pilot or Sail skill tests.

Diplomatic Immunity

You are subject to the laws of your own nation while abroad.

Some countries will not recognize diplomatic immunity in foreigners, or even those from specific nations. The Director must make this decision on a case-by-case basis, but if she allows it for a country once, then she should always allow it.

Diplomatic Immunity does not mean that you can never be arrested in the country you are in. It means that you can be arrested for any crime that your country prosecutes. If you perform acts that the country you are in cannot charge you for, but also will not tolerate, they can have you removed from their country and not allowed in. They can also file official complaints with your own government, which can have serious repercussions when you return home.

Famous

You are a well-known public figure. When you pick this gift, you must decide and announce in what way you are famous. Are you an actor, musician, or politician? Describe the details so that you and the Director can deal with your fame appropriately.

You gain a +1 to all tests made to impress people. This will only work in places where you can be recognized.

Fame always comes with a price. You can draw a crowd whereeever you go, and will have a more difficult time moving about unnoticed. You will suffer a -1 to all tests when trying to not be noticed in a public area. This includes Disguise skill tests and may include Hide tests in certain situations.

Favor

Someone owes you a very big favor. This could be someone of some power in a government or organization. However, whoever it is, the favor he owes you is big and can be very useful.

You or the Director must decide who the person is that owes you this favor, and why. There are two ways to handle Favor:

One Big Favor: The person can owe you one very big favor. For instance, you could have saved the life of an important person and he feels the need to return the favor. With this type of favor, the person will only help you once, and then the debt is paid. Once the debt is paid, this gift is *gone*. To balance this limitation, the favor can be very big indeed and would be something that you may wish to hold onto for a dire emergency.

Recurring Favor: The person owes you a big debt, much like the other method. However, the person intends to repay it by many small favors instead of going out on a limb to help you once. Each favor he pays you will not be as heavy and useful as the big favor, but will still be quite useful.

Be careful when calling in on a recurring favor. If you do it too often, he may decide that he has paid the debt and will no longer help you. It is possible that if you abuse this debt, he will even get angry!

Foreign Tech

You are good at figuring out how to use technology that is alien to you.

If you have any levels in a skill that is comparable to the technology you are trying to use, you can manage to figure it out and use it with some difficulty. For instance, if you are a US Air Force fighter pilot and you try to steal a Russian MIG, you can attempt to fly with a penalty to your Pilot skill even though you have never seen the controls of a MIG before and you do not know how to read

Casting

Russian.

You suffer a -2 to your tests when using this technology. The amount of time it takes to figure it out enough to use it is up to the Director. She could have you make a separate skill test to determine how long it takes you to figure it out.

In most science fiction shows, they often have a leading character stealing or needing to pilot a spacecraft owned by some alien race he has never encountered before. Somehow, he always manages to figure it out and fly it. That is the nature of this gift.

Grapevine

You have access to a big gossip chain that you can use to get information and to spread information.

You gain a +1 to all Gather Information skill tests within the range of your grapevine. You can also seed information, either truthful or false, with a good chance of the information leaking to all who has access to the same grapevine.

The size of the grapevine depends on how many of this gift you take. For just one, it can span an entire company, school, organization or small town or village. Stack one more onto it will expand it to a small city.

High Pain Threshold

You can withstand pain like a trooper. You gain +1 bonus to your Defense Factor toward damage. This can be stacked only once to create a total bonus of +2.

Increased Income

You got a raise or promotion and are now living in a higher lifestyle.

Casting

Raise your Standard of Living by one Level.

This can be stacked as often as the Director allows. The Director may choose to limit your Standard of Living to Superb or less.

Inheritance

You have inherited something from a recently deceased relative or acquaintance.

This can be money an item or even some real estate. The value of this inheritance depends on how many times you took this gift. In order to stack it, you must purchase the multiple gifts at the same time, because once you take the gift, you get the inheritance. You cannot get an extension to an existing inheritance later in time (unless, of course, if you come up with a good story around it and the Director approves).

Example: *You purchase one Inheritance gift. The Director says that your very old great-uncle, whom you used to visit, has passed away. He willed you his estate, a large mansion on ten acres of property in the Scottish Highlands. This sounds great, until you find out that all the animals that graze on the land mysteriously dies and the mansion is quite dilapidated and has a reputation for being haunted. This balances out the size of his inheritance with the value, as well as planting the seeds for some great episodes.*

Keen Sense

One of your senses is very sensitive. When you take this gift, pick a sense, whether it be sight, hearing, taste or touch. You gain a +1 to all Notice tests when using this sense.

This gift can stack.

Lucky

Some call it coincidence, while others call it luck. Whatever the reason, things tend to go your way.

You gain one additional Luck Point that returns at the beginning of every session.

This gift can stack to add any number of Luck Points to your pool.

Never Forget a Feature

When you take this gift, you must pick a feature of a person. Commonly chosen features include face, voice, smell, mannerisms, etc.

Whenever you come into contact of the key feature of a person you have once met, you instantly remember the person. If it has been a long time since you last saw the person, or your only meeting was fleeting and insignificant, you must make a Notice test in order to recognize the person. The Director will decide how difficult the test will be.

Example: *Vicki and Dave have been trying to solve the mystery of the Snow Ghost and are now chasing after the apparition. They can hear its demonic cackling as it disappears around a corner. The Director makes a Great Notice test for Vicki, getting a Superb. "Vicki, you know that cackle!" she declares. "The waitress at the soda shop made that same cackle when she spilled the strawberry shake all over the local bully."*

No Identity

There are no records of your existence anywhere. All tests used to find out who you are or to locate you, such as Gather Information, suffer a -2 penalty. You have no Social Security Number, and thus you have no license, no credit cards, no loans and no job (unless you are being paid "under the table"). This gift can be a double-edged sword, as although you are much harder to track down, you are also not recognized as a person in society.

You cannot take this gift if you already have the Presumed Dead gift.

Offensive Driver

You are trained to use your vehicle like a weapon.

You gain a +1 to all Drive tests when trying to run a car off a road, force your way through traffic, or any other form of aggressive vehicle maneuvering.

Passionate

You are stubbornly passionate about a specific job, person, task, place or item.

When you take this gift, choose something that you will be passionate about. It could be a person, a place, a job (or a certain part of a job), or even an item. You are heavily focused on the object of your passion, almost to the point of obsession, and you gain a +1 bonus to all tests when dealing with the object of your passion. You can take this gift one more time to increase the bonus +2.

Because of your passion, you will find it very difficult to turn aside from the object of your passion, even when you know you should. Whenever this happens, the Director may have you make a Will test in order to curb your passion and turn away. The Difficulty Level of the save will depend on how strong the temptation is and how logical the need to turn away. The Director should decide on a Difficulty Level based on the situation, and then add your Passionate bonus to it. This way, the more passionate you are, the harder it is to turn away from it.

This gift cannot be stacked. Since this gift is all-consuming, it leaves little room for another all consuming passion.

Patron

You know someone of wealth and power has taken you under his wing. He grants you favors and protection

Casting

in exchange for certain services.

When you take this gift, you must define whom this patron is, and possibly even create him on a character sheet. You must also decide what services he requires of you and what kind of favor and protection he can and will offer. The Director will help to keep this balanced.

It is possible to lose this gift if you abuse his help and protection or neglect your responsibilities to him.

Perfect Timing

You always seem to be at the right place at the right time. Whenever it would be really good luck for you to be at a certain place when an event occurs, the Director can make a Luck Roll for you to see if it happens. If the roll succeeds, then you find yourself at the right place at the right time!

Of course, for dramatic reasons, the Director may just decide to forego the dice roll and place you in the right place.

Presumed Dead

You are believed to be dead. All records of you show that you are dead. If you had been wanted by the law or anyone else, they will no longer be looking for you. You have some of the freedom of anonymity, but you must be careful not to be seen by anyone who knows you. All Notice tests for anyone who knows what you look like suffer a -1 penalty to recognize you, because they do not expect to see you alive.

Keep in mind that this is different from the No Identity feat, as you do have records: you have a Social Security Number, and your fingerprints are on file. If you suddenly turn up alive around people who think you are dead, there could be real trouble!

You cannot take this gift if you already have the No Identity gift.

Quick Draw

You can draw your weapon as a free action. Normally, drawing a weapon takes a half action.

Quick Reflexes

You can react quickly in times of need.

You gain a +1 modifier to all Initiative tests. This gift can stack.

Rapid Reload

You have been trained to reload a firearm quickly. Reloading a firearm requires a half action. Reloading a firearm normally requires a full action.

Rapid reload assumes that the weapon has a mechanism for quick reloads, such as a magazine. If the weapon does not have such a mechanism, then this feat does not apply. For instance, Rapid Reload will not apply when reloading a revolver, except when a speed loader is used.

Refuge

You have a safe house or special place where you can go to hide or be alone.

When you take this gift, you or the Director must decide exactly what and where this refuge is and why you have access to it.

How safe this place is and how comfortable and easy to get to it is depends on how many gifts you spend on it. One gift will give you nothing more than a shack in the woods up on a mountainside, or perhaps a nicer place that's not nearly as safe.

You can stack this gift to have more than one refuge.

Savoir-Faire

When you do something, you do it with such flair and finesse that it never fails to impress those who see it.

You are always so smooth that even when you make a mistake, those who witness it may think that you meant to do it.

This is very important when trying to impress and instill people's confidence in your abilities. It does not affect the game's flow, but can add spice to your roleplaying.

Shot on the Run

You are able to shoot a ranged weapon while running with no penalties.

Normally, you take a -2 penalty when firing while running.

Skill Specialization

You can focus on a specific part of a skill, giving you a bonus when working on the subject of your focus.

When taking Skill Specialization, you must choose both a skill and a focus for that skill.

You gain a +1 on all skill tests within your chosen focus. However, you will also suffer a -1 penalty to all tests with that skill that are outside of that focus.

This gift does not apply to all skills. Some skills cover a spectrum of things. For instance, History covers all of the world's history. You can take Skill Specialization to become a specialist on one facet of history, like ancient Egypt or American History. There are some skills, however, that are not broad enough to allow this gift. For example, you cannot pick a specialization for the Concentration skill.

Example: *Jack the archaeologist buys Skill Specialization and chooses the Archaeology skill and Ancient*

Casting

Egypt as his focus. Because he specializes in Ancient Egypt, he gains a +1 bonus to his Archaeology skill tests when dealing with Ancient Egypt. However, when confronted with artifacts from Sumer or Babylon, he suffers a -1 to his Archaeology skill tests when trying to understand the meaning of the images on them.

Once you have applied Skill Specialization on a skill, you cannot use Skill Specialization on the same skill again, unless the Director approves.

Sucker Punch

You can stun a person when making an unarmed attack.

You must declare that you are using this gift before your attack. When you successfully strike and damage your opponent with an unarmed attack, the victim must make a Fair Stamina test or be stunned for one round.

It may be stacked only once.

Tough Hide

You have skin that is tougher than normal, providing you with natural armor.

Add +1 to your Defensive Factor for every time you take this gift. You can choose to increase this bonus to +2 per gift if you limit the type of damage that can be soaked by your armor. For instance, if your hide will not stop piercing weapons, but will stop all slashing and bludgeoning weapons, the Director may let you increase your bonus.

Trustworthy

When you promise to do something, you will do everything in your power to make it happen.

People trust you, and it is not just because you have a trusting face, but because you always work hard to keep your promises.

You gain a +1 in all social skills used to try to convince someone who knows you to trust you.

You must also make a Fair Will test to deliberately break a promise.

Two-Weapon Fighting

You can fight with two weapons with only a -1 penalty.

Normally, you suffer a -2 penalty when fighting with two weapons. This penalty is reduced to -1 when you have this gift.

Well-Traveled

You have been to many places in the world, and thus have gained much experience with traveling and other cultures.

You gain a +1 to all Cultures skill tests and to any tests that concern knowledge of traveling. You will also gain a +1 bonus to all social tests when trying to impress people with your worldliness. This last bonus only applies when the Director feels it would make sense.

Fault Descriptions

Absent-Minded

You spend much time deep in thought and heedless of what is going on around you. Most people can think while performing other tasks. You cannot. When you are thinking about something, you tend to be preoccupied with that thought and thus find yourself not paying attention to what you are doing. As a result, you often find yourself getting lost because you were thinking while walking, or bumping into people, and other such clumsy things.

Table 4-2: Faults				
Absent-Minded	Cursed	Hunted	Multiple Personality	Softhearted
Addiction	Decreased Income	Hunting	Obligation	Stubborn
Alienated	Defeated	Impulsive	Obsession	Submissive
Ambitious	Easily Distracted	Indecisive	Outlaw	Tunnel Vision
Amnesia	Enemy	Intolerant	Overconfident	Unlucky
Amorous Heartbreaker	Finicky	Lazy	Overly Talkative	Vain
Attention Hog	Foolish Bravery	Lecherous	Pacifist	Vendetta
Blunt & Tactless	Jinxed	Lost or Forbidden Love	Phobia	Violent when enraged
Bossy	Glutton	Low Pain Threshold	Practical Joker	Vow
Code of Behavior	Gossip	Machismo	Quick-Tempered	Worry Wart
Compulsive Behavior	Greedy	Manic-Depressive	Rivalry	Zealous behavior
Coward	Gullible	Melancholy	Secret Identity	
Curious	Handicap	Mistaken Identity	Socially awkward	

Casting

Addiction

You have a strong physical and emotional need for something that can be bad for you. This is usually for a narcotic drug, but can be anything that is either illegal or very bad for you. You cannot take this merely to be addicted to things that will not play a negative role in the show, such as cigarettes or caffeine.

You must make a Good Will test in order to resist the need. You must make this test every day to avoid feeding your addiction. If you fail the test and do not have access to it, you will have a cumulative -1 to all tests that day until you either satisfy your need or until you make your next Will test.

This penalty is cumulative for each day you fail the test. So, if you fail your Will test for two days in a row and do not satisfy the addiction, you will suffer a -2 to all tests.

You can get rid of this fault, but it will take hospitalization, which may mean your character will miss some episodes. Even then, the fault does not go away completely, and you should not erase it from your character sheet. The temptation could return.

Alienated

You have managed to make those you work or live with unfriendly with you.

When you take this fault, you must define who you alienated and how. In addition, you must decide to what extent you alienated them. Do they hate you? Do they want to kill you? Or do they simply not trust you or like you?

You suffer a -1 penalty to all social skills when dealing with those you have alienated.

Ambitious

You have goals and are not about to let anyone get in your way. You want to go places and to become more than what you are. As a result, you are more willing to go out on a limb to make that happen.

Amnesia

You cannot remember who you are.

Amnesia has many forms. The most notable cases involve a complete memory loss concerning your identity. However, it could just be that you cannot remember some specific important event in your life.

The best way to handle amnesia is to let the Director fill in the blanks and use it as plot points in the show. After all, the best way to roleplay an amnesiac is if you

Casting

don not know who you are either! You could create a character with the name "John Doe" or even leave the name blank. Since your Director will have to do some work to fill in the blanks, you may need to consult with her before choosing this fault. She may not be up to the challenge.

Amorous Heartbreaker

You have a habit seducing people and using them for sexual favors and then leaving them. You have even gone as far as letting them think you love them when you have no intention of taking the relationship any further than casual sex. Unfortunately, this has given you quite a reputation, and you will have a difficult time seducing or romancing anyone who has heard of you.

Spend some time working out the details of how your character deals with this fault. It will add spice and even plot points for the show.

Attention Hog

You feel an overwhelming need to be the center of attention wherever you are.

Whenever you are in a situation where someone else is getting the attention, you will try to "one-up" him and steal the attention of those around you.

The Director may choose to require a Will test to prevent this fault from taking control. If you fail the test, you will try to steal the attention away from someone else.

Blunt and Tactless

You have no bedside manner. You say what is on your mind when you think of it, regardless of how it would be received by those who hear it. As a result, you come across as course and tough, and you have a way of alienating people.

You cannot take this fault if you have the Savoir Faire gift.

Bossy

You feel the need to always take charge of a situation. You cannot help trying to take command of a situation, even when you know that someone else is more qualified. You do honestly feel, however, that you are a born leader and that you can see just about any situation to a successful completion.

You may need to make a Will test to force yourself not to try to take over when someone else is in charge. Even then, you may continuously offer "advice", which will come over more as if you are trying to tell your boss what to do.

Code of Behavior

You believe in a certain set of principles that govern what you feel to be proper or right behavior. You will never willingly or knowingly do anything to break this code, and the guilt will haunt you if somehow you do manage to break it.

This code must limit your behavior in some major way, or it will not be enough to justify this fault.

You must write down the principles of your code and submit it to the Director for approval. The Director will keep this and make sure you adhere to it.

Any attempt to ignore or break your code would require a Great Will test. Breaking from your code will put you off for that day. You should roleplay that out in your character's mood and attitude. Try to find ways to make up for this breach of behavior.

Compulsive Behavior

You have a constant irresistible urge to perform an irrational act.

You must choose a specific irrational act to be compulsive about. A common compulsive act would be the constant twirling of hair, but although this makes a good example, it is not nearly severe enough to be worth a fault. It should be something that can become a problem in the show, but cannot be something that will take momentum away from the show.

Example: *Treating inanimate objects as though they had feelings. For example, if you unwrap a sandwich, you will not throw the wrapper away. Instead, you will carefully fold it up and tuck it gently away and save it for a proper "burial." You might not specifically bury it, but you will find a humane way to dispose of the poor wrapper. Now, you know very well that the thing is just trash and has no feelings, but you cannot help but treat it that way. If anyone asks why you do it, you would not be able to answer him, because you really do not know.*

Any attempt to ignore an impulse would require a Great Will test. Failure means that you once again fall victim to the impulse. You will feel instant gratification when you finally do take care of it. If you remain in a position where you can still satisfy the impulse, you will not be able to concentrate on anything else and must make a Great Will test every round until you leave the situation or you give in and fix the problem.

Coward

You are easily scared.

Every time you enter a dangerous or scary situation, you will become scared. As described in Chapter Six: Filming, you must make a Will test to determine how you deal with your fear. However, there is one difference. You are always crippled by this fear, so even if you succeed in your Will test, you will be affected by your fear. The Will test will be at least Great, but could be higher if the situation is dire.

The best a coward can hope for is to face his fears. If you succeed in your Will test, you will suffer from the

Casting

Face Your Fears effect and thus live with a penalty to all of your tests.

Curious

You are so curious that you are likely to put yourself into dangerous positions.

When your curiosity is peaked and satisfying your curiosity could put you in danger, you must make a Will test to successfully resist the temptation to investigate.

Cursed

A curse has been placed on you.

If you picked this at character creation time, you must decide what the curse is and work out the details of how it works with the Director. If you pick it afterwards, discuss it with the Director. She may want to decide what the curse is and work getting it into an episode.

The curse can be just about anything, but it has to be serious enough to create a real problem for your character.

Decreased Income

You lose your job or get a pay cut and are now living in a lower lifestyle.

Lower your Standard of Living by one Level.

This can be stacked to decrease your Standard of Living as far as low as Terrible. You cannot lower your Standard of Living below Terrible.

Defeated

You have failed in some task and feel determined to make up for it.

This failure could be a major defeat in some kind of competition that is important to you. A rival archaeologist always manages to get to the important artifact before you. You are a vice cop who busted a major drug lord, but he managed to pay off the judge and get away.

Whatever the case, this defeat haunts you constantly, and are determined to make it right. This is very much like the Obsession fault, except that it has a specific cause. Unlike Obsession, however, it is possible to eventually make up for this defeat and lose the fault.

Easily Distracted

You find it nearly impossible to concentrate on any one thing, and find distractions all around you. You have a hard time studying with music playing in the background, because you keep thinking about the song that is playing. However, you can't study in silence, because then you're distracted by every little noise.

You suffer a -1 to all Concentration skill tests. In addition, you must make a Concentration test when performing any lengthy task in order to maintain your concentration. The Difficulty Level of the test depends on the amount of distractions present.

Enemy

You have made an enemy of someone. Whoever the enemy is, he will oppose you whenever he gets the chance.

You or the Director must figure out who the enemy is when you create your character. It is possible that the Director will not tell you whom she chose as the enemy, and that you will have to figure it out on your own.

How powerful the enemy is and how often he opposes you will depend on how many times you stack this fault. For instance, if you take this fault just once, the enemy could be someone who is powerful, but is not motivated enough to oppose you too strongly or very often. Instead, he merely causes a problem occasionally, perhaps once or twice a season.

Finicky

You are difficult to please. You insist on getting what you want, exactly what you want. When ordering food at a restaurant, you want the steak just a little bit pink in the middle. You want two vegetables, but do not mix them. Instead, put one on the plate with the steak, and the other in a separate dish. To drink, you will have a ginger ale without the ice. You will describe exactly how you want it to the waiter, regardless of how he or anyone else reacts. If any of your instructions are not followed exactly, you will return the meal. In any event, you feel that you are perfectly right in behaving in this way, and anyone who complains is just being unreasonable.

Of course, this does not only apply to meals. You are finicky about nearly everything. If there are certain things you are more picky about and others that you are not, you should list them for own reference as well as for the Director.

Your pickiness increases the length of time required for most tasks at the Director's discretion. In addition, you may receive a -1 penalty to all social skills when dealing with people who have just witnessed your finicky behavior.

Foolish Bravery

You are very brave, but unfortunately do not think before acting.

When faced with a crisis, you are more likely to take the route of greatest bravery even when other less dangerous solutions present themselves.

In a situation like this, you should automatically take the action appropriate for this fault. If not, the Director may secretly make a Will test to see if you react out of foolish bravery and tell you that you can't resist being the

Casting

hero.

Example: *You are walking past a burning house and hear a scream from within. There is a fire alarm box hanging on a streetlight post beside you and you have a cell phone in your pocket. However, hearing the cry for help, you take a deep breath, duck your head and run bravely into the burning house, ready to save the poor soul.*

Glutton

You eat to excess. Food is always near the top of your thoughts. You do not plan a trip, even a day trip, without planning where your meals will be. "Okay, so I'm going to the museum in Boston. Great. But I don't like the food there, so I suppose I could make a small detour to Quincy Market. There are all kinds of restaurants over there. I can grab something quick and then meet everyone at the museum. I'll only be a little late..."

Your preoccupation with food will get in the way of your ability to accomplish your tasks. You will make sacrifices in any plan you are making to ensure that your meals and snacks are covered. In addition, any meal that you plan must be very large.

When in the presence of food, you will have a difficult time paying attention to what goes on around you. When scheduling a meeting, you will most likely try to schedule it at a restaurant or somewhere where you can have a meal. Unfortunately, when around food (especially large amounts of it), you must make frequent Will tests in order to pay enough attention to anything but the food. You will suffer a -1 penalty to all Notice tests (unless it is to perceive something dealing with food).

You eat like there's no tomorrow. This means that you are not appealing to look at while you are gorging yourself, and will suffer a -1 to all social skill tests during this time.

Your gluttony presents a physical challenge as well. If you do not roleplay out regular heavy exercise, the Director may impose penalties to your Stamina as your character develops and gains weight.

Gossip

You cannot keep a secret.

When in possession of a secret, you must make Will tests to keep from telling people. Granted, you will only willingly tell friends and colleagues, but if you do not even want to tell them, you must make a Will test or tell them without even realizing it until it is too late.

When an enemy wants the information, you will not suffer any penalties, as you are motivated not to tell. However, if the enemy is clever enough to engage your ego, perhaps to imply that you are too worthless to have anything of value, you must make a Will test to prevent blurting out a secret.

Example: *You have been working with friends to investigate a crime and you found someone who claims that a crooked cop is behind it. You are being questioned by the police and you're afraid that the detective questioning you is the bad cop. Of course, you know better than to tell him about your witness. There's no way you're going to tell him. No, no, no, not you. Your lips are sealed.*

The detective suddenly turns away from you, saying, "I don't know why I'm wasting my time with you. You're nobody. You would never know anything of any real value."

"Yeah, right!" What's this guy talking about? Nobody? I'm no nobody! You make your Will test and fail. "You think I don't know anything, well that's where you're wrong. I know enough to put you behind bars for 30 years! When we get Howard to testify about what he saw the other night, your goose'll be cooked!" Your jaw drops and your eyes bug out as you suddenly realize what you just said. Aww, not again, you think as detective turns and walks back over to you, looking pleased with himself...

Greedy

You obsessively desire a specific type of thing.

In most cases, the object of your desire is money, and lots of it. You could be greedy about other things though. You could be greedy for artwork, ancient artifacts or other things of value. Whatever you choose as the object of your desire, it must be something that will cause a negative effect in the game. You may need to discuss it with the Director.

You are miserly when it comes to the object of your desire. You will never lend any of it out, and you will always try to acquire more. This is your Achilles' heel, as you are unable to resist this and willing to do almost anything to acquire it.

Gullible

You are easily deceived or conned.

You suffer a -2 penalty to all Sense Motive tests to determine if someone is bluffing or lying.

Handicap

You have a physical or mental illness or injury.

Of course, you must decide exactly what the injury is. It can be anything from a fatal allergy to the loss of a limb or a mental illness. In any event, the injury must be debilitating enough to create a challenge in the game.

56

Casting

What penalties are involved will be based on the type of handicap that you have. The Director must work that out with you.

Hunted

Someone is hunting you, either to kill you or at least to do something bad to you. It could be someone trying to capture or kidnap you, arrest you or some other such undesirable thing.

Either you or the Director must determine who is hunting you, and how dangerous he is. The Director may choose to make this person a recurring character in the show.

Hunting

You are searching for someone for one reason or another. You are dedicated to the task of catching this person for whatever reason you are hunting him for, and will do all you can to succeed.

You must decide who this is. The Director will decide how difficult the task will be and will need to work this storyline into the show.

This is a fault that requires effort from the Director. She should consider this a golden opportunity to add a fun subplot to the story. She will need to make sure that you can make occasional progress in your hunt. The person you are hunting could be someone related to the story of the show, and could make an appearance in some of the episodes. This could be the nemesis, or even someone who had been victimized by the nemesis.

Impulsive

You tend to act without thinking. When you see something you want, you reach for it without thinking about the consequences. This causes no end of trouble, as you have a tendency to put yourself into danger on a regular basis.

If you actively try not to rush into a particular dangerous situation, the Director may require a Will test to avoid to do so.

Indecisive

You have a difficult time making up your mind.

Most decisions that you need to make, especially when you do not have time to consider the options, will be very difficult to make. You should definitely roleplay out the conflict as you struggle to make your decision (even if you, the actor, have already made your decision).

Any snap decisions can take time to make. The Director may require a Will test in order to make the decision quickly.

Intolerant

You are unwilling to tolerate differences in opinions, practices, or beliefs, especially religious beliefs. This also includes intolerance to various conditions of birth, like poverty, sex, race, and such.

If there is a limit to your intolerance, you must decide on it when you take this fault.

You suffer a -2 penalty to all social skill tests when dealing with someone whose beliefs differ from yours. You will show little to no respect for any such people, and may even resort to argument. This can work with other faults to turn a bad situation into an explosive one. For instance, if you also have Violent When Enraged or Blunt & Tactless, you could cause trouble wherever you go!

Jinxed

Bad things happen to you so often that it feels like there's a storm cloud always hanging over your head.

No matter where you go or what you do, trouble seems to find you.

Some call it Murphy's Law, which states that if something you do can go wrong, it probably will. This is the story of your life.

How this fault is used is left completely up to the Director.

Example Symptoms of Manic-Depressive	
Manic	**Depressive**
Increased energy & Strength	Sad, despairing mood
Irritability	Lack of energy
Racing thoughts	Poor self-esteem
Increased interest in activities	Sleep problems (too much or too little)
Overspending	Feelings of guilt
Rapid mood changes	Decreased sex drive
Inflated self-esteem	Crying easily, suicidal or even homicidal thoughts
Increased sex drive	Change in eating habits
Poor judgment	Preoccupation with failures and inadequacies

Casting

Gifts & Faults

Lazy

You have an aversion to physical labor.

When confronted with the need to do any physical task, you will balk and try to come up with a non-physical alternative. Quite often, this will be more expensive or take more work in the long run. Usually, these workarounds will not do the job nearly as well or as quickly as if you had just gotten off your butt and done the work.

You may be required to make a Will test whenever you need to do any strenuous task.

Lecherous

You are a glutton for sexual activity. You are sexual in just about everything you do. When you meet someone of the appropriate sex for your orientation, you instinctively size the person up as a potential bed partner.

Because of your hypersensitive libido, you appear very sexual to those around you. This could cause members of the opposite sex to be more attracted to you. It could also cause others to respect you less. An example of the latter would be a man who also has the Socially Awkward fault speaking to a woman's chest instead of to her face.

Your sex drive is so powerful, that you often find yourself falling victim to it. In a real sense, your libido controls your actions. When dealing with an attractive person, you will be vulnerable to her wiles.

Lost or Forbidden Love

You are deeply in love with someone who is lost to you in one way or another. It can be someone who has died or disappeared, or could be someone that for one reason or another you cannot be with.

You or the Director must create the character who you love, unless another actor plays that character. You must also decide in exactly what way she is lost to you. Perhaps she simply has no interest in you, or is married to someone else. Whatever the case, you need to work this out.

This is a good sub-plot to the show, and should take focus in an episode every now and then.

Low Pain Threshold

You cannot stand pain.

Whenever you suffer pain, you must make the Will test as described in the Fear section of Chapter Six: Filming. The Difficulty Level will depend on the severity of the pain.

If you succeed in your Will test, you will still be affected, and must Face Your Fears. This means you will suffer a penalty of -1 to all of your tests until your pain is treated.

Example Pain Threshold Difficulty Levels	
Wound Type	Level
Scratch	Poor
Light Wound	Fair
Severe Wound	Good
Incapacitated	Great
Near Death	Unconscious

Machismo

You suffer from an exaggerated sense of masculinity. You stress physical courage and virility. You believe in dominating women, and you are prone to aggressiveness.

Mostly, you are full of bluff and bluster, and are not to be taken seriously, but you do tend to be hard to handle. When you shake someone's hand, you practically break it. You insult other men's masculinity in order to make yourself seem all the more physically impressive to women. You dominate women when you can, and tend to be more attracted to the less outspoken ones. You speak in loud boisterous voice, full of bass and masculine tones.

Most characters who suffer from Machismo are male and have Good or higher Brawn.

Manic-Depressive

You suffer from massive mood swings.

You are always in either one state or the other, and never anywhere in between. The following is a breakdown of some of the symptoms of each state:

When in each state, you do not necessary (and should not) have all of these symptoms. You must pick a few and exhibit them.

Each day, either the Director or perhaps a dice roll will decide what state you are in. Each state may last a day or longer. It is recommended that the manic state be the strongest and longer lasting or the character may be hard to play and could cause a problem with the gameplay.

Melancholy

You occasionally suffer from bouts of sadness or depression.

The Director should determine when you feel this way, as well as how long it lasts. It will not happen all the time. When it does, you will feel gloomy and sad. You will not talk much and will be rather anti-social.

Mistaken Identity

Someone else looks so much like you that people are always mistaking you for him.

58

Casting

You or the Director must decide whom you look like and the Director should play him. The person should be someone of some fame (or infamy) so that it can be a real problem. It would be ideal if the Director could find a way to work it into the story of the show.

The two of you look so much alike that it would take a person who has passing acquaintance with either of you a Great Notice test in order to tell that you are not who he thinks you are (or visa versa). Someone who knows you or the other person well can tell with only a Good test.

Multiple Personality

You literally have more than one personality that can take focus at any time.

You can take this fault multiple times, gaining one additional personality every time. Therefore, if you took this fault twice, you will have three distinct personalities, including your original one.

You must fully define each personality, even to the point of filling out separate character sheets. Obviously, all physical traits will be the same, but the skills and some of the mental traits may differ. You may even have different gifts and faults, although all personalities will always have the same Multiple Personality fault.

You or the Director must decide what the trigger will be for each personality to break through. When that trigger happens, you must make an opposed Will test against the other personality's Will or the switch will occur.

Every now and then, as determined by the Director, you must make an opposed Will test against the active personality in order to regain control of your body and mind.

Obligation

You owe someone or a group or organization a debt of service. This could be a legal or moral agreement that must be adhered to by law or by your own code of ethics.

You or the Director must decide what the obligation is, how long lasting it is, and how heavily it will affect the show.

Whatever the obligation may be, there will always be penalties or punishment if you fail to comply. The Director should decide on the details of these penalties, and they may or may not be known to the character.

Obsession

You are almost constantly preoccupied with some fixed idea or unwanted feeling or emotion.

You must decide exactly what you are obsessed with and how strongly you are bound to it.

You suffer from a nearly irresistible urge to pursue the source of your obsession. Any attempt to resist it requires at least a Good Will test.

Outlaw

You are wanted by the law of a particular country or kingdom.

The country you choose must be one where you either live in or will need to frequent. Otherwise, this fault will be harmless. The Director must take care to make sure that this fault represents a significant challenge to you.

You must also decide what you did to become an outlaw.

You live in constant fear of recognition. At any moment, the proverbial jig could be up and you could be arrested. Every cop makes you nervous, as does anyone who stares at you. You read the local police blotter very carefully. You are afraid to visit anyone that you know and love because they are sure to be watched by the authorities.

Essentially, you might as well be dead. You may have a Social Security Number, but using it will get you caught for sure. Your fingerprints are not only on file, but they are constantly being compared to others in an attempt to find you. This will severely limit your ability to take a job or do anything public.

Overconfident

You think that you are capable of handling tasks that are beyond your abilities.

You tend to overly optimistic about any task that you face. If it is a challenging task, you will think it's easy and will treat it as such. A seriously dangerous task, you may feel is merely challenging, and will not be likely to use as much care as you would have otherwise.

This is something that is usually just roleplayed, but the Director may force a Will test if she feels it necessary.

Overly Talkative

You talk way too much, and often way too fast. This mostly only occurs when you are excited, but could happen any time when it seems theatrically opportune.

The problems that arise from this fault are many and varied:

Failure to Hear or Understand You: Because you speak very fast and with many words, people tend to have a difficult time understanding you. This can cause people to tire of you and not want to listen to you. Often, they just shut you out and not even listen!

When a person has tuned you out or when you are just rambling almost incoherently, the listener must make a Notice skill test or Concentration skill test just to get the gist of what you are saying. The Difficulty Level would depend on whether the person is trying to listen or has tuned you out.

Annoying: People tend to be annoyed with those who talk too much. Because of this, you suffer a -1 to all social skills when dealing with anyone who does not also have the Overly Talkative fault.

Slips: You accidentally let some information slip during your constant stream of chatter that would best have been left unsaid. Luckily, this will usually happen when the listeners are having trouble understanding you, and you may be saved simply by the fact that they fail their Notice tests.

When you have information that you do not want to slip, the Director may require a Will test to hold it in. The Difficulty Level may depend on how excited you are when you say it.

Pacifist

You are strictly against violence.

You not only will refuse to resort to violence yourself, but will hold any people who will in contempt. You may even tend to preach to people about peace and non-violence.

You may be able to fight in self-defense, but it may take a force of will, and thus a Will test. However, in a case where it's clearly fight or be killed, you will fight without much hesitation, but the threat must be severe and obvious to avoid having to make the Will test.

When fighting against your better judgment (when you succeeded in your Will test), you will suffer a -1 to your attack rolls for the duration of the fight, or until the situation changes in a way that will fully justify in your mind.

Phobia

You have an unreasoning fear of a particular thing.

You must choose a specific phobia or object of your fear. It could be one of the documented phobias, like claustrophobia (a fear of tight or enclosed spaces), or it could just be a thing like "bugs."

When you encounter the focus of your phobia, you will make your Will test as described under Fear in Chapter Six: Filming. Your Difficulty Level will be at least Great.

If you succeed in your Will test, you will have to Face Your Fears, and suffer a penalty to all of your tests. Suc-

Casting

cess is a relative term when a phobic person is dealing with his mania. You cannot escape it, so the best you can hope for is to live with it.

Practical Joker

You love to trick people in a mischievous way that can cause the victim embarrassment, discomfort or indignity.

From whoopee cushions to a pie in the face, you love to make people laugh at the expense of another.

If you cannot come up with one on your own, you can make a Reasoning test to drum up the plan for a practical joke off the cuff and make it happen.

When presented with a perfect opportunity for a practical joke, you will find it difficult not to take advantage of it. Of course, you do understand the meaning of discretion. That is, you would never do it in a dangerous situation. For instance, if you are a cop, you would not play a practical joke on your partner during a stakeout, unless it was simple and harmless (like telling him the attractive suspect they're watching from another apartment is getting undressed when she isn't).

Quick-Tempered

You are quick to take offense to other people's actions and words.

You behave as though everyone is likely to say and do things to intentionally offend you, whether you actually think that way or not. Therefore, if someone says something that can possibly be construed as offensive, you will not only take offense to it, but will make it blatantly obvious that do. You have a short temper and will get angry easily.

Rivalry

There is a specific person with whom you are always trying to compete.

You must define who this person is, and why he is your rival. This character should be fully created, and played out as a supporting character by the Director. The Director may choose to create the character herself.

This character will play a recurring role in the show.

Secret Identity

You have another identity that must remain secret.

Perhaps you are a super hero, or a secret agent or just someone who is living a double-life. Whatever the case, you have another identity that needs to be kept secret from the other.

The risk of discovery and the importance of keeping the identity a secret must be great enough to present a challenge to you.

Single Minded

You focus completely on one task to the exclusion of all else. This usually happens only with tasks that are important to you personally or professionally, but could happen with anything you concentrate hard on. Definitely, if you make a Concentration skill test, then this will take effect.

When working on a lengthy task, you will be unaware of what is going on around you. Just to notice someone who is standing next to you and talking to you would require a Notice test. During these times, you completely ignore any background chatter that may be going on around you.

However, your tremendous focus does not go unrewarded. You gain a +1 to all lengthy tasks.

It is quite common for a character to only suffer from this fault when focusing on a specific type of task. For example, the man who believes he has been abducted by aliens will only suffer from Tunnel Vision when he is studying UFOs.

Socially Awkward

You are not good at dealing with social situations.

You should decide in what way are you socially awkward. For instance, you could just be painfully shy.

You suffer a -1 to all social skills.

Softhearted

You are kindly and affectionate. Being softhearted, you are susceptible to pity and have a hard time holding a grudge. You tend to forgive and forget, and can be meek.

If someone gives you a "sob story" to make you feel bad, you are likely to believe it and feel sorry for him, even if you do not like or trust the person.

You suffer a -1 to all Sense Motive tests when someone is using Bluff to make you feel pity. You also suffer a -1 penalty to all tests when opposing social skills used against you while you feel pity for him.

Example: *You catch a young punk who just picked your pocket and has taken a clue to the mystery you're trying to solve. When you confront him and demand it back, he starts sobbing and tells you a sad story about how he was kicked out of his home by his abusive step-father and was forced to live on the streets and he's had to eek out a living washing car windows and dealing with rude people who throw things at him when he does it and now he's forced to steal just to survive and...*

You make a Sense Motive test, with a -1, to see if he's bluffing and fail. At this point, you feel very sorry for him. He then uses his Persuasion skill to talk you into letting him go (without giving back the clue). You roll your Will test at a -1 (because you already feel pity for him) and succeed. "I'm really sorry, but I need that thing you took.

Casting

Look, why don't I give you some money in exchange. Fifty bucks'll get you farther than that little thing anyway."

Submissive

You feel the need to let others dominate you.

Usually, this is only in certain circumstances. Some people feel a need to be dominated in professional matters, some in the home, and still others sexually. Although there are some people who are submissive in all facets of their lives, this would probably make a dysfunctional character in the game.

You must pick an area or areas in which you are submissive, then roleplay that out.

Stubborn

You will not budge from any decision you make.

When you make a decision that you feel strongly about, it is always the best decision there is, with no exception. No one can talk you out of it or change your mind.

Any attempt to back down will require a Will test. The Difficulty Level depends on how important the decision is to you.

Unlucky

You have very bad luck.

You lose one permanent Luck Point, so that you have one less Luck Point that returns each session.

Vain

You love yourself, and are excessively proud of your appearance and accomplishments.

You suffer a -1 to all social skills when dealing with people who do not agree with your opinion of yourself.

Vendetta

You are involved in a bitter, destructive feud with someone or some people.

A person, family or group of people has seriously angered you to a point where you would easily resort to violence if you run into any of them. This is usually caused by the murder of a family member of some other serious attack by the offending party against you or your family.

You must define exactly what the cause of the feud is, and who are involved. The Director should create any characters that are necessary and have them as recurring characters in the show.

Whenever you encounter one of these people, you will immediately be violently disposed toward them. No roll is necessary. However, if you are in a situation where it would be bad to outright attack the person, you must make a Good or Great Will test to hold back. The Difficulty Level will depend on how badly you want to hurt the person and how bad the consequences would be if you succeeded. Perhaps if you want to kill the person and you are in public, you would need a Great Will test to not attack him, but if you roll at least Fair or Good, you would hold back enough to not try to kill him, but to just beat him senseless instead.

Violent When Enraged

When you get very angry with someone, you are predisposed to violence.

If you do not automatically make the decision to resort to violence in such a situation, the Director may secretly make a Will test for you. If you fail the test, she will tell you exactly how enraged you are and that you cannot hold yourself back.

Worry Wart

You worry about everything. If anything can possibly go wrong, you feel certain that it will. This will cause anxiety and may even prompt you to make rash decisions and to take actions when patience would have been better.

A Will test may be required in any situation where you are worried about something and you think there could be something you can do about it. If you fail your test, then you will suffer a -1 to all tests while the situation lasts

Zealot

You have an enthusiastic devotion to a cause, ideal or goal, and you will tirelessly strive to further it. This ideal or goal is the center point of your life, and you will stop at nothing to ensure that this goal is met or furthered.

You are like an idealist gone to the extreme. An idealist has a belief in an ideal, but is not necessarily driven to actively enforce it. In addition, the cause that a zealot follows is not necessarily unrealistic. In fact, it could be very realistic, good and correct. It is just that you tend to overreact in regards to the cause.

You suffer a -2 to all tests when trying to turn your back, even temporarily, on the object of your zeal. During any time when you have done this, you suffer a -1 to all tests until you have made things right with your cause.

Props

Chapter 5

Casting

Props

The Props Department

Hello, and welcome to the props department! I see that you all have your parts and are ready to "get into character." Well, you've come to the right place!

This warehouse, where the props department lives, is chock full of all kinds of clothing, equipment, vehicles and of course, weapons. Right here, we've got everything you need.

Now, let's start the tour. Please, follow me—and don't touch anything!

Standard of Living

Before you can start deciding what possessions you want, you have to know how much you can get. Vinnie here will describe the Income system that you'll use to handle money and determine your standard of living. He'll also give you all the instructions you need for choosing your possessions.

Virtually no television shows deal with the specifics of the cast's money and income. After all, you never see the star of a TV show figuring out how much money he has to see if he can afford to buy something he needs.

Instead of having a monetary system that gives the characters a specific amount of money and salary, *Now Playing* uses a simple system that merely works with the character's standard of living. This is a more abstract way of dealing with money, but after all, that's how it's handled in TV You don't know how much money the starring character of your favorite detective show makes, but you do know that he lives in a dingy apartment with sparse furniture, drives a cheap beat up car and wears the same few suits every day.

The following sections describe how the Standard of Living system works and how you can decide what props you can own.

Income

The amount of props you can own is determined by your Income trait. The scale is the same as with all other traits: Terrible through Superb.

All characters start the game with a Fair Income.

Each level of Income gives you Resource Tickets that you can use to spend on props. All props are sorted by how expensive they are in Tickets. There are only a handful of bins, which makes it easy to purchase items.

You can raise or lower your Income trait by taking the Increased Income gift or the Decreased Income fault respectively. See Chapter Four: Gifts & Faults for details.

The different levels of your Income, with examples of how they would apply, are described below. The number of Resource Tickets you earn each episode is listed beside the level in parentheses.

Terrible (1 Tickets)

You are homeless. You have no job and no income, and have no one whom you can depend on for financial assistance. The few Resource Tickets you begin with represent those items that you either always had or you had managed to beg, steal or forage for.

Poor (2 Tickets)

You are poor. You have money and a home, but not much of each. You cannot afford a house, nor could you afford an apartment and expect to furnish it and own anything else. Instead, you would most likely rent a room. You cannot own a car, and you would not own many (if any) expensive items, and you would probably not want to own anything that would be hard to move, since you do not own a car.

Mediocre (3 Tickets)

You can afford an apartment or studio, and can even furnish it sparsely. Any car you would own would be old and beat-up. You would not own many expensive items.

Table 5-1: Standard of Living Resource Tickets		
Income	Tickets	Description
Superb	10	Rich: owns more than one home, vehicles, lots of expensive items, etc.
Great	7	Upper middle-class: owns big house, multiple new cars, plenty of big items, etc.
Good	5	Middle-class: owns house or condo, new car, some big items, etc.
Fair	4	Lower middle-class: Rents a decent apartment or owns a small house or trailer, owns a used car, and a few big items.
Mediocre	3	Lower class: rents an apartment, owns an old car, and a couple big items.
Poor	2	Poor: rents a room, has no car, and has little to no big items.
Terrible	1	Homeless: owns only a handful of small items.

Casting

Fair (4 Tickets)

You can rent an apartment or even own a small house. You would most likely own a used car, but a decent one. If you did own a new car, you would not be able to afford a good home. You can own a small number of expensive items.

Good (5 Tickets)

You make a good living. You can own a nice house, like a split-entry, ranch or small garrison. You can own a new car. You can own some expensive items like personal computers.

Great (7 Tickets)

You make really good money. You can afford a big house (like a large colonial with vaulted ceilings), but not a mansion. You can own more than one new car, and plenty of expensive items.

Superb (10 Tickets)

You're rich. You can own more than one home, or a mansion. You can own multiple cars and have many expensive items.

Acquiring Props

Much of your character's possessions do not need to be requisitioned. These items define your standard of living. Items that you do not need to requisition are your home, car, clothes, and any props that would normally be required by your occupation (i.e., a detective would automatically own a revolver and some ammo).

Resource Tickets

Each level of the Income trait gives you a certain number of Resource Tickets. Each "bin" in Table 5-2: Prop Bins and Resource Ticket Costs has a Ticket cost associated with it. You simply trade in Tickets to pick your props from the bins.

This is very much like getting prizes at a carnival. Each game you play gives you tickets. When you're done, you trade in the tickets for prizes. There are several shelves at the prize booth, where the items on each shelf

Optional Resource Tickets

The use of Resource Tickets can be optional. The Director may choose to let you simply decide what props you should have.

You know your character and you know his standard of living. Simply use your common sense to choose only those props that your character would have with that income.

Of course, if you use this method, you must always gain your Director's approval of all the props you take.

The advantage of this method is that it eliminates the need of any game system rules for choosing props, thus making the task much easier. The problem with it is that it is very subjective and the cast can easily become unbalanced. Because of this, many Directors will not prefer this method and may make you redo your prop choices if you try to bring him into a new show.

Table 5-2: Prop Bins and Resource Ticket Costs		
Bin	Cost	Types of Props
0	$0	Flashlight, food, notebook, film, pen, floppy disk.
1	$100	Camera, cell phone, gun ammunition, palmtop computer.
2	$200	Katana broadsword, standard computer parts.
3	$300	Digital camera, pistol, handheld GPS.
4	$400	Longbow, rifle.
5	$500	Shotgun, Taser.
6	$600	Machine gun.
7	$700	Assault rifle, crossbow.
8	$800	Surveillance system with monitor and cameras.
9	$1000	Personal computer.
10	$1200	Notebook computer

Casting

Props

have a different cost in tickets.

When you create your character, you start with the amount of Resource Tickets that your Income trait allows. You can then use these to outfit your character.

At the beginning of each episode, you gain the amount of Resource Tickets owed to you by your Income trait. This means that at the start of your first episode, you will essentially have twice the amount of Resource Tickets that you would normally get: you get one helping of tickets for creating your character, and the other helping at the start of the episode.

You do not need to spend all of your Resource Tickets right away. You can save them up for buying something big later on during the game.

You can spend tickets before an episode begins, or during the episode. If you requisition props during the episode, the Director may require that you roleplay the scene where you acquire the props. It is also possible that the Directory may not allow you to requisition anything if your character is not in a position to be able to buy anything.

Cost of Props

All props are sorted into bins that are based on their cost. There are six bins. Table 5-2: Prop Bins and Resource Ticket Costs lists the types of props that fit into each bin. Each bin has an approximate price in early 21st century U.S. currency. This is included for your convenience, and does not mean that all equipment costs use that currency. The reason for using Resource Tickets is so that you can play a game that is generic in regards to currency. After all, if you are playing a show that takes place in Ancient Greece, you would not want to use dollars and cents!

The table does not attempt to list every possible prop that you can acquire. Essentially, you can requisition anything that would be available to the character in real life (or in TV). If you need to requisition a prop that is not in any of the bins listed in the table, you must decide which bin it would fit into based on its monetary worth. Simply compare the prop's cost with the costs of the other props in the bins.

Example: *You are trying to add a piece of custom computer hardware that your character needs during the episode. You know that its price in real life is around $500. Looking through the bins, you find that one bin contains revolvers. A revolver normally costs around $500. So, the new piece of computer equipment fits nicely into that bin next to the revolver.*

Realism vs. Television

When playing a game that involves the enacting of tactical situations, it is easy to feel that a high level of realism is desirable. This is quite true in most cases, and even for many roleplaying games. However, this is not true for *Now Playing*. The reason has to do with the game's focus: television.

Television deals primarily with story and characters, and it has very little time for much else. Therefore, you never see much effort spent on the tactics of a combat scene. Yes, you may see the cast form a plan and execute it, but you will not see them worry about how many bullets were fired, what the maximum range is for the weapon is, and how bad the recoil is. The director simply is not concerned with any tactical detail that can take momentum away from the scene.

Some shows may pick one or two things that they feel is important to handle realistically, but will not put the same effort on everything. For instance, a courtroom drama may be very realistic in all of the courtroom scenes, but throw realism out the window when showing

Table 5-3: Guns

Weapon	Strength	Range	Ammo	Size	Weapon	Strength	Range	Ammo	Size
Assault Rifle	+7	400 meters	42	Med	Machine Gun	+6	500 meters	42	Med
Bazooka	+10	400 meters	1	Large	Machine Gun, Heavy	+8	500 meters	100	Med
Bow	+3	100 meters	1	Large	Musket	+6	35 meters	1	Large
Crossbow	+3	100 meters	1	Large	Revolver	+2	50 meters	6	Small
Dart Pistol	+0	30 meters	1	Small	Revolver, Magnum	+4	50 meters	6	Small
Dart Rifle	+0	60 meters	2	Med	Rifle	+5	550 meters	24	Med
Derringer	+1	30 meters	2	Small	Semi-Auto Pistol	+3	50 meters	10	Small
Flintlock Pistol	+4	25 meters	1	Small	Shotgun	+6	50 meters	1	Med
Holdout Pistol	+2	30 meters	5	Small	Stun Gun	+0	7 meters	1	Small
Laser Pistol	+8	20 meters	20	Small	Sub-Machine Gun	+5	150 meters	42	Med
Machine Pistol	+3	50 meters	20	Small					

Casting

a cop searching a suspect's house.

Now Playing works the same way. Because of this, you must not expect the details of each weapon to be perfectly accurate. For instance, the stats for the semi-automatic pistol specify only 10 rounds of ammunition per magazine, when there are semi-autos out there that can hold more.

The stats of any prop can be adjusted by the Director on a case-by-case basis, but are intentionally left generalized in the game to preserve the feel of television.

Weapons

Before I open this door, I want to make one thing clear: Don't touch anything! These things are dangerous, okay. So, keep your mitts to yourself.

All right, this section lists and describes all the weapons that are included with Now Playing. *Of course, we don't have every weapon there is, or was or will be, so if you want to bring in some weapons to add to our warehouse, be my guest. Just do me a favor and run it by the Director first. If you have any trouble figuring out the stats, just look at the stuff we already got and go from there. It's really not hard, since there are not many stats to deal with.*

The weapons are listed in tables, complete with all statistics. They are also described, at least briefly, in this section.

This section tells you everything you need to know to decide which weapons you want and how to use them. It also details all of the types of armor that are common in TV shows.

To understand how to deal with each type of weapon, refer to Chapter Six: Filming.

Creating Weapons

If there are any specific weapons that you need for your show that are not listed here, you can create the weapon without much trouble.

The only game-system specific attribute of a weapon is its Strength. How to determine weapon strength depends on the type of weapon you're creating. The sections below describe how to create both melee and ranged weapons.

Melee (Muscle-Powered) Weapons

Melee weapon strength is determined by a combination of size and sharpness. The following table summarizes the weapon strength modifiers and what they apply to:

Table 5-4: Strength Modifiers for Melee Weapons	
Type of Weapon	Strength
No weapon, not using Martial Art skill.	-1
Martial Art skill or small weapons (blackjack, knife, brass knuckles, sling, etc.).	+0
Medium-weight one-handed weapons (billy club, machete, shortsword, epee, hatchet, rock, etc.).	+1
Large one-handed weapons (broadsword, axe, large club, etc.), or for light two-handed weapons (spear, bow, etc.).	+2
Most two-handed weapons (polearm, two-handed sword, battleaxe, etc.).	+3
Sharpness (add to other weapon damage: knife becomes +1, shortsword +2, etc.).	+1

Ranged Weapons

There is unfortunately no hard-set rule for determining weapon strengths for ranged weapons. However, *Now Playing* offers a wide variety of ranged weapons from the more primitive to the modern and even one or two futuristic ones. You can use these as templates when creating your own.

Weapon Qualities

The following is a description of the qualities that are listed in the weapon tables:

Table 5-5: Melee Weapons							
Weapon	Strength	Ammo	Size	Weapon	Strength	Ammo	Size
Axe	+3		Medium	Rapier	+2		Medium
Club	+1		Medium	Staff	+3		Large
Club, metal	+2		Medium	Stun Gun, melee version	--	10	Small
Dagger/Knife	+1		Tiny	Sword, broad or long	+3		Large
Hatchet	+2		Medium	Sword, short or bronze	+1		Medium
Mace Spray	--	10	Tiny	Sword, two-handed	+4		Large
Machete	+2		Medium	Whip	+0		Medium
Nunchaku	+2		Medium				

Casting

Weapon

This is either the name of a specific weapon or the name of a type of weapon. The weapon named here can refer to an entire category of weapons that all normally have their own differences, but are treated the same in television.

Example: *The semi-auto pistol makes up a variety of very different guns, but in TV shows, they are always just pistols that are loaded with a magazine. Therefore, they are treated the same way in* Now Playing.

Strength

This is the value associated directly with the weapon that is added to your Offensive Factor when determining damage.

Range

This represents the maximum range of the weapon. This applies only to ranged weapons.

Ammo

This is the amount of shots that can be fired from the weapon before you must reload.

Size

This is the approximate size of the weapon. This uses the abstract sizes Tiny, Small, Medium, and Large. The sizes represent a combination of physical size and weight. These size categories will affect attempts at concealing the weapons. For details on concealing items, see the section Item Concealment in Chapter Six: Filming.

Ranged Weapons

Assault Rifle

This is a high-powered fully automatic rifle used by soldiers during war. The M16 is one of the most well known assault rifles available. They can fire single shots as well as any size burst.

A typical assault rifle has a maximum range of 400 meters.

Bazooka

Also called a "rocket launcher", a bazooka is a shoulder-held weapon with a long metal tube for firing short-range armor-piercing rockets. These are most commonly used to penetrate the armor plating of tanks, gun emplacements and other such targets.

An average bazooka has a range of 400 meters maximum, but is generally only effective up to 200 meters.

Bow

There is a wide variety of different types of bows and arrows in the world. This section will attempt to describe some of the more common ones, and will leave the details of others up to the Director's discretion.

The basic concept of all bows is the same. There is one long piece of wood or fiberglass that has a strong string attached to it. The string is not as long as the bow itself, so when it is "strung" (with the string attached to both tips of the bow), the bow is bent or, well, bowed. The bow has a handle near its center with a small rest for the arrow.

To shoot an arrow, you attach the nock (the slitted part in the back of the shaft) by fitting the string in its slit, and rest the shaft on the handle of the bow. You then grip the string and pull it back, causing the bow to bend even more. You do not touch the nock or arrow at any time; the nock will keep it in place. Once you have taken aim, you let go of the string and the arrow is sent flying through the air toward the target.

Aiming: Because of the great strength required to pull back and hold the string while you aim, the longer you hold the string back, the harder it is to do so. Therefore, the Director can let you take careful aim for more than one round to add a bonus to your attack roll, but you must make a Brawn test for each round. If you fail the test, you must fire immediately or ease the string back and rest your arm.

Longbows & Shortbows: Both of these bows work the same way, except that the shortbow is not as powerful. The range listed for a Bow is based on the longbow. If you want a shortbow, simply decrease the range by one-third.

Compound Bows: These are fancy bows that use pulleys and wires to decrease the amount of work required to hold the bow at ready while aiming. Using a compound bow will remove the requirement of making Brawn tests while aiming. However, compound bows are modern-day inventions, and will not exist in a medieval or fantasy setting.

All bows except for compounds need to be stored unstrung, or it could harm either the bow or the string. A full round is required to string it.

Crossbow

The crossbow is made to take the benefits of a bow and make it usable like a gun. You have a stock like a rifle with a groove that the arrow fits in. It has a bow that is built onto the stock.

To use it, you fit the arrow into the stock, and pull back the string until it clicks into a locking mechanism. Then you just aim and fire it like a rifle.

Pulling back the string is very hard, but the crossbow usually comes with a tool to help pull it back. Still, it will take a full action to load the bow. If you have the Rapid Reload gift, it will take a half action.

Casting

Dart Pistol & Rifle

A dart pistol can be used to shoot one dart at a target. They are single-load weapons, so once you fire it, you must insert another dart before you can fire again.

A dart is like a syringe that can be shot into a person from a distance. Therefore, just about any kind of liquid drug can loaded into a dart. The most common drugs used by dart pistols are tranquilizers. The effects of the drug will vary depending upon the dart used.

A dart pistol has a maximum range of only 30 meters.

A dart rifle has a maximum range of only 60 meters.

Derringer

This is a small, one-shot pistol that dates back to the 19th century. It can only hold one round at a time, so you must reload the weapon after each shot. It has a short barrel and is small enough to fit in a pocket. Although it is a single-shot weapon, it is still popular because of its conceal-ability.

A typical derringer has a range of 30 meters.

Holdout Pistol

A holdout pistol is really nothing more than a "back-up" gun. Most police officers carry two guns, but you never see number two. It is a small handgun on an ankle or some other hidden part of the body that can be easily concealed and used in a pinch. They tend to be small, with not much ammo. An example would be a five-shot snub-nose .38 Special.

A derringer can also be used as a holdout pistol, but they are not as common.

A typical holdout pistol has a maximum range of 30 meters.

Laser Pistol

Laser weapons can vary greatly from show to show, but this is a fine example of a typical TV hand-held laser weapon.

This is a hand-held weapon looking similar to a regular modern-day pistol. However, instead of throwing slugs, it fires a beam of concentrated light of great heat.

The laser pistol has the following three settings:

Stun: This is a non-lethal setting that merely shocks the nervous system, causing the victim to fall unconscious. The victim must make a Superb Stamina test or fall unconscious for 10 minutes.

Kill: This is the normal lethal setting. A short burst of energy is fired, with a weapon strength of +8. Each burst will use up one charge.

Cutting: This setting is used strictly for cutting through metal surfaces. It fires a continuous beam that is extremely thin and powerful. It can cut through most

Casting

metals up to 1 foot thick. Cutting through a 1-foot thick steel plate will take 1 minute per foot, so a 1'x1' square section can be cut out in 4 minutes. This will eat up power at the rate of 5 charges per minute.

A laser pistol is equipped with a 20-charge power pack.

Machine Gun

Machine guns are military weapons designed for causing suppressive fire to force an enemy to keep cover. Machine guns cannot fire single shots, and are therefore not designed for accuracy.

When fired, the spray of bullets may hit anyone in the general area of the target. The Director must decide who would be in the range of the spray. Those that are in the "danger zone" but were not the intended target of the shooter will gain a +1 on their defensive roll.

Machine Gun, Heavy

These are heavy weapons that cannot be carried or operated by a single man. Usually three men are needed to operate the weapon: one for the weapon itself, another for the mount and the third for feeding the ammunition. The gun's recoil is so powerful that it can only be fired while mounted firmly in place. Heavy machine guns are usually mounted on a military vehicle, such as a jeep, or on a tripod. The ammunition usually comes in the form of a long belt of rounds that are fed into the side of the weapon.

The heavy machine gun can fire any type of burst but cannot fire single shots.

Machine Pistol

This is a fully automatic pistol. It looks very much like a normal semi-auto pistol, except with a longer magazine. It can fire single shot, short and medium bursts.

Machine pistols are wildly uncontrollable, and thus add an additional -1 to all bursts fired with this weapon, even if you are proficient with the weapon.

Musket

This is the first rifle that was very reliable, and was popular for around 300 years before it was eventually replaced by the percussion cap weapons.

Muskets were flintlock weapons. To fire a musket, you first pour gunpowder into the barrel, then put the ball into it. When you squeeze the trigger, a large hammer with a piece of flint on it smacks down hard on a steel plate, which causes the sparks as burning bits of iron fly from the flint. Some of the sparks will fly into a hole in the barrel, thus igniting the gunpowder. With a whoosh of flame, the ball is shot from the barrel at the target.

The musket can fire only one shot before it must be reloaded. Reloading takes time and effort, and involves pouring the powder from your powder horn into a powder measure, then into the barrel. Then you put the ball in (and even that requires a special process involving a greased strip of cloth), and then finally using a ramrod to pack it in tightly.

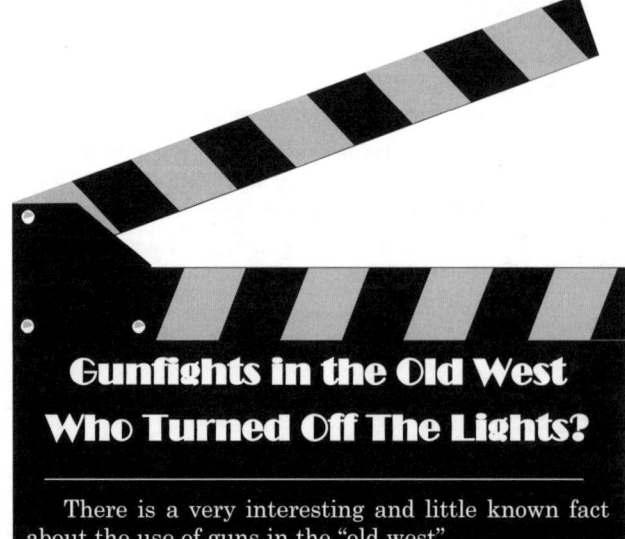

Loading: Loading a musket takes 6 minutes (and yes, I mean *minutes* not *rounds*). Cut this time in half if you have the Rapid Reload gift. Loading these guns is a time-consuming, laborious process, involving pouring in powder, inserting the ball, and ramming it down. There's actually more to it than that, but this gives you an idea of the complexity of the process. If you need a quicker turn-around, carry multiple weapons.

Muzzleloader Pistol

This is the first truly portable pistol, and was popular for around 300 years before percussion cap weapons eventually replaced it.

You first pour gunpowder into the barrel, then put the ball into it. When you squeeze the trigger, a large hammer that strikes something that causes a spark in the chamber to ignite the gunpowder. With a whoosh of flame, the ball is shot from the barrel at the target.

Muzzleloaders were in use until the modern cartridge guns replaced them in 1861.

Gunfights in the Old West — Who Turned Off The Lights?

There is a very interesting and little known fact about the use of guns in the "old west".

When a gun is fired, the concussion caused by the blast can be strong, especially in a tight space such as the barroom of a saloon. The concussion is strong enough, in fact, to snuff out all small exposed flames within a 12-foot radius. Therefore, if you are standing near a kerosene lamp when you fire, you might put it out just by shooting your gun.

So, when a gunfight breaks out in a old west saloon, you might find yourself fighting in the dark right after the first shot is fired!

Casting

Ammo: There are two varieties of the muzzleloader. The most common (which were used up until the early 1800's) had only one shot before needing reloading. In the early 1800's, muzzle-loading revolvers were invented that gave you 6 shots before being emptied. Unfortunately, reloading was just as difficult.

Loading: Loading a muzzleloader takes 6 minutes (and yes, I mean minutes not rounds). Cut this time in half if you have the Rapid Reload gift. Loading these guns is a time-consuming, laborious process, involving pouring in powder, inserting the ball, and ramming it down. There's actually more to it than that, but this gives you an idea of the complexity of the process. If you need a quicker turnaround, carry multiple weapons.

Revolver

This is the standard Police firearm. It has a rotating cylinder that holds the rounds. After the weapon fires, the cylinder turns, loading another round into the chamber. This is one of the most common styles of pistol and has been around since the 19th century.

Revolver, Magnum

This is a more powerful version of the revolver. It is physically larger and does more damage, but otherwise looks and works like a regular revolver.

Rifle

Most commonly hunting rifles, these weapons are not as powerful as the assault rifle, but work in much the same manner. They are single-shot weapons that can hold a magazine storing 24 rounds. Because of its size, it does the same damage as a semi-auto pistol, but is more accurate, and is thus more capable of hitting vital parts of the target.

Semi-Auto Pistol

This is a pistol whose rounds are automatically loaded into the gun from a magazine. A magazine is required to load the weapon, and each magazine can hold 10 rounds.

The magazine is located inside the weapon's handle, and can be released via a switch on the gun. Once a magazine is empty, you can either pop in full magazine, or refill the empty one. Obviously, refilling an empty magazine will take time, as you would need to take each round from a box and fit it into the magazine before putting it back into the gun, but it can save you money, as a 10-round magazine is more expensive than a box of 50 rounds.

Some people are very skilled at switching magazines. If you have the Rapid Reload gift and another full magazine, ejecting the empty magazine and sliding in the full one will be a free action.

Shotgun

A shotgun is a rifle that fires a volley of shot over a short range. These weapons hold one or two rounds and must be reloaded after each shot.

The "rounds" of a shotgun are a plastic shell containing a large number of small pellets called "shot". When the weapon is fired, the shot are projected outward in a cone.

Stun Gun

The stun gun fires two probes at a target up to 21 feet away. The probes are attached to the taser by high-voltage insulated wires. When the probes touch their target, they emit an electrical charge that can temporarily shut down the target's nervous system.

There is another, less expensive version of the stun gun that that is not a ranged weapon. It has the same two probes, but they are fixed to the device itself, and do not fire outwards. This weapon requires a melee attack to work.

When struck, the victim must make a Great Stamina test, or be completely immobilized for 4 minutes. Even if the victim makes his Stamina test, he will still be dazed, suffering a -1 penalty to all tests.

Sub-Machine Gun

This is a lightweight, automatic weapon that fires pistol rounds. It is usually fired from the shoulder or hip and has the ability to fire single rounds.

Melee Weapons

Axe

This really refers to the big-bladed battle-axe, used in ancient days for combat. Any modern axe will act as a hatchet, except with a longer handle.

Some battle-axes have two blades, while some have only one. In any case, they are all big and heavy.

Club

A club is a simple weapon that you can use to beat with. This could be a wooden stick, a cane, a billy club, or any other such cudgel.

There is another category of club in *Now Playing*: Metal Clubs. These are identical to normal clubs, except that they do more damage. Examples of metal clubs would be a crowbar, hammer, pipe, etc.

Dagger

Daggers are generally very large knives used for

Casting

fighting. In *Now Playing*, this category has been broadened to include any large knife, including Bowie Knives, butchers knives, and hunting knives.

Hatchet

A hatchet is essentially a small axe. It is what you would use to cut firewood. The tomahawk is also considered a hatchet in this game.

Mace Spray

This is a small aerosol that can be used to temporarily immobilize or disorient a living target. These are small, look like they could be for perfume or deodorant, and are thus easily concealed. Because of their inconspicuous look, they are quite popular as concealed weapons.

Mace only affect's a target's eyes. When sprayed in the victim's eyes, his eyes will slam shut and he will feel an intense burning that will last 4 rounds. At the beginning of each round of effect, the victim must make a Great Stamina test, or his attention will be completely consumed by the pain and will fall into a fit of rubbing, squirming and screaming. If at any time he makes his Stamina test, he will be able to act, but will be disoriented and have difficulty seeing. When in this state, he will suffer -2 to all all tasks until the sprays effects wear off.

A mace spray has a maximum range of seven feet and can be used 10 times before it is empty.

Machete

A large heavy knife used as a weapon or for cutting vegetation. Although this is a knife, it is larger and heavier than a dagger, and therefore does more damage.

Nunchaku

A pair of hardwood sticks joined together by a chain or cord. The cord is never longer than one foot, and is often shorter. These weapons are a popular choice of martial artists in movies and television because of their very dramatic appearance.

Holding one of the sticks, you swing the other stick in the air, causing it to spin and fly with great speed and power. You strike your opponents with the flying part of the stick.

Rapier

This is a long, straight, slender sword with two edges. It is used as a slashing and stabbing weapon. It is slender, and therefore ineffective against anyone wearing armor. It was used heavily during the Renaissance. Those who study fencing can use a rapier in battle and duels.

Staff

This is the trusty quarterstaff used by Robin Hood and his merry men. It is a long wooden stick, often with a metal shoe on one end. The staff is typically near the height of its wielder.

The staff is often used to aid in walking as well as fighting. Martial artists employ two forms of staffs, called the Bo and Jo sticks. The Bo stick is about as tall as a person, while the Jo stick is about half that height. The Bo and Jo are not metal-shod, but will do the same damage.

Sword

There are many types of swords in the world, all designed for different purposes. Each one is a weapon, but each are designed for a specific method of fighting or for fighting a certain type of foe. The following is a brief description of some of the more common swords used throughout history:

Bronze: During the Bronze Age, shortswords were the primary weapon. The difference lies only in the material the blade is made of. Bronze is a softer metal, and will therefore not last as long.

Broadsword: These swords are long, with a blade about 31 inches long. It has a wide, usually two-edged blade and is designed for slashing. It's hilt is designed for only one hand, although there are some that are called "hand-and-a-half" swords. If you were to hold one of these with two hands, one hand will be mostly gripping the pommel.

Scimitar: This has a broad, curved sword with one edge on the convex side. It is mainly used for slashing. There are many types of swords that are similar to the scimitar, including the saber and cutlass. All of these swords do the damage of a broadsword.

Shortsword: This is a short sword with two edges. It is larger than a dagger and yet shorter than a broadsword. It used mainly for slashing, but can be lethal

Table 5-6: Explosives							
Weapon	Blast Level	Blast Radius	Size	Weapon	Blast Level	Blast Radius	Size
Hand Grenades: Fragmentation	10	6'	Tiny	C-4	32	10'	Tiny
Hand Grenades: Incendiary	12	6'	Tiny	Claymore Mine	40	10'	Small
Hand Grenades: Smoke	10	6'	Tiny	Dynamite	16	5'	Small
Hand Grenades: Tear Gas	10	6'	Tiny				

Casting

as a stabbing weapon as well. Probably the most famous shortsword is the Roman Gladius.

Two-Handed Sword: Contrary to what you see in the movies, this sword is not meant to be used by ultra-muscular men for chopping people in two. Instead, they were meant to be used as anti-cavalry weapons. Those in the front lines would use the two-handed sword to chop at the legs of the horses. Once you are in close fighting, however, you would drop the big, bulky sword and draw your main weapon.

Whip

This is a long, flexible thong that can be used to lash at opponents from a distance. You can whip someone who is up to 6 feet away. Whips are designed to lacerate. This means that they are meant to tear and cut skin. The simplest of whips may only create welts, but most are designed to cause real wounds.

If your whip has a cat-o-nine-tails or some other form of barbs, add +1 to the weapon's Strength.

You can use a whip to disarm an opponent. To do this, make an attack against your opponent. Because you are targeting a specific part of your opponent (his weapon), you attack at a -1 penalty. If you are one away from hitting, then you succeeded at a normal attack, but failed to disarm. When successful, your opponent must make a Good Brawn test or he drops the weapon.

You can also attempt to trip an opponent. To do this, first make a successful attack. Then, you both make a contested Brawn test. If you succeed, the whip has coiled about his legs and you have tripped him.

Explosives

Now, don't worry, these are all locked up and you can't touch them unless you need them.

We've got a ton of explosives here, from your normal sticks of dynamite to C4 and other big time firecrackers. We'll show you the stats for all the explosives we have, and give you some ideas on how to make your own.

Casting

Making Your Own Explosives

The formula for creating your own explosives is simple. All you need to know is how much damage the explosive will do at the center of the explosion, and how big the radius between the Blast Levels is. From there, it's easy to calculate the amount of damage dealt at each Blast Level. Just use the following formula:

> *For each Blast Level, simply halve the amount (rounding up) of damage caused by the previous Blast Level.*

Example: *You've decided that your pipe bomb will do 12 points of damage at "ground zero", and that the Blast Radius will be 6'. So, for every six-foot increment away from ground zero, you halve the damage until you get to zero. This will give you 12/6/3/2/1, for the damages at each Blast Level. Multiply the number of levels by the Blast Radius and you now have a total area of effect of 30'.*

Explosive Descriptions

C-4

C-4, or composition 4, is a powerful explosive designed for military use. Unfortunately, it's stability and sheer destructive force has made it the primary weapon of terrorists. It is easy to conceal, even past most security posts.

C-4 is an explosive like most others. What makes it different is its casing or binder. The binder is what the explosive device is encased in. C-4 uses a plastic binder that has the consistency of modeling clay.

You can mold C-4 into any shape so that you can actually change the direction of the explosion.

The explosive force of C-4 is very great, as it is designed to destroy heavy walls, tanks and other large armored objects. You can stuff C-4 into the cracks of a wall and detonate it from a distance.

It is very stable, and requires an actual detonator to be set off. In Vietnam, soldiers have actually lit C-4 with a match to act as an improvised cooking fire. Normal flame will not detonate it.

Claymore Mine

This is a very popular type of land mine that is made up of a block of C-4 explosive and small ball bearings. When detonated, the bearings become deadly shrapnel. This is what causes it to have a much higher Blast Level than normal C-4.

The detonator of a Claymore mine is weight sensitive. This is so that it can be buried and detonated when someone steps on it.

Dynamite

Dynamite is just one of many types of explosive that work in a very similar way. TNT and nitroglycerin are two others. All of these explosives are chemical in nature and do the same amount of damage in *Now Playing*.

Dynamite is essentially just an enclosed tube containing a liquid explosive, like gasoline, that will combust when exposed to heat. The tube can have a long wick coming out of one end, or could be connected to wires so that you can ignite it with a spark from a distance.

Hand Grenades

Fragmentation: When a fragmentation grenade detonates, a large amount of shrapnel (small bits of sharp metal) is ejected in all directions at high speed. The shrapnel will riddle anyone caught in the blast of a fragmentation grenade.

It is very difficult to treat the victim of a fragmentation grenade, as he will suffer dozens of injuries, all involving tiny bits of shrapnel lodged in the body. Without immediate hospitalization, the Difficulty Level of any attempt to treat the patient's injuries will start at Good, and increase the closer he was to the center of the explosion.

Incendiary: Incendiary grenades burst into flames when detonated. Anyone caught in blast are at risk of catching on fire.

Anyone on fire will take 2 points of damage each round until extinguished.

Smoke: Smoke grenades cause no damage. They simply produce a heavy amount of smoke, causing loss of visibility as well as possibly incapacitating the victim.

The Blast Level does not represent damage. Instead, it only represents a means for determining the size of the area that is affected by the smoke.

Anyone affected by a smoke grenade must make a Good Stamina test or become incapacitated by the smoke. Anyone making the Stamina test will suffer a -2 to all tests until they receive medical aid.

Anyone affected by a smoke grenade must receive medical aid within three days or suffer from permanent lung and throat damage. This will result in a permanent drop of one level of Stamina, and may cause the victim's voice to become raspy.

Tear Gas: Tear gas works like Smoke grenades, but is more incapacitating. The stinging in your eyes and throat are much worse, but actually do little to no lasting damage. In addition to the Stamina test as with smoke, you must make a Will test or lapse into a panic attack and run wildly in any direction in an attempt to get away from the gas.

The Blast Level does not represent damage. Instead, it only represents a means for determining the size of the area affected by the gas.

Casting

Once away from the gas, its effects will fade in 20 minutes, half that if treated with first aid.

Armor

Well, now that you know where to find the weapons, I'll show you were to get the stuff that might just keep you alive. There's a big selection of armor here, from ancient bronze and leather armor all the way to Kevlar vests.

Chain Mail

Chain mail is made of interlocking links of metal, woven into the form of a coat. It is specifically design to defend against slashing and piercing blows, but will work adequately against bludgeoning blows as well.

Chain mail will not stop gunfire or other powerful modern weapons. It will also not stop a bolt from a crossbow, which fire with much greater force than traditional bows.

Concealable Vest

This is very light and smaller version of the Kevlar vest. It follows all of the rules of that armor, except that it's not as thick, and therefore has a worse Defensive Modifier.

Anyone who makes a Great or better Notice test can tell that you are wearing a concealable vest under your clothes. The Difficulty Level is worse at greater distances or in poor visibility.

Kevlar Vest

This vest is made with Kevlar fibers, which offer tremendous resistance to attack while remaining soft, flexible and relatively lightweight. Kevlar vests will stop most forms of cutting or piercing weapons, including shrapnel, bullets and knives.

Because it only offers protection from cutting and piercing weapons, a Kevlar vest will not stop any other type of damage. For instance, someone is beating you with a club, you will not gain any benefit from wearing the vest, and you cannot add its Defensive Modifier to your Defensive Factor.

Anyone who makes a Good or better Notice test can tell that you are wearing a Kevlar vest under your clothes. The Difficulty Level is, of course, worse at greater distances or in poor visibility.

Leather Armor

This is a coat and pants outfit in thick, heavy leather. It is capable of taking in damage from most slashing, stabbing and bludgeoning attacks.

Leather armor will not stop bullets or other powerful projectiles. It will defend against arrows fired from bows and crossbows.

Plate Mail

This is the typical "suit of armor". It is made of large metal plates that have been shaped to fit the curves of the human body. The suit will cover every inch of you, except your joints, which are covered by a leather undergarment.

Plate mail is extremely heavy and cumbersome. Anyone wearing plate mail will suffer a -2 to all Agility tests and skill tests that key on agility and dexterity.

Plate mail is designed specifically to repel swords, arrows and bludgeoning blows. The invention of the musket put an end to the use of plate mail, as a bullet will go right through the armor with no effort.

Riot Armor

This is a Kevlar suit of armor that covers more of the wearer's body, increasing the coverage value.

Riot armor is identical to the Kevlar vest in all other ways.

Riot armor is almost impossible to conceal. Anyone who makes a Poor or better Notice test can tell that you are wearing riot armor under your clothes. The Difficulty Level is worse at greater distances or in poor visibility.

Table 5-7: Armor					
Armor	Coverage	Defensive Factor	Armor	Coverage	Defensive Factor
Concealable Vest	Good	+4	Chain mail	Great	+4
Kevlar Vest	Good	+6	Leather	Good	+2
Riot Armor	Great	+6	Plate mail	Legendary	+6
NOTE: Please refer to the armor descriptions to determine what types of attacks the armor is effective against.					

Casting

Props

Table 5-8: Example Vehicles

Vehicle	Type	Acceleration	Speed (Scale)	Handling	Size (Scale)
Bicycle	Cycle	Poor	Great (0)	Mediocre	Terrible (2)
Canoe	Boat	Poor	Mediocre	Mediocre	Great
Compact Car	Car	Mediocre	Fair (10)	Fair	Mediocre (4)
Fullsize Sedan	Car	Good	Good (10)	Mediocre	Good (4)
Jet Fighter	Aircraft	Superb	Superb (15)	Good	Fair (7)
Midsize Sedan	Car	Fair	Fair (10)	Fair	Fair (4)
Motorboat	Boat	Good	Great (10)	Mediocre	Fair (4)
Motorcycle	Cycle	Great	Great (10)	Mediocre	Fair (2)
Pickup Truck	Car	Poor	Mediocre (10)	Mediocre	Great (4)
Race Car	Car	Great	Superb (10)	Great	Good (4)
Single-Engine Airplane	Aircraft	Poor	Mediocre (15)	Mediocre	Poor (7)
Sports Car	Car	Great	Great (10)	Good	Good (4)
Trailer Truck	Car	Poor	Mediocre (10)	Poor	Superb (4)
Twin-Engine Airplane	Aircraft	Fair	Good (15)	Fair	Mediocre (7)
Two-man Sailboat	Boat	Fair	Fair (10)	Poor	Fair (4)

Vehicles

Mack here will set you up with any vehicles you might need. He'll describe the different types of vehicles and will list the stats for common examples of each type. To learn how to use vehicles, refer to Chapter Six: Filming.

Vehicles look much like characters when viewed on paper. They have attributes, skills, gifts and faults. These all work the same way that they do with characters. The difference is that they do not have the same six attributes, and many of the other traits are different as well.

This section will not describe the Traits of vehicles and how vehicles work. That is described in Chapter Six: Filming. This section will describe a number of example vehicles that you can use in your shows. They can also be used as templates for making your own vehicles.

Keep in mind that the Traits listed for these vehicles are merely examples. Feel free to adjust them to suit your purposes. For instance, you might want to adjust some of the attributes to account for age and condition. Also, you might even want to have differences on a less subtle level, like having a difference between a Corvette and Camaro, even though they are both sports cars.

Note on Scale

Many of the example vehicles show two Scale attributes: one tied to Size and the other tied to Speed. This is because a vehicle could be physically not much bigger than a human, but be an order of magnitude faster. A motorcycle is a prime example of this. Physically, it is no more than twice the size of a human, but can go faster than 100 MPH, where most people can't even run 10 MPH.

The Speed Scale also applies to Acceleration.

Bicycle

Attributes

Acceleration: Poor   Speed (Scale): Great (0)
Handling: Mediocre   Size (Scale): Terrible (0)

Gifts

Bell, basket.

Faults

Not motorized.

Description

This covers all forms of bicycles, and even tricycles, if you'd like. Mountain bikes would have the added gift of "off-road durability". There are others gifts, such as "10-speed gears", and "training wheels" that can be used as needed.

Canoe

Attributes

Acceleration: Poor   Speed (Scale): Mediocre (0)
Handling: Mediocre   Size (Scale): Great (0)

Casting

Gifts

2 Paddles

Faults

Narrow.

Description

This is a long, narrow boat that has seats for two people, one at each end. A third or fourth person can sit in line in the middle. The boat is controlled by one person paddling in the front one side of the boat, with another paddling in the back on the other side. Occasionally, they switch sides, but the important thing is that they both paddle on opposite sides.

A single person could paddle a canoe, but would need to sit in the center of the boat, and continually alternate paddling on each side of the boat.

Compact Car

Attributes

Acceleration: Mediocre
Speed (Scale): Fair (10)
Handling: Fair
Size (Scale): Mediocre (4)

Gifts

Radio with CD player.
Driver side airbag.
Great fuel economy.

Faults

Cramped.
Seats only 4 comfortably.
Hatchback does not stay open.
2 Doors.

Description

This is basic transportation. It's not comfortable, not fast or particularly fun, but it will get you where you want to go without costing a fortune on gas. They can seat four people with relative comfort, but not much more. Cargo space in the trunk is poor. One problem that plagues all hatchback cars is that the hydraulics that keeps the hatchback door open do not work for very long after buying the car. They will eventually begin to fail, and you will find yourself having to prop the door open with your head or shoulders as you put things into and out of the trunk.

Fullsize Sedan

Attributes

Acceleration: Good
Speed (Scale): Great (10)
Handling: Mediocre
Size (Scale): Good (4)

Gifts

Cruise Control.
Traction Control.
Radio with CD player.
Driver and passenger airbags.
Power windows.
Power mirrors.
Power driver's seat.
Remote keyless entry.
Remote trunk release.

Faults

Inefficient fuel economy.

Description

This is the "land yacht" that people make fun of. These were popular in the 70's before anyone cared about fuel economy. There are advantages to it, though. It has plenty of room and is extremely comfortable. It also has more power than the average midsize sedan.

Fuel economy is very poor, averaging around eighteen miles per gallon. When driving one of these cars, you must always be sure there are plenty of gas stations along your route.

There is a good amount of cargo space in the trunk of the fullsize sedan, making it excellent for transporting many people and their belongings.

Jet Fighter

Attributes

Acceleration: Superb
Speed (Scale): Superb (15)
Handling: Good
Size (Scale): Fair (7)

Props

Casting

Props

Gifts

Computer Targeting Device.

4 Air-to-air missiles.

2 Cannons (Strength 5).

Faults

Crash without power.

Must move continuously while flying.

Consumes fuel very quickly.

Description

This is a fast and maneuverable fighter plan. It is powered by a jet engine, and can attain high speeds, even surpassing the speed of sound.

It is equipped with four air-to-air missiles. One hit from a missile will at least force an aircraft to crash, but may cause the entire plane to blow up. Once the fighter has locked onto a target, the missile will follow that target until it detonates. You must make a successful Pilot test at a Difficulty Level of at least Great to avoid being hit by the missile. The Director can make the battle more exciting by requiring several Pilot tests, as the missile may reacquire you before blowing up.

Firing cannons at another aircraft is an opposed Pilot skill test. All vehicles have Wounds like characters, so damage is handled the same way.

The jet fighter has enough fuel to fly and fight for two hours.

Midsize Sedan

Attributes

Acceleration:	Fair
Speed (Scale):	Fair (10)
Handling:	Fair
Size (Scale):	Fair (4)

Gifts

Cruise Control.

Radio with CD player.

Driver and passenger airbags.

Power windows.

Power mirrors.

Power driver's seat.

Faults

None.

Description

This is a comfortable, happy medium between the compact and the fullsize sedan. Its fuel economy is not bad and it is much more comfortable than the compact. It also has enough power to satisfy most people.

Not all midsize sedans have the power amenities that are listed above, but many do. You can adjust the gifts and faults accordingly to make a better fit for the owner's standard of living.

Motorboat

Attributes

Acceleration:	Good
Speed (Scale):	Great (10)
Handling:	Mediocre
Size (Scale):	Fair (4)

Gifts

Faults

Seats 4-8.

No enclosed cabin.

Description

Motoboats move very quickly over the water. They can be a little tough to steer at high speeds. Whenever it hits a wave, there's a jarring impact. Often, the boat will become slightly airborne when it hits a wave, and may rock heavily when it lands on the uneven waves.

Motorcycle

Attributes

Acceleration:	Great
Speed (Scale):	Great (10)
Handling:	Mediocre
Size (Scale):	Fair (0)

Gifts

Great fuel economy.

Faults

Seats 2.

No enclosed cabin.

Casting

Props

Description

They're fast and fun, but not always practical. They can go places where cars cannot, but you wouldn't want to ride one in the winter.

This includes all motorcycles from dirt bikes to racing bikes. You just need to adjust the Speed and Acceleration to cover the type of motorcycle you have.

Pickup Truck

Attributes

Acceleration:	Poor
Speed (Scale):	Mediocre (10)
Handling:	Mediocre
Size (Scale):	Great (4)

Gifts

Cruise Control.

Radio with CD player.

Driver airbags.

4-Wheel drive.

Cargo space.

Faults

Bad fuel economy.

Seats only 2 people, including driver.

Description

These are meant to be a workhorse. They have a large bed in the back for transporting large cargo. They have little room for passengers, but that's okay, since they are designed for a different job. Technically, passengers can sit in the bed, but unless it has a cap, it is dangerous and illegal to do it.

Pickup trucks are versatile, able to drive adequately both on normal roads, and off roads. They are equipped with four-wheel-drive, and can drive across rocky terrain.

One problem they have is that they are very light in the back, which causes its handling to suffer.

Casting

Props

Race Car

Attributes
Acceleration: Great
Speed (Scale): Superb (10)
Handling: Great
Size (Scale): Good (4)

Gifts
Heavy driver restraints.
Roll bars and reinforced cage.

Faults
Bad fuel economy.
Only one seat.
Not street legal.

Description
These cars are designed purely for racing. They are extremely fast and handle very well on dry race tracks. However, they are not made to be driven on the streets, and have no lights, signals or other devices that are necessary for driving on public streets.

Single-Engine Airplane

Attributes
Acceleration: Poor
Speed (Scale): Mediocre (15)
Handling: Mediocre
Size (Scale): Poor (7)

Gifts
Two-way radio.
Seating for 5.

Faults
Crash without power.
Must move continuously while flying.

Description
This is a small recreational aircraft, usually with its wing on top of the plane. It has a single, prop-driven engine.

To make a twin-engine plane, simply increase the all the Attributes by one, leaving the scale alone, then increase the amount of seating.

Sports Car

Attributes
Acceleration: Great
Speed (Scale): Great (10)
Handling: Good
Size (Scale): Good (4)

Gifts
Cruise Control.
Radio with CD player.
Driver and passenger airbags.
Power windows.
Power mirrors.
Power driver's seat.
Remote keyless entry.
Remote trunk release.

Faults
Bad fuel economy.
Seats only 2 people, including driver.
Very little trunk space.

Description
These are the fastest of all street-legal cars. They are wide and low to the ground to add aerodynamics and to allow the car to stick to the road at high speeds. They are fast, great looking, and extremely expensive (some cost more than a house). The downside is that they have little room for storage and have only two seats.

Trailer Truck

Attributes
Acceleration: Poor
Speed (Scale): Mediocre (10)
Handling: Poor
Size (Scale): Superb (4)

Casting

Gifts

Radio with CD player.

CB Radio.

Trailer.

Cargo space.

Sleeping compartment.

Faults

Bad fuel economy.

Seats only 2 people, including driver.

Description

These are the 18-wheelers that spend all their time riding the highways of the world. They are huge and cumbersome, and have little passenger room, but they do have a big trailer for cargo. In the back of the cab is a small sleeping compartment, since most trips that truckers make span many days.

Tanker trucks may have the additional fault of "hazardous materials", if that applies.

Twin-Engine Airplane

Attributes

Acceleration:	Fair
Speed (Scale):	Good (15)
Handling:	Fair
Size (Scale):	Mediocre (7)

Gifts

Two-way radio.

Seating for up to 6.

Faults

Crash without power.

Must move continuously while flying.

Description

This is a small aircraft, but a little larger than the single-engine. It is often used by small companies and occasionally for recreation. It has two prop-driven engines, one on each wing.

There is a larger and more upscale version of the twin-engine. This is the twin-engine jet, such as the Lear. For these aircraft, increase all of its attributes by one, and increase its seating to take up 15 passengers.

Two-Man Sailboat

Attributes

Acceleration:	Fair
Speed (Scale):	Fair (10)
Handling:	Poor
Size (Scale):	Fair (4)

Gifts

Adjustable centerboard.

Jib or Spinnacker

Description

This is the standard day-sailor or two-man racing boat. It has one mast, but can use a jib, or small sail that extends forward from the mast in addition to the mainsail.

The centerboard is a keel (blade-like board that goes down into the water under the boat) that can be raised in shallow water.

The jib is a small sail that is attached to the front of the mast to provide additional coverage.

A spinnacker is like a jib, but is much larger. It is big and round, and looks like a big colorful bubble in front of the mast. It is most useful when there is at least a fair amount of wind.

The Zoo

We have a wide variety of beasties here, from the common dogs and cats to monsters and dinosaurs. Now Playing only stocks one or two of each type of animal, just to give you something to work with.

Camel

Attributes

Brawn:	Good to Great
Agility:	Mediocre to Good (Scale 3)
Stamina:	Great to Superb
Reasoning:	Poor
Perception:	Fair
Will:	Terrible
Scale:	2

Casting

Skills

Run: Mediocre to Good
Jump: Poor to Good

Gifts

Desert Survival, Trainable.

Description

Camels live in hot and dry areas, including deserts. They can live without food and water for three to four days. They are domesticated animals that are often used for riding and baggage carrying. They are herbivores that eat dates, grass, wheat, and oats.

A camel can have additional skills, each one tailored to the specific training it has received. Some examples include riding, driving and packing.

Cat

Attributes

Brawn: Fair
Agility: Great to Superb
Stamina: Fair
Reasoning: Poor
Perception: Great
Will: Good
Scale: -7

Skills

Bite: Good (Strength +1)
Hunting: Great
Jump: Poor to Good
Run: Great to Superb
Survival: Fair

Gifts

Vision, Nine Lives.

Faults

Independent-minded, Curious, Lazy, Vain.

Description

Although cats are domestic animals and make great pets, they are strong-willed (for an animal) and are next to impossible to train. If you ever see a cat "heel" on command, it would be a rare thing and worthy of your amazement.

Nine Lives: Cats are resilient and through amazing feats of dexterity and gobs of luck, they can escape from almost certain death with little to no injury. All cats have 5 Luck Points at the start of each session.

Cobra

Attributes

Brawn: Mediocre
Agility: Good
Stamina: Poor
Reasoning: Poor
Perception: Good
Will: Poor
Scale: -8

Skills

Spit: Great
Bite: Good (Strength +1)

Gifts

None.

Faults

Bad temper.

Powers

Poison (+4 damage).

Description

Cobras are mean-tempered snakes that attack either by spitting venom into its victim's eyes, or by biting.

The poison of a cobra deals +4 to damage. When spit, the damage will only result if swallowed or striking the eyes. Anyone whose eyes come into contact with cobra venom must make a Great Stamina or become overwhelmed by the pain and fall into a fit of rubbing, screaming and cursing. The victim must make the Stamina test each round until either you manage to control the pain, or receive medical treatment.

If your eyes have been affected by cobra venom and you do not receive medical treatment within 5 hours, make a Great Stamina test or become permanently blind.

Casting

Crocodile

Attributes

Brawn:	Great
Agility:	Good
Stamina:	Good
Reasoning:	Poor
Perception:	Mediocre
Will:	Poor
Scale:	0

Skills

Swim:	Great
Bite:	Good (Strength +4)

Gifts

Amphibious.

Faults

Eats anything.
Cold-blooded

Description

The crocodile has been around since before the dinosaurs, and they have thrived. Their only natural predators are humans, who are threatening to do what hundreds of millions of years of evolution has failed to do: drive them to extinction. Humans hunt them for two reasons: they are a threat to the people who live near them, and their skins are valuable for clothing and accessories.

The crocodile is a cunning hunter, and will lie mostly submerged in the water waiting patiently for prey to come by. When it does, it will burst into sudden motion and attack. Its perception is not very good, and it cannot identify ideal food. Therefore, it will simply attack anything that vaguely resembles food.

It is a cold-blooded animal, and must spend much time in the sun warming up before it can be active.

Casting

Props

Dog

Attributes
- Brawn: Poor to Good
- Agility: Fair
- Stamina: Fair
- Reasoning: Terrible
- Perception: Superb
- Will: Terrible
- Scale: -1

Skills
- Bite: Good (Strength +2)
- Run: Mediocre to Great
- Jump: Poor to Good

Gifts
Loyal, Trainable.

Description
These are the normal domestic dogs who range from the tiny Shih-Tzu to the large Great Dane. They are loyal to their owners and make great pets.

Dogs can be trained to perform many tasks. These are treated as skills, and can be tailored to a specific dog or breed. Some examples of these skills are: Hunt, Track, Herding, Guard, Guide, and Tricks.

Elephant

Attributes
- Brawn: Good to Superb
- Agility: Good
- Stamina: Good
- Reasoning: Mediocre
- Perception: Fair
- Will: Poor
- Scale: 8

Skills
- Trample: Good
- Smell: Superb

Gifts
Trainable.

Faults
Males subject to Musth (annual madness).

Description
The skills that a horse can learn are tailored to the type of training it has received. Some examples include riding, hauling, stacking (logs, etc.), tricks.

Falcon

Attributes
- Brawn: Good
- Agility: Good to Superb (Scale 5)
- Stamina: Fair
- Reasoning: Poor
- Perception: Good
- Will: Poor
- Scale: +6

Skills
- Fly: Great
- Bite: Fair
- Claw: Great

Gifts
Courageous, Flight, Trainable.

Faults
None.

Description
Falcons can run through a variety of sizes. The Scale listed above represents only one of them. The falcon's Scale can be adjusted from -8 to -4 to reflect sizes from sparrow hawk to eagle.

Falcons can be trained. They may have additional skills as a result of specific training it has received. Examples of learned skills are manning (a measure of how tame it is), hunt ground mammals, hunt birds, aerial acrobatics, etc.

Casting

Grizzly Bear

Attributes
- Brawn: Fair to Great
- Agility: Fair
- Stamina: Fair to Great
- Reasoning: Poor
- Perception: Great
- Will: Poor
- Scale: 3

Skills
- Claw: Great
- Hug/Crush: Good
- Forage: Great

Gifts
None.

Faults
Berserker.

Description
Grizzlies are temperamental, and can attack in a berserker rage if approached. This does not always happen, but it is frequent enough (and dangerous enough) to stress the use of caution.

Horse

Attributes
- Brawn: Good to Great
- Agility: Good to Great (Scale 4)
- Stamina: Good
- Reasoning: Poor
- Perception: Fair
- Will: Terrible
- Scale: 3

Skills
- Kick: Good
- Run: Good to Great
- Trample: Good

Gifts
Trainable.

Description
The skills that a horse can learn are tailored to the type of training it has received. Some examples include riding, driving, racing, and various tricks.

Lion

Attributes
- Brawn: Fair to Great
- Agility: Fair
- Stamina: Good
- Reasoning: Poor
- Perception: Great
- Will: Poor
- Scale: 2

Skills
- Bite: Good (Strength +2)
- Notice: Good
- Run: Good
- Stalk: Great

Gifts
None.

Faults
Lazy.

Description
Lions are excellent stalkers. All Notice tests to notice a lion when it is stalking you will be an opposed roll versus its Stalk skill.

Lions are lazy creatures, and will usually not attack unless it is hunting or you get too close to its pride (family).

Smilodons live in a pride, where one male presides over several females. The females do the hunting, and the male protects the pride.

All the females of the pride participate in the hunt. A few will lie in wait while the rest chases the prey toward them.

Props

Casting

Props

Smilodon

Attributes
- Brawn: Great
- Agility: Fair
- Stamina: Good
- Reasoning: Poor
- Perception: Great
- Will: Poor
- Scale: 3

Skills
- Bite: Good (Strength +4)
- Claw: Good (Strength +3)
- Run: Fair
- Stalk: Great

Gifts
Keen Hearing

Description

This is the famous "sabre-toothed cat" of Earth's history. It lived in during the Pleistocene era, between 0.1 and 1.6 million years ago. Smilodon lived during the time of the Neanderthals, but did not live in the same area. Other smaller sabre-toothed cats lived in the northern regions where Neanderthals lived, and many of them hunted the now extinct species of humans. Smilodon is now an extinct species of cat.

Smilon's primary weapon is its claws. Like modern lions, the females would hunt by chasing down their prey. Although their jaws sport two tremendous curved fangs, they do not attack with them. They are too fragile to use in a fight. Instead, they grab hold of their prey with their claws, and use their weight to pull it down. Then, they would claw it until it was almost dead, and use the fangs for the death kill.

Because of the clumsiness of the sabre teeth, smilodons do not strip a carcass to the bone, but instead leave much of the inner meat behind for scavengers.

Smilodons live in a pride, where one male presides over several females. The females do the hunting, and the male protects the pride.

Velociraptor

Attributes
- Brawn: Good
- Agility: Great
- Stamina: Good
- Reasoning: Poor
- Perception: Great
- Will: Poor
- Scale: 2

Skills
- Attack: Great
- Balance: Good
- Jump: Good
- Stealth: Good

Gifts
Keen Hearing

Description

Velociraptor is a small carnivorous dinosaur that lived in the Late Cretaceous period of Earth's history. It died out sixty-five million years ago with the rest of the dinosaurs.

The velociraptor is a much smaller animal than it is popularly known to be. It is only approximately three feet tall at the hips, but is five to six feet long. It walks and runs on its hind legs and uses its long, stiff tail as a counterbalance.

The velociraptor attacks by leaping onto its prey, grabbing it with the claws on its "hands," and slashing it with the razor sharp, sickle shaped claw on its feet. This claw is sharp enough and powerful enough to cut a huge gash down the side of its prey, spilling its entrails. The victim may still be alive when the dinosaur begins to eat it.

It is believed that velociraptor hunted in packs, and that they were very intelligent for animals. They were among the smartest of all the dinosaurs.

THE FINAL FRONTIER

"Derelict"

<u>TEASER</u>

FADE IN:

EXT. SPACE

The emptiness of space. Then we PAN DOWN and see an ALIEN SHIP moving slowly through space. At first, it looks fine, but when the engines come into view, it is obvious that they are not running. Now the ship begins to list to one side, but there is no sign of damage. PUSH IN and DISSOLVE THROUGH TO:

INT. ALIEN SHIP

A MASTER SHOT of a hallway that is torn apart by laser fire. There are burn holes in the walls, and the ceiling has caved in, in places, exposing live conduits.

A door slides open and an ALIEN comes out. The alien is humanoid and vaguely reptilian, with very muscular green, scaly skin and a protruding snout. Its eyes are red. It is carrying a laser rifle, which it aims down the hall, first one way, and then the other. Satisfied, it begins to walk quickly, yet cautiously down the hall. PUSH IN TO FOLLOW.

The alien makes its way down the hallway to the junction of another hallway. A large, double paned sliding door is in the wall across the new hallway from where his hallway ends. He cautiously aims his rifle down each direction, and then crosses to the door. He presses a sequence of buttons on a control pad in the wall beside the door, and the doors slide noisily open. The alien looks around nervously as the sound shatters the silence. It steps through the doors, panning his gun around to ensure the room is clear of enemies. CUT TO:

INT. SHUTTLE BAY

It is a very large room, with one small shuttlecraft in it. Large bay doors are opposite the CAMERA. The signs of a battle are here as well. Wreckage and debris lie scattered about. The shuttle looks okay, though.

The alien begins walking toward it, but after a few steps, it sees a SHADOWY FIGURE in the shuttle's doorway. The figure is vague, and looks more like the shadow of a creature, rather than the creature itself.

ALIEN

(Surprised and scared)

(Grunts)

The alien begins firing at the shadowy figure. Balls of bright blue energy hurtle toward the figure, only to go straight through it and erupt inside the shuttle. The alien begins to run back to the door. PUSH IN TO FOLLOW.

INT. SHUTTLE BAY

As it runs through the door, the alien slams the door's controls with one hand. The doors grind shut. The alien turns, aims, and fires at the controls. It erupts in flame and sparks. The alien once again, turns and runs. PUSH IN TO FOLLOW.

The alien runs down the hallway, and finally reaches a turbolift. It does not work. Frustrated, it growls, and then looks nervously back the way it had come.

As though coming to a decision, it turns and runs a short distance to a door. This one opens on a vertical tube with a ladder going straight up. The alien shoulders its rifle and begins to climb. CUT TO:

INT. BRIDGE

The bridge is dimly lit with intermittent flashing from lighted panels. Once more, the room is littered with debris and the walls and ceiling show the scars of battle. Dimly, the sound of a human VOICE can be heard, as though through a radio.

VOICE

This is the Terran cruiser Euphrates to unknown vessel. Do you read? Can we offer assistance?

A door suddenly opens manually, and the alien steps onto the bridge. It grabs its rifle and pans it around, surveying the room. It does not heed the voice.

Satisfied, it then rushes to a console and begins typing. The lighting in the room turns red, and a warning claxon goes off from the panel the alien is working on. PAN AROUND TO LOOK OVER ITS SHOULDER.

A red symbol is on the screen the alien is hunched over. It is alien and not readable, but it appears to be a warning. A voice is heard from a speaker that says an automated message in an unknown language.

Suddenly a sound is heard behind the alien. It whirls around, grabbing for its rifle, which drops on the floor. The alien's eyes widen with terror, and then it snarls in anger and hatred, and rushes past the CAMERA.

Off CAMERA, you can hear the sounds of a struggle. The alien suddenly screams in terror, chokes as though being strangled, and then goes silent.

VOICE

We are sending a shuttle over to your ship. We come in peace. We want to help.

CUT TO OPENING CREDITS

END TEASER

Filming

Chapter 6

Acting

Performing Tasks

Whether you are using a skill, an attribute, or are attacking someone, you are performing a task. All tasks involve rolling dice to determine a modifier and then applying that modifier to the appropriate trait to determine your level of success. This section describes the details of how to perform a task as well as how to deal with the results.

Fudge Dice and Alternatives

Fudge Dice are special six-sided dice that have symbols on them instead of numbers. On each die, two sides are blank, two have a plus sign "+" and two have a minus sign "-". Fudge dice are available at any gaming store, as well as online at http://www.fudgerpg.com/.

If you cannot find Fudge dice, you can use normal six-sided dice, but you would need to do a simple conversion on each roll. Simply apply the following conversion:

> 1 or 2 = "-"
> 3 or 4 = blank
> 5 or 6 = "+"

Making a Test

Whenever you perform a task or need to roll dice against an attribute, you make a test.

To make a test you must roll four Fudge Dice. Add all of the pluses "+" together, and then subtract all of the minuses "-". Ignore the blanks. The result is your test modifier. Then, raise or lower your trait level by the amount of your test modifier. The formula for determining the level of the test is as follows:

> Result = Trait Level + Test Mod + Situation Mod

The levels, and the order that they are in, are listed below:

| Table 6-1: Trait Levels and Modifiers ||
Level	Modifier
Legendary	+4
Superb	+3
Great	+2
Good	+1
Fair	+0
Mediocre	-1
Poor	-2
Terrible	-3

Example: *Jack is using his Paleontology skill to identify the dinosaur that he sees grazing in nearby field. He rolls four Fudge dice, resulting in 2 pluses, 1 minus and 1 blank. He subtracts the one minus from the two pluses, which equals a +1 modifier. His Paleontology skill is Good. He adds +1 to his Good skill, which makes Great. So he has made a Great Paleontology skill test. The Director had already decided that it is an obscure dinosaur and had set the Difficulty Level at Great. Jack barely managed to identify the dinosaur.*

Difficulty Level

The Difficulty Level is the level that your test must match or exceed in order to be successful. For instance, if the Difficulty Level of your Drive Car skill test is Great, then your test must equal Great or Superb (or even higher) in order to succeed.

Situation Modifiers

Sometimes a certain situation may cause the test being rolled to be easier or harder. This is what is called a situation modifier. The Director sets this number and it is applied to all tests that the Director sees fit as long as that situation lasts. For instance, when driving a car in a

Fudge Cards

As a fun alternative to Fudge Dice, you can easily create cards that you can deal instead of roll. Here is how:

On a sheet of card paper, cut out rectangles about 3.5" long by 2.5" wide. Make a deck of them with at least 30 cards. The number of cards you make must be divisible by three.

On one-third of the cards draw pluses ("+"), on another third draw minuses ("-"), and leave the final third blank.

To use them, shuffle the deck at the beginning of the gaming session. Whenever you need to roll dice, deal out four cards instead, and treat the results the same as if they were Fudge Dice. You could shuffle between deals, or just once until you have gone through the deck.

Acting

snowstorm, the driver may get a situation modifier of -2 to all Drive Car tests during the snow storm. This modifier is applied

Opposed vs. Unopposed Tests

A task can be either opposed or unopposed. An opposed task means that the target of your task has the ability to try to stop or counter your task. With an unopposed task, there is no one who can try to stop you. The difference between them is only the way that the Difficulty Level is determined.

Opposed Test

With an opposed test, your opponent also makes a test. The result of your opponent's test becomes your Difficulty Level. The type of test that your opponent makes depends on the situation and is generally determined by the Director.

Example: *Jack the cop is trying to shoot the suspect with his revolver. He makes a Handgun skill test and his result is Good. The suspect then makes an Agility test, resulting in Good as well. Since Jack needs to reach or exceed the suspect's test, the shot managed to hit the suspect.*

Unopposed Test

With an unopposed task, the Difficulty Level is not defined randomly. In these cases, the Director must decide on a Difficulty Level that is appropriate for the task.

Secret Rolls

Sometimes the Director will make test for the cast member. This is done in those cases where the character does not know what is going on, and therefore it should not be announced to the actor.

Example: *Jack is walking down a path from the road to bushes where the body of the latest killing was found. The Director knows that he is walking past a beeper that the killer had dropped, but it is not beeping right now and Jack is not actively looking for clues. The Director rolls a Notice test for Jack without telling his actor. The test was a failure, so she keeps her mouth shut and doesn't let on that there is anything interesting with what he's doing.*

Relative Degree

This represents how well your test fared against the other participant in an opposed task. It is a number that represents the difference between the two tests.

For instance, Jack is trying to run Jill off the road. Jack made only a Fair Drive Car skill test, while Jill made a Great Drive Car test while trying to resist Jack's attempt. Since Great is 2 higher than Fair, the relative degree would be a -2 from Jack's perspective and a +2 from Jill's. Apparently, Jill was prepared for Jack's attempt and had no trouble at all with staying on the road.

Beyond Superb and Below Terrible

It is possible to make a test whose result is higher than Superb. Simply refer to any level higher than Superb as "Superb +1, Superb +2, etc.". It is sometimes important to note the exact level of your test, as determines how well you succeeded and the Director may base her results on it.

The same goes for tests that fall below Terrible. These would be Terrible -1, Terrible -2, etc.

If the Director has chosen to use the Legendary level in the show, then one level higher than Superb is Legendary. All tests that roll above Legendary are considered to be Legendary +1, Legendary +2, etc.

Automatic Success

Some tasks that you may take are so easy they do not require a test. For instance, as long as you have any levels whatsoever of the Computer Use skill, you will not need to make a roll to succeed at sending an e-mail on your computer. These tasks are usually obvious, but it's ultimately up to the Director to decide.

Critical Successes and Failures

Critical successes and failures add a touch of flair to the game play. Some Directors may choose to exclude this rule from their shows as they could take away from the show's atmosphere.

Critical Successes

A critical success occurs when the character does not just succeed at a test, but instead does so with exceptional flair. Your Seduction skill test leaves the woman ready to tear off her clothes for you; or your defensive Agility test was so good that get the chance to counter with an immediate attack, even if you already attacked that round.

When all four dice roll a "+", you have the option to spend one luck point to have a critical success. The actual effects of the critical success are up to the Director and can differ for each situation. In any event, the task is wildly successful.

A test that results in a +4 after modifiers does not cause a critical success. A critical success only occurs if all four dice have a plus on them.

Acting

Critical Failures

A critical failure occurs when all four dice roll a minus. When this happens, you not only automatically fail your test, but you do so quite horribly.

Example: *Jack had succeeded in stealing a CD with vital computer data from the villain's office and is now hiding outside the window on a narrow ledge. The Director tells him to make a Balance skill test. Jack rolls and all of his dice turn up minuses. The Director grins and says, "You momentarily lose your balance. You manage to stay on the ledge and even keep quiet, but you dropped the CD. It falls three stories to land on the head of a guard, who now looks up right at you!"*

When you score a critical failure, you can pay one luck point to avoid the critical failure. In the above example, the Director might describe a momentary fumbling with the disk before managing to keep hold of it.

As with critical successes, all four dice must roll minuses in order to score a critical failure, regardless of modifiers.

Attributes vs. Skills

At a glance, attributes and skills both look similar. They both have levels and can be used to make tests. It may not be obvious how they differ in game terms.

You always use skills to perform tasks.

Attributes are used in two ways:

Untrained Skills

When you try to use a skill untrained (at the default level), the default skill level will increase to Mediocre if the attribute that the skill uses is at Good or higher. For instance, you are trying to run, but have never purchased any levels of the Run skill. If your Brawn is Good or higher, the skill defaults to Mediocre. If your Brawn is less than Good, you must use the default level of Poor.

This does not work with skills that default to non-existent.

Spectacular Failures

If you fail by a wide margin, for instance, by three or more levels, you may make a test of the attribute that corresponds with the failed skill. A success means that you manage to salvage something from the failure. Failure means that the skill failed as normal.

Example: *Detective Powers is chasing after a suspect. He doesn't know who the suspect is, but he knows that he has something to do with the murder, and runs when he sees him. He decides to try to tackle the suspect. The Director calls for a Jump skill test. Powers rolls the test and fails miserably. Therefore, he makes a Brawn test, since Brawn is used for jumping. His test succeeds. The Director decides that Powers grabbed the suspect, but failed to keep a grip on him. Not only did the suspect remain standing and running, but also the detective fell flat on his face. However, because of his successful Brawn test, he was able to grab the suspect's coat, tearing the pocket open. A small piece of paper with a phone number on it fell to the ground. Therefore, he may have failed to stop the suspect, but he managed to find a clue that could help him catch him.*

The Use of Luck

Spending Luck Points

You can spend luck points as described below. You can only spend luck points to benefit yourself. For instance, you cannot use your luck points to increase another character's Defensive Factor.

Panache

You can spend a luck point to complete a successful task with a touch of flair that is nothing short of impressive. You must first succeed in the task as normal, making whatever test is necessary, and then you can spend the luck point to add the flair to it.

Any supporting cast that witnesses it will be impressed and may act more favorably toward you. This can be very useful in a seduction or when trying to convince an otherwise doubtful person.

You cannot spend luck points in this manner on any task that has already required luck points just to succeed. For instance, James tried to tumble through a window to make a grand entrance into a crowded drawing room. He rolled his Tumble skill test and failed by one level, so he spent a luck point to push up his skill test result by one to make it a success. Because he already spent a luck point to increase his test roll, he lost his chance to succeed with panache. In fact, the Director may describe the result as being bungled!

Modify Tests

You can spend a luck point to alter the dice roll of any test by one level, either up or down. You can do this *even after the roll has been made*, as long as the Director has not described the effects of the test.

For instance, if you need a Great Tumble skill test to successfully dive through the blast doors before they close, and you only rolled a Good, you can immediately spend one luck point to raise test to a Great, which allows you to succeed.

You can also spend luck points to increase your Offensive and Defensive Factors in combat. Therefore, if someone tries to hit you and succeeds, you can spend luck points and add them to your Defensive Factor, thus making the attack miss.

Acting

You can spend as many luck points as you want to modify a single test, except that you cannot spend more than you have.

Reduce Damage

You can spend a luck point to reduce intensity of the wound by one level. This will make a Light Wound become a Scratch, or an Incapacitated become a Severe Wound. As with modify tests, you can spend the luck points even after the damage has been assigned, as long as the Director has not yet described the effects to the actors.

The Director may describe the result as though the wound appeared worse than it really was.

Favorable Conditions

If the Director allows it, you can spend luck points to cause a favorable condition to be present in the game. For instance, the cast is locked in a maximum-security prison and need to escape. One actor may spend luck points to make one of the guards be a cousin of his who will help them escape.

This use of luck points is completely up to the Director. This will not fit in all styles of shows and must be used with caution. In addition, the Director must decide on the cost for a specific condition based on how much it will help the cast. In any case the Director has the right to veto any suggested condition.

Inspiration

Sometimes you simply run out of options and cannot think of what to do next. In a case like that, you can spend luck points to get a clue from the Director in the form of an inspiration or intuition. The Director will set a cost for inspiration, determine the content and describe it in a way that fits in with the situation.

As with favorable conditions, the Director reserves the right to disallow inspirations.

Acting

Luck Rolls

There are times when you may need to make a Luck Roll. Depending on the situation, you or the Director can roll four Fudge dice and add the number of Luck Points you have to the roll. The lucky event occurs if the result is Fair or better.

This is used in two ways: by the Perfect Timing gift, and as a secret roll by the Director when she wants decide if a good thing should happen to you. In the latter case, it can help the Director when she needs to make a decision regarding your character. If she can't decide, she can make a Luck roll. There may be other uses for the Luck Roll that the Director may come up with.

Fear

Fear can be a very debilitating emotion. When struck down with fear, you enter a world where nothing else exists except the fear. Loss of control becomes a serious threat, as you become unaware of everything that is happening around you, and you focus on that fear. Fear has many faces and its effects range from a knot in your stomach, to the hairs rising on the back of your neck, to total panic where nothing matters except getting away from the source of your fear.

A Matter of Will

When dealing with fear, your Will attribute is your best friend. It is what can save you from complete loss of control.

When you face a frightening situation, make a Will test. The Director will choose the Difficulty Level based on how terrifying the situation is. In addition, if you are already predisposed to that type of fear, due to a Phobia or some other fault, the DL will be even higher.

If your Will test succeeds, you will be unaffected by the fear. Surely, the fear will still be with you, but it will not be strong enough to affect your abilities.

If the test fails, the Director will choose one of the following effects:

Face Your Fear

You will face your fear and do whatever it is you were going to do. However, you will suffer a -1 to all actions for as long as the source of the fear is present. You will be shaking, and on the verge of retreat the entire time. Your nerves will be so tense that any shock or surprise, no matter how trivial, may set you off. As a result, you will have great difficulty concentrating on your tasks. If another surprise does happen, you can either re-roll the Will test with a penalty, or just choose how to behave. It's up to you and the Director.

Flee in Fright

You will run away. This may do this physically, or you may do this mentally. If you do not physically run away screaming, you will have retreated mentally. This could have the effect of you freezing in fear, unable to move or think. In essence, you are paralyzed. Your mind is either fully focused on the source of your fear to such an extent that you are completely unaware that you are not moving, or your mind has retreated to some "happy place" where the fear cannot reach you. Either way, the result is the same.

It is possible that you do move. You could curl up on the floor in a fetal ball, suck on your thumb and become a gibbering ball of emotion.

One final method of flight is simply to pass out. It would be the same as the Knockout effect that is described in the Subdual Combat section later in this chapter.

Duration of Fear

Once you the source of your fear is gone, you will no longer suffer from its effects. You may not recover immediately. It could take you some minutes, or even up to an hour or more, depending on the seriousness of the fear. The Director must decide how long it will take you to recover.

Item Concealment

There are two considerations for determining the difficulty of concealing an item. The first is how you plan to conceal it, and the second is the size of the item.

The Director must decide on a Difficulty Level for the attempt based on how you plan to conceal the item. She then modifies this Difficulty Level by applying the item's size. The table below lists the different sizes of items and the modifiers they represent.

| Item Sizes and Concealment Modifiers ||
Item Size	Modifier
Tiny	+0
Small	+1
Medium	+2
Large	+3

Combat

Combat in *Now Playing* works very much like any other skill test. The attacker makes a skill test with the weapon he is using and the defender opposes that test

Acting

with an appropriate defensive skill. For instance, if Jack is shooting a revolver at Joe, Jack would make an opposed Handgun skill test against Joe's Agility test.

Combat is necessarily more complex than a simple skill test, though, as it must handle offensive and defensive maneuvers, wounds, and even death. Because each character's life is on the line, a certain set procedure must be defined in order to ensure that combat is handled fairly. The rest of this section explains the rules for handling combat.

Types of Combat

There are two main types of combat: melee and ranged. They are both treated the same way, as far as determining whether you hit your target, but they differ some in how damage is assessed.

Melee Combat

Melee combat is any combat that is not ranged. That is, if you are brawling or fighting with swords, knives, or sticks, you are in melee. The stronger you are, the more force you can put into each blow. For that reason, your Brawn will have an impact on the amount of damage you cause on your opponent.

Name Cards for Initiative

Every actor can hold a 3x5 card that has his character's name on it (and the actor's name if they are all strangers). The Director will also have a card for each Supporting Character or group of characters.

When initiative is decided, lay the cards out on a table in order of initiative, including the card(s) for the Supporting Cast.

This will make it easier to keep track of who goes next during combat. If one character holds an action or changes his initiative order during combat, you can simply move the card.

Ranged Combat

Ranged combat involves the use of any type of distance weapon, such as a gun, bow and arrow, sling, or even thrown weapons. Since the force of the weapon is pretty much the same for every attack, there are no modifiers to damage based on any of your character's attributes.

Initiative

This determines the order in which people get to act. Although combat generally happens simultaneously, people react at different speeds, and one person may be able to act before another.

Initiative Order

Initiative is the order in which everyone acts during each round of combat.

To determine the initiative order, everyone who is actively ready to enter combat must make an Agility test. The order in which everyone acts is in this order from highest to lowest. This includes Supporting Cast (the Director may choose to roll once for all Supporting Characters for simplicity). If there are any ties, those characters will act simultaneously.

Once everyone has made his Agility tests, the Director makes a list of each character, starting with the one who rolled highest, and going down from there.

Surprise

Some characters may be surprised, and will therefore not get a chance to act during the first round of combat. All surprised characters are not added to the initiative order until the beginning of the second round. The actor can roll with everyone else, but not act yet, or he can roll at the beginning of the second round.

Combat Rounds

A combat round is six seconds long. Each round, everyone involved in the combat may take actions of six seconds in duration or less. To simplify this, each action that you may want to take will be either a free action, half action or full action.

Free Action

A free action is something that takes so little time as to be negligible. For instance, picking up a pistol that is sitting on your lap would be a free action, because it would take no more than one second to do it.

The Director can allow you to take any number of free actions during one round, but may limit it depending upon the specific actions you wish to take and the situation.

Acting

Example Combat Scene

SHOW: Boston PD: The Beat.   EPISODE: Crime and Punishment   SCENE: Bob's Surplus

Director: You're responding to a silent alarm at 129 East Hollis Street. You know the place to be Bob's Surplus, a pawnshop that has been robbed three times in the past six months. It's 9:52 PM. The store closed at 5:00. It's smack-dab in the middle of a city block. It has one door opening onto the street, and one door opening onto a back alley. The back alley door is much harder to break into and all the previous break-ins were in front.

Officer Cullen: I have Powers drop me off one block from the place then drive by without shining any lights. I don't want the perp to suspect our presence. He'll drive around back and check that out while I walk up the road toward the store's front. I'll stop right before the beginning of the store's windows.

Director: Everything goes as planned. Powers drives the squad car around the corner and parks out back. You're walking up the sidewalk nearing the storefront when the door opens and a man steps out. He's about 5' 8" tall and 170 lbs. He's dressed in very baggy blue jeans and is wearing a dark sweatshirt with a hood that is wrapped tightly around his face. He's wearing gloves and is carrying a full backpack on his back. He looks first in the other direction, and then looks directly at you. For a moment you both freeze as your eyes meet.

Cullen: Is there anyone else on the sidewalk? Is he armed? How well lit is the place?

Director: There is a young couple walking leisurely toward him from the corner where your partner had turned down. His hands are empty. There are streetlights, but the one in front of the store is out, so visibility is poor right where he is.

Cullen: Crap! I can't shoot with the civilians there. I draw my gun, aim it at him and yell "Police! Freeze!"

Director: Let's roll Initiative! <Rolls 4 Fudge dice, resulting in +2 and adds it to his Fair Agility> He rolled Great.

Cullen: <rolls 4 blanks for a +0, so his Good Agility stands> I've only got a Good.

Director: As you're reach for your gun, he bolts, racing down the street past the pedestrians.

Cullen: Okay, I still shout, but I'll do it as I run after him. If he does not stop by the time I've passed the people, I'll shoot at him. As I run, I'll turn on the radio and yell "In pursuit of suspect on foot. He's heading toward the corner of...what's the side street...Pine.

Powers: That's the street I drove down to get out back, right? I'll jump out of the car and run to cut him off, drawing my gun as I do. "I'll cut him off," I yell into the mic.

Director: He's almost at the corner when you're clear of the people, and you can tell he's getting ready to turn down Pine Street. Take your shot.

Cullen: I'll take three shots. <Rolls a Gun skill test, for a +1 added to his level of Good>. Great for the first. <second roll is -1> Fair, and finally...<third roll is +1, but has a -1 because it's the third shot>...Good.

Director: <rolls the suspect's only Agility test to oppose the shots, rolling +1 to his Good Agility. This makes a Great> The first shot struck his shoulder. He twisted and you can hear him curse, but he still manages to round the corner. The other two shots missed. <the Relative Degree is Great (shot) minus Great (Agility) or 0. The weapon strength is +2 for a revolver, which is just a Scratch>.

Director: Powers, you round the corner from the back of the building and start running toward East Hollis. You get about halfway when you hear three shots fired and a man in baggy jeans and a hooded sweatshirt round the corner. It looks like he got hit in the right shoulder. He just drew handgun. When he sees you, he comes to a stop and raises the gun. Roll your Initiative.

Powers: <rolls -3, added to Good Agility> Aw, Poor!

Director: The suspect fires. <rolls +1 added to his Good gun skill> He makes a Great shot!

Powers: <rolls +3, added to Fair Agility> Superb! I shoot him. <rolls +4, added to his Good gun skill> Superb +2!

Director: <rolls -2, added to his Fair Agility, making Poor. RD is 7, +2 for revolver is +9, a Near Death> Wow! Your shot hit him square in the chest, quite possibly hitting his heart. With a jerk, he falls unconscious to the ground.

Acting

Half Action

A half action is something that you do that will take three seconds or less. This could involve moving into position, dodging or parrying an attack, or making a normal attack like stabbing with a knife. Generally, you can take two half actions in one round.

Full Action

A full action is an action that requires a full six seconds to accomplish. If you were taking careful aim before firing your gun, this would take a full action. Reloading a revolver without the use of a speed loader will take a full round, unless you have the Rapid Reload gift.

The Attack Roll

When making an attack, the two combatants make opposed tests. The attacker makes a test using the most appropriate skill for the weapon, such as Handgun. The defender makes a defensive test with whatever trait seems most appropriate. For instance, if she has the Dodge skill, she should use that, but if she has none, then it would be a straight Agility test. Whoever made the highest roll is the victor.

The Director may give each combatant a situation modifier, based on the difficulty of the attack or defense, and any other factors that may apply to the situation.

So, a simple attack roll can be illustrated with the following formula:

Attack Test + Modifiers v.s. Defense Test + Modifiers

Loading Weapons

Loading a weapon takes a full action. If you have the Rapid Reload gift, loading is reduced to a half action.

Drawing Weapons

Drawing a weapon is a half action. Drawing a weapon is a free action if you have the Quick Draw gift.

Surprised Opponents

A surprised opponent cannot defend himself, and therefore does not make an opposed test. Instead, the Director must decide on a difficulty level based on the situation. From that point on, the attack works as normal.

Simultaneous Attacks

Two combatants who fall into the same position in the initiative order (their initiative rolls came out the same) are attacking simultaneously.

Since both combatants are attacking, neither will get to roll a defensive test. Instead, the Director must decide on a Difficulty Level for each. Both combatants will make their attacks. Because both attacks were made at the same time, both combatants can take normal damage if they both hit.

Two Weapons

Fighting with two weapons simultaneously is very difficult. You will suffer a -2 penalty on all attacks while fighting with two weapons. This penalty is reduced to -1 if you have the Two-Weapon Fighting gift.

Shields

Shields do not work like body armor. Instead of absorbing damage, they can prevent the wielder from being hit. This is because a shield is not attached to your body, but is merely an obstacle you can put in the way to block an attack.

Shields apply a penalty to your opponent's attack roll for melee and/or ranged attacks. The size of the shield determines the size of the penalty. The table below summarizes the penalties for the most common types of shields.

Shields are also cumbersome, and can get in the way of various tasks that you may try to perform. The table below also lists the penalties to all skill tests that the Director feels would be affected by the shield.

Shield Penalties			
Shield Size	Melee Penalty	Ranged Penalty	Skill Penalty
Small	-1	0	-1
Medium	-1	-1	-2
Large	-2	-2	-3

Multiple Combatants

When you fight multiple opponents, you are at a great disadvantage.

Each combat round, you must choose which opponent to attack. Every other opponent will gain a +1 to their attacks because you have left yourself open to them.

You can choose to fight defensively. You must declare

Acting

this at the beginning of the combat round. For that round, none of your opponents receives the bonus. Instead, you receive a -1 penalty to all attacks because your efforts are divided between fighting and defending.

All-Out Attack & Defense

All-Out Attack

An all-out attack is a furiously frenzied attack, where the attacker goes berserk. The ferocity of the attack is enough to throw the defender off guard, as well as to increase the force of the attack.

An all-out attack adds a +1 to your Offensive Factors, and an additional +1 for damage. However, if the attacker ties or loses the opposed test, the other combatant wins, gaining the +2 damage bonus. This is because a all-out attack comes with the price of a decreased defense. While making an all-out attack, you put all of your effort into the attack, and therefore leave yourself open to attack by your opponent.

All-out attacks only work with melee attacks.

All-Out Defense

Just as you can put all your effort into your attack, you can also put extra effort into defense.

In an all-out defense, you can use your combat skill for your opposed defensive test. However, if you do so, you will not be able to attack that round.

If you make a successful all-out defense, you can make a Notice test to find a tactical advantage. This will give your opponent a -1 to his attack roll in the next round when you exploit that tactic.

Physical Considerations

There are certain conditions that can affect combat:

Off-Hand

You suffer a -1 penalty to all attacks made with your off-hand. This penalty does not apply if you have the Ambidexterity gift.

Fighting Blind

You suffer a -2 penalty when fighting in the dark. This penalty is reduced to -1 if you have the Blind Fight gift.

Shooting While Running

You take a -2 penalty when firing a weapon while running. No penalties apply if you have the Shot on the Run gift.

Multiple Weapons

You suffer a -2 penalty for fighting with two weapons at once. This penalty is reduced to -1 if you have the Two-Weapon Fighting gift.

Called Shots

You can aim a shot or strike at a specific body part, but it will be difficult at best.

The result of your attack test must be at least a Good or Great (depending on the complexity of the shot). Therefore, even if you win the opposed attack test, you still need a Good or Great to hit the specific target you aimed at.

Example: *John the police officer is in a face-off with a suspect whose gun is aimed at him. If John shoots, he had better kill him with the first shot, or he's a goner. John decides that if he does not shoot, the suspect will, so he takes aim at his head and fires.*

The Director decides that a head-shot would only require a Good shot to hit. John and the suspect make their rolls. John only gets a Fair, but the suspect does worse in his Agility test and gets a Poor. Because he didn't get a Good shot, John failed to hit the suspect in the head, but he still won the opposed test, so instead, he hit the suspect in the chest. The suspect will now get to fire at him!

Guns

Most weapons assume that you cannot fire or strike more than once in a single six-second combat round. Guns, however, are the exception to this. It is quite easy to empty a magazine of ten rounds or more in the space of six seconds. Of course, the accuracy of those shots will suffer, so it is not always a given that you would want to fire multiple shots in one round.

You can fire up to 12 shots in 6 seconds. Every two shots beyond the first will suffer a cumulative -1 to its attack roll. Therefore, the first two shots will have no penalty, the third and fourth shots will suffer a -1, the fifth and sixth will suffer -2, and so on.

Bursts

Firing bursts are meant to work as suppressive fire and not to kill individual targets. This is because a burst fires a large amount of rounds in a poorly controlled area of effect. You cannot expect many of the bullets to hit their target.

This is handled in the following manner:

First, choose a type of burst, from Short, Medium or Long. Then, make your attack roll as normal. A successful attack means that you hit your target with at least one round. The Relative Degree of the attack will determine exactly how many rounds struck their target. Table

Acting

Table 6-2: Burst Success			
Relative Degree	\multicolumn{3}{c}{Number of Bullets to Hit Target}
	Short	Medium	Long
+0	1	1	2
+1	2	2	5
+2	3	3	10
+3	4	4	15
+4	5	5	20
+5	5	6	25
+6	5	7	30
+7	5	8	35
+8	5	9	40

6-2: Burst Success illustrates how many rounds strike for each type of burst.

Suppressive Fire

Suppressive fire means that you are not trying to hit any specific target, but are merely trying to blanket an area with fire to keep your opponents at bay. In this case, you are not really expected to hit a target.

Table 6-2: Burst Success only applies if you are aiming at a specific target. If you are performing suppressive fire, then you would do the following:

The attacker does not make an attack roll. Instead, the Director decides on a Difficulty Level, and those within the area of effect of the burst must make an Agility attribute test to avoid being hit. The Relative Degree of any failed test can be applied to Table 6-2: Burst Success to determine how badly the character was hit.

If anyone within the area of effect of the suppressive fire was already behind cover, he does not need to make the Agility test.

Explosives

In television, explosions happen fast and furious, and little attention is put to the details of how they work. For this reason, the system for handling explosives is quite simple. It may not be fully accurate, but it is accurate enough to work well in a show.

There are only two attributes to an explosive, and these attributes are all that is needed to handle any explosion. These attributes are described below:

Blast Level

This represents the amount of damage caused to anyone and anything at "ground zero" of the explosion. You could consider this to be the weapon's Strength.

It is also used to help determine the total range of the blast and how damage dissipates as it spreads outward from the center of the explosion (See Blast Radius below).

Blast Radius

The amount of damage caused to anything that is at the center of the blast is equal to the Blast Level. The Blast Radius determines the size of the circle within which that damage is applied. For instance, if the Blast Level is 12 and the Blast Radius is 6 feet, then anyone within 6 feet of the blast will take a full 12 points of dam-

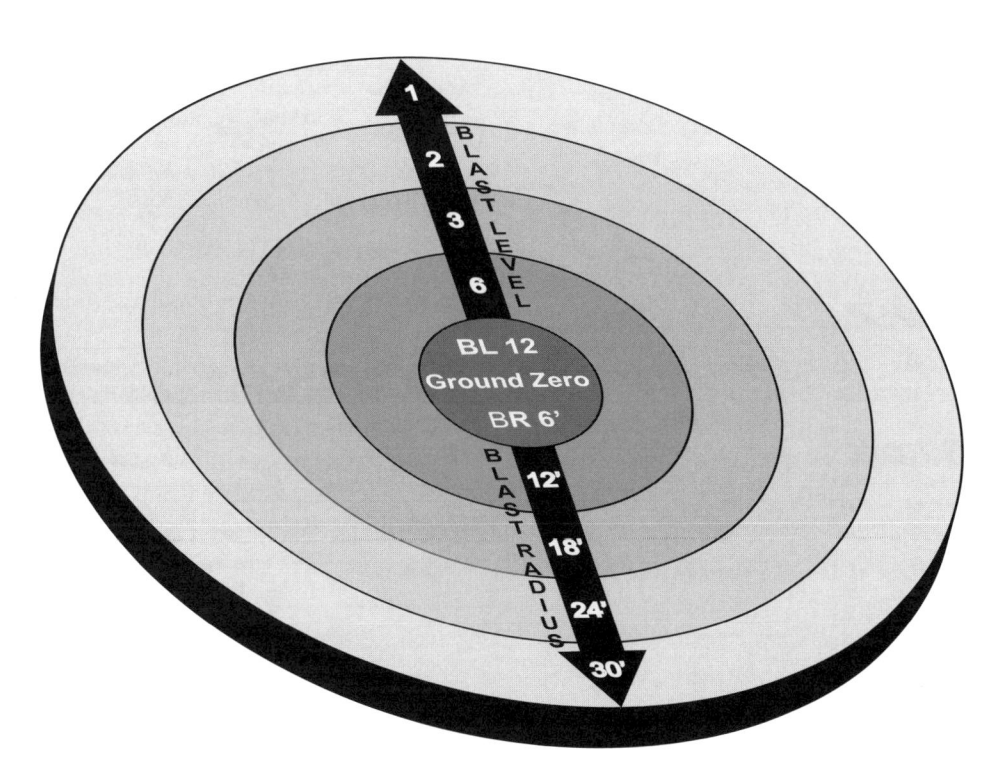

Acting

age.

The force of the blast dissipates at a rate based on both the Blast Level and Blast Radius. For each Blast Radius beyond the center radius, the Blast Level is cut in half (rounded up). This continues until the Blast Level reaches zero or less.

Example: *Jack is leading a group of soldiers across a clearing in the jungles of Vietnam. He steps on a landmine, which detonates. The mine's Blast Level is 12, and the Blast Radius is 6'. Because he is stepping on the mine, he takes the full 12 points of damage, easily putting him well beyond the Near Death wound. He disintegrates. His team, however, are not so close to the blast's center. The closest soldier is 11 feet away. That is within 2 Blast Radii from the location of the mine. Therefore, the Blast Level is halved only once. He takes 6 points of damage, giving him a Severe Wound. The soldier behind him is 15 feet away. This is 3 Blast Radii away, so the Blast Level is halved twice, first from 12 to 6, then from 6 to 3. He takes 3 damage, giving him a Light Wound. Those within 4 Blast Radii take 1 point and those beyond that are out of the blast's range and take no damage.*

Using Barriers with Explosives

A simple way to handle barriers like walls when dealing with explosions is to give the barrier a number of points to represent how strong it is. Then, when the explosion occurs, subtract the amount of damage caused by the explosion from its strength points. If there's any damage left over, the barrier was destroyed.

Once an explosion has destroyed a barrier, simply use the number of damage points left as the Blast Level for each level beyond.

Example: *John was standing on the other side of an apartment wall when a bomb exploded in the hallway on the other side of the wall. The Director decides that the sheetrock wall has a Strength of 10. The Blast Level when the explosion reaches the wall is 16. The wall bursts asunder and anyone on the other side receives 6 points of damage. If John was one more Blast Radius away from the wall, the damage would be 3.*

Injury & Death

Determining Damage

Once an attack has succeeded, the Director must determine how badly hurt the victims are.

Determine the amount of damage dealt by the following formula:

$$Damage = RD + OF - DF$$

Relative Degree (RD)

This is the difference between the two opposed tests (the attack an defense rolls). This determines just how good a hit the attack was.

Offensive Factor (OF)

This is the sum of all damage modifiers. The most common Offensive Factors are described below:

Brawn: When the attack was made with a strength-based weapon (fist, sword, club, etc.), your Brawn is added as an Offensive Factor.

Weapon Strength: Most weapons have a strength modifier that represents and damage it causes beyond the Brawn of the wielder. For instance, guns will do great damage without the aid of the wielder's Brawn, and a sword's sharpness will also increase the amount of damage caused.

Scale: Apply your character's Scale as an Offensive Factor.

Defensive Factor (DF)

This is the sum of all defensive modifiers. Some of the more common Defensive Factors are described below:

Armor: Armor does not prevent you from being hit in combat. Instead, it merely soaks some of the damage of the blow. The bonuses for any armor that the blow struck are applied as Defensive Factors.

Scale: Apply your character's Scale as a Defensive Factor.

Damage Capacity

Some people are just very hard to kill. It happens from time to time in real life, and happens more frequently on television. Therefore, there must be a way to let a person brush off injuries beyond the simple Defensive Factor. This is called Damage Capacity.

Every time you take damage of at least a Light Wound, make a Stamina test. The result of the test will determine how well you can handle the injury, as detailed in the table below:

Stamina Test Results for Endurance	
Great or better	reduce severity of the wound by one level (Severe Wound to Light Wound, etc.).
Mediocre to Good	No adjustment.
Poor or worse	Increase severity of the wound by one level.

100

Acting

Recording Your Wounds

The final result of the damage formula is the number of wounds taken by the victim. To determine the level and severity of the wound, consult Table 6-3: Wounds.

Simply compare the amount of damage taken (the result of the above formula) and find where it fits in the table in the Damage row. That would indicate the level of injury. Place a letter that represents the injury level in one of the circles of that column ("S" for Scratch, "L" for Light Wound, etc.).

Example: *Jack was stabbed by a knife. The relative degree was 3, the offensive factor was +2, and the defensive factor was +1, then the resulting damage would be 4. Looking on the table, 4 is shown as a "Light Wound". The actor will write an "L" in the circle under "Light Wound".*

Wound Overflow

Let's say that in the above example, Jack had already received one Light Wound, and has now been dealt one more Light Wound. On his character sheet, the circle for Light Wound is already filled. Therefore, he must put his mark in the next available circle upward, which would be a Severe Wound. He would write an "L" in a circle under Severe Wound. He still puts the "L" in there because the injury is technically still a Light Wound, and since Light Wounds heal more easily than Severe Wounds, it is important to keep track.

Wound Levels and Their Effects

There are five different levels of wounds: Scratch, Light Wound, Severe Wound, Incapacitated, and Near Death. Each one has its own meaning and effects. These wound levels are described below:

Scratch

A Scratch is equivalent to any wound that is so small as will not be of much concern. A graze from a gunshot, or some other minor injury would constitute a Scratch. You can survive a few of these injuries without effort, but they do add up.

Light Wound

This is a serious wound, serious enough to have an impact on your tasks. The Director must decide on the type of injury and add a -1 penalty to all traits that would be affected by the injury. For instance, a sprained ankle or knee would result in penalties toward Agility and any skill that requires the use of your legs, such as Jump and Climb.

Alternately, if you do not want that level of complexity, the Director can simply apply the -1 penalty to all tests.

Severe Wound

This is a nasty wound, and will have a drastic effect on you. The Director must decide on the type of injury and apply a -2 penalty to all traits that would logically be affected.

Alternately, if you do not want that level of complexity, the Director can simply apply the -2 penalty to all tests.

Incapacitated

The injury is so severe that you are unable to act. You are still conscious, and can think, but even speaking will be tough and reduced to gasps and hoarse croaks.

Any attempt to do very simple tasks, such as crawling, opening a door, or grabbing an item will require a Stamina test. The Difficulty Level will be at least Good, but could higher depending on the task being taken and the circumstances around it. A failed Stamina test means that you fall and possibly pass out for 1 to 3 rounds (roll a Fudge die and treat a minus as 1, blank as 2 and plus as 3).

Near Death

Not only are you unconscious, but you will die within one hour (and possibly less) without medical help. No one recovers from Near Death on his own.

Automatic Death

Sometimes there are cases where no roll is necessary to kill someone. For instance, slitting the throat of an unconscious victim requires so little effort or risk that death is guaranteed.

Non-Lethal Combat

Sometimes when in combat, you really do not want to hurt your opponent, but merely knock him out or stun

6-3: Wounds

1, 2	3, 4	5, 6	7, 8	9+
Scratch	Light Wound	Severe Wound	Incapacitated	Near Death
○ ○ ○	○	○	○	○

Acting

him. In addition, some shows are non-combative by nature, but must still have a way of handling brawls and other forms of fighting. A sitcom is a prime example. Some sitcoms have fights, but it is important that they never end in anyone getting very hurt. This is where non-lethal combat comes in.

To fight non-lethally, you must declare to the Director your intention before you attack. If the Director agrees that it can be done with the type of attack you are going to make, then you can do it.

A non-lethal attack is identical to a normal attack. Damage is calculated the same as always, but the list of wound types are different. The names and descriptions are different, but their effects are essentially the same. These wound types are described below:

Bruise

A Bruise is equivalent to any wound that is so small that it will not be of much concern. A punch on the shoulder, a kick in the shin, or even an "Indian sunburn" are all types of Bruises. You can take a few Bruises before they start to cause a real problem.

A Bruise has no effect on you. You can take three Bruises before they begin to spill over into the next wound.

Hurt

Now you are taking a beating. When you are Hurt, your abilities begin to suffer. A head butt, a punch in the kidney, and even the pain of receiving too many Bruises are all types of Hurts.

> You suffer a -1 to all tests related to the injuries

The Director should decide on the nature of the injury in order to figure out what skill and attribute tests are affected.

Daze

You have taken such a beating that you are dazed and having a tough time continuing. Whether you took a huge blow, or are suffering from the constant punishment of lesser injuries, you are now in serious risk of losing the fight. You see stars and have a hard time focusing on your target.

> You suffer a -2 to all tests related to the injuries

Stun

You can no longer act. Usually, you will fall down and remain conscious, although it is possible that you will remain standing, and stagger about helplessly.

Any attempt to do very simple tasks, such as crawling, opening a door, or grabbing an item will require a Stamina test. The Difficulty Level will be at least Good, but could higher depending on the task being taken and the circumstances around it. A failed Stamina test means that you fall and possibly pass out for 1 to 3 rounds (roll a Fudge die and treat a minus as 1, blank as 2 and plus as 3).

Knockout

You fall unconscious. You will remain unconscious for 10 to 20 minutes, depending on how serious the Knockout was. You will remain unconscious for 20 minutes if the strike was 2 or more points higher than needed to make a knockout, or if the knockout occurred as a result of wound overflow from Stun. Otherwise, you will remain unconscious for only 10 minutes. A successful First Aid or Treat Injury test will halve the amount of time you are out.

Body Armor and Damage Reduction

In *Now Playing*, armor does not help to prevent you from being hit, and therefore does not add any bonuses to your Defense. Instead, it will absorb some of the damage of the attack, if the attack successfully struck the armor.

All body armor has a Defensive Factor associated with it. Add this bonus to all your other Defensive Factors when you are struck in combat.

Most forms of armor do not stop all types of attacks. For instance, a Kevlar vest will not stop a bludgeoning blow. The description of each type of armor will specify what types of attacks it will defend against.

Coverage Level

Armor does not cover your entire body, and thus will not always protect you from every attack. Each type of armor has a Coverage Level. The Coverage Level specifies how well the armor covers you. When an attack successfully hits you, compare the Relative Degree to the Coverage Level. If the attack succeeded by the armor's Coverage Level or less, then it struck the armor and you will not take full damage. If the attack succeeded by more than the Coverage Level, then the blow got past the armor and the armor's Defensive Factor will not apply.

Fatigue

There are times when you will need to keep track of a character's endurance, and apply penalties to his tests as he grows more tired. You can use the following simple mechanic:

Stamina Loss

Every time a character's endurance is stressed, the

Acting

Director may call for a Stamina test. If the test fails, the character temporarily loses one level of Stamina. If the stress is particularly bad, the Director may choose to have a minimum number of levels lost even if the character passes the Stamina test. For instance, if the character succeeds, he loses one level, and if he fails, he loses two.

A character with a Stamina of Terrible is bedridden, and cannot perform any physical action. A character with no Stamina at all is in a coma.

Regaining Stamina

You regain Stamina lost due to fatigue back at a rate of one level for every ten minutes of rest.

Healing

How wounds heal really depends on the type of show you are running. If the show puts much detail into healing and medical topics, such as a medical drama, then you would want to use a more detailed method for working healing. However, most shows do not put much emphasis on the healing of wounds.

Now Playing includes two separate methods for handling healing. The Simple Healing method, which works best for most shows, and the Detailed Healing method, which is almost strictly for medical dramas. Of course, you can adjust these methods to fit your shows in any way you want.

Simple Healing

The process for healing depends on the Wound Level. The process for each is described below:

Scratch

These almost do not count as wounds. All scratches heal at the end of the scene in which they were inflicted. No skill tests are required to heal them.

Light & Severe Wounds

These require a successful First Aid or Medical skill test to heal. If the Director chooses to, she could require proper medical equipment, but this is not necessary, since this is TV.

A Good skill result will heal all wounds of this type by one level. This means a Light Wound heals completely or a Severe Wound becomes only a Light Wound. A Great result will heal two levels and a Superb will heal three.

Healing these wounds take some time. About an hour or two of rest and care will be needed to heal these wounds.

Incapacitated

This type of injury requires more care. The same rules apply for Incapacitated as for Light & Severe Wounds, and the same skill test will apply to it, but it takes more time. A minimum of four hours is required to heal an Incapacitated Wound, and the patient will remain incapacitated for at least half that time.

Near Death

This requires hospitalization. The patient's wounds are so severe that medical attention must be given within one hour of receiving the wound, or he will die. A Fair First Aid or Medical skill test will stabilize the injury so that he will not die right away, but the wound will remain as Near Death until he receives full hospital care.

A stabilized wound that does not receive proper treatment will need stabilization again in four hours. Each time, the Difficulty Level will increase by one.

Example: *Jack was injured in a rockslide and received a Near Death wound. Tara performs First Aid on him, receiving a Good. This is enough to stabilize the injury. However, they are trapped in the cave and cannot get help. Four hours later, his wound becomes unstable again and he will die an hour later if she doesn't help. She once again makes a First Aid test, but now she needs at least a Good to succeed. She got a Good, just barely stabilizing his injuries again. She is worried that he will not last another five hours here.*

Detailed Healing

This is designed specifically for medical dramas and other shows that require much detail when dealing with the treating of injuries. Because of this, the process is more complicated.

The process requires a diagnosis, treatment and perhaps some surgery.

The system works similarly to the Simple Healing method, except for the following differences:

Treating Individual Wounds

The Simple Healing method requires only one skill test to heal all wounds by one or more level. The Detailed Healing method requires a separate skill test for each individual wound.

When treating an injury, you must first choose which wound on the patient's wound table you want to treat.

Diagnosis

Before treating an illness, make a Diagnosis skill test. The result will determine if you were able to diagnose the illness or injury properly.

Acting

Treatment

Once you have diagnosed the illness, make Treat Injury tests. There may be multiple tests involved, depending on how many wounds must be treated.

Surgery

If surgery is required, make a surgery test. Of course, you cannot just make the test. You have to roleplay it out. This could mean planning out what surgical procedures need to be made, and making several tests for them. In this way, you could succeed in stopping the internal bleeding, but fail to fix another more serious part of the injury.

Vehicles

Vehicles look much like characters when viewed on paper. They have attributes, skills, gifts and faults. These all work the same way that they do with characters. The difference is that they do not have the same six attributes, and many of the other traits are different as well.

This section will describe each of the important traits for dealing with vehicles, and will then include the definitions of some of the more common vehicles shown on television.

Attributes

Vehicles do not use the same six attributes that characters have. Instead, they have their own that are specific to them. These are described as follows:

Acceleration

This represents how quickly it can increase speed. This is equivalent to a car's "0 to 60" rating.

When two vehicles begin a chase, both drivers make their appropriate skill tests for the type of vehicle they are driving ("Drive Car" for a car, "Pilot Airplane" for an airplane, etc.), and add Acceleration attribute's modifier to it.

Example: *Jack is racing Pete in a drag race. He's in a suped-up Charger and Pete is in a Camaro. The Director has decided that the drag strip is long enough to require 3 Drive tests for acceleration to determine the winner. When Jack's girlfriend waves the flag, both Jack and Pete make their Drive Car skill tests. Jack rolls +1. His Charger has an Acceleration attribute of Great, which has a modifier of +2. This makes his total +3. He adds it to his Good Drive Skill to give him Superb +1. His car leaps forward with a loud squeal and zooms ahead in a cloud of smoke. Howev-*

Acting

er, Pete rolls +4. The Camaro only has a Good Acceleration and his Drive Car is only Fair. However, his phenomenal roll gives him a total modifier of +5. When he adds this to his skill level, the result is Superb +2. Pete's Camaro manages to outrace Jack in the first leg of the drag race.

Handling

This represents how difficult, or easy, the vehicle is to maneuver. This also results in a modifier to the driver's skill test. Use this attribute whenever the performance of the vehicle itself has a factor on the task.

Usually, Use Handling only when something goes wrong. For instance, if you try a maneuver and fail badly, another Drive test may be required, modified by the Handling attribute, in order to avoid losing control. Although you can include Handling's modifier to all Drive tests, this could overly complicate game play.

Example: *In the above drag race, neither driver applied Handling to the first leg of the race. In the second leg, Jack rolls and gets a result of Great. Pete, however, does very badly, and gets a result of Poor. The Director declares that Pete's Camaro begins to fishtail and swerve, and that Pete needs to make Good Drive Test to avoid crashing. Pete makes a Drive Car test and rolls a -2. This is not good, because the Camaro has Mediocre Handling. This roll results in a total modifier of -3, which, subtracted from his Fair Drive Car skill, makes Terrible. With a loud screeeeeech, the Camaro spins, then flips, rolls three times, and stops after sliding for fifty feet on its roof. The Director must now decide how badly hurt Pete was, and whether the car's fuel ignites!*

Speed

This merely represents the vehicles maximum speed. In a television show, it is really not necessary to accurately gauge a vehicle's speed in miles per hour. It is really only important to note how much faster the vehicle can go compared to the others in the scene.

This does not really modify any tests, but is instead something that the Director and actors can use to determine how many times the driver must make Acceleration tests to reach top speed and how far apart the vehicles are at the end of each round.

Size

Again, this is an abstract value that represents the differences in the sizes of the vehicles. For instance, an "econo-box" sub-compact might have a Mediocre size, while a 1970's muscle car would have a Good or Great size.

Scale

This works exactly as it does with characters. For instance, a compact car would have a Fair Size and a muscle car would have a Great Size. These attribute levels are relative to other cars. However, because their Scale is 2, making its size much greater than that of humans. A small single-engine prop-driven airplane would have Mediocre Size compared to other planes, but its Scale would be 4, making it bigger than the muscle car.

Skills

There are far too many potential skills for vehicles to list and describe here. Luckily, almost all of them are simple enough to just use your common sense. However, a few will be described here for your convenience:

Auto Positioning

This system communicates with satellites to determine your current position and display it in an onscreen map. APS units and services have differing levels of quality. Some are not terribly accurate or reliable, and others just do not have service in many areas.

When you try to use this feature of your vehicle, make this skill test for the vehicle. A failed result means that either the results were inaccurate or incomplete, or that service was not available at that time.

Traction Control

This can be either electronic traction control or four-wheel drive. In any case, you can use this skill when trying to have the vehicle drive over tough terrain.

Autopilot

These are for vehicles that have a computer-controlled autopilot feature, such as an aircraft or spacecraft. It replaces the need for you to make your own piloting tests. Once you have programmed in the course, the autopilot will take over.

The same rules apply for Autopilot as for Pilot. Therefore, any normal maneuvering will not require a skill test, but any type of maneuver that is out of the ordinary or challenging will.

Targeting System

This represents a computer-controlled targeting system. This would oppose the defensive skill or attribute test of the target.

Gifts

Vehicle gifts are those things that are part of the vehicle that do not have variable results when used. As with skills, there are too many gifts to list here, so only a few have been included for your convenience.

Acting

Filming

Weapon

The vehicle has a built-in weapon, such as a heavy machine gun emplacement or a laser turret. Of course, you should also list the weapon's Strength when adding this gift to the vehicle.

Hyperdrive

This is just an example of a special form of engine that extends beyond the normal type of engine for the vehicle. For instance, a ship that has hyperdrive would also have standard engines for slower than light speed travel.

Atmospheric Drive

This would be for a spaceship that can travel both in space and in a planet's atmosphere. Not all spaceships can do this, so it would be a gift.

Faults

These are problems with the vehicle. They could exist due to damage or wear-and-tear, or it could be a design flaw. The following are just a few examples.

Non-Standard Parts

This will make the vehicle difficult to repair.

Unattractive Exterior

This may or may not be very bad, depending on the vehicle's use. If it is a passenger ship, then this can cause people to take a different ship.

Temperamental Engine

The engine has a problem that causes it to stall or fail to start on occasion. Often, a good swift kick or smack in the right spot will fix it, but not always. For some reason, it always seems to pick the worst times to happen...

Cramped & Uncomfortable

This will have a big effect on morale during long trips.

Magic

Anatomy of a Magical Spell

There are four elements of a spell. Each one is necessary for any spell to be cast. They represent a person's natural ability to perform magic, his skill in casting the spell, the energy required to cast it, and his skill in handling that energy.

Mana

Mana is an energy that exists everywhere in nature. Mana exists in all living beings, as well as in some sacred objects. Magic uses mana as the "fuel" for its spells. You must direct a certain amount of mana toward each spell, and it will not succeed if you do not have enough.

Magical Aptitude Power

This special Power grants the innate ability to perform magic. Of course, anyone can perform parlor tricks and illusions, but only those gifted with Magical Aptitude can perform feats of true magic.

This allows the character to gather and manipulate mana to his own ends.

Handle Mana Skill

When you take the Magical Aptitude Power, you automatically gain the Gather Mana skill with a default of Terrible. It is through this skill that you would gather up mana to spend when casting your spells.

Ritual Skill

Each spell that you would learn requires taking levels in the Ritual skill. As is described in Chapter Three of *Now Playing*, you must pick a specific ritual when taking this skill. For instance, a magician could have a Good Divine Fortune skill and only a Fair Levitate Object skill.

Of course, purchasing each magical spell as a separate skill means that you will develop those skills slowly, but that adds both realism and balance with the rest of the cast.

Performing Magic

Casting Spells

Casting a spell is not easy and is fraught with peril. Even the simplest and most harmless of spells includes a certain amount of risk. Casting a spell is not something to be done lightly!

The following steps are required to cast a spell:

Gather Mana: Make a Handle Mana skill test. This will determine how much mana you manage to pool up for the spell. The Mana attribute of the spell being cast defines the Difficulty Level. The invocation will be guaranteed to fail if you do not gather enough mana for the spell.

Perform Ritual: Make the appropriate Ritual skill test for the spell that you are casting. All of the mana you have gathered will be released and will take the form that the spell has woven for it. Whether the Ritual succeeded or failed, the mana has been released and will take whatever form the failed Ritual has woven for it. If you failed

Acting

your Ritual test, the result of the spell will be a bastardized form of the spell you attempted.

Dismissal: If your spell failed, you have one chance to dismiss the mana you have just released and thus prevent the spell from taking form. This requires a Dismissal whose Difficulty Level is that of the amount of mana spent on the spell. This will be either the value of the spell's Mana attribute, or the amount of mana you had gathered, whichever one is lower. If you succeed in dismissing the mana, the spell will have been cancelled before it could take full form. If you fail this as well, then the spell will take such form as the Director chooses.

Concentration

If there are distractions during the course of the casting, the Director may require occasional Concentration skill tests to ensure that you are not disturbed. A failed test could mean a penalty to your tests, or it could mean a failure of one test, depending on the Director's choice.

Failed Spells

As long as enough mana was used to cast the spell, the spell will succeed in casting. However, any mistakes in the performance of the casting ritual will cause the spell to take a form that is different from that in which you had planned. This is a very important distinction, because it means that there is great risk in performing magic. If you mess up, the consequences could be dire!

When you fail a ritual, you will have the opportunity to attempt to dismiss it. You will need to do this right away before the spell's effects can fully manifest. To dismiss the spell, you must perform the Dismissal described above. A successful dismissal means that the spell is gone and will have no effect in the world.

If you fail to dismiss an improperly cast spell, it will take effect. The effects will definitely be different from those that you had planned. The exact nature of its effects are decided by the Director, but should be based on the Relative Degree of the Ritual skill attempt. A ritual that almost succeeded would have only a minor difference in its effects. A ritual that failed badly would have wildly unpredictable effects that may only vaguely resemble those of the original spell.

Example: *At an outdoor festival, Max the Magician casts a Levitate Object spell on his beautiful partner to cause her prone form to rise five feet into the air. He rolls his Handle Mana test and succeeds. Now that he has pooled up enough mana, he then rolls his Levitate Object Ritual skill test. He needed a Good roll, but rolled Terrible instead. The Director decided that the spell does levitate his partner, but it does two things wrong: it lifts her very quickly, like three feet per second; and it does not stop at five feet. In fact, she continues to rise until she is lying one hundred and fifty feet in the air! The Director, taking pity on the actor playing the poor partner, decides that if Max succeeds in another Levitate Object spell, he can have her float gently down to Earth. Of course, if he fails...*

Mana

Mana is a natural energy that exists in all living beings. Almost every culture has a belief in the existence of mana. The Chinese call it Chi, and the Japanese call it Ki. Mana is the most essential component in performing magic. It is to magic as electricity is to a television.

When casting a spell, you must first pool up mana from yourself, others and the local environment. The spell's ritual is used to weave the mana into a form that the spell requires, and then releases it into the world. If you cannot pool enough mana for the spell, then the spell will fail. If you pool enough mana, but make a mistake during the ritual, then the mana will still be released, but will have taken the form of your mistake. Unfortunately, the magician only knows what form the mana will take when the ritual is done properly, so the results of a poorly done ritual will be unpredictable.

Handling Mana

Each spell has a Mana attribute. That represents, in a way, how much mana is needed for the spell to work. The more mana that is required, the more difficult the Handle Mana skill test will be.

The Mana attribute is the Difficulty Level of the Handle Mana skill tests.

Places, Objects & Times of Power

Myths and legends all state that some items carry more mana than others. Certain symbols, such as the pentagram, and items such as crystals, crystal balls, and tarot cards are all examples of these things. Also, there are certain places that seem to radiate more mana than other places. Stonehenge, churches and temples, and ancient burial grounds are said to be focal points of natural energy. And finally, there are certain times that are said to convey more power than normal. Halloween night is a prime examples, as are the other solstices.

The Director may choose to add a bonus to all Handle Mana and Ritual skill tests when any of these factors are present.

Pooling Mana from Other Sources

Normally, your Handle Mana test will only pool mana from yourself and from the ambient mana pool. In order to pool mana from another living being, you must either have its consent or force it out. Either way, the other "donor" must be involved in the ritual. If he gives consent, he would take some active part in the ritual. The only way to force mana from another creature would be to ritually sacrifice it.

Creating Spells

Creating spells should be simple. You must decide what the spell will do when cast properly, as well as any limitations it would have. Then, figure out how difficult it would be to cast on a scale of Terrible to Superb. Finally, using the same scale, decide how hard it would be to pool up enough mana to cast the spell.

Example Spells

Divination

Mana: N/A

The subject asks a question about his future and the fortune teller then performs the Divination Ritual skill to divine the answer.

This spell requires so little mana that you do not need to make a Handle Mana test. Instead, you just perform a Divination Ritual skill test. The Difficulty Level will depend on the difficulty of the divination being done.

A successful Divination test means that the fortune teller has discovered something about the subject's future in respect to the question being asked. The answer will always be vague and could have more than one interpretation.

This is among the most harmless of spells. A failed Divination will simply give you a wrong or very misleading reading.

Levitate Object

Mana: Varies

This spell allows you to lift an object into the air and have it suspended for a length of time.

The mana required for this spell depends both on the weight of the object and the height to which the object is to be lifted. A small object like a spoon would have a Mana attribute of Mediocre. A piano would require Great Mana.

After making your successful Handle Mana test, you must then succeed at a Levitate Object Ritual skill test. As with all rituals, a failure will have unpredictable results.

Once you have successfully lifted the object, you must make a Handle Mana test every other round to maintain the spell. If you fail your test, the spell is broken and the object drops to the ground.

Converting Systems

It is not practical to include rules on converting every game system to *Now Playing*. However, two specific types of game systems are widely used. This section will describe how to convert between those systems.

Standard 3-18 Scale

There are many games whose traits fall within a scale of 3-18. You sum up the rolls of three six-sided dice to determine each trait. The following chart illustrates how to convert between them:

FUDGE Level	3-18 Level
Superb	18+
Great	16-17
Good	13-15
Fair	9-12
Mediocre	6-8
Poor	4-5
Terrible	3 or less

Percentile Scale

The table below illustrates how to convert traits whose values are percentages to *Now Playing*.

FUDGE Level	Percentile Level
Superb	98-100
Great	91-97
Good	71-90
Fair	31-70
Mediocre	11-30
Poor	4-10
Terrible	1-3

Game System Focus

If you decide to convert *Now Playing* to another game system, you must always remember the focus of the game. Television is a very character oriented medium. Much more emphasis is placed on the interactions between characters than on the action. Some systems are heavy in rules, and drill down into the details of tactics. You should be wary about what rules you use in your game, because if your focus shifts towards the action, your "show" may become just a "game."

A good rule of thumb when using another roleplaying game system for your show is to look at the types of mechanics that are used in *Now Playing* and try to use only similar mechanics in the other game. For instance, if your game system has detailed rules on the effects of weather, right down to character movement rates during blizzards and earthquakes, you may want to simply omit these rules and play them by ear. In a *Now Playing* show, these details are better left up to theatrics rather than to the game system.

Directing

Chapter 7

Acting

Directing

The Job of Directing

Directing a game in *Now Playing* is a very busy job. You must wear several different hats all at the same time, and you never get a break. However, the rewards are tremendous. There's nothing like coming up with a story and watching your friends have a great time acting it out. It lets you be creative in ways that you may never have thought possible.

The following is a description of each of the jobs that you will have as a Director:

Storyteller

The episodes that you run are stories, and you have to describe the events that take place in a way that will peak your actors' interest. Consider each description a story. Make it vivid and interesting. It must keep them on their toes and make them want to keep playing.

Actor

You must also play the roles of everyone that the leading cast encounters during the show. This means that you have to know and play quite a number of characters in each episode. Try to play each role as though you are your own. The more passion you put into the characters, the more fun it will be for the actors to roleplay with them.

Referee

You control the game system. You have the final word in any decision that must be made regarding the rules. Many of the skills leave details up to the Director. You must use your best judgment when working out the details.

In most cases, the actors will not need to bring a copy of the rulebook with them to each gaming session. You, however, will want to have it handy to look up any rule that you cannot remember.

Mother Nature

Finally, you control the environment. You can decide to make it rain, or to make it windy or snow. Sometimes you can use the environment to help guide the cast down a certain course of action.

Prepare for the Session

Learn the Show & Episode

If the show is one that really exists, watch some episodes back to back. Pay close attention to the mood set by the show, and what the supporting characters were like. Think about how you would describe some of the scenes in the episodes as if they were the episodes you are going to direct. It is important to describe the scenes in a way that would build the mood of the show.

If the show does not really exist, then read about it. Try to decide what kind of mood the show should have and then prepare yourself for building that mood.

Know the Actors

You always have to remember that the show is not just for your benefit. It must be appealing to the actors as well. You most likely know the group you are playing with. Think about them, and consider how well they will enjoy the episode you have in store for them. It is quite possible that you will feel the need to adapt the episode to make a better fit for the personalities of the actors. This is especially true with store-bought or pre-made episodes.

The actors can be easily distracted. You must make sure that the episode engages their minds and emotions. You must make them really want to pay attention, and that can only happen if you adapt the episode to fit their personalities.

Know the Leading Cast

Just as you must cater to the actors, you must also cater to the characters they play. Always make sure that every character has a major role to play in the episode. You have to remind yourself that every actor is playing a starring role. Any actor whose character does not get a chance to shine will be disappointed and bored.

Don't Allow Just Any Character

Making sure that the entire leading cast will play important, active roles can be a very difficult task. If you let the actors play any type of characters they want, you will aggravate this problem. You must, and I mean must, review every character concept that your actors come up with. It is extremely easy for them to create characters that you will never be able to work into the plot of your show without giving them supporting or even incidental roles. This has been a very common mistake among unseasoned Directors throughout the entire history of roleplaying games.

When an actor comes up with a concept for his character, you must review it. Come up with a plot hook that will let the character fit into the show. Then, decide if that hook is good enough to let you come up with ways to make him a star in every episode. If he is not good enough, figure out why. It is quite possible that he only needs some minor adjustments. Come up with these adjustments, and discuss them with the actor. You should be able to work out a concept that you both like. If not, you may need to send him back to the drawing board.

Acting

Balancing the Cast

When reviewing the characters, you must keep balance in mind. The game system, with its hard limits on the acquisition of traits, does a good job of keeping each character in balance with the others. However, you must also make sure that there is a good balance between the leading and supporting cast. You must make sure that any adversaries will present the level of challenge that you had in mind for the leading cast. It would be a tragedy for the final showdown to end quickly with little effort from the leading cast. Alternately, it would also be bad if the leading cast had little chance against the enemy.

Power Gaming

There are actors who pride themselves on making the most powerful characters allowed by the game system. They do not cheat; they simply study the rules to find every loophole and trick in order to make the most powerful character possible. People call them Power Gamers. Some people like them, and others do not. However, since they do not actually break any rules, you really cannot fault them.

You must take extra care when reviewing the characters that they create. It is quite possible that a power gamer will create a character that is too powerful for the show you are running. Allowing the character into the game could force you to make your adversaries more powerful. This can cause that character to outshine the others and cause great problems in the game. Now, I am not saying that you should not allow the character in. Instead, you could apply limits. Have him make certain adjustments to bring the character into balance with the others.

Premade Characters

In most cases, it is best if the actors create their own characters. Sometimes, however, you may want or need to supply characters that have already been created. Premade characters are great for any game where you cannot have the actors take the time to create their own characters. Running an event at a gaming convention is one good example of a situation where premade characters are ideal.

Another time when premade characters are desirable is when you still have room for more actors in your game. Create enough extra characters that you can be hand out if any new actors join the game.

Whatever the case, if you create a few characters, be sure they follow all the rules that you put down about characters for your show. Try to show as much attention to detail when creating the character as you would if you were going to play her. This will ensure that the characters will be every bit as complete and good as the ones that the other actors made.

Gender Switching

Some actors like to play characters of the opposite sex. Some do it for the roleplaying challenge. Others do it simply because the character they were creating just made more sense as that gender. Of course, there could be any number of reasons, but the fact remains that you are likely to run shows where at least one actor roleplays another gender. This is perfectly normal and okay. And, as a matter of fact, you may certainly find yourself having to roleplay the opposite sex, since you must play all supporting characters.

For whatever reason you do it, you should always use care when playing a cross-gender character. Avoid stereotypes, and try to play the character accurately. If you find that you cannot play him properly in the gender he was created in, do not even try. Just announce the character's gender and then play him like normal.

Prepare for Absentees

There are two ways in which an actor can be absent from the session: either he gives you notice that he will not be attending, or he just does not show up. Both require prep, but you need to handle them in different ways.

For planned absentees, it is easier. You must make sure that none of the scenes or beats of the session do not depend on those who are not showing up. This should not be difficult at all, but you should give it at least a little thought before the session.

For no-shows, it can be more difficult. This is because you won't know until it's time to start the game. Either you must make the same types of changes as a planned absentee on the spot, or you plan for them beforehand. Planning unexpected absentees can be tricky, but it is possible. The key is to make sure that none of the important scenes or beats of the session depend on anyone. This may not be hard with some shows. If all the characters are cops, for instance, it should not be hard to focus certain events on any of them. Some may be tougher, and it may be that you really cannot change the focus of some beats. You will just have to play around them. Sometimes, I will create more than one scene for a particular beat of the episode. Each of these scenes will focus on a different character and will handle the beat in their own way. This way, I can just choose which scene I want based on who shows.

You should decide on a minimum number of actors for your session. That is, it may come to a point when there will not be enough actors present to justify running the session. This may depend on which characters are not coming, or it may be just a matter of numbers. Whatever the case, you should decide this up front.

Getting Into Character

Now Playing is all about acting and TV shows focus on the interactions between the characters. You must

Directing

111

Acting

treat each supporting character as though she were a leading character. Play her with feeling and passion. All supporting roles must be compelling.

Don't Forget Who the Stars Are

A common mistake to make is to have a supporting character outshine the leading cast. This is just about the worst thing that you can do as Director. Having a supporting character defeat the nemesis, especially when one of the leading characters was able to do it, is anti-climactic. It will deflate the energy of the episode and leave actors feeling robbed.

This is difficult when you are proud of the supporting role you created. You will want that character to shine. However, you will have much more fun with the character if you make the actors want to deal with her. You can only achieve that if you roleplay her passionately, while still keeping her in a supporting role. The cast will not want to deal with anyone that will outshine themselves.

Preparing the Scenes

It always helps to have a good idea of how you plan to run the session. The problem is that the cast will drive the episode in a direction that you never expected. So, how can you prepare for the session when you cannot predict the direction in which it will go? The one scene that you can predict is the first scene. This is because you will place the cast in the scene and provide the appropriate stimuli for them to react to. Prepare the scene. Beyond that, you should be able to come up with a list of possible scenes that the cast may end play out. Prepare some of those as well.

You most likely already have a general idea of the scenes that you hope or expect the cast do play out. Take a notebook and a pen and start jotting down notes to help you be ready for running the scene. Having some of the details written down will mean that there will be less for you to make up on the spot. This will have the added bonus of minimizing inconsistencies in your descriptions of the scenes.

The Set

Decide what the set looks like. Describe it several times to yourself, and takes notes. Sketch out a map of the set, if a diagram is more to your liking. Expect the cast to ask you questions about the set, and prepare some of the answers. Do not spend too much time on this. You cannot expect to know everything that they will ask. Instead, focus on the important information.

Supporting Cast

What supporting cast members will be involved in the scene? Decide on the details of each character: why is each character is in the episode, how is he dressed, and what kind of mood is he in.

Each supporting character must serve a purpose in the episode. TV studios always work on a tight budget, and they will never cast a character that is not necessary in the episode. Before creating character concepts for the supporting cast, decide what characters are needed. For instance, if the episode is a murder mystery, you may want multiple suspects to keep the cast guessing. You will also want witnesses, enough of them to help you distribute the clues during roleplaying. Once you have decided what you need from a supporting cast, you can then work out the details of them.

Season Beats

Some shows have a storyline that spans entire seasons. When creating the episode, you most likely will have assigned one or more of the season's plot beats to this episode. Somehow, you must make that beat happen in the episode. Decide what scene or scenes it will happen in and figure out how it will happen. Often, the beat will be an event that takes place during the episode. Those are the easiest to plan because it has no bearing on what the cast is doing at the time. Occasionally, however, the beat will directly involve actions taken by the cast. These are much trickier. Hopefully, you will have had the foresight not to expect a character to take a specific course of action. If you did, then there is a good chance that the beat will never happen. You could come up with a number of different ways in which the beat can happen, and then choose the most appropriate one based on what the cast does.

For more information on beats, see Chapter Nine: Writing Episodes.

Rehearsing Scenes

I once ran an adventure show about dinosaurs running amok in South American rainforests. The cast was not supposed to know yet that the animals they were sent to investigate were dinosaurs, but the actors knew. My first challenge was to somehow grab them and pull them into the story; make them forget that they already knew about them, and just send them on a wild ride that will keep them on their toes throughout the rest of the game. This was going to be tough, since they already knew what they were up against. I knew I needed a scene that was specifically designed to set the mood and to get their adrenaline pumping. The mood I wanted was one of desperation bordering on panic. I had to make them truly fear for their characters' lives.

I devised a scene that would to do just that. They wanted dinosaurs, I'll give them dinosaurs. However, it could not be just any dinosaur. It had to be a T-Rex. Nothing else would show them the sheer magnitude of what they were up against. I also knew it had to be mostly show, and I knew that a supporting character would die. After all, I had to put them in touch with their own mortality.

After I created the scene, I ran through it several

Acting

times by myself, aloud, in my car during my commute to work. My commute is an hour long, so I had plenty of time. I would begin describing the scene just as I would when I run it with real actors. I would also play their parts, making decisions that seemed right at the time. I ran through it several times and committed not only the details of the scene to memory, but style of describing it as well. When I finally directed the episode, that scene went so well that it left the actors stunned! I still get compliments about that scene to this day.

Rehearsing a scene has the following benefits:

Learning the details: Rehearsing helps you to drive home the details of the scene, so that you can see it in your head clearly, when you finally run it.

Identifying problems: Sometimes you cannot find problems in your scene until you have run it. Having a dry run will help you weed out the problems and leave you with a scene that flows beautifully, and is consistent with the episode's story.

Immersion: There is no way to help you really get into the episode than to run a scene. By performing a dry run by yourself, it puts you fully into the story and gets you psyched up for running it live. You will find yourself much more focused when running the scenes that you have rehearsed, as opposed to those you did not.

Getting into character: When you run through the scene, roleplay the various supporting characters that appear in it. This will make great practice for the real thing.

Gear

This can serve as a checklist to make sure that you have everything you need to run a smooth gaming session.

Dice

It practically goes without saying that you will need to bring Fudge dice for yourself. You should only need the standard four Fudge dice for yourself. However, never forget your actors. Some of them may not have Fudge dice, and those that do may forget to bring theirs. Granted, everyone can share a few sets of dice, but it will be nicer if everyone has their own set of dice to use for the session. You can buy Fudge dice in "GM Packs" that have five sets of dice and a dice bag.

Notes

Always remember to bring any notes you have written about the show, the episode or the session.

Blank Character Sheets

These are very useful if a new actor joins the game unexpectedly. You may not need them often, but they're a real lifesaver when the need arises.

Supporting Characters

The character sheets of your supporting characters. Without them, it will be very tough roleplaying them. They may be playable, as you probably remember what they are like, but it's doubtful that you'll remember their skill and Attribute levels.

The Leading Cast

The Director should always have her own copy of the character sheets of the entire leading cast. These can serve a dual purpose. You will need to refer to these when making secret tests against them. In addition, if the actor forgets his character sheet, you can always lend him yours.

Using Props

Sometimes props can be useful when running a game. Props can add to the atmosphere of the episode. This can include simple items like toy guns, but it is often the more inventive props that can add a lot to the game.

Some shows are famous for their soundtracks. In these shows, the music you hear during the scenes is almost as important as the events taking place. For a show like this, you can literally create a soundtrack for your episodes. I hand-select several songs for each scene, make MP3s of them and store them on my notebook computer. I then make a play list for each scene. That way, at the start of each scene, I can simply run the play list for that scene. I would recommend selecting several songs for each scene, as you cannot judge how long each scene will take. You can also make your player repeat.

If you do include a soundtrack, it is very important that you do not play it loud enough to distract yourself or the actors. You must also be careful not to spend too much time messing with it. It must be something that always remains in the background.

You can do the same thing for sound effects. For instance, if you are running a popular science fiction show, you can make a collection of sound files of laser guns, space ships and other common sound effects from the show.

Whatever props you use, you must be very careful not to let them get out of hand. That is, if you or the actors spend much time just dealing with the prop, then it could actually harm the flow and atmosphere of the game.

The Session Begins

You have already prepared as much as you can for the session. You have arrived at the game, and you have all of your gear. Now it is time to set up.

Acting

The Gaming Environment

You should give some thought to the room where you play. It should be comfortable and have little distractions. It should be private so everyone can feel free to play his role without inhibition. Ideally, everyone should sit at a table with comfortable chairs. The least amount of distractions that are there, the better it is.

You should sit at the head of the table so that no one will be sitting directly on either side of you. You will need some privacy, as you have notes, maps and other paraphernalia that the actors should not see.

I have a small whiteboard that is easily portable. I keep it in my car and bring it to every game. That way, I can draw a quick sketch of a map or tactical area for a combat scene. I could even list the initiative order for combat on the whiteboard. They are very handy and not expensive.

A Set Starting Time

Tardiness has been the bane of my existence as a Director. Every gaming group I have been a part of has had trouble getting every session underway. The problem is that if you say that the game starts at eleven o'clock, many people will roll in between eleven and twelve. Then there will be the expected conversations where people discuss what has happened in their lives since the last session. If the game starts near a mealtime, then people may order food. By the time you get things going, a couple hours have slipped by.

You have a schedule to follow. You have prepared your session and are expecting a certain amount of time to run it in. It is your unfortunate duty to rein everyone in and make sure the game gets underway when at the predetermined time. Play hardball. Tell everyone ahead of time when the game starts, and do not feel bad about saying that anyone who is late will miss some of the game. Then, when the time you give comes, start the game. Make all out-of-game conversations end and get it started. The actors should not mind, since this is why they have all come.

Handling Late Arrivals

Do not stop the game when someone shows up late. Just politely let him know that the game is in progress. If his character is with the rest of the cast, then you must pause when it is convenient and give him an update of

Acting

what has happened. Of course, any opportunities that he would have taken had he been there are lost to him. That is his punishment for being late. If his character is separate from the rest, so much the better. Only fill him in on those events that his character would be aware of.

Unexpected Absentees

This can be a disaster if you do not use a set starting time. It is common for a Director to want to wait for everyone to show up before starting the session. The problem is that if one or two of the actors do not show at all, you may well have wasted the entire session. By the time you realize that they are not coming, too much time has been wasted, and you no longer have time to do all you wanted in the session.

Because you have prepared for unexpected absentees, and you start the game without waiting for late arrivals, you should not have any problems with them. If they show up late, you should handle them as explained above. You have already prepared for no-shows, so you will not have a problem there.

The only problem occurs when those that do not show or are late bring the count of actors below your minimum for the session. At that point, it may not be worthwhile to begin the session until more people show up. Unfortunately, there is no way around this.

Recruiting a Scribe

It can be very helpful to have someone take notes on the events of the session. If your game runs once a week or even less frequently, it can be downright necessary. This lets you keep a running log of everything that goes on in the game. You can use this to help you figure out Experience Point awards, and even for coming up with a plan for the next session.

It is important that someone other than you take the notes. This is because you are the busiest person in the game, and this would be one responsibility too many. You could easily be too busy just taking notes that you do not have time to run the game. This should be easy for an actor.

Teaching New Actors

Sometimes a person who has either never played *Now Playing*, or has never played a roleplaying game at all will join the game. This means you will be in the position of having to teach the game. It is important for everyone else that you don't spend much time doing this up front. This is where the simplicity of *Now Playing* can be a big advantage. Explain just the basics

Obviously, having him create a character for the session you are about to run is out of the question. Instead, give him his choice of the premade characters that you brought to the game. If the character is on a character sheet, it would be much easier for him to understand.

Briefly explain the differences between Attributes and skills, and then describe his specific gifts and faults. Focus on the fact that Attributes refer to physical and mental abilities that are mostly genetic, where skills deal with learned abilities. Explain that Attributes improve only slowly over time, if at all, where skills can improve steadily.

Describe how to make tests. Have him make a sample skill test or two. Explain the levels and that the dice roll is only a modifier to the trait being tested.

Finally, explain the basics of combat. Do not go into any detail. All you need to do is explain that combat works the same as any other skill test, just that your target level is the result of your opponent's defensive skill test. Run through a mock combat round.

The above explanations should take no more than ten minutes. That should be all he needs to get started. Then you begin the session. The best way for him to learn the nitty gritty of the rules is by playing it. For instance, explain Wounds when he suffers some!

Recapping the Last Session

This is necessary if you meet once a week or later. Briefly describe the major events that took place. You could read some of it from the notes your scribe had taken during that session. If you want, you could start with "Previously on..." and use that as your teaser.

Do not spend much time on your recap. Make it quick and concise. You want everyone to be up to speed on what has happened, but you do not want it to become yet another delay in the game.

Scene One

The first scene in an episode is one of the most important. It must introduce the episode, as well as any new characters. It must also grab the actors' interest, and pull them into the story. It must make them want to play. The first scene sets the stage for the rest of the episode, and it will be what the actors base their first impressions on. If they do not like the first scene, you will be hard-pressed to make them like the episode.

Given its great importance, the first scene must directly involve the entire leading cast. It must be exciting. The episode must start on a high point.

Simultaneous Scenes

Sometimes it is not possible to involve the whole cast in one scene. That's okay, as long as you find some other means of directly involving all of the actors early in the session. One ideal way is to run more than one scene simultaneously.

Have multiple "Scene Ones," and frequently cut between them. Two of the leading cast comes to the office at night to find themselves in a fight with some prowlers.

Acting

Example of Setting the Mood

SHOW: Dinosaur Island   EPISODE: Predator   SCENE: T-Rex

Director: You're all walking down the main path. It is hot and humid and you're all sweating. Bugs are out in droves. The rainforest is heavy on both sides, and the tall trees create a canopy over the path, keeping the light dim. The path is about 10' wide. You have heard various animal sounds as you hike along the path. Some you recognize and others you do not. Suddenly, you hear a sound that causes you all to stop short. It is a loud, bellowing call echoing across the island. It was rather loud, but sounded at least a mile distant to the east of the path. Whatever it was, you all bet the animal was big.

Dr. Cartwright: I've got Animal Studies. Can I identify the sound? <Her skill test is Great>

Director: You've never heard a call like that before. It doesn't sound like any animal you've ever heard of. However, you feel certain that it was a mating call.

Anthony: Well, the critter's at least a good mile off the road. Shouldn't be a problem. Let's get a move on.

Director: After a good 10 minutes of walking, you see a game trail that crosses the path.

Anthony: I'll examine the tracks. "Dr. Cartwright, can you help identify these tracks?" <make Animal Studies skill test, getting Fair>. Cartwright gets Good.

Director: You see a motley assortment of tracks, but most of them you cannot recognize. Some have three clawed toes. Doctor, the only kind of animal you know of that has three toes are birds. But these are very big. Each toe is approximately one and a half foot long! Anthony, some of these tracks are fresh.

Anthony: "We'd better cross and put some distance between us and this trail. Let's go!"

Director: The two of you cross the trail with no trouble. Then, you suddenly hear that call again, off to the right. Now you hear another call coming from the left. This one chills you all to the bone. It was loud, very loud. And it was real close. Dr. Cartwright, you have no doubt that this is one huge carnivore.

Dr. Cartwright: I quietly wave for the rest to follow and move quickly, but carefully down the path.

Director: You suddenly hear loud, booming footsteps that shake the earth. The trees on the left side of the game trail are shaking, moving and cracking as something comes lumbering up. Suddenly, the trees burst open and the largest land animal you have ever seen in your life comes crashing onto the path. There is no mistaking what you see. You've all seen plenty of pictures of this beast during your lives that the name comes easily to your lips. You are all staring at a Tyrannosaurus Rex. It stands on its two legs, with its body leaning forward, its back almost horizontal. It's using its long, stiff tail as a counterbalance. You estimate the beast is about 45' from nose to the tip of its tail. Its head is already among the trees on the other side of the path when it suddenly stops. It swings its head around to face down the path in the direction you were going.

Cartwright: What do I know about T-Rex? <Makes a Great Paleontology test>.

Director: You know that it's a solitary carnivore, and the current belief is that it cannot distinguish shapes unless they move.

Cartwright: "Everybody freeze!"

Director: The T-Rex turns its head to stare at Cartwright. Its head leans forward and dips slowly downward. Its head comes to a stop only three feet from the head of one of the hired help, Pablo. Pablo tries hard not to move. He's sweating and shaking. The dinosaur snorts. Its breath is foul, and smells of rotting flesh. Pablo looks at the massive jaws with its six-inch serrated teeth, then slowly down to his machete. Then, every so quietly, the slightest hint of a whimper escapes his lips.

The T-Rex, with one fluid sweep of its head, opens its jaws, snatches Pablo up, tips its head up high and swallows the poor man in one big gulp.

A stunned silence sweeps across the team, broken only by the sound of gulping and burping on a grand scale.

Glenn: "Run for it!" I run down the path away from it as fast as I can!

Director: The T-Rex takes one step onto the path and emits a deafening roar that breaks everyone from their shock. Suddenly, the call is answered by the familiar mating call. The T-Rex stands up, and cocks its head to one side as if listening. It takes one last look around at the small scraps of food running around on the path. Then it turns and charges down the game trail in search of its mate. All that is left of Pablo is an old machete.

Acting

Meanwhile, the other two are driving to have an emergency meeting with a client, only to discover that they are being followed. The followers will try to run them off the road if our heroes do not lose them.

Start one, and then cut after only a few minutes to the other. Never stay long on one scene, and always cut at a climactic point. Frequent cuts will give the impression that both scenes are taking place at the same time. Cutting on a climax will keep the suspense rolling.

It may be a good idea to keep all of the simultaneous scenes short. Of course, you have no idea what the actors will do, so you cannot guarantee they will be short. If you plan the scenes to be short, though, they should still run short. If not, refer to the Controlling the Flow section later in this chapter.

The Scenes

Now it is time to run each scene. You may have many of these planned out, but in all likelihood, you will be making most of them up as you go along. After all, you can never accurately predict what the actors are going to do in any given situation. However, none of this should be hard. You know the sets, the supporting cast, and the story. Use them to drum up new scenes on the fly.

There are tricks that you can use to keep the cast on track. They are described below in the Challenges of Directing section.

Describing the Scenes

This is when you put on your storytelling hat and tell the actors what is going on around their characters. The better your descriptions are, the more they will enjoy the game. It is so very easy to lose the actors' interest simply by giving bland descriptions.

You may be running a premade episode, or you may have written down some of your descriptions prior to the session. Resist the temptation just to read the descriptions verbatim. If you read them, you are almost guaranteed to lose their interest.

You should have already become familiar with all the written descriptions. When it comes time to describe a scene, reread the description silently to yourself. Then, describe it in your own words, without consulting with the written description.

Don't Over-Describe

In some roleplaying games, it is good to describe the scene in vivid detail, so that the actors get a complete view of their whole surroundings.

This is *not* a good idea when running a TV show.

The sets of a television show are not detailed. They contain only what is necessary to drive the plot. You must do the same. In your head, you may envision this beautiful scene that is rich with detail. You may have pictured some details that you would love to describe to the actors that really have no bearing to the plot of the show.

You must be careful not to describe too much. Not only does it break the TV atmosphere, but it also can bore the actors. After all, it is possible that they don't think all those details are as great as you do. Focus only on what is necessary for the scene, and it will run more smoothly.

Reining in your descriptions will also have the benefit of keeping your sessions down to a reasonable amount of time.

Director Theatrics

Build atmosphere when you describe a scene. You can do it partly in your choice of words, but mostly by the delivery. In a horror game, I once saw a Director stalking around the table, describing the scene as he did so. When one character heard a quiet noise, he would stop his stalking right behind the character's actor. Then, he would suddenly lean forward and whisper into his right ear, "You think your hear something off to the right. Sort of a little click, click, clitty-click (he would make this as a sound effect) on the rocks nearby. You can't see anything moving. It's all very dark." Then he'd shrug and stand up, and give a dismissing wave of his hand. He'd begin stalking again, and as he walked away, he said, "Ah, it was probably just a mouse. Yeah, that's it. Gotta be a mouse." The actor was left with a vivid image of what the Director described. He later said that as the Director was whispering to him, he was completely unaware of everyone else in the room, and could actually see the scene in his mind. He also had the same sense of foreboding and tension that the character had.

Feel free to get up and move around. Act out some of your supporting characters in a more physical way than the other actors. When a supporting character approaches a leading character, you do just that. Walk right up to him, put your hand on his shoulder and say, and speak to him.

Personal Perspective

When you describe what a particular character sees, do it through that character's perspective. How would describe the sound of the slow dripping of blood to a character who has not yet seen the blood? It all depends on the character's personality. Whenever you hear a sound that you cannot immediately identify, you instinctively fit the sound to something that is well known to you. If the character you are describing it to has a drinking problem, you might describe the rather thick drips of blood as "like good vodka dripping from the bottle."

Resolving Actions

After you have described a scene, the cast is going to act. They will talk to each other, they will talk to supporting characters, and they will tell the Director what

Acting

actions they are taking. It is now time to take off the storyteller's hat and put on the referee hat. It is your job to decide the outcome of every action the cast takes.

Difficulty Levels

Whenever an actor rolls the dice, you must decide on a Difficulty Level. As described in Chapter Six: Filming, the Difficulty Level is the level that the actor must roll for his test in order to succeed. You should decide on the Difficulty Level before the dice are rolled, so that you will not be biased by the results. Of course, if the roll is a contested test, then the Difficulty Level is merely the results of someone else's dice roll.

Be fair when deciding on Difficulty Levels. Base them on how tough you believe the task to be. Keep in mind, though, that there is no fun in always making the tests too easy or too difficult. Having some tests be extremely difficult is okay now and then, but you do not want frustrated players on your hands. In contrast, you do not want them bored. Picking good Difficulty Levels is a skill that may take some refining throughout your career as a Director.

Director's Discretion

Sometimes it just seems appropriate for theatrical effect to make a particular test succeed of fail, no matter what the result of the dice roll is. This is perfectly acceptable behavior for a Director, as long as you follow two important rules. First, do not make it obvious that you are doing this. It could take away some of the fun from the actor who just rolled, and it may give away your intentions, which is never good. Second, do not make a habit of it. It is perfectly normal to ignore the results of a dice roll occasionally for dramatic effect. However, if you find yourself doing a lot, then you are taking much of the control the actors have over the situation away from them.

Secret Tests

Sometimes you need a leading character to make a test for something that he will not be aware of if the test fails. For instance, if the cast is being followed, you may need them to make Notice skill tests to discover their shadow. If you announce that everyone needs to make a Notice test, all of the actors will suddenly be aware that something is going on around them and they will be likely to metagame. You have copies of everyone's character sheet, so you can make the rolls for them.

You have the right to make trait tests on behalf of the actors whenever a situation like this arises. This way, if their tests fail, you can simply not describe it to the actors and they will be none the wiser.

Here is a good trick: Every now and then, roll the dice as though you are making a secret roll even though there is no real need to do so. This will add enough randomness to make it impossible for them to assume that something is going to happen just because you rolled the dice.

One last word about secret tests: do not go overboard. Only make secret tests when the situation calls for it. If there is no harm in having the actors roll, then let them. After all, the characters belong to them, and they have a right to make those rolls themselves.

Commercial Breaks

You are probably laughing right now at the notion of including commercial breaks in your game. Well, you should; it is funny. However, there is some logic behind it. A lot of thought goes into deciding just when to break for commercials. Therefore, you should give game breaks just as much thought.

Most TV shows take four or five commercial breaks. Each break happens between the acts. This is because each act handles a certain phase of the episode, and there is a natural pause between them as one act resolves and the next begins. Since your episodes will also have acts, it is a good idea to follow the same format. Bathroom breaks, ordering food, and other such activities can really kill the momentum of your episode if you allow them to happen at any time.

So, tell everyone that you will all be taking breaks at certain key points during the course of the session, and that you would like the game to run uninterrupted until each break. Of course, if someone really needs to leave for any reason, he can. You should stress that any unnecessary breaks must happen during the scheduled breaks.

Acting

Another important hat that the Director must wear is that of the actor. In fact, the Director has the most intense acting job of the whole game, for he must play the parts of every supporting character in the show. This section will offer some advice that may help you get into your parts, and keep the actors in theirs.

Playing Supporting Characters

The supporting cast is the key to a successful TV episode. Since television shows focus more on the interactions and relationships of the characters, it is vitally important that the entire cast be well-developed and fun to deal with. The dialogue between the leading and supporting cast must be fun. The actors should be inspired to have full conversations with the supporting cast.

You must treat each supporting character as if it were a leading role. Nothing can kill an episode quicker than a flat and lifeless supporting cast. They must all be interesting in their own ways. Watch a few episodes of your favorite show, and pay close to each supporting character. You will find that even the most insignificant character has something about him that makes it fun to watch the stars interact with him.

Acting

Handling Accents

Using a flavored accent can add a lot to the charm and atmosphere of the setting. However, not everyone can do a good job of imitating an accent. If you cannot adequately use a particular accent, then you are better off to drop it completely than to try and fail. A bad accent can distract from the game.

Co-Directing

If you are running a show that has a large number of supporting characters, you could opt to have another person help you direct. This other person will only wear the actor's hat, and will play some or all of the supporting roles. Of course, this means that she will need to be privy to at least some of what you know about the episode. This is why she is a Co-director. She must know about the episode in order to play the roles in a way that would be beneficial to the story.

Co-directing is an effort in teamwork. You and your co-director must work as a team to run the game. You must divide the responsibilities, and then work together to pull it off. The benefits can be enormous, though, as one Director can focus fully on roleplaying the supporting cast, and the other can focus on the other many tasks of directing. This means that the supporting cast will get the attention they deserve, which is important.

Co-directing is not always necessary, and can sometimes be more of a burden than a bonus. If you have only a few supporting characters, and the episode is rather short, there will be no need for a co-director. In a case like that, the effort of coordinating your efforts may outweigh the benefits you would get from it.

Maintaining Balance

Sometimes you may find that the characters fall out of balance during the course of the episode. This could happen because a character finds a special item or artifact that gives him powers that far exceeds that of the others. It could happen because the actor is power gaming, and has become more powerful than you had thought he would be. Whatever the case, you will need to take steps to ensure that all the characters are in balance with each other.

Earned Faults

One way that you can fix an unbalanced character during the game is by having him gain a new fault. You would have to find a way to introduce the fault in the story of the episode, so that it makes sense. This is a great way to do it, because it adds plenty of roleplaying opportunities and can add to the fun of the game.

Acting

Directing

Level with the Actor

Sometimes there is just no good way to add balance to a character in-game. In these cases, you may just need to take the actor aside and discuss the problem with him. He should understand, and the two of you can work out a solution. Always remember that you are the boss. If he pushes back and is unwilling to compromise, you must make the decision yourself. An unbalanced character can ruin the game for everyone, so you must resolve these situations when they happen. This is why it is so important to review each character before allowing him into the game.

Leading vs. Supporting Cast

Sometimes you may find that the leading cast is not powerful enough to defeat the nemesis, or an incidental character is in danger of defeating a leading character. You always must take care to ensure that the supporting cast is not too powerful. However, no matter how well you prepare, you will still sometimes have this situation.

Fixing balancing issues between the leading and supporting cast is rather easy. This is because you do not have any actors playing the supporting roles, so you can change them at will without anyone knowing. You should just be careful not to change anything about a supporting character that the actors have already seen or experienced. This could cause continuity problems that can confuse or annoy the actors.

Power Gaming

There are actors who study the game system rules in search of ways to make their characters overly powerful without breaking any of the rules. If there are any holes in the game system that can allow a character to be unbalanced at creation time, these actors will find them and exploit them. They often pride themselves on their ingenuity, and brag about how clever they were. Their primary goal, however, is to have the most powerful character in the game.

People call these actors power gamers. Power gamers quickly gain this reputation, so you probably already know which people in your group are power gamers. Pay close attention to balance when reviewing their characters. The problem with power gamers is that although their characters are usually unbalanced and unacceptable in your game, they have not broken any rules. Therefore, you must be understanding when you have him fix his character. You can congratulate him for his cleverness, but then tell him that the character will not work in your game as is.

Resolving Disputes

It is almost inevitable with a large group that disputes may arise regarding the game system. Often, the disputes are between actors, but sometimes they can direct them at you. This is when you put on your referee hat, and arbitrate the dispute.

Of course, you are the boss, and in the end, you make the final decisions. The problem is that you do not want anyone to be angry or resentful. Try to resolve the disputes in a way that they all can live with. It is times like this where *Now Playing*'s flexibility can be its downfall. There are people who memorize the rules and call them out whenever someone deviates from them. What you must stress to these people is that the rules of *Now Playing* are not set in stone. They are given mostly as a guideline, and can be adapted as needed to suit your game. Explain this to them. It may be all you need to do. Sometimes, however, you may find it beneficial to formalize some of the adjustments you make to the rules so that everyone understands and accepts them.

Awarding Luck Points

At the beginning of every session, every character has a certain number of Luck Points. Most characters start with only three, but they can increase that number by taking the Lucky gift, and decrease the number by taking the Unlucky fault. These are just the number that they begin each session of the game with. During each session, you are encouraged to award the characters with additional Luck Points when an actor does something special.

There are many good reasons to award Luck Points to a character. The following are some examples of common behavior worthy of Luck Point rewards. Of course, you have complete control over the awarding of Luck Points.

Good Acting: You should reward exceptional acting with Luck Points. *Now Playing* is all about acting; it is the most important part of the game. Now, some actors always do a great job with the acting. You should not reward them for their acting, or they will end up with twenty Luck Points, or more, by the end of the session. Instead, find other ways to reward them. However, you should definitely reward an actor that is very shy and quiet when he rises to the occasion and does a good bit of acting.

Quick Thinking: Another good cause for rewards is when an actor thinks quickly in a time of crisis, and manages to succeed in a task that no one expected him to. For example, if he finds himself outnumbered and surrounded by thugs all brandishing guns, and manages to escape unharmed, he deserves a reward. In fact, I would consider him extremely lucky, so Luck Points would just make sense!

Sacrifice: If a character makes a great sacrifice to help a fellow character, his good deed may warrant a reward. Again, if this is normal behavior for that actor, then do not reward it. Only unexpected exceptional behavior deserves rewards.

Penalties

Sometimes an actor does something that is just

Acting

wrong. If he chooses to do something that his character just would not do, you can penalize him by costing him a Luck Point. Of course, you should never want to punish an actor for his behavior, but there may be times when he does something that angers the rest of the group. Costing the actor a Luck Point might be a civil way of dealing with the situation.

Balancing Luck

The problem with awarding Luck Points to the leading characters is that it gives them an extra advantage over the supporting cast, and can greatly unbalance the game. There is a nice way to help maintain that balance.

You can keep a pool of Luck Points for the entire supporting cast. Every time a leading character spends a Luck Point, it does not go away, but instead goes into your Luck Pool. Whenever you want, you can spend Luck Points out of this pool for any supporting character. This can make the leading cast think twice before using their Luck Points.

Challenges of Directing

There are many challenges that you must face when directing a *Now Playing* game. This section will discuss some of these challenges and offer advice on how to deal with them.

Everyone's a Star

Most TV shows star only one or two characters. However, a roleplaying game usually needs four or more starring roles, because that is how many actors you have in your game. You must remember that every character portrayed by an actor is a starring role and must share the limelight with all the others. This can pose a special challenge because if you are not careful, the game will lose that TV feel. This section will describe several ways to work around this issue without losing the feel of your TV show.

Alternating Stars

Some TV series' have a large cast of leading characters. They handle this same issue by alternating starring roles. For instance, one episode will focus on three specific leading characters, and the others take a supporting role. In the next episode, two or three different leading characters take the focus. This will continue throughout the course of the season.

The important thing to note here is that although the story of the episode focuses on only a couple cast members, the supporting characters can still have much to do.

This method can work in *Now Playing* only if the actors do not mind taking a supporting role on occasion. Not all people are going to like this idea, so you would need to discuss this with the actors before taking this approach.

Multiple Plots

This approach is common among crime dramas and medical dramas. A crime drama may have six or seven leading roles. Teams of two or three detectives each investigate a different crime. Sometimes the crimes have some crossover, where both crimes are related. This can cause the teams to work together on occasion to solve their crimes.

When handling this kind of show, you must frequently cut between plots so that no one has to sit out for long.

Controlling the Flow

The most important single rule you can learn about Directing a roleplaying game is: **You cannot directly control the flow of a roleplaying game.**

In television, the director has complete control over the flow of the story. She can call "cut" as soon as she sees anything happen that she does not like. After all, she can always call for another take until they get it right. This makes perfect sense for a television show.

This, however, is not television. The goal of *Now Playing* is to reproduce the feel of a TV show, but it does not want to reproduce the feel of *filming* a TV show. Every scene in a roleplaying game can only be done in one take. You can never call "cut." Once the actors have played out the scene, it is done, no matter how they did it. I know how it can feel to have worked hard on a story for your episode and then find the actors handle it differently than you had envisioned it. It can be tough, but you have to learn to deal with it—or better yet, to enjoy it!

You have to understand that the actors are playing their roles the way that they feel is appropriate or fun. If you start telling them what to do, they will no longer be having fun, and they will want to quit. You must give them that freedom or the game will be a disaster.

A Touch of Subtlety

If you have never directed a roleplaying game before, you are probably shaking your head, thinking "but the story requires them to stay on track. If they go off on a tangent, the story won't work." Well, it is true that they run the risk of trashing your episode without trying. However, it is vitally important to avoid taking an adversarial posture toward your actors. The goal of *Now Playing* is for all of you to have fun. Let them have fun. There are still tricks you can play to keep them on track.

The key to maintaining control over the flow of the episode is in subtlety. Through subtle manipulation of all of your existing tools, it is quite possible to keep the actors on track without restricting their feeling of freedom. This is where the true art of directing comes into play. If you are new to directing, it may take several ses-

Acting

sions or episodes to really get the hang of it. However, if you take the advice given in this section, you will become a successful Director.

Set Goals That Engage

Set clear goals for the cast that their actors will feel strongly motivated to reach. Take notice that I said to motivate the *actors*, not just the cast. Although the actors will try to play their roles accurately, if they are not properly motivated to attain the goals you have set, they will be very likely to wander.

Make all their goals short-term. If it will take a long time for the cast to reach the nearest goal, you will most likely lose the actors' interest. If the goal is many sessions away, the actors will most likely either lose interest or get frustrated. If each goal is no more than two four-hour sessions away, the actors should not lose interest in them.

Example: In a Renaissance period game, the cast was a group of adventurers in Spain. The nearest goal that the Director had set was that one of the adventurers had inherited a castle in Germany and needed to go there to claim it. The problem was twofold: the journey to Germany would take many, many sessions; and the goal was really not very interesting to the one who received the inheritance, and not at all to those who did not. As a result, they seemed more interested in buying bulls in Spain and sending them to Russia, where two of the characters hailed from. This frustrated the poor Director to no end. Ultimately, the episode was doomed.

The "Support" in Supporting Cast

As Director, you control the supporting cast. You can use them to give the leading cast a gentle shove into the right direction when they stray from the goal. This is why they are called "supporting cast." You can use them to not only support the leading cast, but to support the storyline as well.

Example: The leading cast is made up of detectives who have been trying to track down a murderer. The detectives, however, are having trouble figuring out the clues that they have found and are getting lost in their investigation. They begin to follow leads that do not really exist. The Director decides that they need a little help, something to put them back on track. In this case, giving them more evidence or clues will be the most subtle and effective way. She knows that she can either have the murderer strike again, or have a new witness come forth. She decides that they need something exciting at this point, so the murderer is going to strike again. One witness that they had already interviewed would make sense as a next target, so that is what she does. She can be sure to leave a new useful clue at the new crime scene for the cast to find.

Manipulating Events

Sometimes if the cast has gone off on a tangent and needs a little shove in the right direction, you could create an event that will give them the inspiration they need to get back on track. Creating new clues, bringing in a new witness, and hearing rumors are all good methods of helping the cast get back on the story.

The important thing is always to maintain continuity. Do not introduce events that confuse or contradict the story. Make sure your event fits in well with the storyline and that it feels like it had been planned all along.

As Director, you cannot just suggest a course of action. Every time the Director speaks out of character, she shatters the atmosphere and tension of the scene. You can only interact with the cast through your supporting cast.

Example: You are playing a cop show. The cast, two cops, are standing around the crime scene looking for more clues. They are stumped. There are, in fact, no more clues at the scene, but there are witnesses in the slummy tenement across the street that might drop more clues. The problem is that the actors do not even think to go door-to-door asking questions. Therefore, you decide to have one of the witnesses leave the building and get noticed. You describe the following: "Bob, frustrated at not finding any more clues, you glance around you and your eye rests on someone. A young man, probably in his early twenties, is standing on the sidewalk just outside the door to the tenement across the street. He is staring right at you. When your eyes meet, he stands still as stone, looking very nervous. Then, he drops the box of cigarettes he was holding and bolts into a run down the road." The Director decides to have any chase end with the witness going around to the back of the building and trying to climb the fire escape and back into the building through a window. This will result in the cops catching this witness and potentially having to deal with others as well.

Director Theatrics

Good storytelling can be as much a physical act as it is verbal. You can stalk around the table, allowing yourself to use more of your body in acting out your roles. If you pace around the table as though there were no reason, it puts you in a great position to surprise the actors at crucial moments. In a suspenseful moment, you can have a supporting character sneak up on a leading character and surprise him. And, of course, you can do it for real!

Example: In an episode of a horror show, two characters were trudging through hip-deep water in a sewer. They were trying to escape one or more bizarre creatures that they could hear following them. The suspense was mounting. The Director accidentally dropped her pen, which bounced under the table. She went down to get it, and grabbed one of the actors' legs and yanked him suddenly under the table. The actor screamed, and when they were both face to face under the table, the Director described the creature that just pulled him under the water.

Acting

Metagaming

It is almost unavoidable that the actors are going to learn details about the events in the game of which their characters are not aware. Metagaming is when the actor takes advantage of this information, and adjusts the behavior of his character based on that information. Most actors do not mean to metagame. However, it is hard to pretend you do not know something that you really do, and it can be even harder to keep track of what your character does and does not know.

This means that from time to time, your actors are going to metagame, whether they mean to or not. You must always assume that they did not mean to, but you should also chastise them for it. There are a number of great ways to handle this.

Whatever method you choose, you should announce your intention to the actors before you begin the game.

Simple Reminder

You could just remind the actor that he is metagaming, and perhaps make him change his actions if they do not coincide with his character's knowledge. After all, why punish a person if you do not need to?

Lost Luck

Whenever someone is caught metagaming, you will take one Luck Point away from the offending character, and add it to the supporting cast's Luck Pool. You will be surprised how quickly everyone will pay close attention to what they are doing!

Bad Luck

Cause the offending character to fall into a bad situation by seemingly bad luck. For instance, if the offending character is sneaking in the enemy's lair shortly after his actor metagames, you can simply have him trip at the wrong moment, step on a loud branch, or trip a motion sensor. Now his cover is blown and he is in trouble!

Distractions & Tangents

Just about all gaming groups suffer from this. Clearly, any group where the members are friends will have the temptation to chat and converse about out-of-game topics. This has been one of my greatest challenges as both a Director and an actor.

The solution to distractions is mostly a simple force of will. Whenever you realize that you have been distracted, stop whatever it was you were doing and immediately get back to the game. If you see others being distracted, you can switch the action to their characters. Engaging them in some kind of action or in-game activity is the best way to end a tangent.

Tempo

Keep the tempo of the game fast. If the cast is separated, do not spend too much time with one group. Switch scenes frequently so that everyone remains active.

Immersion

Use the Director Theatrics described above to immerse the actors-and yourself-in the story. This keeps everyone focused on the game, and eliminates most distractions.

The "Support" in Supporting Cast

The supporting characters are not stars. You must never let them shine or save the day. If you ever see a supporting character outshine a leading character, you have a problem. There is nothing that will frustrate the actors more than to be one-upped by the supporting cast.

No Director ever wants this to happen, but it does. The following are two examples of how this can happen.

Director Pride

You usually create your supporting cast yourself. Quite often, you will be especially proud of one of the characters. Roleplaying this character will be so fun, that you may start to treat her like a leading character. This is fine, as long as you remember to show restraint when the climax comes. However, it is all too easy to go overboard and steal the limelight at a crucial moment.

The following example is true story:

Example: In a Renaissance swashbuckler show, the leading cast had come to an old abandoned port town where they knew their pirate nemesis had his secret base. One of their men, a supporting character, had been kidnapped by their nemesis, and was being held in one of the buildings. The cast split up to find him. One leading character found their friend and fought a duel with the nemesis. The fight was going badly, but all was not lost. The actor had some tricks up his sleeves that he had not yet used. However, the Director had not been able to roleplay his favorite character for two sessions, as he had been kidnapped. He was anxious to play the character, and when he saw his chance, he took it. His favorite supporting character managed to escape his bonds, grab the pirate's flintlock pistol and shot him in the head.

The actor's excitement deflated. He was angry. He yelled at the Director. Unfortunately, the angry actor was quite justified. The Director had overstepped his bounds, and had his favorite supporting character save the day, just as the true star of the show was about to do his final trick and dispatch his greatest enemy! The Director tried to fix his mistake by having the pirate survive with a deformed face, and have him come back with a vengeance. Luckily, the actors were satisfied with this and the game continued. He also apologized, which helped.

Acting

Unbalanced Game

The game has been running for a while already, and you suddenly realize that the leading cast is greatly inadequate for dealing with the nemesis. The cast already knows how powerful the nemesis is. You will throw out all continuity if you make such a drastic change at this stage of the game. Your options are limited at this point.

The following example is a true story that describes the wrong way to handle this situation:

Example: In a modern-day occult thriller, the cast has been trying to solve the mystery behind a series of kidnappings and murders. The cast is made up of young occult practitioners, and they have discovered that the serial killer is himself an occultist. They continue their hunt for the killer, and find out that he is extremely old and powerful. The actors and Director realize that they are out of their league. The Director decides to solve the problem by introducing several new supporting characters who are all powerful occultists. They have the power to stop the killer. At this point, the leading cast inadvertently takes a more supporting role as they become dependent on the new characters.

He could have let the cast discover some ancient tome that has a spell that they could use against him. He could also have introduced a magical artifact that could have helped the cast destroy him. In any event, he could have solved this problem by much nicer methods. Instead, he introduced powerful supporting characters that dwarfed the leading cast, which made them feel useless.

Ending the Session

Ending the session on a good note is tremendously important. The final scene of the session is the one that makes the most lasting impression, so you want it to be big. You also want to prepare them for the next session, especially if the session did not end the episode.

The Climax

You always want to end the session on a climactic point. It should be a high-action, high-energy scene that really gets them going. You want the actors to look forward to the next session, and a climax is the only way to make that happen. In addition, the only time a TV show does not end on a climax is when the story ends on the episode, and then it ends with a short tag after the final climax scene. In all cases, the climax was either the final scene, or right before it.

Cliffhangers

If this is not the final session of the episode, you should definitely end on a cliffhanger. Think about all of the two-part TV episodes you have seen in your life. How many of them did not end on a cliffhanger? I will bet the answer is very few, and those that do, you cannot remember. Cliffhangers in your sessions have the same effect on your actors as TV cliffhangers do with their audiences.

Ending with the Act

You will want to end your session at the closing of an act. This will create a sense of closure that is necessary for your session. You want the cast to leave the game feeling they made progress. If they are still in the middle of things, they may not have that feeling. In addition, by putting such a long break in the middle of an act, you will destroy the momentum that the act was trying to build. Close the show at the end of an act even if it means ending the game a half-hour early. You can use that time to talk and socialize, and even to prepare for the next session.

Awarding Experience Points

Award experience points to the cast. Collect the notes from the scribe, and use those to help you if you need them. The actors will want this as a sign of progress.

Do not be too free with experience points. Keep in mind that it only takes one EP to raise a trait from Poor to Terrible, and two to raise it from Fair to Good. You should not give out more than three EP to any one character in a session. The following table could help you figure out how to distribute EP:

Experience Point Awards	
EP	Accomplishments
1	Participated in the session.
2	Character performed moderate use of skills and abilities.
3	Character made extensive use of skills and abilities in difficult and even dangerous situations.

Scenes from Next Week

You can give the actors a basic idea of what to expect for next week. Of course, you do not want to give any important details away, but if you can give a brief sales pitch of the next session without doing that, it would be good.

What Does the Cast Plan To Do?

Find out what the actors plan to do in the next session. Write them down in your notes. You can use that information to help you plan for the next session.

Screenwriting

Scene 1 Shows

Scene 2 Writing Episodes

    Dr. Steve Stone stopped in his tracks and stared in amazement at what lay before him. He had been squeezing down short, narrow passages ever since he and his companions had entered the ancient Egyptian tomb. Now, he suddenly found himself standing in the entrance to a chamber, and he stood in awe as he surveyed the room. It was approximately ten feet square with another passageway opposite him. The walls were covered with hieroglyphics and other ancient Egyptian pictures. But it was the sarcophagi in the center of the room that held his attention. There were three of them, sitting side by side in the center of the room with their feet pointing toward them. They were made of gold, and were elaborately decorated. Stone guessed that it was the lost Pharaoh and his wife and son. This will be a find for the history books, he thought as he entered the room, gesturing for his companions to follow.

    "Careful," whispered Dr. Edward Talis, his most trusted colleague, and doctor of archaeology back at Harvard. "The place is most likely booby-trapped." He motioned toward the floor. "See the bones. Something killed these people before they could defile the sarcophagi." Stone and Talis knelt and studied the floor, while Catherine Plummer, an archaeology student from Talis' class, examined the walls. At length, Stone shook his head. "I see nothing to account for these bones. My guess is they were trapped when the entrance was blocked."

    "The hieroglyphs talk about a curse," Plummer said, running her hands gently over the glyphs. "It says that death will come to all who dare to desecrate the tomb."

Screenwriting

Stone waved a hand in dismissal. "They all say that, but it's hogwash. Come on, let's check out the sarcophagi." He stepped up to the nearest sarcophagus, and a rock slab under his foot slid downward ever so slightly. At that moment, a large rock slab slid down from its hiding place in the ceiling to completely seal the doorway they had entered from. Another slab slid down the other entrance, but stopped short about three feet from the bottom, stuck on some debris. They could hear some rumbling in the walls, followed by a hiss of escaping air. They all looked around wildly, wondering what was happening. Suddenly, snakes began pouring out of small holes in the walls. There were hundreds of them, and they were all racing toward them.

"Run!" shouted Talis, and he bolted for the jammed doorway. They all hurriedly crawled under the slab and ran up the passage. Catherine had to leave her bag behind in her hurry to leave the room. They ran up the passage as quickly as they could, the snakes in hot pursuit. As they ran, they could see three-foot wide shafts spaced evenly along the walls, three feet above the floor. "What are those for?" Catherine puffed as they ran, but no one answered.

Up ahead, Stone could now see a doorway at the end of the passageway. It looked inviting, and he wondered briefly if it could give them any escape from the snakes. He stopped suddenly, and Catherine almost ran into him. Talis heard them and stopped, turning around. "What is it, Dr. Stone?"

Stone shook his head. "I don't know. I just don't like it." He looked down the hall at the approaching snakes. "The room looks too inviting. I think it's a trap."

"Then what do we do?" Catherine asked, staring nervously at the slithering mass that was working its way up the passage toward them. "We can't go back, and we can't kill them all."

Stone looked at one of the shafts. "I don't think they can reach these shafts. It's our only chance!" With that, he grabbed the lip of the nearest shaft, hoisted himself up, and slid down, feet first.

"You idiot!" shouted Talis, but he saw no alternative. He helped Catherine climb in, and then slid down after her.

***

When the three archaeologists landed, they all looked around, their jaws hanging in disbelief. What they saw was not only completely unexpected, but unbelievable as well. The place was filled with whiteness, as far as the eye could see. There were no structures, walls, or anything here. Simply nothingness. Above them, they could see the opening to the shaft, framed in white emptiness. Stone wondered if he was in heaven.

Someone else was here. Standing about ten feet from them was a young man, approximately eighteen years old. He was dressed in jeans, and wore a t-shirt that sported a fiery dragon. He was tall and thin with shaggy black hair. He was facing them with a puzzled, and slightly frustrated look on his face. He ran his hand through his hair absently as he stared at the adventurers, bent in thought, as Stone and the others stood up. "Where are we?" Catherine asked, but the young man ignored her.

Suddenly, he grinned. "I've got it!" he shouted, looking altogether pleased with himself. "All right, I know what I'm doing." He lifted a tome from the whiteness by his feet, and flipped through it until he found the page he was seeking. He turned his back on the others and began to chant in an unintelligible language. At one point, he stooped and rolled four small cubes on the floor. Each one had markings on them. He examined the results of his roll, and continued his chanting.

The others suddenly became aware of a change in the scenery. The whiteness was fading, and in its place was the jagged brown of a natural cave. The light faded until the only illumination came from the electric lantern that Talis held. As the cave solidified and became whole, the young man faded until he was gone completely.

They were now in a subterranean cave. Stalagmites and stalactites riddled the chamber and their voices echoed. One rough passage led away from here.

Stone cleared his throat and shook his head, then said, "Well, I guess we go through there," and he began marching toward the passage...

Shows

Chapter 8

Screenwriting

The Show

In *Now Playing*, the show represents the setting of your game. In roleplaying game terms, this is your campaign setting. The show defines the world and environment in which the episodes are run. It describes the atmosphere of the show and its mood. It decides if the show is a serious drama, a science fiction show, a cop show, or whatever. It also defines any plot that may exist for the show. This could include a timeline of events, a history, and special information that the cast members will know.

There is more to creating a show for *Now Playing* than is normal in other roleplaying games. There are many elements of television shows that need to be taken into consideration while designing your show. Much of what is discussed here can also be applied to existing roleplaying games in order to add that TV feel.

The rest of this chapter describes these elements and helps you put them all together to create your show.

The Formats

Almost all shows you see on television today fit into one of a few established formulas or formats. These formats dictate the focus of the show, the atmosphere and even the duration of its episodes. The format is the most basic element of a show, and is the first decision you must make when creating your own. The following formats are currently in use today:

Thirty Minute Comedy

These shows get their name from the length that they run on TV. The most common of these are the Situation Comedy, or "sitcom." These rely almost completely on character interaction, and usually have almost no action. In each episode, the characters are thrown into a sticky, and potentially embarrassing, social situation, and they have to find a way out.

Structure

These comedies are short, running for thirty minutes on TV. An episode is made of two acts with optionally a teaser, or tag, but usually not both. For details on acts, teasers and tags, refer to Chapter Nine: Writing Episodes.

Sixty Minute Drama

This is the most common type of show to roleplay. Several of these dramas have already been released as successful roleplaying games.

Like all shows, dramas put great emphasis on the cast. However, each episode of a drama must tell a story. Each drama may have some humor in it, but it is primarily a serious work of fiction. Each episode is sixty minutes long on TV to accommodate the larger storyline.

Structure

Each episode of a drama will have four acts plus an optional teaser and/or tag. Syndicated dramas often have five acts plus the teaser and tag to allow for more commercial breaks. Each act of the syndicated episode will, of course, be shorter since the shows run the same length as network dramas, but with more commercial breaks.

TV Movie

The "Made for TV Movie," as it is often called, is normally a two-hour event that runs very much like a two part episodic drama. These have become quite popular, and can serve many uses, even in your game. Many networks use the TV movie as a means of testing the popularity of a show. If the movie is a success, then they are justified in starting a series. You can do the same for your game. If there is a show that you think would make a great RPG, but you are not sure if your gaming group will get into it, work it up as a TV movie and run a big one-time event. If they love it, go ahead and plan a season of episodes. If not, move on to the next show idea.

Structure

Because this works pretty much as an episodic drama that is twice as long, the TV movie should have eight acts with a teaser and a tag. The tag is important in the movie, because you must assume that there will be no sequels. You will need the opportunity to wrap the show up nicely and provide closure. Of course, you should be careful not to eliminate the possibility of a sequel, unless you are one hundred percent certain that you will not want to continue the show.

Reality Shows

Reality shows can be tricky. Some of these shows that have been aired on television do not have any discernable plot and would not work well as a roleplaying game. However, some reality shows would work out well, and of course, you can always invent your own.

A good example of a reality show that could be a fun roleplay, would be one where a group of normal people is left on a deserted island with a small amount of supplies. They are given a goal, something that they must accomplish, and they have to learn to work together to succeed.

An example of a reality show that would not work is where each contestant is subjected to some kind of stimulus and he must deal with it or lose. Although technically, you can play this type of show, it would involve almost no actual roleplaying, and will therefore be quite boring.

Screenwriting

The difference between the two examples is that the former can actually have a story and character interaction, where the latter has neither.

Structure

If you want to run a reality show, structure it like an episodic drama. Give it four acts and perhaps a teaser and almost definitely a tag to sum up.

The Serial

A serial is a show that tells one big story. Each episode can equate to a chapter in the story. Most shows are a standard series, where each episode is a self-contained story. There is no overall story that ties the episodes together. In this way, you can play the episodes in any order that you want, without worrying too much about the continuity of the show.

Like a standard series, each episode of a serial must be a short, self-contained story that has its own beginning, middle and end. However, many of the episodes will help to tell part of the main story and keep it moving throughout the season. Because of this, you need to plan a serial out in some detail to make certain that the story always progresses.

Adapting a Real Show

Turning a real TV show into a roleplaying is generally not hard. The trick is to take a show that was designed around a specific storyline and cast of characters and make it work with new characters and perhaps a new storyline. This section will point out some challenges that you will face and offer some solutions.

Well-Known Storylines

This is a concern for anyone who is trying to run a serial with *Now Playing*. The problem with this is that most of the people who will play your show will already be familiar with the story that the real show has told. This will take away all of the mystery and freshness from your game. If you run a show that tries to follow the same storyline, two things will happen. There is always at least one critic in the group who will complain about every plot point. The second is that your show will almost immediately deviate from the storyline and take you in a direction that the story may not be prepared to support. There are two solutions to this problem, as described below.

Vary the Story

If you really like the story, then keep it. However, you should intentionally change the story so that even those who have watched the entire series will have no idea what is going to happen next. Also, tell the actors that you did this. By modifying the storyline, you will have made it your own and it will, therefore, not be bound by the continuity of the original story. Now if anyone tries to poke holes in the story, you can say "but this isn't that story!"

Make a Spin-Off

Throw out the story that has already happened and make your own. It's possible that you could assume that the events in the original story have taken place, and that your show is starting where the other left off. Alternatively, you could simply say that the other show never happened, and start fresh.

Creating your own storyline is arguably the best thing you can do. This gives your nearly full control over the show and lets you be as creative as you want. This also means that your actors will have absolutely no clue as to what is going to happen. The only limitation you will have is that you must keep all of the setting's elements. If you don't, then you're no longer playing that show; you've created a brand new show entirely.

Changing the Cast

It is a foregone conclusion that most actors will to want to create their own characters. This holds just as true for *Now Playing*. Of course, there are always those few actors who do not want to bother creating their own characters, but they are so rare that you should not expect to have any of them in your show. Using the original cast of the show can be great for conventions or other games when you don't want to take the time of having everyone create characters. The problem is that the actors will rarely become attached to them, and thus not play them as well as they would otherwise.

This simple fact means that you must make sure that the show you run will work with a cast that is different from the original. In addition, you must put some thought to what types of characters would work in your show. A good way to handle it is to let the actors come up with their own character concepts and then describe them to you. Consider each one in turn. Think about how you can work each character into the show. Ask yourself the following questions:

How Would You Cast Him?

Every character must have a specific role to play in the show that will make him indispensable. It must also make sense for him to be there. For instance, in a sci-fi show about the adventures of a space explorer ship, it may be very difficult to cast a thief. Although he may be useful from time to time, the Director would be hard-pressed to find a logical reason for him to be a member of the crew. However, a doctor would be very easy to cast, as every starship would need medical personnel.

This is a question that you could make the actor answer. Let him come up with a good reason for being in

Screenwriting

the show, and you decide if it makes sense.

Would He Have a Leading or Supporting Role?

Often, an actor would come up with the concept for a fascinating character that ends up having little to do in the game. Just because a character is interesting, does not mean that he will fit well in the show.

For instance, in an FPI serial that focuses on UFOs, having a character that can sense ghosts may find himself doing menial work that has nothing to do with his special abilities. Only on rare occasions would his sensitivity be of any use.

If an actor does create a very interesting character that would only be useful on occasion, you may choose to keep him as a supporting character and bring him in as a guest star.

Would He Have a Place in Every Episode?

This is actually related to the last question, but is worth asking anyway. If you cannot think of more than a few episodes in one season where the character would have a vital role, you might want to recommend that the actor make a different character. The last thing you want is for an actor to have nothing to do simply because the character is not a good fit for the show.

The Setting Elements

These are the guts of the show. Although you can play out the same cast that the real TV show features, it is always recommended that the actors create their own. Playing the real cast can be great for a one-time game, but the actors are not as likely to feel as comfortable in their roles than if they created them themselves. You could use the real cast as supporting characters. As for the storyline, you should make it your own. You can take the base storyline and modify it to fit your needs. You can also scrap the original storyline and run your own. In that case, you will be better off running your show as a spin-off.

The Concept

If you had to sum the show up in one or two sentences, that would be the concept. If the show is a serial, be very careful not to confuse the entire storyline as the concept. Generally, the concept will be much smaller and would serve as the seed for the story.

Watch the pilot episode of the show, if you can. If not, watch a few episodes of the first season understand it. If the show has a web site-and I would be surprised if it does not-go there. The home page will probably have the basic concept neatly spelled out for you.

The concept is the most basic building block of the show. Since almost every other aspect of the show will be subject to change by you, it is important that you fully understand the concept.

Example: The show FPI, which is included in this book, has the following concept: The cast are all members of a formal civilian group of people who investigate cases of the paranormal. They read or hear about UFO sightings, Bigfoot encounters, ghosts and other paranormal phenomena, and they go to investigate them. They use both scientific and spiritual means to prove the existence of these phenomena.

The World

Now that you know what the concept is, you must isolate the physical aspects of the setting. This would be to identify the time period, technology level, and the existence of anything out of the ordinary.

Example: In FPI, the world is identical to the world of today, set in modern times. The difference is that UFOs, ghosts, and mythological creatures may, in fact, really exist.

The Atmosphere

This represents the mood of the show. Is it dark and ominous, or is it light and humorous? You must identify the atmosphere of the show. It is important that all episodes of the show build the same atmosphere. Without that, there will be no sense of continuity, and the actors will feel as though each episode is a completely different game.

Research the Show

No matter how well you know the show you want to adapt, you should always do some research on it. Videotape some episodes. Then, take a notebook and pen, and watch them. Pay close attention to all the elements that have been discussed in this section, and study how they handle them. The following are some useful things to watch for:

Separation of Acts

In a one-hour episodic drama, there are usually four or five acts. Each one ends at a commercial break. Each time they return from a break, ask yourself this question: "Did they just change the focus of events in the episode?" If your answer is yes, then you probably just found the end of an act.

Count the number of acts that you find in each episode. They should always be the same. Look for patterns in the goals of the acts. As discussed in Chapter Nine: Writing Episodes, many shows follow a set formula for determining their acts. Identifying any such pattern can be helpful in creating episodes that maintain the feel of your show.

Screenwriting

Teasers and Tags

Do the episodes have teasers? Do they introduce plot or do they introduce characters? Identify whether they often involve the leading cast, and if not, think about how you can make your episodes involve the cast in the teaser without changing its atmosphere and goal.

Placement of Clues

If the show is a mystery, pay close attention to every clue that is laid out. Keep in mind that not all of the clues may be found by the cast. It is quite possible that the Director purposely left extra clues behind to help the audience solve the mystery. You should find that the best mysteries involve many small clues, rather than a few big ones.

Creating Your Own Show

Creating your own show is always much easier than adapting an existing show. This is because you do not have to study the show and learn what the Directors had done. Instead, you already know everything about your show's setting, and you just need to flesh it all out.

Your show should have all of the same elements that an existing show has. Otherwise, it will not feel like a TV show. So, go be sure to decide on a format and define any overlying story arc. Work out all of the setting elements. Define the show's concept, world and atmosphere.

Powers and Technology

Now Playing is a rather generic game, as far as setting is concerned. This means that there will sometimes be elements of your show's setting that is not fully supported by the game. However, the game system has been designed with this eventuality in mind, and it should be very simple to add any settings elements that you need. Powers and technology are two most common elements that you may need to adapt into the game system. This section will help ensure that your task is a simple one.

Powers

Chapter Two: Creating Characters tells you all of the mechanics for creating and purchasing Powers. This section will give you some tips on where to begin and how to create good, balanced Powers.

Limit the Scope

The easiest way to make a Power that is out of control is to not impose any limit on its effects. You must always ask yourself "Is there any way that he could abuse that Power?" and impose limits on the power that will prevent that abuse.

Example: The actor is creating a superhero that can change the molecular structure of objects (like turning glass to stone, wood to glass, iron to water, etc.). The Director decides that it is too powerful, and so comes up with the following restrictions:

1. He cannot make changes on an atomic level—changing coal to diamond is okay because they are both carbon-based, but steel to wood is too difficult.

2. It does not work on living tissue.

3. Determine the size of the item affected by gauging how much energy he puts into it. This results in fatigue- and thus Stamina loss. The larger the object, the longer it will take to change, and the more Stamina is lost.

Adjust the Cost

Never forget that a Power has a cost. Each Power costs two or more gifts to acquire. When you consider allowing a Power for a character, think about how much the Power is worth. The psychic ability to read a person's aura may only be worth two gifts, while the ability to plant a thought in a person's mind may be worth three or more. This means that a Power is at least twice as powerful as a gift. If the Power that the actor wants doesn't seem more powerful than most gifts, let him have it as a gift.

Remember that the more expensive a Power is, the more faults he is going to take to pay for it. That can be a good way to judge how much to charge for a Power. Is the Power really worth taking two faults for?

Technology

Science Fiction shows offer a special challenge for *Now Playing* Directors. Each show defines their own technology that will differ, at least to some degree, from those of other shows. It would be impractical, and perhaps impossible, to cover all the types of technology used in all shows in this book. However, *Now Playing* is designed to make it easy to adapt these technologies to your game. Use the following guidelines to help you adapt the technology of your show to the game system.

Vehicle Stats

Use existing vehicles as templates. In most cases, you can find a vehicle that is similar to the one you want to deal with. Keep in mind that if you are dealing only with having the vehicles interacting with other vehicles, you do not need to worry about Scale in reference to humans. For instance, when dealing with aerial combat, set the most common size of aircraft to Scale 0, and then work from there. In most cases, all the aircraft would have the same scale, and would only differ in the normal Attributes. The trick is that they only need to differ from each other, and not be based on humans.

Example: You are creating two space fighter ships for

Screenwriting

your sci-fi show. These crafts will only fight each other and other spaceships, and will never attack a human directly, nor a traditional aircraft. The Director decides that she might as well use the Jet Fighter in the Props chapter as one of the spaceships, and then modify its Acceleration and Handling stats slightly for the other ship.

Large Ships

Large ships must be treated in two ways, depending on if you are handling combat or regular navigation and use. This section will discuss the latter.

You usually do not need to do anything special for the normal operation of a ship. When the cast is operating a ship and are just setting course and doing ordinary tasks, no game system traits—Attributes, Gifts, Faults, etc.—are necessary. In fact, unless the cast is trying to do something tricky or dangerous, no skill tests should even be required.

Example: Lt. Green is the navigator of a large starship. He is told to set a course for Alpha Centauri. Since that star system is on all of the star charts, he does not need to make any Navigation skill tests to succeed. However, if he must manually navigate his way through an asteroid field, then he should make many Navigation or even Pilot skill tests.

Large Ship Combat

Watch a episode of a sci-fi show that focuses on the crew of a starship. Pay close attention to how they handle starship combat. What you will notice is that they do not put much emphasis on details of the starships themselves. That is, they do not care about any differences in the speed, handling or acceleration of the ships. They may care about the maximum speeds, and on the number and power of the weapons and defenses, but that is about it.

If you treat large ships in your show the same way, you do not need to put much thought into defining the ship's Attributes. Simply choose a Strength trait for your weapons, and a Defensive Factor for them to represent how much punishment they can soak without suffering damage. Also, if the ship has some kind of shielding, define that Defensive Factor as well.

Deciding on the Strength of a weapon can be simple. Just decide how many hits it would take to breach the hull of the ship. The hull will have its own Wounds. Consider a Hull Wound of Incapacitated as a breach. This would mean that if the hull sustains 7 or 8 points of damage, after subtracting your Defensive Factors, it has been breached.

Record Wounds for specific parts of the ship. (i.e., each main weapon battery, engines, hull, etc.). That way, during combat, you can handle attacks to specific ship systems.

See the full-page starship combat example as an illustration of how this works.

Weapons

A very large selection of weapons is included in Chapter Five: Props. If the weapon you want is not listed there, then you can take the closest match and tweak it to your tastes. Table 5-4: Strength Modifiers for Melee Weapons, also in that chapter, gives you guidelines on how to decide on a Strength trait for your weapon.

If a weapon is ultra-powerful, you should find some kind of drawbacks to it. For instance, having a devastatingly powerful pulse cannon might require five minutes to recharge after each use, leaving the ship or character defenseless until then.

High Tech Devices

Using high tech devices will require the use of a skill. What skill to use will depend completely on the device in question. Some devices will definitely require a new skill just for using it. Others, however, should be able to use skills that already exist. For example, a futuristic portable medical scanner, if it were standard equipment for a doctor in the show, would only require a First Aid or Treat Injury skill test.

Do not forget usefulness of the Foreign Tech gift. This is a gift that most characters in a futuristic sci-fi show

Screenwriting

Example Starship Combat

SHOW: The Final Frontier   EPISODE: The Targon Encounter   SCENE: The Battle

Director: The Targon battlecruiser has dropped out of hyperspace and is approaching. It is currently 500 kilometers off your port bow.

Captain: Tactical!

Lt. Smith: <rolls Tactical Systems test> Good.

Director: The Targon ship has two forward pulse cannons, one aft pulse cannon, and one fore and aft torpedo bay. The forward cannons are located on the top and bottom of the ship can can pivot to fire in various angles. She is equipped with an energy field of unknown configuration.

Captain: Hail them.

Director: They do not respond to the hail. Lt. Smith, they are powering up their weapons.

Captain: Red Alert! Raise shields, and bring weapons online. Evasive maneuvers!

Director: <rolls Targeting skill for the Targon ship, getting a Great> Lt. Crandal, make your Navigation test.

Crandal: I'll try zig-zag downward. <rolls Poor> Darn! Poor.

Director: You fly underneath the Targon ship, but you react too slowly. A well-aimed shot from her lower cannon strikes your upper laser cannon. It takes 10 damage, minus 4 from your shields for a total of 6.

Lt. Smith: That's Incapacitated! Sir, our upper laser cannon is damaged, but still functional.

Captain: Lieutenant, fly right up at their belly, and give 'em everything you've got. Pull out of the way at the last second!

Crandal: Aye sir! <rolls Superb Navigation> Superb! I'm flying up at him.

Lt. Smith: Can I locate the weakest section of the ship's hull? <rolling Tactical Systems>

Director: The exact center of the Targon ship has the least energy shielding and is fairly narrow. They apparently put more shields around their weapons and engine systems.

Lt. Smith: I target that point and fire a steady burst from the lasers and as many torpedoes as I have time to fire right at that point! <rolls for each weapon, getting Good, Legendary, and Great>

Director: <rolls Poor Navigation for the Targon ship> Wow! All weapons hit their mark. <calculates damage> With a huge explosion and a shower of debris, the Targon ship splits in half. However, a large chunk of debris is careening toward your ship, and it's only a hundred kilometers distant!

Crandal: Yikes! <rolls Fair Navigation> Fair!

Director: You try to pull away, managing to avoid a head-on collision. However, the wreckage strikes the main hull with great force and slides down the length of the ship.

Crandal: I'll blow all my Luck points to have it avoid the engines, if you'll let me!

Director: You now have no more Luck. The wreckage strikes the aft cannon and caroms off to float harmlessly into space. <Calculates damage> However, the hull takes 6 points of damage and the aft laser takes 8. <This is a Severe Wound and an Incapacitated>

Lt. Smith: Sir, our hull has suffered severe damage, and our aft cannon is offline. Looking for hull breaches now <looks enquiringly at the Director>.

Director: <Shakes head> None.

Lt. Smith: Whew! No breaches. All other systems functional.

Captain: Bring us about. Hail the Targon vessel.

Director: This time, they respond. Audio only.

Captain: Targon vessel. This is Captain Horatio Edwards of the starship Excalibur. Disarm your weapons, lower what shields you have left, and prepare to be boarded.

Screenwriting

have. It gives them the ability to pilot an alien spacecraft, fire alien weapons, and so on.

The Cast

The Leading Cast

The Leading Cast is the group of characters that the actors play. They are almost never created just for one or two episodes. They are an integral part of the show. Because of this, they will have a tremendous impact on the atmosphere and feel of the show. You must make sure that each cast member fits nicely in the setting of your show. Of course, you should always let the actors create their own characters, but you still have the final word as to whether the character will work in the show or not.

Everyone's a Star

Most TV shows have a leading cast of only a few characters. However, most gaming groups have up to six or more actors. This means that you may need to adjust the setting of your show to allow more leading characters. The danger in this, of course, is that if you are not careful, some of the characters may end up in a supporting role. You must remember that everyone in the game is a star, and therefore must have a strong role.

There are some creative ways around this. You can have more than one plot in each episode, with two groups of characters working each plot simultaneously. You can cut back and forth between the two, thus keeping them all busy and ensuring that they are all in the limelight.

Another method is to let some of the characters play strong supporting roles. Some actors would love to try out a different character each time. This way, an actor can play a guest star that appears either in only one episode, or occasionally throughout the season.

The Supporting Cast

There are three types of supporting roles in a TV show. One is the regular character that appears in most episodes, but never takes center stage. He is the police commissioner who always chews out the stars for their reckless behavior, or the wise guy co-worker who is always cracking jokes. These characters support the show, by adding some dynamics to the setting.

The other type of supporting role is the short timer. This character only appears in one episode. He is there strictly to support the plot of the episode and to give someone for the leading cast to work off.

The third role is the regular guest star. He can be either a strong character that helps drive the plot forward, or a incidental character that adds flavor or helps in some small way. The strong character could be the mysterious woman who hires the private eye to find out what her husband is doing. She spends a lot of time with the character and acts as the private eye's partner for the episode. The incidental character could be the druggy snitch that the cops come to for information.

Whatever the role, the supporting characters must be colorful, because they add spice to the show and give wonderful roleplaying opportunities. Define their personality, and even build a bit of background to them. Give the actors a sheet of paper that describes everything they know about these characters. Even describe one or two events that involved the character and one of the leading cast members. This can give the actor something to work with when roleplaying scenes with him.

The Nemesis

The nemesis or archenemy is a very important character, and is not like any of the other supporting roles. He must be a complete and fully defined character, as much so as the leading cast. After all, he's the stars' alter ego, and must be formidable. The scenes where they face off must be spectacular, and they will never be if you don't put much effort into him. Do not think of the nemesis as a supporting role. He's a starring role that the Director happens to play! Of course, as colorful as he is, he must never outshine the leading cast.

Casting the Roles

Some distinct steps govern the process of casting the roles for your show. With most roleplaying games, the actors would create their characters with some guidelines given by the Director. Then, the Director would look them over and give approval. Finally, all the actors would hear about each other's character and come up with ideas on how they all know each other. This is not a formal procedure, but it is a common practice.

In *Now Playing*, you must use a more formal approach for casting in order to preserve the feel of a show.

The Character Concept

As discussed in Chapter Two: Creating Characters, the actor will come up with a concept for the character based on the description of the show's setting. This concept is the nucleus of the character; the basic idea that inspires the actor and makes him want to play it.

Background and Back Plot

Once the actor has a concept for his character, he discusses it with the Director. The actor knows the character's personality and the Director knows the show and the story, so together, they work out the character's background.

The actor only knows the basics of the setting, so

Screenwriting

there is only so much that he can come up with for the character. The Director, however, knows all the details about the setting and the story that she wants to unfold throughout the series. She can help come up with all the interesting facts about the character. Since the actor will need to roleplay it, he will need to be involved in this process to ensure that everything that is decided upon really fits how he wants the character to be portrayed.

The end result is a character that is quite detailed. He has the concept that the actor originally started with, and is embellished with lots of history and knowledge that will be indispensable when roleplaying. After all, how can you have your character speak from experience when you have no idea what experiences he has had?

Example: *The captain of a starship could be given the following information: brief history of the commands and ships he served on, first-hand information on any alien races encountered, first-hand knowledge of specific starships or of certain classes of starships, etc.*

Formal Character Creation

This step includes all of the work detailed in Chapter Two: Creating Characters. It involves purchasing all of the character's traits and filling out the character sheet. Of course, the actor should do this, and have it reviewed by the Director. The choices that the actor needs to make should be quite easy by now, since the actor knows the character so well.

Relationships

Even before the pilot episode is run, the cast of characters has a history. After all, the show does not begin with the cast's birth. Each character in the show will most likely already know about some or all of the others. It is very important to figure out exactly what kinds of relationships each character has with the others. This will, of course extend to the supporting cast as well as the leading cast. For a very small show that has a limited number of regular characters, this task would be rather simple, and would require no special techniques. It is for the more complex shows that the relationship wheel can come into play.

The Director will take the character and figure out who knows whom. Quite often, this will also be a collaborative effort between the actor and Director, but it is not always so.

The Relationship Wheel

The Relationship Wheel is a tool that you can to help figure out the relationships of the cast. It is great for helping you remain consistent for all characters. For instance, until I started using the Relationship Wheel, I would often write up relationship papers for each character that were inconsistent. That is, I would tell Jack that he has worked with Sue on several occasions, but then tell Sue that she does not know Jack. The Wheel makes it easy to keep things straight as you are developing the relationships between the cast members.

To create the wheel, focus on one character, and then follow these steps:

Step 1: On a blank sheet of paper, write the character's name in the center of the paper, and then write the names of each leading and supporting character in a circle around it.

Step 2: Pick one of the characters in the circle and figure out how he knows the one in the center. If they know each other, draw a line connecting them.

Step 3: Mark the line in a way that tells you what kind of relationship this is. For instance, for one game, you may need to distinguish between whether the characters know each other professionally, personally or by reputation only. You can do this by using different colors, putting a letter or word on the line, or however you want to mark them.

Step 4: If the center character knows the outer one, put an arrowhead on the end closest to the outer character. If the outer character knows the center one, put an arrowhead by the center character. If they both know each other, put one on both ends.

Step 3: Move to the next character and do the same.

When you have finished, you will have a complete Relationship Wheel for the center character. You will know exactly how that character knows each of the other characters in the show.

When you create the Wheel for the next character, always refer to the Wheels you've already created so that they all correspond. This is what will eliminate inconsistencies.

When you have fully completed, you can then write up a more formal description of each relationship if you so desire. In some shows, the Wheel alone may suffice. You can then hand a copy of the Wheel and descriptions to the actors, only giving each actor the Wheel for his own character. You should keep a copy of all the Wheels for herself.

Choosing a Genre

The following sections are written with creating a new show in mind. However, when adapting an existing show, you should read about that genre in order to gain some useful insight.

The rest of the sections of this chapter will describe a different genre of television drama that is ideal for roleplaying games. They will also offer tips and suggestions on how to make the games run smoothly.

Screenwriting

Shows

Action & Adventure

The Action and Adventure is a high-adrenaline show that thrusts you through a whirlwind of action and leaves you breathless when it's over. Although they also focus on the characters like all other shows, the plots have more importance.

Build the Excitement

Excitement is the primary key to an Action and Adventure show. Build the excitement quickly and keep the thrills coming throughout the episodes. Cliffhangers are your friend. Use them to good advantage. The cast should feel breathless by the end of each session.

The Archetypes

The following sections describe some of the more common formulas for action shows. You can choose on of these as a template, or create your own.

Adventure

These shows are all about people who, in one way or another, go on a perilous adventure each week, nearly losing his life in the process. Perhaps the show is about an archaeologist who is willing to take any risk to recover ancient treasures. Or perhaps it could be about an investigative reporter who will do whatever it takes to get the story. Whatever the situation, the leading cast has a certain knack for getting into trouble and has a flair for getting out of trouble in spectacular ways.

Martial Arts

Some of the best of these shows come from Hong Kong, but these days, they are everywhere. The shows center on a cast that are martial arts experts. They could be cops, mercenaries, or secret agents.

The key skill in these shows is, of course, Martial Arts. For these shows, you can choose to expand the rules for Martial Arts to add some more detail to the combat scenes. There may be some free martial arts rules for Fudge posted on the Internet that you can make use of.

Screenwriting

You can just use the existing rules for the Martial Arts skill without any problems, however. It's really up to the show you are doing and the feel you want it to have.

Superhero

These are about the wildest of all action shows, and the one that will stress the bounds of the game system to its limits. Superhero shows have many challenges to overcome when creating the characters and deciding how to handle combat. The two most important challenges are when dealing with superpowers and combat damage.

Each super hero is likely to have at least one superpower. Use the Superpower game tweak described below when to help you create your superheroes.

Most superhero shows have the heroes and archenemies taking a severe amount of damage without serious injury, even though their superpowers do not prevent it. You can do this by using the Non-Lethal Combat system combined with Fatigue to handle the heavy punishment that the superheroes take.

Westerns

The Wild West was an exciting time and place. There were Indians, outlaws, train robberies and wild animals galore. It was so dangerous out there, that it is hard to believe that we were actually able to tame it. Of course, it was people like the cast of your show who managed to tame the Wild West and bring it under control.

Adapting a western for *Now Playing* is pretty simple. You need to understand the time period, and make sure that you disallow any equipment that is out of date. However, all of the common weapons of those days are already available, and no additional traits are necessary.

Game Tweaks & Tips

Artful Dodger

Do not forget this gift. It was included in *Now Playing* specifically for shows like this. This will make a character more difficult to hit.

Luck

Distribute more Luck points. You can start the characters off with more than the standard three, or you can just be more generous when awarding them.

Wire Fu

Some martial arts shows are very theatrical. They are nicknamed Wire Fu because the characters leap inhumanly high and far while doing battle in mid-leap, and the actors wear wires to make this happen.

Allow a new gift called Wire Fu. This gift allows them to make these great leaps, and allows them only a -2 penalty to their combat while leaping. To actually perform the leap, they would simply use the Jump skill.

Superpowers

Superhero shows assume that nearly everyone has at least one superpower. By requiring the heavy cost for Powers, it severely limits all of your heroes. A minor tweak is needed to allow all characters to have superpowers without crippling them.

All characters in a superhero show gain one two-gift Power for free, in addition to the one free gift that they already get. If the character does not have a superpower, then he can split the Power into two gifts, or shift them to other traits as he wishes.

Cop Shows

A Mix of Genres

What you will find if you watch a variety of cop shows is that they are made up of a mixture of other genres. Many are action shows that focus on the crimes being committed. Some are serious dramas that focus as much on the characters as on the crime itself. Still others borrow heavily from mysteries and thrillers.

You need to fully understand which genres your show borrows from and strive to maintain that mix. Without it, you may find that you are no longer playing the show you wanted.

A Good Crime

In a cop show, you need a good crime. Of course, as you will see by the archetypes, not all cop shows revolve around a specific crime, and some do not need to be very detailed or large. On the other hand, many require a richly detailed and planned out crime, full of mystery, suspense and the potential for action. In these cases, look to the Mystery genre for ideas, and just apply them with the atmosphere of a crime drama.

The Archetypes

The following sections describe some of the more common formulas for cop shows. You can choose on of these as a template, or create your own.

The Beat

The main cast is made up of street cops or highway patrol, and the plot of each episode is to simply patrol the beat. During the course of the episode, they may respond to a handful of crimes. Most often, the individual crimes are not what are important to the episode. Instead, the

Screenwriting

episode is about the characters themselves, and some of the events that take place are designed to have an impact on something that is going on in their lives.

With this type of cop show, you have the opportunity to run a game that has no real plot, but just a collection of encounters. A liquor store robbery, a quick foot chase after a purse-snatcher, or even a gang war scene are some examples of the encounters that you can throw at the cast. In cases like these, you do not even need to focus on the cast's personalities, depending upon what the actors want.

Consider making one suspect pop up from time to time with a final standoff at the end. For instance, say the cops are highway patrol officers. They notice a big, beat-up car driving along the highway with a light out. They pull him over. A quick check with HQ shows no priors on the vehicle. As the cops walk toward the car, one of them spots something odd about the trunk. When he walks over to inspect it, the driver suddenly starts the car and peels out, bursting into traffic. The cops get back in their car and give chase, but he manages to get away. Later, they run into the car again somewhere else on their beat. After a few chases and incidents, they finally corner the suspect, only to find out that he is the guy responsible is a wanted serial killer.

This type of cop show is geared more toward action than toward drama.

Crime Drama

Where the beat archetype deals with uniformed street cops, the crime drama usually deals with detectives. Because of this, it focuses more on the particulars of the crime and the investigation that takes place to solve it.

These serious dramas are designed to focus heavily on the characters. Some crime dramas walk a fine line between emphasizing the crime being solved and the characters that are solving them. In all cases, it is a dark, emotional ride.

When creating an episode of a crime drama, pay attention to the leading cast. Finding a way to make one of the cast members emotionally involved in the case will add to the drama and roleplaying of the episode.

The Drama

Dramas are very serious shows that involve adult themes. In almost every drama, half of the focus of each episode is on the events that take place, court cases to be tried, and so forth. The other half is on the relationships of the cast. You should try to find a good balance between the two, and if you can make the events effect the cast in a personal way, so much the better.

The Archetypes

Courtroom Drama

People seem to love watching court cases, both real and theatrical. There have been a variety of courtroom dramas that have thrilled audiences over the years. There is something exciting about a good argument and when both counsels deliver an excellent closing argument, the tension can really mount.

Go and watch a few court cases. Most cities allow anyone to sit in the courtroom and watch the proceedings. That will give you a good feel for how a court case flows. Of course, it's easier to just watch a stack of episodes, which is also recommended, but actually attending one may give you more insight.

The Process: What is the series of events that drive a courtroom drama? Usually it starts with someone walking into the cast's law office. What then? The process of trying a court case generally follows certain steps:

Step 1: The prospective client shows up at the law office and has a meeting with one or more lawyers to describe the case. The lawyers will then decide if they want the case. If so, they will discuss it with the client and will try to get all pertinent information.

Step 2: The lawyers and clients of both parties meet at the law office (it does not matter which office) and try to settle the case out of court. Sometimes the case ends there, but where's the fun in that?

Step 3: Eventually (in TV, anyway) the case goes to court. There is usually a summary hearing, which is mainly to introduce the case to the judge. For a small case, this may be the only time the case goes to court, but for a big case, this is usually just to let the judge decide if it is worthwhile.

Step 4: The trial begins and the witnesses are called and questioned. Usually the prosecution begins calling witnesses. After the prosecution questions the witness, the defense gets a chance before the witness is excused. This continues until the prosecution has no more witnesses. Then it is the defense's turn to call witnesses. This will continue until all witnesses have been questioned.

Step 5: Sometimes one side will try to make an offer to settle and end the trial. It's ultimately up to the client to decide whether to take it or not. Sometimes the lawyer whose client is making the offer makes the offer to the other lawyer, just between them. By law, the client must be given the offer, but sometimes the lawyers can make a decision about how they want to handle it ahead of time.

Step 6: If all offers are refused, then the closing arguments are given in a separate session. Then, the jury retires to decide on the verdict. When they have decided, a new session is called and the verdict is given.

Screenwriting

Daytime Dramas

Also known as Soap Operas, the daytime drama is one of the most popular types of drama on the air. The secret to their success is twofold: the characters are all people with normal professions that are more beautiful and glamorous than real people; and their plots focus on hot, steamy relationships. These are the "bodice-rippers" of television.

The important thing to remember when creating your characters is that they must all be beautiful and "perfect." When someone does something wrong, it must be a shock. Another important thing to keep in mind is that any personality that you initially develop for your character is very likely to change during the course of the show. As a matter of fact, his personality may make a complete turnaround from good to evil, prim and proper to sleazy.

Make good use of the Relationship Wheel described earlier in this chapter. It is important to set up some very intricate relationships between the entire cast, even at the outset of the game. After everyone has created their characters, the Director should use the Wheel and her own ideas to set up the initial relationships before the game begins. She would then have to write up the details of each relationship for each character, being careful not to let people know about things that their characters would not know.

Medical Drama

Medical dramas most often take place in a hospital, but could be set in any medical facility. For instance, it could be a wartime show, where the doctors work near the front lines. Whatever the setting, however, the drama is mostly about the struggle between life and death, either for the patients or for the cast. Like all dramas, the show will focus on the cast's lives and relationships, but will always put some emphasis on the cases that are brought in.

Medical dramas may need to use the Detailed Healing rules described in Chapter Six: Filming. Using this method can make an emergency room scene every bit as exciting as a combat scene, if run properly. Keep the pace fast and furious, because every second counts. If the actors know something about medicine, then play on that. Describe symptoms and let them try to actually come up with the answers. If they are stumped, they can pay a Luck point to get an inspiration. They may blow a few Luck points during the surgery, but the Director may then award them one if they actually save the life and roleplay the scene well.

Romance

Intriguing Company: Romance shows are all about relationships. The key to a good romance is a well-developed cast. Make sure that there are many potential pairings and a varied assortment of characters. Will there be one woman that all the men are trying to woo, or are there enough women to go around, and it is all a matter of who gets whom? Each character should have a very detailed background and personality, with high emphasis on likes, dislikes, hobbies, etc. After all, how can you find true love if none of the characters have anything in common?

Exotic Locales: Where will it take place? Make sure the setting is romantic. A Caribbean or Hawaiian beach is a common choice. Lots of sand, surf and tanned bodies can add to the atmosphere.

Danger: Add some excitement to your show. A storm at sea can really put your chivalry to the test! Do you try to console the frightened woman, or do you brave the storm to and save the boat. Either one can win the love of the right woman if you play your cards right.

"Hey, Baby!": This kind of show is all about charisma. How well you schmooze is equally as important as how well you dress. Help the actors get into your character. Give them plenty of opportunity to try out their pick-up lines. Do not say what comes from your heart, say what comes from your character's heart. In addition, when someone makes a play for you, do not forget that it's not you he wants, it's your character.

Humor or Heartache: Make sure you remember the atmosphere of the show. There are some very serious romances on TV, mostly in mini-series, that cover some very heavy social topics. However, most are more light-hearted, with almost as much humor in them as drama. Whatever atmosphere you go with, be consistent. A show that flip-flops from comedy to serious drama and back again can lose its appeal very quickly.

Situation Comedy

Sitcoms, as they are usually called, are the most common of all American TV shows. They are short and sweet, and intended strictly to make people laugh. Each sitcom follows the Thirty Minute Comedy format, and so each plot cannot be very detailed. The focus of a sitcom is always on the cast; how they interact, and how they deal with the crazy situations they are always thrown into. As a result, the plots are almost completely inconsequential, and do not usually need to be detailed or deep.

The Quick Laugh

This type of sitcom focuses heavily on the comedy stylings of the individual cast members. Often, it focuses on one character in particular, but the entire cast always contributes in much the same way.

These are the shows that are filled with one-liners and often star a famous stand-up comedian. The plots are very simple, and are designed strictly to allow for a great number of jokes. Like all sitcoms, the plot will put the cast into a potentially embarrassing situation that they must find a way out of. However, the actual resolution of the situation is not what is important, and is often down-

Screenwriting

Shows

played and not climactic. Instead, the importance is on the funny jokes that the stars can let loose during the episode.

This type of sitcom is difficult to roleplay. This is because there is extremely little action, and the dialog and interaction that occurs is mainly jokes. The actors who play the game must be adept at improvisational stand-up comedy.

The Crazy Situation

This is the best type of sitcom to roleplay. In this show, the cast is thrown into some kind of wild and crazy situation they must find a way out of. In these shows, it is the things that the characters do to resolve the situation that is funny. Of course, during the course of the episode, the cast will be throwing one-liners when they are appropriate, but that will is not the focus.

Example: The show is about a young woman who has been having a hard time finding a decent job because of her gender. She has managed to get a job at a big firm by passing herself off as a man. She is now one of her boss' chief employees. In this episode, her boss fixes her up with his beloved niece. Of course, she cannot say no to the date, and must take her out. Crazy, embarrassing, and very funny times lay ahead!

Mysteries & Thrillers

Mysteries and thrillers run hand in hand. A thriller is nothing more than a mystery that has a dark atmosphere and keys on suspense. A mystery involves the viewer intellectually, where a thriller involves him emotionally.

A Good Mystery

The key to running a good mystery is clues. Many roleplaying game scenarios can be run without much planning and with the Director coming up with the details spontaneously. However, that does not work well with a mystery. You need to plant clues in the game for the characters to find, and that means that you must do at least some planning.

An easy mistake to make is to drop only a few big clues for the characters to find. You must expect that they will not find all of the clues, so if you only leave a few clues, then they may fail to solve the mystery just by missing one of them. Instead, drop many small clues so that if they manage to pick up more than half of them, then they have a good chance of solving the mystery. Watch an episode of your favorite thriller or mystery show and write down every clue you find, including those that the characters in the show failed to find. You will be surprised at the high number of clues present in the episode.

The Role of Suspense

Suspense is a thriller's best friend. With a thriller, you need to keep the cast on the edge of their seats and nervous, almost afraid, of what they will find on the other side of the door.

Thrillers are most often dark and moody, with elements taken from horror movies. Dark, foggy nights, big bald trees with gnarled branches and roots, creaky steps and doors, all add to the thrill and suspense of the game. Thrillers are all about atmosphere, and you must be sure to build it up for every episode.

The Archetypes

The following plot concepts are common in mysteries and thrillers. Some only follow one or two, but others will have episodes that fit into all three. These are not hard-fast rules to follow, though, so use your imagination and use whatever you think will apply to your game.

Murder Mystery

This is closely related to the crime drama, but where a crime drama puts as much focus on the relationships of the main characters and their personalities, a murder mystery focuses heavily on the crime at hand, and on the collecting and analyzing of the clues.

Quite often, the main characters are not in the law enforcement community, but just always manage to find themselves in a position of having to solve a mystery.

Occult Thriller

In an occult thriller, the cast must deal with various aspects of the paranormal. Like others of this genre, these are dark and mysterious shows, dealing with the macabre. They are usually aimed at adults and mingle elements of horror movies into the story.

A haunted house, a disturbed burial site, and a bizarre cult are good examples of occult thrillers. An episode usually starts with some kind of crime or event that draws the characters in without seeming very out of the ordinary. But once they begin to unravel the clues, they find themselves involved in something beyond the realms of modern science.

Make your episode dark and spooky with lots of surprises that will keep them on their toes. These shows are more thriller than mystery, and the mood should reflect that.

Screenwriting

Science Fiction

The Archetypes

The following plot concepts are common in sci-fi shows.

Futuristic

The most common setting for a futuristic sci-fi show is to focus on the adventures of a particular starship or space station. The cast will be her crew and the vessel, whatever it is, will be the central setting. These shows can either fit into the action and adventure genre, or the drama.

For these shows, you will need to leverage the Powers & Technology section found earlier in this chapter to outfit your cast with the proper technologies.

Modern Day Thriller

A sci-fi thriller usually deals with UFOs and aliens, but sometimes includes high tech mysteries and government conspiracies. They are thrillers, like any other, but often with a darker mood.

Some sci-fi thrillers have one central plotline that runs throughout the series, working rather like a serial, and building up to some climax at the series' end. However, not all of the episodes are directly related to the plotline. This adds some flexibility to the show, allowing the actors a breather from the intensity of the plotline.

When dealing with an ongoing plotline, it is often best to start the characters at the beginning, when they know nothing about it. Let their search for "the truth" be their motivation.

Creature Hunt

Lone people walking the city streets late at night are being killed in a manner that defies logical explanation. Something is out there, stalking the night, watching with inhuman eyes for its next victim.

The creature hunt focuses on some kind of beast that is not known to science. This could be a mythical creature, like Bigfoot and the Loch Ness Monster, or it could be something completely new—something made up. In any case, the cast finds themselves hunting this thing, or perhaps just trying to escape from it.

One method to take when creating this kind of show

Screenwriting

Shows

is to flip through one of the many monster supplements and look for a creature that inspires you. Then pull it from its fantasy setting and design a story that would explain its existence in our world. You may not even need to figure out exactly how it came to be, but just how it managed to escape detection. Of course, you will need to define why it has suddenly become known to the cast.

You can find creatures in this manner in other Fudge games, as well as a variety of other game systems. Chapter Six: Filming has rules on converting trait levels from other common systems to Fudge.

It's recommended, however, that you create your own creature. This is best for two good reasons: you are more likely to end up with a creature that best fits your show, and you can guarantee that the actors know nothing about it. The latter is critically important when running a mystery show.

Cartoons

Saturday Mornings

Cartoons have graced the TV screens of Saturday mornings for decades, giving children of all ages something to look forward to when their weekends begin. Over the years, a wide variety of cartoons were spawned, most of which starred lovable and interesting animal characters. People of all ages loved to watch mischievous animals with human qualities running amok and causing trouble wherever they went. Whether they were always trying a clever plan to escape from the zoo, or just trying to avoid the hunter, their antics kept Saturday mornings filled with laughter.

The Archetypes

There are three major archetypes to cartoon TV shows. Slapsticks and Silly Sitcoms are most often found on Saturday mornings, but can now be seen at all times on cable channels. Primetime Sitcoms are different, and tend to have more mature themes and audiences.

Slapstick

The silly hunter is walking quietly through the woods, shotgun in hand. He is following some tracks, and is eager to hunt down his prey. A ways ahead of him is a chipmunk. This chipmunk is walking on two legs and is carrying a large stamper in the shape of a rabbit's foot. He stamps it on the ground occasionally as he walks, snickering to himself at his joke. Finally, he gets to the hole in the ground that sports its own mailbox that says "Racer Rabbit." Quickly, the chipmunk hides and waits for the hunter to find the hole.

This is a prime example of a slapstick cartoon. They usually star animorphic characters (animals that have human characteristics) that compete against each other in some way. Like all slapstick shows, the competitions are usually quite violent. However, no matter how violent they get, the characters never really get hurt. Sometimes they see stars, sometimes they may even get their heads flattened, or become squishy like an accordion, but they always fully recover.

Handling these shows in *Now Playing* is easy. Simply use the Non Lethal Combat rules and apply some simple judgment calls when deciding what happens. For instance, you can say that if the character gets a dazed, he sees stars. If he falls off a cliff and suffers a Stun or Knockout, he squishes and walks like an accordion.

Each episode normally runs for fifteen minutes, which is one-quarter of the length of a drama, and therefore only has one act. You can plan out the same number of beats if you like, but beats are not very necessary in these shows.

Silly Sitcoms

These are like normal sitcoms except for the following three differences:

1. They are aimed at children, and thus have sillier plots.

2. They normally star animorphic characters like the slapstick cartoons.

3. Some are only fifteen minutes long.

When you take a slapstick cartoon and a real sitcom and put them together, you get a silly sitcom. The plots are aimed at children, but are usually not slapstick in nature. They are more like real sitcoms, but with silly plots. The characters are the same kind of silly animals that the slapstick shows have, but they are not nearly as violent. Now, this does not mean that there is no slapstick in these shows, only that there it is not the focus.

The example of the zoo animal who is always trying to escape is an example of the silly sitcom. At the beginning of the episode, he tries to escape and is caught. Then, something happens that puts the zookeeper in trouble. Although the zookeeper is his nemesis, our hero still likes him and does not want anything bad to happen to him, so he spends the rest of the episode trying to bail the zookeeper out, with hilarious results.

Treat these like normal situation comedies, but with some of the elements of the slapstick cartoon.

Primetime Sitcoms

These are simply normal adult sitcoms that merely happen to be animated. Sometimes they introduce something that is unrealistic, or impossible in real life, but this is not necessary. For instance, the show could be exactly like a regular sitcom, except that the show is animated and the sitcom family owns a talking dog.

Treat these shows exactly as you would regular situation comedies.

Writing Episodes

Chapter 9

Screenwriting

Anatomy of an Episode

If you want your episodes to feel like a TV show, you need to know how TV episodes are structured. This section describes some of the tools and structures used in making real TV episodes. Along with each description are some tips to help you create your own episodes for roleplaying.

The Act

Acts are a major division in a show. Each act marks the change of a focus in the story. In fact, this change is so big that you can even name your acts. Each act is made up of scenes that contain several beats. The act provides the topic or goal of the beats and the scenes implement the beats.

The Scene

The scene is what you use to implement your acts. A scene is the canvas on which you, the Director, and the actors paint a piece of the story. The scene is made up of a plot point that needs to be acted out, a set in which the scene takes place, and all of the supporting cast members and items that may have a part to play in the plot point.

Generally, you never cut to a new location or time. If you break to a new location or scene without flowing naturally to it, you are cutting.

The Beat

The beat is the most basic element of an episode. Each beat describes one major plot point of the story. Here is an easy way to think of it: If you had to describe what the episode is about in five sentences or less, each sentence would be a beat.

A beat can be something that could take a long time to roleplay out, such as a battle with a foe. However, there can be beats that take very little time, but are still pivotal points in the story. An example of this would be having the cast read an article in the newspaper about their biggest foe breaking out of prison. Both of these beats are vitally important to the story, yet one takes up much time in the roleplay, while the other does not.

The Teaser

The teaser is a small scene shown at the beginning of the episode that sets the stage for the story to come. This will always contain an event that will try to capture the audience's attention and convince them to stay tuned after the opening credits and commercial break.

You can use this tool in the same way in *Now Playing*. It is just as important to capture the interest of the actors and give them a taste of the excitement that is to come.

Show: Operation: Earth.
Season: One.
Task: Planning the Beats

Beat 1: Government discovers increase in UFO sightings worldwide. Starts agency to investigate them.

Beat 2: UFO encounters seem to have some hidden agenda.

Beat 3: UFO starts dogfight with USAF fighter results in both craft crashing. Pilot is missing from downed UFO and must be found.

Beat 4: Several missing people are found alive, but do not appear quite right. Alien abduction is suspected.

Beat 5: Large alien mothership sighted by satellite telescopes is heading this way. Several isolated attacks by smaller UFOs signal impending invasion.

In a television episode, a teaser usually has one of two focuses. On is to introducing the main characters by having some event happen to them. The other is to introduce the plot without involving the characters. An example of the latter would be to start with a merchant ship in the Arctic Ocean that has some kind of encounter with a UFO.

Obviously, in *Now Playing*, you cannot have a teaser that does not involve the leading cast. It is important that they are involved in every scene. In addition, you should never describe any events that the leading cast will not have known about. However, you can properly introduce the plot while still involving the leading cast-or at least one or two cast members.

The teaser is not required, but is a very effective way to start an exciting episode.

Goal of the Teaser

The ultimate goal of the teaser is to peak the interest of the audience-or the actors in our case. In television, the teaser is short, and always cuts to both the opening credits and commercials after it has finished. Your teaser should also be short, and perhaps you can then take a

Screenwriting

break yourself. That would be a good time to order food, or break out the snacks. The nice thing about running the teaser first is that it gets the actors pumped up for the game, so they will be less likely to take their time on breaks.

The teaser must always be a cliffhanger. This is your chance to capture the interest of your actors. You want them to be anxious to continue playing.

Example: A US soldier, a leading character, is quietly trudging through a swampy forest in Vietnam. He has been separated from his platoon, and is searching for them. However, he knows he is deep in enemy territory and quite worried. It is dusk and in the dense forest, visibility is poor. Animal noises are all around him and he is painfully aware of the sound of his feet in the shallow water.

Suddenly he is fired upon. Vietnamese soldiers are firing from up ahead. Jack, his actor, decides to duck for cover and return fire. The Director tells him he is obviously outnumbered and cannot find a safe way to escape. Jack decides there is not much else to do but take as many down as he can before he falls. He fires again.

As he sticks his head above the trunk of a fallen tree to fire, he sees a large, fast moving shape dart through the trees to disappear behind the large boulder where the enemy is. The thing moved like an animal, but he has no idea what it could be. He hears screams of terror and pain as well as gunshots. The shape finally darts off again to disappear into the trees. There are no more gunshots and all is silent. The animal sounds, which had stopped during the incident, gradually return. Jack finally decides to carefully approach the boulder. What he finds is the remains of four Viet-Kong soldiers brutally mangled by some kind of creature. Like all soldiers, he had been briefed on the various animals that live in this place, and none of them are a match for what he just witnessed. It just does not look right.

The teaser ends here, with the soldier all alone with this unknown menace that seems even more terrifying than the enemy he had feared only a few minutes earlier.

The Tag

The tag is like the alter ego of the teaser. It is a short scene that plays at the end of the episode. It sums up the events of the episode and wraps things up nicely. It is in the tag where plot seeds are planted for later episodes.

It should be short, like the teaser, and is used to tie up loose ends. It is not always necessary, but can be a very useful tool when setting the scene for future episodes.

Planning the Season

Although this may be important for television, it is not terribly important in a roleplaying game. However, you should put some thought to this topic. After all, the actors are going to be trying to develop their characters throughout the course of the show, and having a good overall plan of the season can help to ensure that they get the chance.

With a serial, you should plan some key events for the season itself. You can even think of the season as being a very large episode. Work out a handful of beats that you can use to describe your goals for the season. Then, keep these beats in mind when you are creating your episodes. At least half of the episodes of your season should have one of the season's beats in it. These will be your important episodes for the season. The two obvious candidates are the season opener and finale. The rest should be scattered throughout the rest of the season. It's good to have a few episodes that have nothing important to do with the show's storyline. These can be a nice break from the intensity of the show.

The beats that you line up for the season must be very generic. It is the job of the episodes to expand on them and fill in the details.

An example would be the hypothetical show "Operation: Earth" shown in a nearby sidebar. It shows the five major beats of season one of the show. It nicely illustrates the flow of the story throughout the season. Each beat is designed to appear in an episode that is evenly spaced throughout the season. As the beats progress, the intensity and importance of each one increases. The middle beat, number three, is of special interest and could be made into a two-part episode. Beat one would be the Pilot and beat five would be the season finale.

Campaigns

In roleplaying game terms, a campaign is a large, ongoing storyline that the actors play week after week. The story is long, detailed, and often complex. Because it is meant to run continuously for a long time, it is much more detailed than the average TV show. The question then comes, "Is it possible to run a campaign in *Now Playing*?" The answer is yes!

The key to running a detailed campaign as a TV show is the combination of the serial and planning the season. With a serial, you have a single storyline that stretches across one or more seasons of a show. There is a real sci-fi TV show that has done just this. They had a complete, detailed story already planned to last five seasons. The story was about a war. Each season dealt with a different aspect of the war, from rumors of war, to the coming of the war, to the war itself, and finally the aftermath and reconstruction. The story was detailed, and the setting was rich and fully developed. In essence, it was a complete campaign.

This means that you can run a complete campaign by following a few simple steps:

1. Break the story into acts. These acts will be the show's seasons.
2. Determine several beats for each season. If you have the story already in mind, this should be simple.

Screenwriting

3. Plan each session as an episode. This means to make each session a complete episode by it its own beginning, middle and end. Work it out so that they still work toward the main goal, while still being self-contained.

Step 3 may be the most difficult part. The following example should help to illustrate how you can do it. The example uses a fantasy setting to make it more like a standard RPG campaign.

Example: In the campaign, a party of adventurers has set out on a great quest to seek the tower of an evil wizard and recover a sacred item that had been stolen. The item has tremendous magical powers, and in the wrong hands, the item could be used for great evil.

In one episode, the party enters a town, weary from their journey. Immediately, they can sense that something is not right, but they are not sure in what way. In fact, this town is the result of an early experiment the wizard had made with the item. The cast must figure out what had happened to the town, possibly repair the damage, and get supplies that they need to complete the quest.

The example illustrates a short, episodic adventure that is very much a part of the major story.

Goal of the Episode

Every episode is part of a bigger entity: the show. You must first ask yourself what effect you want this episode to have on the show. Are you trying to drive a major storyline forward? Are you trying to increase character development? Are there new aspects of the setting that you are trying to introduce? These are all common goals of a typical episode. It is important to consider this when designing an episode because the actors are living through the seasons of the show, and they will be sensitive to the direction that the show is taking.

Understanding the goals of your episode is also important for determining the type of episode that you are creating. For instance, if you are trying to drive home a major plot point of the main storyline as well as introducing new characters and setting elements, you should consider making it be a season finale or opener.

You should always ask yourself how important these goals are to the actors and the roles they play. Upon answering this question, you may realize that they would not be interested at all. This does not mean you should not run it; it may be vital to the main story arc of the show. Instead, you may need to find a way to make it more interesting to them without losing sight of your goals.

Example: The goals of the pilot episode of Operation: Earth are as follows:

1. Introduce the setting of the show. This would consist of showing how the U.S. government has become concerned with the frequency of UFO sightings and the legitimacy of the evidence. This episode will focus, in part, on the formation of the Earthwatch project, which is tasked with investigating UFO sightings and assessing any threat they might cause.

2. Introduce the cast. There must be plenty of situational interaction for them.

3. Provide Beat 1.

Episode Formats

Most episodes are standard and follow the same format. However, there are certain special episodes that you must treat differently.

Pilot

The pilot episode can be very tough to write because it does so much. The pilot must introduce the entire show as well a providing a good story to involve the actors. You must introduce every aspect of the show. This includes the setting, the cast (both leading and supporting) and the atmosphere. This is quite an undertaking, which is why the pilot episode is usually twice the length of a standard episode.

Season Finale

Like all endings, the ending of a season must be big and climactic. It must be the most important and pivotal episode of the season. It should bring closure to at least one aspect of your story arc while leaving some questions unanswered for the next season.

This is also an ideal place to introduce new story elements and making casting changes. After all, this is where one phase of the life of the show ends and another begins.

Season finales are not a complete episode in themselves. They always end on a very climactic note and cut to a black screen that says, "to be continued..." What is worse is that the viewer must wait a few months for the next season to begin before seeing the conclusion of the story in the season opener. You should always end a season with a cliffhanger just like this. Just take care not to make the wait for the opener too long. Unlike a TV show, the longer you wait between sessions of your game, the more the actors will forget what happened, and become separated from the emotion of the episode. A wait of a week or two is usually fine, but a wait of a month or more could ruin the excitement of the both the finale and its subsequent opener.

Season Opener

Just as the season finale must be more important than its season's opener, the opener of the next season must be even more important. The season opener is usu-

Screenwriting

ally part two of last season's finale, and must finish whatever story it began. This episode will set the stage for the entire season, so it must be full of energy.

Two-Part Episode

Sometimes the plot that you come up with is just too big to fit in a standard four-act episode. That is fine. There is a precedent for that called the two-part episode, or the "made for TV movie." Both work in much the same way.

You must work out twice as many acts as is normal for the show's format, since it will be twice as long. The fourth act should be climactic, but of course, not conclude the episode.

These episodes should be on a grander scale, having a more pivotal role in the overall story of the show. However, you must be careful not to let them outshine your season finale.

Planning the Episode

This section discusses the steps involved in creating a *Now Playing* episode. Doing this amount of planning may not be traditional for a roleplaying game, but it is essential if you want the game to feel like TV. The work involved really is not difficult, nor is it very time-consuming. It just takes a little thought and planning up front.

Decide what the atmosphere is going to be like, and if it is going to be a standard episode or one of the special ones described earlier.

The following are the steps that you should take when designing your episode. They are laid out in the order that they should be handled.

Initial Concept

Most episodes begin life with a basic idea. This idea could be a beat that you set down for the season, or it could be simply an inspiration. Some of the best episodes are those inspired by newspaper articles or stories you hear about on the news.

Once you have a concept, figure out the goals of the episode. These may be based on the progress of the season's storyline, or perhaps a situation with your gaming group. For instance, if you have just added a new actor to your group, one of your goals would be to introduce the new character into the show.

Defining the Acts

Decide what you want each act to focus on. Most shows use the same format for determining the acts for just about all of their episodes. Each act should have a specific goal. If the beats in the act are specific enough, you can come up with a name for it.

For example, one popular science fiction show separates each episode into four acts that follow the same formula. Here are the acts they have with a handy title and brief description:

Act 1 - Introduction: This act introduces the plot of show. Here they will encounter an alien ship, or send a team down to a planet. The show explains why they are there and what they plan to do.

Act 2 - The Plot Thickens: During this act, the plot laid out by Act 1 is expanded on, with some kind of problem or challenge building up by the end of the act. For instance, a member of the crew discovers that the friendly aliens have some hidden agenda that appears hazardous to his crew, but he does not yet know what it is.

Act 3 - Conflict: The plot twist that was built up by Act 2 is now brought forth and the cast must is affected by it. They now have their work cut out for them. They

Screenwriting

Writing Episodes

struggle with it, and pave the way for the final resolution. They find out that the aliens need their ship and plan to strand the crew on their dying ship and steal theirs. Attempts to stop them do not succeed, but put them in a position where they have one last chance to save their ship.

Act 4 - Resolution: This is when the cast devises a plan to end the conflict and resolve the situation. They put the plan into action and, hopefully, succeed. This is all very climactic.

The above list of acts also works for most mysteries and dramas. For mysteries, consider Act 2 as an investigation that feeds the cast clues that give them mostly what they need to solve it, but throws them a curve to lead them down the wrong path. Act 3 has them discovering the misdirection and finding the clues necessary to solve the case. Act 4 has them catching the villain or otherwise bringing the case to resolution.

Now, the question you probably have in mind is, "How can you make sure that the cast does what the acts say." Well, the answer is you cannot. There are tricks you can do to help lead them in the right direction. These tricks are described later in this chapter.

As described in Chapter Eight: Shows, the one-hour drama has four acts. You will need to plan your acts. This is described later in this chapter.

148

Screenwriting

Standard Formulas

Most network dramas have their own formula which each episode will follow. The formula governs the goal of each act in the episode. In this way, they can put out episodes quickly. This can also work in a roleplaying game.

Example: There is a sci-fi show whose episodes follow this formula:

Act 1 - The Bait: The ship has an encounter that catches their attention. It could be a derelict ship, a first contact or some spatial anomaly. Whatever it is, they choose to deal with it.

Act 2 - The Twist: During the course of dealing with the encounter, there are hints that something is not quite right. Perhaps one of the leading characters does something that greatly complicates matters.

Act 3 - The Conflict: All Hell breaks loose because of the events of Act 2.

Act 4 - The Resolution: The cast works out a plan to set things to right and they execute it. In most cases, the plan is successful.

Placement of Beats

Each act should have about four to five beats in it. These beats will define the act and help you decide on what scenes you need to prepare for.

Creating Your Beats

Each act normally has four to five beats. You must decide what each beat will be. Here is a good method to use when planning your beats:

Take one sheet of lined paper. On the first line, write "Act 1:" followed by the title of the act, if any. Then, skip five lines and write "Act 2:" and its title. Repeat this process until you have all of acts listed. Then, use each of the blank lines to write in your beats. Do not use more than one line for a single beat! If you need more than one line, you are getting into too much detail. A beat is meant to just list an important plot point. Be brief; there is plenty of time elsewhere to expand on it. Setting up the paper like this will help keep your beats in check. You should never need more than five lines of 8½" x 11" paper to list your beats.

Planning Scenes

Once you have listed the beats for all of your acts, sit down with a notebook, pen, and your list of beats. Study each one, starting with the first. Think about how you could make the beat happen in the episode. You can start by asking yourself if the first beat will be in the first scene. After all, it is quite possible to have more scenes than you have beats. If not, you will need to figure out what scenes may come before it.

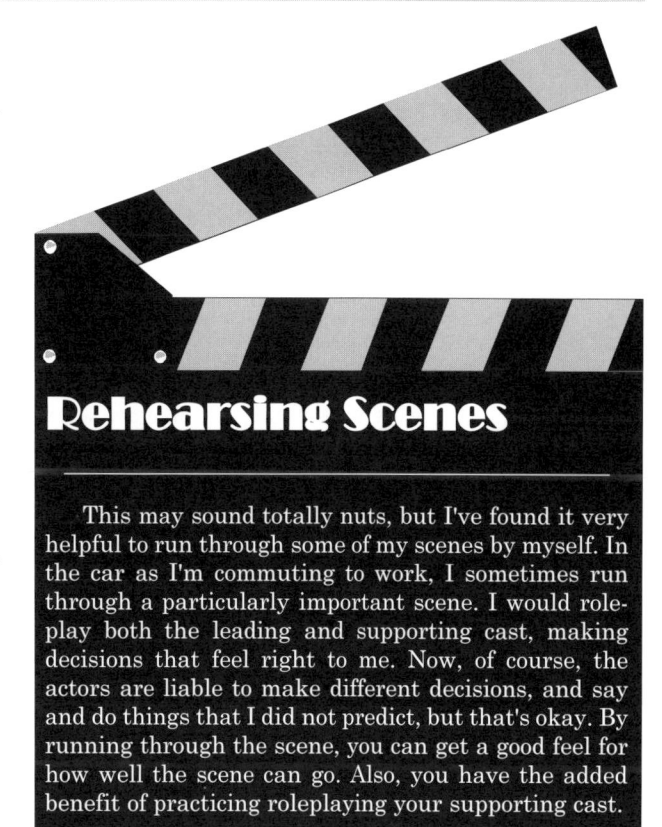

It is hard to plan a scene when you have no idea what the cast is going to do. The goal of the scenes is not to force the cast down a particular course of action, but instead to help minimize the work you must do on the spot to prepare scenes as you go. In most cases, there is a number of scenes that are obviously likely to be played out. If you can flesh out the details of these scenes, you will be that much more prepared for the session.

The first scene of the episode is always the hardest, and is the only one that you have much control over. This scene introduces the plot of the episode, as well as immersing the cast into it. How will you start the show? You know what the goal of the scene is: either to make the beat happen, or to do the necessary prep for the beat. You know the cast, and you know the setting. Just think up a way to work it all together, and then let the actors do what they do best.

Casting the Supporting Cast

Defining the acts and beats may identify some of the supporting cast members that are required for the episode, but in most cases, you will still need to find more. By laying out some of the scenes, you can identify what supporting cast you need in more detail. Some may only be useful in the scene you define for them, but others may be useful even if their scenes are never played.

Rehearsing Scenes

This may sound totally nuts, but I've found it very helpful to run through some of my scenes by myself. In the car as I'm commuting to work, I sometimes run through a particularly important scene. I would roleplay both the leading and supporting cast, making decisions that feel right to me. Now, of course, the actors are liable to make different decisions, and say and do things that I did not predict, but that's okay. By running through the scene, you can get a good feel for how well the scene can go. Also, you have the added benefit of practicing roleplaying your supporting cast.

Screenwriting

Example Episode Plan

SHOW: Operation: Earth.   EPISODE: Missing Persons

Concept

There are places on this Earth where the local population believes beyond all doubt in the existence of Extra Terrestrials. They believe this so fully because of the frequency and, perhaps, level of encounters with them. What is it about these places that make them such a hotbed of UFO activity?

The people of a Carver Mill, Maine have been the subject of study and experimentation by Extra Terrestrials for many decades. Most of the population have either not been experimented on, or have only been abducted a few times. These people all believe in UFOs, and are wary of them, but are more than willing to talk about them. The changes to their behavior is more subtle. However, those that have been abducted many times will not only avoid the subject, but will make any "outsider" who asks too many questions regarding UFOs feel very unwelcome: "Why don't you just go back to the big city where you belong."

Members of the Foundation for Paranormal Investigation, a civilian UFO group, disappear while investigating sightings in the Allagash wilderness of Maine.

Act 1: An Unexpected Case

Beat 1: A cast member receives word from a contact in the FPI about the missing team.

Beat 2: The Agency officially sanctions a trip to the Allagash to investigate.

Beat 3: The FPI contact volunteers to come and demands it if necessary.

Beat 4: The case that the FPI team investigated involved a UFO landing in the Allagash.

Act 2: Carver Hill

Beat 1: Everyone in town believes in UFOs more completely than anyone they've seen before.

Beat 2: People speak freely about UFOs and offer clues about the sightings.

Beat 3: Many people remember seeing the team, but have no idea where they are now.

Beat 4: There is something very odd about these people. They all behave strangely, but it's hard to tell how.

Act 3: Hidden Agenda

Beat 1: Some of the townsfolk offer differing stories about the whereabouts of the missing team.

Beat 2: Some of the townsfolk don't like all their questions and try to make them unwelcome.

Beat 3: Those that don't like them have private meetings and give the team the creeps.

Beat 4: A local guide knows where they went. Volunteers to help.

Beat 5: MiB threatens them not to enter the Allagash. Team suspects unfriendly townsfolk.

Act 4: The Allagash

Beat 1: The Allagash is a big wilderness with rivers, rocky hills, and thick forests that makes travel hard.

Beat 2: They have the odd feeling about this place that just can't pinpoint. Are they being watched?

Beat 3: They're first camp is vandalized while they sleep. They now have no supplies. Guide is gone.

Beat 4: The FPI team's camp is found. It looks untouched as though they were there, then just disappeared.

Beat 5: A UFO sighting and distraction by unfriendly townsfolk end in the mysterious return of the FPI team.

Screenwriting

Guest Stars

Jelena Koslova: The FPI member that contacts the team. She is taken from the FPI show in the Now Playing book.

Initial Supporting Cast

Friendly Townsfolk: One generic character can be created to represent many people. They have Great Tall Tales skill.

Guide: Use the friendly townsfolk character, but add more outdoorsman skills (Track, Camping, Climb, Forage, Hide, etc.).

Unfriendly Townsfolk: The same character sheet as the friendly townsfolk might be usable here. Give them Great Bluff and Good Intimidate skills and Good outdoorsman skills.

Men in Black: Take the unfriendly townsfolk character, add Superb Intimidate skill.

Gray Aliens: They should only be seen, not interacted with. No character creation necessary.

Teaser

Set: FPI Chapter meeting house. It's the basement of a house that has been turned into a laboratory. There are tables set up with computers, printers, and copiers. There are papers strewn about on the tables. The lighting is dim and the walls are concrete. Some pictures of the paranormal are taped to the walls.

It is now 1:30 AM on October 15. Jelena is there, talking on a radio.

Background: Jelena belongs to a chapter of the Foundation for Paranormal Investigation. The rest of her chapter, made up of three men, has gone to the Allagash wilderness in northern Maine to investigate some recent UFO sightings. They had begun their investigation in Carver Hill, Maine, but are now camping deep inside the Allagash wilderness.

It's Mike Carter's voice. "We're camping in the wilderness now. It's pretty thick and rough out here, not to mention cold. The others don't like it, but I find it refreshing. We think the latest sightings happened not far from here. We're setting up the monitors now." There's a little static, that goes away shortly. "It's hard to see through the trees, but I think it's a clear night. There have been sightings every night over here for the past week, so we should see something tonight." The static comes back and makes it hard to hear.

He will respond to anything Jelena says. He has not yet seen anything bizarre, but he may say something like "...something odd about...Carver Hill...not happy with us." Unfortunately, that's the most she can get out of him.

All of a sudden, he breaks off and says "What the...Joe! Are you getting this?" More static. "...You won't believe it. It's...look at...colors! I think..."

All static now. Communication has been completely lost. All attempts to reconnect fail.

[CUT TO BREAK]

Additional Background

Jelena does not have much knowledge about UFOs, nor has any real interest in them. That is why she stayed behind. Any attempts to contact the FPI Head Office ends with no help coming in the near future. The FPI investigates; they do not rescue.

She has a friend in Project Earthwatch that might be able to help. This is one of the leading cast (name Jack). Their Agency is proactive and might be able to help. She does not have his phone number, but does know where he lives.

Scene 1: Meeting in Jack's Apartment

Set: Small, one bedroom apartment. Living room/dining room combo is messy with case files strewn on the floor and tables. The TV is on with the news playing. He is on the couch reading an old case report when Jelena arrives.

This scene is left completely up to the actors. Supply information that either would know as necessary.

Screenwriting

Writing Episodes

Dragging or Guiding: Handling the Cast

No roleplaying game should drag the cast along a pre-defined course of action. That is a sure-fire way to lose actors. However, letting the cast loose on a setting with little to no guidance often results in chaos and ultimately confusion or boredom. A properly designed scene will offer gentle guidance and a reminder of the plot without cramping the actors and hindering their creativity.

Treat each scene as a mini-setting. This will paint a nice, vivid background for the cast and give them something to work with. Then, use the supporting cast to add spice and to keep them focused on the plot.

The Set

The set for each scene is very important. Paint a good picture of what the scene looks like in your head, and do the best job you can of describing it to the actors. Write them down.

Sometimes the set may be too complex to simply envision in your head. In these cases, map them out. This is usually done for buildings and other complex structures. Provide a special copy of the map for the actors. The actors' map should not show any places that their characters would not know about.

Supporting Cast

Watch some TV shows and pay close attention to the supporting characters. What you will find is that each character has a purpose in the story. One may be there to introduce clues to the mystery, or to provide red herring- an obvious suspect meant to throw off the investigation. Still others are there to help fill out the story. For instance, its doubtful that you can have your FBI agents investigating a crime without them meeting up with the local law enforcement.

The supporting characters on TV are not always as flat as you may think, and should definitely not be flat at all in the game. Give them a bit of a background and motivation. Some of them may not need as much development as a leading character, but he should be a complete character nonetheless. It is with the supporting cast that you can best keep the cast on track, and the better you define them, the more you can do with them without them seeming unrealistic.

Cameos and Guest Stars

Just as some shows introduce a character from another show, you can sometimes do the same. This is usually done with the supporting cast. For instance, if the Director was an actor in another show, she might bring her character from that show into her show as a supporting character. These cameos are best kept to a minimum and characters such as these rarely become permanent characters in the new show.

A guest star is a cameo that is played by an actor and shares the top billing in the episode with the leading cast.

Tailor the Show

Always keep in mind that the leading cast is the most important part of your show, because it what the actors will be playing. You must custom build the episodes of your show to the cast. Unlike most real TV shows, the cast will most likely be large, and they must all play an important in the episode.

Stars and Focus

It is very difficult to make an episode that does not put most of the focus on one character. There are some shows that do it, but most focus on one character. In *Now Playing*, it is okay to put the focus on one character in the episode, as long as every character gets focus on an episode, and that the entire leading cast is still the stars of each episode.

There is a distinct difference between having focus in an episode and being the star of it. When the focus of the episode is on you, the plot will center on you, but you do not necessarily get to be the only one to shine. In fact, it could be the other characters who play out the climax in order to save your life! When you are the star, the episode shines on you, and everyone else takes a back seat. The writer of an episode should always try to avoid making any one character the star. If the plot needs to have someone in the center, that is fine, as long as he only has focus and does not get to steal the show. Everyone must share the limelight in every episode.

Part Time Characters

Sometimes there will be an actor in your gaming group that is not going to be able to come to all the sessions of the game. He will still want to be in the game, but cannot be a regular character. You must find a way to write him into the show as a part time character. This means that you can include him into any episode at a moment's notice, but if he is absent, the episode will not suffer. This is a tricky task, but it can be done. Here are some guidelines to making this work smoothly:

— Think about the actor's character concept. Make sure that he has plenty of abilities that can be important, but not crucial, to the show.

— Make sure that the plot of the show does not center on him. The show must be able to go on without having to play him as a supporting character.

— Ask the actor if he would not mind his character being run as a supporting character when needed. You should avoid doing this whenever possible, but sometimes it may be necessary. For instance, if the cast is taking a shuttlecraft down to a planet, and you want to make sure that he is with them for the next session, you will want to bring him along.

FPI: The Show

Scene 1 FPI

Scene 2 The Paranormal

Scene 3 The Big Dig

Scene 4 Haunted Holiday

Saudi Arabia, February 19, 1991

9:42 PM

When Colonel Joseph Buckingham came slowly to consciousness, the first thing he was aware of was that he hurt all over. The second was the horrid smell of burned flesh. He was freezing and in agony from the dozens of flesh wounds and burns that covered his body. He could not see, but was aware that he was lying face-down in the sand, and the only thing he could hear was the sound of canvas flapping in the wind.

He remembered now. He had been taking a stroll along the perimeter of the camp in the early morning before dawn. They were going to bug out today to take up an attack position outside of Kuwait, and he was anxious to get under way. He heard a noise, like the wail of a banshee, and then it struck. It must have been Scud, he thought. He heard the explosion and felt himself be blown away by the blast. He must have lost consciousness after that, for he remembered nothing more until now.

His eyes were starting to clear. Good. Sit tight until you can see, he thought, better to play dead until you know who's around. Soon he could see that the camp was completely destroyed and looked like there were no survivors. Dead bodies and wreckage were strewn all over, and the ground smoldered in places.

He tried to move, but couldn't. Straining to look back, he saw that wreckage from a truck lay across his *legs. Blood was everywhere, but it didn't look like he was bleeding now. It was then that he realized he could not feel his legs. Well, he thought, that settles it; I'm going to die. He relaxed and rested his head on the ground looking out to the side. I think that's Jenkins' body over there, he thought idly, the young man's poor wife won't be able to handle this. He was now becoming used to the notion of death, and a calmness fell over him.*

It was then that he saw it. A pair of jet black arms suddenly rose out of the sand, no more than twenty feet away. The bare, bony arms rose straight upward from the sand. Their fingers were long, with sharp, claw-like nails. They remained that way for a long moment, then bent downward at the elbows, the palms of those bony hands placing themselves firmly on the ground. With a strain of muscle, the arms pushed and a body emerged upward from the sand. In just a few seconds, a figure was crouching on the sand of the desert. Although the creature had pulled itself out of the sand, the sand had not moved, and even now appeared completely undisturbed.

The Colonel could not believe his eyes. The thing looked vaguely human, but it was horribly wrong. It was gaunt and emaciated, its ribs clearly visible through its jet-black skin. Its arms were unnaturally long, and the Colonel believed that they would drag on the ground when it walked. It was its head, though, that was the most disturbing. It was shaped like a human head, but it had no features. No mouth, no nose, no ears. All it had were eyes. Those eyes! They were human-shaped, but were big and red. A shiver ran through him when he looked at it, and he knew in his heart that it would be best not to let it know he was alive.

The thing crouched in the sand for a few moments, looking around slowly, as though surveying the place. Finally, it moved over to one of the corpses and began pawing at it as though searching for something. It was Jenkins. The thing was pawing at his face, his hands, all of his exposed areas. Then, it began to open Jenkins' clothing to paw at his chest and stomach. Buckingham was filled with rage at the defilement of his man, but knew he could not do anything to give himself away.

More of these things began to appear now. First he saw the hands rising out of the sand, then they climbed out as though climbing out of a hole. Each one looked around, crouching like the first. Then each would pick a different soldier and do the same thing to it.

What the Hell are they and what are they after, he thought as he watched helplessly from his position not far from the first of those devils. That one had finished with Jenkins, and now hopped over to another corpse even closer to the Colonel. Soon, he knew, one of them would come to him.

My gun! Of course! He always had his sidearm with him. Now, if he could just reach it without attracting attention. Quietly and carefully, he slid his hand down to his side, inch by inch, until he felt the cold steel of the .45's handle. Ever so gently, he removed it from its holster. Now that it was ready, he relaxed a bit.

An early morning breeze raised a small cloud of dust in front of his face. He coughed. It was not loud, but it was enough. The thing closest to him, and two others instantly raised their heads, staring right at him. His eyes met those of the first one, and it chilled him to the bone. Those inhumanly red eyes stared back at him, devoid of any hint of emotion, neither for good or evil. In that icy gaze, he forgot all about his gun. Time seemed to stop as they stared at each other.

Suddenly the thing lunged at him, its long bony fingers reaching out for his head...

FPI

chapter 10

FPI: The Show

The Foundation

Welcome, friends. I am glad you all could make it. My name is Dr. Arthur Shepard, and I have called you here to offer a proposition that you may find to your benefit. First, I'd like you all to read this:

> **Bigfoot Is an Eco Terrorist**
>
> In Silverton, WA, Bigfoot killed five loggers that have been chopping down trees in his forest, experts claim. This is the latest of a long campaign of eco terrorism by the big hairy ape. According to a surviving logger, the mysterious ape-man began by bellowing threats and spiking trees and logging roads. Now, it seems that he has turned to murder. "All five loggers were torn to pieces," claimed the local sheriff, who has begun a search of the forest to find the ape-man and its cohorts.

Anyone who has read some of the sensationalist rags out there has seen articles like this. Of course, you know that it's all a load of bull—just fun stories made up to sell their "paper." After all, the concept of Bigfoot spiking a tree is absurd.

But what if I told you that this story is true? I was there. I saw the tracks. I even saw the bodies. And more importantly, I saw the Sasquatch. Now, I can see the look of incredulity on your faces. Well, the rag that printed it did embellish…quite a lot, really. But the core story was true: Bigfoot was in that forest and it did have something to do with those deaths. Just because a story is wild and difficult to believe does not mean there is no truth at all to it. Always remember that!

We are in a scientific age where everything that is accepted as truth must first be proven. Anything that cannot be proven is dismissed as "paranormal" and considered to be nothing more than a wild story. It is arrogance to claim that the extent of existence ends with the extent of our knowledge. There are things out there in the world that we do not yet understand, but exist nonetheless. However, popular culture, as evidenced by the article I showed you, has convinced the masses that the paranormal is nothing more than fun stories to tell to you children at bedtime, or to give people a scare in the movies.

The Foundation for Paranormal Investigation is dedicated to proving the existence of the paranormal. We are made up of intelligent, well respected people from all walks of life who have a passionate interest in matters of the occult and paranormal. We investigate these cases with an impartial, objective view with the purpose of gaining additional knowledge that can be added to our already great collection. We are not ghost hunters. We do not necessarily intend to destroy ghosts or other entities. Our goal is knowledge.

Our areas of study include, and are not limited to: ghosts and other spirits, demons, possession, angels and religious phenomena, UFOs, magic, psychic powers, and even super-human powers.

The Foundation recruits people from all walks of life who have a passionate interest in the paranormal, and who have skills that can be useful. Since our primary goal is knowledge, we need scientists, who can study it objectively with all the latest technology at their disposal. We need magicians and psychics, who can lend their experience and understanding to the cause. It's important to understand that the Foundation neither wants to prove or disprove it. We just want the truth. Some of our members do not believe in the things they are investigating, while others do. Most simply keep an open mind, and believe it when they see it and learn it. We also have great need of those with investigative skills, as nearly all cases have mysteries to be solved. We need members who are good at dealing with people, asking the right questions and extracting the facts from fiction in their stories.

So, if you are interested in becoming members and feel that you can contribute to the Foundation's goals, you are invited to stay. All those who aren't should leave now.

Very well, now that only those who wish to join are present, I can begin to tell you about the FPI.

History of the FPI

To tell the history of the Foundation for Paranormal Investigation is to tell the recent history of its founder, Colonel Joseph Buckingham.

Colonel Joseph Buckingham

Colonel Joseph Buckingham is a decorated colonel in the British army. He comes from a very respectable and wealthy family with many ties and connections. He now lives in a posh and old mansion near Elgin, Scotland. Being a career military man, he never had time to get married, and his current obsession has not changed that. He lives alone with his servants and the occasional friend.

His family is highly respected among members of the British government and aristocracy. They have accrued great wealth and power, and can call in favors from important persons when necessary. His family line, for as far back as they have traced it, has been a military one. Each generation boasts at least one great officer. His father was a flying ace in the Royal Air Force, receiving many medals of valor. His grandfather was a general in the British army. He has found his granddad's reputation to be hard to follow.

Joseph was also a successful military man. He is a born leader, with an uncanny skill at reading a person's body language and knowing exactly what to say or do to gain his trust and respect. He is also a great tactician. It is the combination of these qualities, along with many

FPI: The Show

years on active duty that allowed him to rise to the rank of colonel by the age of thirty-eight.

The Incident in Arabia

In 1991, during the Gulf War, Colonel Buckingham and his troops were awaiting final word to mobilize and enter Kuwait. Early in the morning, the camp was struck by a missile and was wiped out. He had lost his legs in the attack and very nearly lost his life.

He had regained consciousness for a brief time before the rescue choppers arrived. It was then that he had his first brush with the paranormal. He saw some horrific beings climb out of the sand of Saudi Arabia to paw at the exposed flesh of the dead soldiers. He says that these things were vaguely humanoid, but were short and thin as though starving. Their arms were abnormally long and their fingers ended in claws. Their skin was jet black and hairless, and their heads were devoid of all features save their eyes, which were red. They looked hideous and evil, but when one met his gaze, he could see no emotion in its eyes at all, which he said unsettled him more than anything else. When one of those things saw that he was alive and awake, it lunged at him and he lost consciousness.

To this day, he is not sure what they were. He didn't think they were ghosts, but they also didn't fully fit the profile of demons or devils. But one thing was certain: they were not human, nor were they any other type of known animal. They went from body to body, pawing at the corpses of his men, and there was nothing he could do about it.

I was a field medic back then, and was the one who found him on the site. He was mess and I originally thought he was dead. It was only by chance that I noticed him breathing as I was putting him into the body bag. After all, he appeared so obviously dead that I didn't even think to check for a pulse! To make up for my mistake, I took it upon myself to see to his care personally. When we first spoke of the incident, he didn't mention the things he saw, but I could tell that he had seen something that had shaken his soul. I know, because I have rescued the dead in many parts of the world, and I have seen many things that should not be. Eventually, he confided in me, for he could tell I was a trustworthy man. I must admit that I had never seen things like those beings he described, but I believe him. His injuries did not extend to his brain and he showed no other signs of mental instability. He was indeed quite sane. Besides, my own experiences have taught me that things like this can exist, so I took his word.

I did not need to caution him to keep it secret. He is a brilliant man, and had not become a colonel by making rash decisions. No, he knew not to report his experience. However, with my aid, he managed to conduct a bit of an investigation anyway. There were reported to have been no signs of any intruders in the camp between the time of the explosion and the arrival of the rescue teams. Also, nothing seemed to be missing from any of the bodies, and everything seemed normal, given the circumstances. The only interesting thing was that every corpse had unusually low levels of serotonin. There was no medical explanation for this, but in the absence of any evidence of tampering, it was logged merely as a peculiarity, and no investigation was made of it.

Founding the FPI

Colonel Buckingham has spent every day since then in a search of an answer. Being a cripple, though, has given him one gift: time. He is still technically a colonel in the army, but is on "extended inactive duty." Now he devotes all of his time to studying the paranormal. He has spent countless days in libraries reading about every ghost haunting and U.F.O. sighting, but has not come any closer to understanding what he had experienced. It seems that no one has ever reported seeing the beings that he had seen, and it frustrated him to no end.

I remained close to him ever since we met at the devastation in Saudi Arabia. I visited him in his mansion whenever I was leave. I told him all of the stories of my experiences, and he wrote them down. He began to collect all the stories he could, and took notes on the legitimacy of each one. When my tour of duty ended, I moved in with him. Together, we worked to research and document all the cases of the paranormal we could find.

Eventually, we knew that simply reading and taking notes would not be enough. We had to investigate cases as they happened, to view the scenes while they were still fresh and to interview the witnesses while they were still focused on the events. This was beyond us, as he was crippled and I was his doctor.

We hired a team of scientists and psychics to investigate one case. It was a haunting in a Yorkshire mansion. The team brought in state of the art equipment to monitor everything that went on in the mansion, and the psychics worked to speak with the spirits. The results were better than we had ever imagined! It was then that we realized what we had to do. Colonel Buckingham used his wealth and connections to found the FPI and make it all happen. This was back in 1996, and the Foundation has grown greatly since then. The amount of quality information that we have received as a result is incredible!

You will be amazed at the things you will learn and experience as chapter members of the Foundation for Paranormal Investigation.

Organization

The Foundation works as a group of individual chapters. Each chapter is self-sufficient and has access to the resources available at the head office.

FPI: The Show

Chapters

The Foundation is made up of many chapters. Each chapter is a group of members who works together to investigate any cases that they feel are relevant. A chapter may contain any number of members, and can have any form of internal organization that the chapter decides upon. In all cases, the chapter must have a Chapter Head, who is the official liaison to the Head Office. Most chapters have one or two members whose task it is to write up the reports of their missions that are to be submitted to the Head Office for inclusion into the Library.

Chapter House

The Chapter Head can buy or rent a place for the chapter to meet, if he wants. In many cases, though, the chapter will simply use the home of one of the founding members and save their money for equipment or travel.

Chapter Head

The chapter head is the official leader of the chapter. In most cases, he is the founder of the chapter, but there are some that elect a new head from time to time.

The chapter head is in charge of the administration of all chapter duties, and has the final say about taking each case.

Any chapter member can have access to the Head Office and its resources, but usually only a Chapter Head can get an audience with the Colonel himself.

Charter

The official goal of every FPI chapter is to investigate cases of the paranormal and to issue reports on their investigations to the Head Office. These reports must be thorough, objective and as accurate as possible. The Foundation's intent is to build the world's largest repository of accurate knowledge of the paranormal.

One common misunderstanding is that the FPI is a group of "busters" who hunt ghosts with the intention of destroying or removing them. On the contrary, it is their job to study and observe them. In most cases, they have no interest in removing them, as that would take away the subject of their study. Some chapters, however, have been known to accept payment for getting rid of unwanted spirits, but that is always done *after* they have gotten all the information they can about them. After all, learning how to dismiss or destroy spirits would make one hell of a great report to the Head Office, and a few extra bucks on the side can't hurt either!

Resources

The primary resource of the FPI is the Head Office and its library. The Head Office is really Colonel Buckingham's home. It is a very large mansion on many acres of land near Elgin, Scotland. It sits on the top of a hill surrounded by woodland, and is out of sight from most roads.

The library is extensive, containing copies of books on virtually all topics of the paranormal. All of the common or popular books are available in the library, as well as many that less common or even rare. They have an extensive card catalog that can be accessed by a computer via the Internet. The Chapter Head can request a username and password for any of his members so that they can have access to the card catalog and database.

One nice feature of this database is a special rating key for each book, article, video or other item that describes how reliable or accurate its information is. It will also contain cross-references to all Foundation reports that expand upon or contradict the information it contains. This can be invaluable to all FPI members.

Funding

By default, the Head Office provides little funding to a chapter. Each chapter is meant to be self-sufficient and must therefore provide for themselves.

However, there may be times when the Director feels that the Head Office would aid the chapter. This is possible, and is more common in the lending of equipment, and less common in dispensing money.

Because each chapter must fend for itself, many chapters will perform services for money. Some have been known to accept money in return for ridding a house of an unwanted spirit. Of course, the chapter would study it and learn as much as they can about it for their own records before they complete their hired task.

Handling Investigations

Always remember that while investigating a case, you are representing the Foundation for Paranormal Investigation. You must present yourself in a professional manner. The Foundation has a reputation of performing intelligent and objective investigations, so you must always present yourself in that manner.

FPI: The Show

Each chapter has the right to pick and choose which cases they would like to investigate. It does not matter how you find out about the case, as long as it involves a topic that is of interest to the Foundation. Before beginning your investigation, you must report to the Head Office and notify them of your intentions. This will help eliminate the possibility of having more than one chapter investigating the same case. Also, the Head Office can help you best if it knows what you are doing.

Occasionally, the Head Office will assign a case to a chapter. Those cases must be taken. Also, if the Head Office contacts you and tells you to abandon a case, you must comply. Aside from these two rules, you have complete autonomy in your investigations.

The Head Office

The Head Office is the residence of Colonel Joseph Buckingham, founder of the FPI. It's located

Chain of Command

As founder of the FPI, Colonel Buckingham is the man in charge. He oversees the Foundation and its work. Sometimes he'll intervene, but that is only in extreme cases or when he feels personally involved in the topic at hand. For the most part, he lets the Foundation run itself and simply watches. The Colonel reads every report that is submitted and will comment on them from time to time.

Below him is myself, Dr. Arthur Shepard. Some call me co-founder, but really I just helped the Colonel with his researched and suggested some ideas. However, I take a much more active role in the Foundation. I oversee all of the chapters, and will even recruit members and start chapters as I see fit. I have almost complete autonomy, as the Colonel fully trusts my judgment. He has overruled some of my decisions, but those cases are rare, and I must admit, usually quite justified.

After myself, the chain of command falls on the individual chapters, beginning with each chapter head. Any command structure below that level is defined by each chapter and will only be recognized within that chapter.

There is a Head Office Manager who will oversee the day-to-day affairs of the Head Office. All chapter heads must accept the Manager's authority when visiting or dealing with the Head Office.

Security

Security is a topic of great importance to the Foundation, and covers many areas. I will try to cover the most important security rules now:

Information: You are not (and I repeat: *not*) to submit any of the reports of your chapter's investigations to anyone outside of the Foundation. Doing so may be grounds for immediate dismissal. The Foundation has every intention of making its information available, but it reserves the sole rights to how and when. Releasing a report to the wrong audience or at the wrong time could cause great damage to the FPI's reputation, and that will not be tolerated. If you want to disclose a report to an outside party, then you must first get permission from the Head Office.

Resources: This one is simple: no one who is not a member of the Foundation for Paranormal Investigation is allowed access to the Foundation's resources. There are no exceptions. This includes access to the Head Office, any records in a chapter house, and the computer network and Internet site. If you feel the need to give a non-member access to a Foundation resource, it must first be cleared by the Head Office. Non-compliance of this rule will be punishable to the full extent of the law.

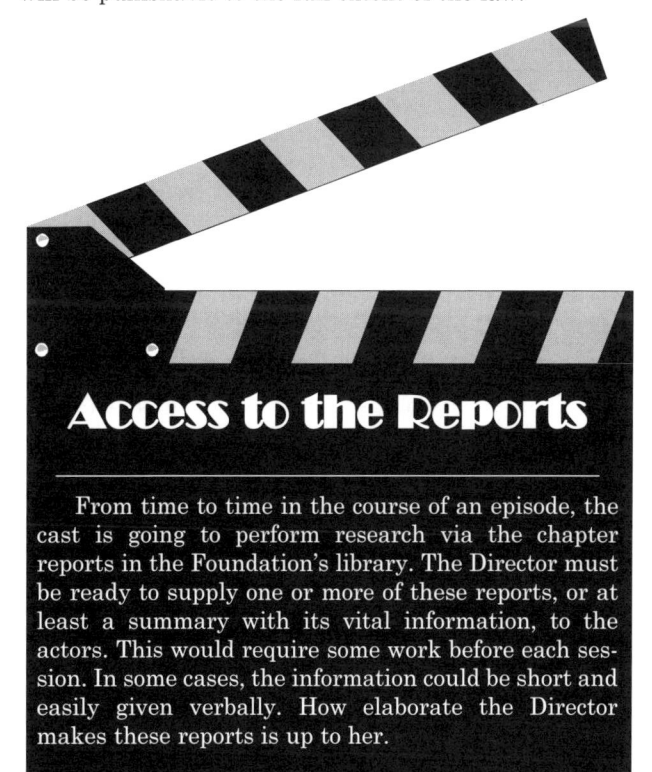

Access to the Reports

From time to time in the course of an episode, the cast is going to perform research via the chapter reports in the Foundation's library. The Director must be ready to supply one or more of these reports, or at least a summary with its vital information, to the actors. This would require some work before each session. In some cases, the information could be short and easily given verbally. How elaborate the Director makes these reports is up to her.

The Library

The library contains hundreds of books on the various topics of the paranormal. It also contains hard copies of all of the reports submitted by Foundation chapters. All of the reports are available online via the Foundation's Internet servers. The library itself has a number of computers set up to access the online site as a research aid.

The library is located at the Head Office in a separate building that was built on the grounds with an enclosed passageway connecting it to the main mansion.

There are currently around five hundred reports on file in the library (and online). Most of them are inconclusive in their findings and are often about similar phenomena. However, all of the reports are well done and well researched. It is safe to say that none of them are made up of hearsay and conjecture.

FPI: The Show

Art of Ghost Hunting

Hunting for ghosts presents a particular challenge in that there has never been any solid proof of their existence. For a long time, all we could go by was first-hand accounts from people who have seen them. Nowadays with modern technology, we can attempt to scan for them, monitor them, and even record them on film and tape.

Amateur and professional ghost hunters have used a variety of methods to investigate ghost sightings. This section will describe the process for some of the more common methods. Many FPI members will utilize a variety of these methods during one investigation. This is advisable since no one method is reliable, and having positive feedback from several different detection methods will provide more concrete information.

NOTE: The Foundation for Paranormal Investigation cannot vouch for the validity of any of these methods. However, they are all acceptable practices when investigating cases of the paranormal, as long as all the findings are properly recorded, and the members remain objective.

Electronic Voice Phenomena

This is the art of capturing the voices of spirits on tape. Thomas Edison was the first person to claim to have heard spiritual voices on audio tape. He said that if you amplify the recording and listen carefully, you could sometimes hear a voice speaking when you know there was no one in the room at the time when you made the recording. This phenomenon has been named Electronic Voice Phenomena, or EVP.

Human voices always fall within the audio range of three hundred to three thousand Hertz. EVPs take the form of Extremely Low Frequency voice recordings, and fall in within the range of one to three hundred Hertz.

This is perhaps the most common method of ghost hunting, simply because it is the easiest. However, the sounds that you hear are usually so distorted and rough that they could easily be explained away as interference or defects in the tape. Like all methods of ghost hunting, Electronic Voice Phenomena are not conclusive evidence of the existence of ghosts. They can be very useful, however, to those who believe because they include actual spoken words that may be a message from beyond the grave.

Capturing EVP

Required Equipment: Portable tape recorder, blank recording tapes, computer, and audio editing software.

Take the tape recorder, and put a blank tape in it. Walk quietly around the place that you suspect to be haunted while recording. Occasionally speak to the spirits in a soft, soothing voice. Ask it questions that you think it will want to respond to. It is important to leave plenty of silence between your questions. Even if a spirit is present, you will never hear EVP with your naked ear; it is far too low a frequency for that. If you do hear a spiritual voice, then it is not an EVP and you are very lucky!

Once you have spent plenty of time recording the silence of the area and asking your questions, turn off the recorder. It is now time to analyze the recordings.

Analyzing the Recordings

Before you can study the recordings, you must first transfer the recordings to a computer. Connect the tape recorder to your computer's line-in connector, then fire up your audio editing software. Play back the tape while recording it to your computer.

The software will show the sound waves of the recording. You now must select a section of the recording where the sound waves show silence, then zoom in on it, and play it back. You will hear the hiss of the tape loudly, but you may hopefully hear a voice in the background.

This process will require both a Computer Use skill test and one or more Notice skill tests. If the Computer Use test fails, then the recording could not be transferred in a quality good enough to make out anything. If the Notice tests fail, then you could not pick out any Electronic Voice Phenomena.

Electro Magnetic Frequency

Another common tool for ghost hunters is the Electro Magnetic Frequency (EMF) detectors. Every living animal emits electro magnetic energy. There are different types of EMF, and an EMF detector will pick them all up. This simple meter measures the amount of electro magnetic frequency emissions in the area.

Many ghost hunters have noted a distinct pattern of high levels of EMF in places that are known to be haunted. Because of this pattern, the EMF detector has become a staple weapon in a ghost hunter's arsenal. Although there has been no conclusive evidence that these devices detect the presence of spirits, the Foundation for Paranormal Investigation uses these to help gain as much information about the spiritual phenomena as possible.

No skill tests are required to use these devices, as they are so very simple to use. Simply turn it on and walk around the suspected area. The meter has either a needle or LEDs that will show the level of EMF detected.

The detector will show the following ranges of emissions:

Magnetic Field: 0-100 microteslas
Electric Field: 0-100 volts/meter

FPI: The Show

Environmental Changes

Many people have reported sudden unaccountable changes in the environment when seeing a ghost. In most cases, this is in the form of a gust of icy wind or a sudden drastic drop in temperature. Sometimes other barometric changes occur, according to the accounts of witnesses. For this reason, ghost hunters often bring barometers and other gear used to monitor weather conditions.

Psychic

Some ghost hunters claim to have the psychic ability to be able to detect and even to see ghosts. These Sensitives merely walk around a haunted area in a relaxed state. Some claim to feel "vibrations" left behind by the spirits. Others claim to feel their presence much like a person can sometimes sense that he is being watched. Still others claim to feel sensations, like intense cold or a tingle when touched by a ghost. Some psychics seem to be more likely to see an apparition, and some have even been known to speak to them.

Although the Foundation for Paranormal Investigation is open to the concept of psychic phenomenon, the use of psychics as a means of detecting ghosts is not accepted on its own merits. A reported incident with a psychic must be corroborated by other measurements, such as EMF, EVP, or bizarre environmental disturbances.

> A character must have the Sensitive Power (such as Jelena Koslova) in order to sense the presence of ghosts psychically. See the Sensitive Psychic Power in Chapter Eleven: The Paranormal for details.

Show Plotlines

The first half of this chapter and the following chapter all describe the setting of FPI. However, before you can play it, you have to define a show. The show is the combination of a storyline and a cast that is placed in the setting.

This section describes a number of different show ideas that you play with FPI. Of course, you can always think up your own storylines, but these can give you a good idea of what can be done with this setting.

FPI: Shadow Games

When in Saudi Arabia during the Gulf War, Colonel Buckingham had an experience that changed his life. The shadowy creatures that he saw pawing at his fallen comrades were working together toward some end. The Colonel has made it his life's goal to find out what these creatures are, and what they were doing. It is the primary goal of the FPI. Any chapter that comes across reports of Shadow People or any other similar being is required to investigate.

In this show, reports of Shadow People have been on the rise. As the FPI members investigate these reports, they find a pattern in their behavior. At first, this pattern only adds to the mystery, but as time goes on, the cast begins to learn of a sinister plan forming behind their actions.

FPI: Invasion

Scattered among other cases, the cast investigates some UFO reports. At first, these reports all appear random and unrelated. As the investigations continue, however, they begin to see similarities in the incidents, and begin to uncover a conspiracy that may end in an invasion. The cast must find out who is behind the conspiracy, and what the aliens are doing.

FPI: Armageddon

Some of the cases that the cast investigates seem to have religious implications. As the investigations unfold, the cast begins to realize that signs of the apocalypse are occurring, and that this may be the beginning of the end of mankind!

FPI: Psi Conspiracy

There is a secret agency within the U.S. government that studies and experiments with psychic abilities. It is unsure what they are intending to do, but they are taking a strong interest in anyone who exhibits psychic ability. Many of the psychics that the FPI has investigated have disappeared mysteriously. Does this agency have anything to do with the disappearances? It is up to the FPI to find out! This show can begin without the FPI's knowlege of the agency, and can focus on the quest for the truth.

FPI

There is actually no need to have a storyline that runs throughout the course of the show. In this show, the episodes are all independent of each other, and can be played in any order. Each one is just a new case for the cast to investigate.

The Cast

The following are characters that were created specifically for FPI. Some are designed as leading characters, and some are meant to be supporting roles. It is always recommended, though, that you create your own characters for the show. You will always become more attached to characters you create yourselves than ones that you borrow from someone else!

FPI: The Show

The Foundation

Jelena Koslova
Leading Character
Gypsy Fortune Teller & Sensitive

Brawn: Fair **Reasoning:** Good
Agility: Fair **Perception:** Great
Stamina: Fair **Will:** Fair
Luck: 3 **Income:** Fair

Skills: Concentration (Fair), English Language (Fair), Move Silently (Good), Mythology (Good), Notice (Great), Occult Knowledge (Good), Perform Divination (Great), Research (Good), Russian Culture (Good), Séance (Good).

Gifts: Attractive.

Faults: Tunel vision when dealing with spirits.

Props: Deck of tarot cards, deck of playing cards, pouch of rune stones, incense & burner, small flashlight.

Jelena is a Rom Gypsy who moved to the United States with her family when she was five years old. She is now a US citizen, but has close ties with her family and her culture. She is at odds with her family to some extent because she is not willing to accept some of the traditions of her people. For instance, her family has pre-arranged a marriage for her to another Gypsy. She wants no part of it. He seems like a nice enough man, but she firmly believes that she should be allowed to make her own choices.

She is a Sensitive. This means that she can sense, see, and sometimes speak with spirits of the dead. She can make a Notice skill test to sense the presence, or perhaps see a ghost. To speak with them requires a Concentration skill test. She must be able to speak the language that the ghosts know.

Along with this ability, her family has taught her the skill of the Séance, with which she can use the energies of others to help her initiate contact with the spirit world. If the Séance skill test is successful, she can add the number of people in the séance to her skill tests for contacting the spirits. It will also force a spirit to come to them.

She is very fascinated with the spirits and her gift. Whenever she is dealing with spirits, she may become totally fixated on it, to the exclusion of all else. The Director may call for a Will test to remain aware of what's going on around her.

She joined the FPI so that she could learn more about spirits, the dead, and other powers like her own. The FPI wanted her because of her obvious talents.

Physical Description: She is an exotic beauty. She has the curves that drive men crazy, and she capitalizes on them by wearing provocative Gypsy clothing. Her light skirts that show off her curves and in the right light, you can see the shape of her legs through them. Her blouses are always low-cut. She wears a single hoop earring, and her long, wavy black hair partly covers one side of her face. She wears light slipper-like shoes.

Christina Mariani: Christina is a free spirit. She is a scientist, but spends little time in the lab. She always prefers working on location in the ocean, or on the shores of exotic locales. Jelena respects this and feels that it is healthy for her spirit. However, Christina is also impulsive, which has gotten them all into trouble on numerous occasions.

Mike Malone: He's a cop, and there's no mistaking that. Sure, he's a private investigator now, but he used to be a cop, and he still acts it. Whenever they get into a tight situation, he always takes charge. Not that there's anything wrong with it. This team needs leadership, and so far, he's been quite good at it. Mike's a tough man, and not one to cross. But he is a good man, and true to his word.

Mike seems to have special feelings for Christina, although Jelena doesn't think that she realizes it.

Dr. David Walker: Walker's a doctor; a man of medicine and research. He has a mellow attitude, and is not quite the active person that Mike and Christina are. Jelena gets the feeling he does not respect your work.

Nicholas Wu: He is a professor of physics who is very enthusiastic about all forms of science. He is responsible for the large amount of equipment in the FPI van, but he does gather a lot of good data. He's witty and friendly.

FPI: The Show

The Foundation

FPI he joined right away.

His primary interest in the FPI lies in medical phenomena. However, he is interested in just about any case that his chapter investigates. The more he learns about the paranormal in general, the more knowledge he will have to apply to the cases that directly concern him.

David feels a moral obligation to help those who are injured. This has caused him to miss out on important aspects of a case simply because he had chosen to stay behind to look after an injured person. However, he considers the field practice he has gotten in the FPI to be a good experience. His training has been strictly in hospitals, and performing field medicine like a paramedic is rather invigorating.

Christina Mariani: As a capable scientist, David respects her. She is also quite pleasant and helpful. However, she has a tendency to being bold and daring, and in his opinion, she spends too much time in the field, and not enough in the lab. A good scientist is grounded in research and experimentation, not in gallivanting around the globe to play with fish! Science, however intriguing, is not an adventure. David has lost count of the times that he has treated her as a result of some brave, but foolhardy adventure that she had undertaken. He just hopes that some day she'll learn to tone down the excitement, and focus on what's important.

Mike Malone: He's a cop, and there's no mistaking that. Sure, he's a private investigator now, but he used to be a cop, and he still acts it. Whenever they get into a tight situation, he always takes charge. Not that there's anything wrong with it. This team needs leadership, and so far, he's been quite good at it. Mike's a tough man, and not one to cross. David has had to treat several poor souls who got in his way; of course, each one had gotten on the wrong side of the law, and the violence was justified.

Mike seems to have special feelings for Christina, although David doesn't think that she realizes it. But David doesn't mind. In fact, it means that Mike is always there to keep her out of trouble when things get bad.

Jelena Koslova: Jelena is a Russian gypsy, and frankly, David believes she is a fraud. However, she does lend a different perspective to the team, and has great knowledge of the occult.

Nicholas Wu: David relates with Professor Wu better than with the rest of the team. He is a physics professor, so he is a scientist through and through. He seems to be most interested in psychic phenomena. It is not David's line of interest, but he cannot argue with his findings.

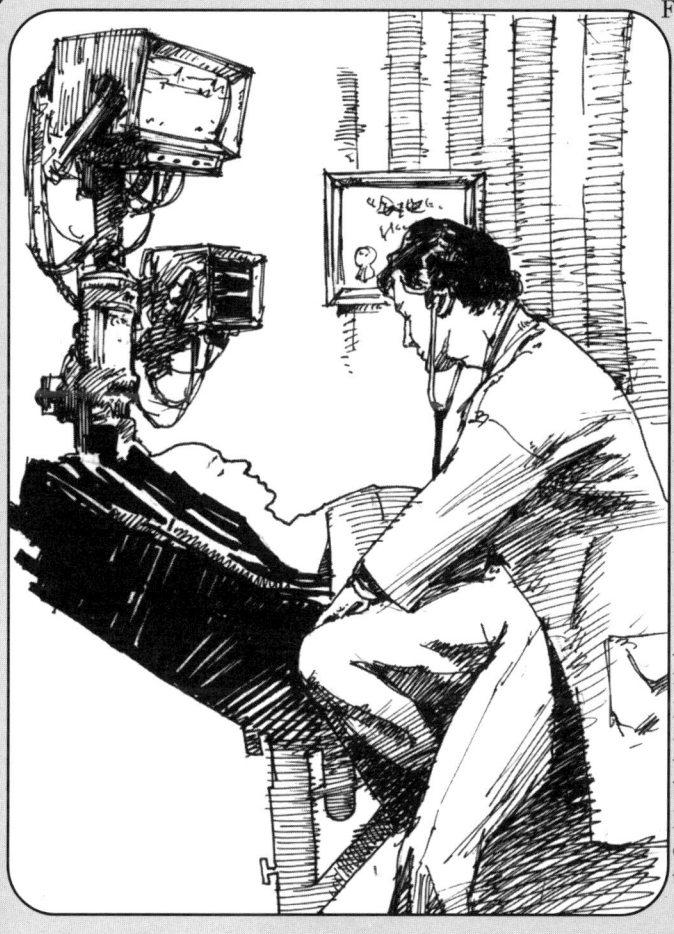

Dr. David Walker
Leading Character
Medical Doctor

Brawn: Fair   **Reasoning:** Great
Agility: Good   **Perception:** Fair
Stamina: Fair   **Will:** Fair
Luck: 3   **Income:** Fair

Skills: Autopsy (Great), Computer Use (Fair), Diagnosis (Good), First Aid (Great), Notice (Good), Parapsychology (Mediocre), Research (Good), Treat Injury (Great).

Gifts: Always keep your cool.

Faults: Obligation to help the injured.

Props: Medical kit, palmtop computer, cell phone, pager.

He is a doctor of medicine at a local hospital. He is very rational and clear thinking. However, he has seen things in his years as a doctor that cannot be explained by science. He became passionate about understanding these bizarre phenomena, and when he learned of the

FPI: The Show

The Foundation

Professor Nicholas Wu
Leading Character
Physics Professor & Parapsychologist

Brawn: Fair **Reasoning:** Great
Agility: Fair **Perception:** Good
Stamina: Fair **Will:** Fair
Luck: 3 **Income:** Fair

Skills: Computer Use (Great), Concentration (Good), Diplomacy (Mediocre), Forensics (Good), Parapsychology (Good), Photography (Great), Physics (Great), Research (Great).

Gifts: Contact (MIT Forensics Professor).

Props: Notebook computer, palmtop computer, 35mm camera, Film (10 rolls), handheld tape recorder, 10 tapes, EMF Detector, nightvision monocular, cell phone.

Professor Wu is a physics professor at a local college. He is taken by the awesome majesty the subject. The way that nature maintains perfect balance in such a complex system fascinates him completely. He brings this emotion into his lectures, which manages to pass this passion onto his students. For this reason, he is the most popular science teacher at the college.

He recently had a student that exhibited a strange ability. He was able to move objects without touching them. He simply concentrated on the object, and it would move. Confused about it, he came to Wu to see if they could figure out how it works. He was hoping Wu would be able to explain it as a naturally occurring phenomenon. The last thing he wanted was to be considered a freak.

Wu was fascinated by it. He performed dozens of experiments, but was ultimately unable to figure out how it worked. However, he was able to detect and measure electro-magnetic energy that emanated from the student whenever he used his power. Wu decided that this must be a natural phenomenon, and that it is not something outside of the realm of science. He just had to figure it out.

Wu became very passionate about this. He began to study psychic phenomena in detail. He attended a lecture on ghosts by a gypsy woman named Jelena Koslova. What she said fascinated him. If psychic ability exists, and he is now certain that it does, then there may be some truth to the phenomenon of spirits. He spoke with her afterwards, and learned about the FPI. He joined immediately.

His enthusiasm for investigating the paranormal is extraordinary. The van is always overpacked with equipment whenever they take a case.

Christina Mariani: Christina is as exciting as she is smart. As a marine biologist, she's very capable. But she's adventurous, always wanting to go out on location. She says you can't study living things in a lab, because you have to know how they live in their natural habitat. Nicholas believes there is truth to that. Dr. Walker doesn't seem to agree with her point of view. He thinks she's reckless. Nicholas thinks she brightens up the team, and adds spice to their investigations.

Mike Malone: He's a cop, and there's no mistaking that. Sure, he's a private investigator now, but he used to be a cop, and he still acts it. Whenever they get into a tight situation, he always takes charge. Not that there's anything wrong with it. This team needs leadership, and so far, he's been quite good at it. Mike's a tough man, and not one to cross. He's got a big chip on his shoulder, though, and Nicholas thinks it can get him into trouble. He's always getting hurt, as you can easily tell by the scars whenever he takes his shirt off.

He's got thing for Christina, which is fun to watch, because Mike tries hard to be professional with her.

Jelena Koslova: Jelena is a Russian gypsy, and plays it to the hilt. Nicholas is not sure if all of her abilities are real, but she's still a valuable member of the team. Besides, she's exotically beautiful, and she is the only one who can take his mind off his work without trying.

Dr. David Walker: He is a medical doctor. Nicholas has had some good scientific conversations with him. He has been a lot of help to the team with his extensive medical knowledge. Of course, with Mike around, it is always good to have a skilled doctor on the team.

FPI: The Show

Mike Malone
Leading Character
Private Investigator

Brawn: Good
Agility: Fair
Stamina: Fair
Luck: 3
Reasoning: Fair
Perception: Great
Will: Good
Income: Mediocre

Skills: Bluff (Mediocre), Brawl (Great), Criminology (Fair), Gun (Great), Stealth (Good), Gather Information (Great), Interrogate (Good), Intimidate (Good), Research (Fair), Run (Fair), Notice (Great), Sense Motive (Fair), Shadow (Good).

Gifts: Keen Eyesight (+1 to all sight-based Notice tests).

Faults: Bossy, Decreased Income.

Props: Flashlight, Revolver (Strength +2), Box of 50 rounds, cell phone, Swiss Army knife, pocket notebook & pen, investigation kit (fingerprinting kit, rubber gloves, etc.).

He was once a tough-as-nails police detective who worked in the homicide division of the New York Police Department. He was trying to catch a serial killer. He found the killer, but what he saw shook him to the core. The killer turned out to be some kind of bizarre creature. He shot the thing three times in the chest and back, but it ran away.

In the aftermath, Internal Affairs walked all over him. Although he was not fired, he was fed up with the process and quit. He went into business for himself as a private investigator, and soon found out about the FPI. He joined up right away. The more he could learn about this stuff, he reasoned, the better prepared he would be when he went up against another one!

Mike tends to try to take the lead in any situation, sometimes even when he does not have the right to do so. He'll just automatically assume the lead and start blurting out orders.

Christina Mariani: Mike likes Christina and has great respect for her talents. Like him, she's a person of action, ready and willing to jump in and get things done. She's also very smart, and very attractive. Although he tries to keep a professional relationship with her, he is quite taken with her. After all, an attractive woman who's personality fits his own is a hard woman to resist. But, since he has to work with her, he tries to keep things cool.

Mike feels he has to watch out for Christina. She is quite impulsive, and although she's intelligent, she has managed to get herself into deep trouble by taking unnecessary risks. He could not bear to see anything bad happen to her, and he can't prevent her from entering into dangerous situations, so he keeps close to her and acts as her protector.

Dr. David Walker: Walker's a doctor; a man of medicine and research. He has a mellow attitude, and is not quite the active person that he and Christina are. This has sometimes slowed down their investigations, but his skills have nevertheless proven quite useful.

Jelena Koslova: Walker's a doctor; a man of medicine and research. He has a mellow attitude, and is not quite the active person that he and Christina are. This has sometimes slowed down their investigations, but his skills have nevertheless proven quite useful.

Nicholas Wu: Walker's a doctor; a man of medicine and research. He has a mellow attitude, and is not quite the active person that he and Christina are. This has sometimes slowed down their investigations, but his skills have nevertheless proven quite useful.

The Foundation

FPI: The Show

The Foundation

Christina Mariani
Leading Character
Marine Biologist

Brawn: Fair **Reasoning:** Great
Agility: Fair **Perception:** Good
Stamina: Good **Will:** Good
Luck: 3 **Income:** Fair

Skills: Balance (Fair), Computer Use (Good), Concentration (Fair), Cryptozoology (Good), Drive Motorboat (Good), First Aid (Mediocre), Nature Lore (Great), Mythology (Mediocre), Notice (Fair), Photography (Good), Research (Great), Sail (Fair), Swim (Good).

Gifts: Passionate about Marine Life.

Faults: Blunt & Tactless, Impulsive.

Props: Palmtop computer, cell phone, sample jars, tweezers, small plastic bags, rubber gloves.

She is a marine biologist fresh out of college. She is very energetic and athletic, and takes a very active approach to her studies. Instead of spending most of her time in a lab, she likes to go out and study marine life in its natural habitat. Because of this, she has taken her studies to a variety of places around the world. She is an accomplished diver and feels almost more at home underwater than on land.

During her explorations, she has seen animals that she could not identify. Of course, in all cases, she never got any proof, and therefore never went public about them. She joined the FPI so that she can attempt to learn more about these creatures and to have access to the resources she needs to gather proof.

If anyone can find adventure in the field of marine biology, it is Christina. She is bold and daring, and is not squeemish in the least. This mix tends to make her impulsive, and she will often walk right into dangerous situations without thinking about the consequences.

Whenever she feels there is something that needs to be said, she will just come right out and say it. She pays little heed to ettiquette, and will come straight to the point, no matter how rude. This is not intentional, and in fact, she will never think that she said anything wrong.

Mike Malone: He's an ex-cop that still acts like he still is one. He now works as a private eye, and does a good job of it. Christina mainly sees him through work with the FPI. He is every bit a man of action, and so they're always the ones to go first into danger, which happens all too often with the FPI. She knows that he likes her, but in what way, she's not sure. He obviously respects her for her skills and her active nature, but she's not certain if there's anything more to it.

Dr. David Walker: Walker's a doctor; a man of medicine and research. He has a mellow attitude. This has sometimes slowed down their investigations, but his skills have nevertheless proven quite useful.

Christina gets the feeling that Dr. Walker does not appreciate her adventurous approach to science. He is very much the kind of person who thinks that scientists should spend most of their time in the lab doing research and experimentation. He doesn't seem to understand that science is alive and very closely tied to the Earth. There is only so much that you can learn about something when you have separated it from its natural environment.

Jelena Koslova: She's a gypsy and is very spiritual. She is quite exotic and very interesting to talk to. Christina likes having her come on the investigations.

Nicholas Wu: He's a passionate scientist who is almost obsessive about psychic phenomenon. He is very much into technology, and tends to overpack the van on every trip. But he does always produce a lot of good data for our case reports.

FPI: The Show

Matt Hawkins
Leading or Supporting Character
Investigative Reporter

Brawn: Fair **Reasoning:** Fair
Agility: Good **Perception:** Great
Stamina: Fair **Will:** Good
Luck: 3 **Income:** Fair

Skills: Area Knowledge (Good), Brawl (Mediocre), Climb (Fair), Direction Sense (Fair), Disguise (Fair), Dodge (Fair), Folklore (Mediocre), Forgery (Fair), Gather Information (Great), Notice (Great), Photography (Good), Pick Lock (Fair), Read Lips (Fair), Research (Good), Run (Fair), Shadow (Fair), Stealth (Good), Swim (Fair).

Gifts: Perfect Timing (the Director can make sure you're at the right place at the right time, whenever it makes good theatrical sense).

Faults: Ambitious, Curious.

Props: Handheld tape recorder, 2 blank tapes, cell phone, notebook & pen, camera, 4 rolls of film, fake ID.

He has always wanted to be an investigative reporter ever since he was a kid. He would rat on his friends all the time just to be the one to "get the story." This has not made him very popular with his peers, but he never really cared much about that.

He graduated from Boston University with a double degree in Broadcasting and Journalism. He got a job in the Channel 12 news department, first as a journalist, writing the stories that the anchors read. That was not enough, though. One day, he snuck onto a crime scene and got the inside scoop on a very controversial police case. He recorded it himself and showed it to his boss. He's been an investigative reporter ever since.

Matt commonly uses unethical methods to get his stories. He has disguised himself and posed as various officials to get onto a crime scene, and has taken advantage of people to further his own ends. Nothing gets in the way of his ambitions. In short, he's a jerk—a very successful one!

Matt has become almost obsessed with the FPI. He has bumped into them on a few occasions, and found that they draw good stories to them like magnets. He keeps tabs on them, spying on them every now and then to see what they're up to. They're a big organization, with money and resources in other countries. However, so far, he has been able to find out about the one chapter and knows next to nothing about their organization. Matt suspects that there's more to them than just a bunch of ghost hunters...something more sinister!

Christina Mariani: She is a marine biologist who does work for the Aquarium, and a member of the Foundation for Paranormal Investigation. She's gorgeous and spunky. Someday, Matt will make a more pro-active investigation of this group, and Christina will be his way in...through her pants, if he gets his way!

Mike Malone: He's an ex-cop from New York that is now working as a private eye. He's tough and smart, and is Matt's biggest stumbling block in his investigation of the FPI. Malone is tough and doesn't take kind to people poking around. However, he's also a great person to watch, as he's always stirring up trouble with the group.

Dr. David Walker: Walker's a doctor at one of the hospitals here in Boston. You've seen him working with Malone and Mariani, so you assume he's a member of the FPI, but you don't know what his involvement really is.

Jelena Koslova: She's a gypsy and is very hot! However, she seems to understand him a little too much. He's not sure if there's has something to do with being a gypsy, but he keeps his distance, just in case.

Nicholas Wu: He's an eccentric scientist who is nuts about technology. He thinks he can hunt and study ghosts by using lots of fancy gadgets and machines.

FPI: The Show

The Foundation

Dr. Arthur Shepard
Supporting Character
Medical Doctor

Brawn: Fair **Reasoning:** Great
Agility: Fair **Perception:** Good
Stamina: Fair **Will:** Good
Luck: 3 **Income:** Good

Skills: Anatomy (Great), Autopsy (Great), Biology (Great), Brawl (Fair), Computer Use (Fair), Concentration (Fair), Cryptozoology (Good), Diagnosis (Great), Dodge (Fair), First Aid (Great), Hypnosis (Fair), Notice (Fair), Occult Knowledge (Good), Parapsychology (Good), Research (Great), Sense Motive (Fair), Treat Injury (Great).

Gifts: Always keep your cool, Well Traveled, Patron (the Colonel).

Faults: Obligation to care for the Colonel.

Props: Code that people should avoid physical risk at all cost.

Doctor Shepard is a very serious man. He has been everywhere and seen a lot, and it has been a sobering experience for him. He has seen many strange things and that's what made him sympathetic to the Colonel's story.

He met Colonel Buckingham in Saudi Arabia during the Gulf War. The Colonel had been badly injured during a bombing attack, and he was the doctor who patched him up. Dr. Shepard was very good to him, and the Colonel told him his story. Shepard did some investigation into the matter for him, but discovered nothing. Still, he believed the Colonel, because he had heard of similar incidents by other believable sources.

After the war, Shepard chose to work for the Colonel, who was honorably discharged after losing both of his legs in the attack. He is now his personal doctor and confidante. He helped his friend with his research into the paranormal.

When the Colonel founded the Foundation for Paranormal Investigation, Shepard took an active role. Shepard is the Chapter Coordinator. He oversees the creation of new chapters, and makes sure that they are all following the proper procedures. He and the Colonel read every report that comes in, and he will send feedback to the chapters if anything was not done properly. He has, on occasion, disbanded several chapters that were repeatedly negligent in their duties.

Colonel Joseph Buckingham
Supporting Character
Retired British Military Colonel

Brawn: Fair **Reasoning:** Great
Agility: Fair **Perception:** Great
Stamina: Good **Will:** Great
Luck: 3 **Income:** Great

Skills: Area Knowledge: Middle East (Good), Computer Use (Fair), Cryptozoology (Good), Culture: Arabic (Fair), Notice (Good), Occult Knowledge (Fair), Parapsychology (Fair), Politics (Great), Research (Good), Gun (Good), Diplomacy (Great), Comaraderie (Fair), Interrogate (Great), Intimidate (Great), Sense Motive (Great).

Gifts: Increased Income (twice), Inheritance, Passionate about the paranormal.

Faults: Handicap (twice): lost both legs.

Joseph was also a successful military man. He is a born leader, with an uncanny skill at reading a person's body language and knowing exactly what to say or do to gain his trust and respect. He is also a great tactician. It is the combination of these qualities, along with many years on active duty that allowed him to rise to the rank of colonel by the age of thirty-eight.

In Saudi Arabia, he lost both of his legs in a bombing attack, but more importantly, he saw strange creatures desecrating the corpses of his comrades. This made him obsessed with the paranormal, and it has become the primary focus of his life, now that he has retired.

He has a special relationship with Dr. Arthur Shepard. He met the doctor in Saudi Arabia, and he was very open to the paranormal. He confided in the doctor, and found that he not only believed him, but was ready to help him investigate. Since then, he has taken Arthur on as his personal doctor, and spends much time with him. The doctor lives in the Colonel's mansion and works hard with the FPI.

The Colonel founded the FPI as a means for him to get as much research and investigation done on the paranormal as possible. Since then, his library has grown immensely with reports from the various chapters. He still has not discovered any more information on the shadow creatures that he witnessed, but he is still hopeful.

FPI: The Show

Episode Guide

This is the episode guide for season one of FPI: Shadow Games. You can take these simple episode descriptions and build a full season of FPI with them. You can also pick and choose the ones you want, or you can throw them all away and run your own season. In any case, this guide is a good example of a planned out game.

101 - Shadows

The FPI team investigates a house whose owners claim is haunted by black figures skulking in the shadows.

102 - Haunted Holiday

Mike Malone's cousin invited him and his colleagues for a visit, only to find that the house's previous owners still live there.

103 - The Big Dig

The team is called in to help the Boston police department solve the case of missing workers in an undersea highway tunnel that is still under construction.

104 - Experiments

The subjects of psychic experiments back in the seventies cause havoc in a small town in upstate New York.

105 - Ghost Ship

The ship that had been bearing Christina's cousin is sighted again after being lost as sea for seven years.

106 - Sasquatch

Sightings of Bigfoot draw the team to Washington State, where they are hunted deep in the forest by an unknown creature.

107 - Terror

Trapped in a building that is blown up by terrorists, one member of the team witnesses mysterious black beings that take an interest in the bodies of the dead.

NOTE: One actor can play his normal character, and the rest can play supporting characters.

108 - The Triangle

The team takes a boat into the Bermuda Triangle to investigate strange happenings.

109 - Gothic

The team visits the house that a famous author of gothic horror once lived in, and finds the source of his inspiration.

110 - MKU

A man with special psychic abilities comes to the FPI for help, but is being hunted by a covert government agency.

111 - Aztec

The team investigates a newly found Aztec tomb that is said to be cursed.

112 - Walking Dead

The member of the team sees an acquaintance walking down the street-one that had died in a building explosion!

NOTE: The character that sees the dead man is the one who was trapped in the building in episode 107. That's where the man had died. There is a connection here between the black creatures and the dead man.

113 - Invisible Enemy

The team investigates an abandoned house after hearing on the news that two youths claim to have been assaulted by ghosts inside it.

114 - Missing Persons

The team is peril as they help police investigate the disappearance of an entire family inside a house that has the reputation of being haunted.

115 - Monsters

People in a small town are being attacked at night under bizarre circumstances, and each one appears linked to a child's nightmares.

116 - Target

The FPI chapter house is broken into, and the only things stolen are the reports concerning shadow people.

NOTE: This should be about a conspiracy dealing with shadow people.

117 - G.H.N.E.

A ghost-hunting group with acquaintances in the FPI disappears while investigating a supposedly haunted wood in Massachusetts.

NOTE: The title of this episode represents "Ghost

FPI: The Show

Hunters of New England," a fictional ghost-hunting group. Feel free to change the name as you see fit.

118 - Future Tense
A young woman who claims to be able to see the future has predicts the death of an FPI chapter member.

119 - Abduction
While investigating a routine report of a UFO sighting, the team finds themselves involved in something much more complicated...and dangerous.

120 - Night Stalker
A string of serial murders in Boston lead the team to believe that the killer may be a vampire.

121 - Limelight
The producers of a TV special about ghost hunters convince the team to spend the night locked in an ancient English castle with other ghost hunting teams.

122 - Ghouls
Graves are being desecrated in a small New England town, and the team suspects a paranormal culprit.

123 - Final Act
A stage magician performs an act claiming to be able to defy death, and apparently succeeds.

124 - Shadow Alliance Part I
Colonel Buckingham himself sends the team to Iraq to investigate a top-secret report that an entire platoon was wiped out in an Iraqi attack, and then suddenly reappears unharmed.

FPI: Invasion Key Episodes

These are some of the key season beat episodes that can be played in *FPI: Invasion*. You can use these in your shows or create your own. The importance of these episodes is that they help to drive the story of the impending alien invasion forward. Each of these episodes has a plot that is very important to the overall storyline, and by placing them throughout the season, it will keep the actors' interest.

101 - Night Lights
People in a small town in upstate New York exhibit strange behavior after witnessing mysterious lights in the sky.

108 - Circles
The team investigates a rash of crop circles that have appeared across the United States.

112 - Fourth Kind
The team is called in to investigate the disappearance of a three loggers in the forests of Washington State.

118 - Subjects
The team receives a call from a distressed woman who claims her husband and son had been abducted by aliens and returned, only to deny it when they arrive to investigate.

124 - Ghost Town
The entire population of a small midwestern town disappears shortly after UFO sightings were reported.

FPI: Armageddon Key Episodes

The following are some key season beat episodes that you could use when playing *FPI: Armageddon*. You can use these in your shows or create your own.

101 - Signs
The team investigates some recent cases that resemble signs of the apocalypse.

108 - Sins
A serial killer's ritualistic methods make the team think that he believes he is a warrior of Satan.

112 - The Walking Dead
The dead seem to be rising from their graves in a remote Alaskan town.

118 - Fallen Angel
An old woman approaches the team and tells them about an angel that was captured by a paramilitary group in Florida.

124 - Catastrophe
Several catastrophes happening at the same time cause the team to suspect a coming Armageddon.

The Paranormal

Chapter 10

FPI: The Show

The Paranormal

What is Paranormal?

The dictionary describes the paranormal as "Beyond the range of normal experience or scientific explanation." Most people think of ghosts, magic and UFOs when they hear the word. Well, certainly that is the popular conception of the paranormal, and it is the focus of the FPI However, the key phrase to consider in the above definition is "Beyond the range." The goal of the Foundation is to extend the range of normal experience and scientific explanation so that we can better understand paranormal phenomena.

Psychic Powers

This summary report refers to psychic powers as abilities to perform acts above the human norm through thought and will alone. Psychic powers do not require rituals or other tools in order to be used. The psychic merely concentrates and through his own force of will, causes the event to occur.

There are literally hundreds of different reported cases of psychic phenomena, yet they all fall under a certain group of categories. These are described below.

It is interesting to note that in virtually all cases, no psychic power was great enough to perform more than one specific type of task, and are not flexible enough to encompass the abilities of an entire category. For instance, I met a man who could see into a person's past simply by making physical contact, skin to skin. However, the only past event that he could see was the very last time the person was injured. Most of the time, he would only see the person get a paper cut or a stubbed toe. Occasionally, however, he would see the person attacked by an assailant, and possibly even be able to identify him.

MK-ULTRA

During World War II, the CIA started this program to experiment with hypnosis as a means of mind control. Their goal was to create couriers that are resistant to torture. In most cases, the courier would not even know that he was carrying secret information. The information could only be retrieved by using a special post-hypnotic suggestion.

Supposedly, they were successful, at least to a certain degree. They employed the use of hypnosis, drugs, and psycho-surgery in order to create the desired effects.

The research of MK-ULTRA continued into the 1970's, when it was supposedly disbanded. There are those who believe that the project is continuing under a new name, and perhaps under a different branch of the government. There have been rumors of the Navy using telepathy and ESP as a means of locating submarines.

Clairvoyance

This is defined as the ability to see events and objects that are beyond the capability of the senses. This includes seeing future events, past events, object reading, and even the ability to travel through objects with your mind and see things far away.

There is specific information on some of these abilities. This information is described below.

Object Reading

This happens when the psychic holds an object in his hands and concentrates on it. Eventually, he may see images or flashes of a vision of events that occurred in the object's presence. In most cases, the vision seen is of one particular type of event, such as a violent act or a time that the object was touched by a living being. Exactly what the psychic sees is up to the psychic, but it will always be from a limited range of visions.

Out of Body Experience

The psychic puts himself into a trance and then forces his consciousness to leave his body and travel to another place. In this manner, he can travel through any barrier, and go anywhere he wants within a specific range. He can hear, see and smell, but cannot touch and cannot be seen. There have been reports of Sensitives and other psychics being able to see the wandering spirits of living psychics, but they have not been substantiated.

Game Rule Implementation

A character can spend two or more gifts for the Clairvoyance Power.

When you take this Power, you must choose which skill you will automatically get: Read Object or Spirit Walk. Once you choose, you will never have the ability to perform the other skill. For instance, a person with Read Object Clairvoyance skill will not be able to Spirit Walk.

There is no range for Object Reading. The psychic must be touching the object with his skin for the Power to work.

The distance you can Spirit Walk depends on the number of gifts you spend on the Power.

Distance = 1 mile X number of gifts spent

Empathy

Empaths claim that the personality and emotions of every living being are displayed in their aura. Empaths claim they can interpret the subtleties of the aura and learn much about a person's emotions and personality.

According to them, they can identify a person's behavior before he acts and can even sometimes know more about it than the person himself.

Although the energy fields radiating from living things have been photographed and even monitored, there is no proof that connects these energies with the mind.

Game Rule Implementation

A character can spend two or more gifts for the Empathy Power.

The range of a psychic's power is line of sight.

Interpret Aura: This Power comes with the Interpret Aura skill with a default level of Terrible. Each Gift you spend for this Power above two will add one free level to this skill.

Precognition

This is the ability to look into the future. The ability to divine the future or give prophecy has been around throughout history. From the Oracle at Delphi to modern day Gypsies and fortune tellers, psychics have claimed to see glimpses of the future when they enter certain places of power or by touching certain objects. They all say that when the visions come, they are quick and not always easy to interpret.

Many of the reported cases have been proven to be hoaxes. A very large number of people pretend to have this ability as a scam to trick other into giving them money. There are, however, enough convincing cases to warrant keeping this topic open.

Tests have been run on subjects during some of these visions, and it has been determined that in most of the convincing cases, the subject honestly believes that he is seeing the vision. This has been proven by studying brain wave patterns, heart rate and other physical evidence. This still does not prove that the visions are real, but merely that the subject *believes* them to be.

Fortune Tellers

Some psychics who have lesser precognitive abilities require the use of special tools to perform their divination. This includes such tools as tarot cards, tea leaves, the palms of their subject's hands, to name a few. These people often perform their art for money. Most of these people have no actual precognitive ability, but there are some who do. However, those that do have the gift have much lesser psychic abilities.

Game Rule Implementation

A character can spend one or more gifts for the Precognition Power. If the character only spends one gift, however, he will only have the ability of a fortune teller.

The Art of Fortune Telling

Fortune Tellers have less psychic power than others (if they even have any). A fortune teller can buy the Precognition Power with only one gift. However, they will need to use the following method for performing their divinations.

1. Make a Perform skill test opposed by the patron's Sense Motive skill or Perception Attribute. This will determine how convincing he is in the act.

2. Make a Concentration skill test. If you fail, then you cannot successfully perform your divination.

3. Make your Divination skill test. If you succeed, you find out something about the future which you can then pass on to the subject.

Note that the result of a successful divination will be very vague at best. It will be accurate, but up to interpretation. For instance, if the patron is going to be approached by a mugger dressed in black, the divination may have the result "Beware of a dark stranger."

A successful Perform test will mean that you were quite convincing to the patron even if your Divination test failed. In that case, your patron may believe a lie.

This means that the Divination skill will only work if a successful

Divination: This Power comes with the Divination skill with a default level of Terrible. Each Gift you spend for this Power above one will add one free level to this skill.

Psychokinesis

Psychokinesis is the production of motion in physical objects through the use of mental will. At a quick glance, this definition sounds the same as that of telekinesis, but it is different on a very basic level. Psychokinesis deals with creating motion *within* the object by manipulation of its cells. Telekinesis moves the object itself.

The most common cases of psychokinesis have involved such tricks as bending spoons and stop watches with only the subject's mind. There have been reports, however, of psychokinesis being used on a much larger level. There was a report of a man in Tibet who used psychokinesis to slow down his metabolism while he was stranded in the mountains. This allowed him to survive in the frozen wastes while waiting for rescue. There was another report of a man who could make metal items hot to the touch by causing its cells to move so rapidly that they would heat up. Neither of these reports has been substantiated, though.

Game Rule Implementation

A character can spend two or more gifts for the Psychokinesis Power.

The range of a psychic's power depends on the number of gifts spent.

> Range = 10 feet X number of gifts spent

Affect Object: This Power comes with the Affect Object skill with a default level of Terrible. Each Gift you spend for this Power above two will add one free level to this skill.

Sensitive

A Sensitive can see, speak with and sometimes even summon spirits of the dead. Cases of this have been reported all over the world. Of all psychic phenomena, this is probably the most difficult one to prove. To prove that someone can see ghosts of the dead, you must first prove that the ghosts exist, and then somehow prove that he truly can see it. To date, there has been no evidence to support this ability. However, because there has also been no evidence to discount it, these phenomena will still be studied.

Game Rule Implementation

A character can spend two or more gifts for the Sensitive Power.

The range of the psychic's power depends on the number of gifts spent.

> Range = 100 feet X number of gifts spent

The Sensitive can feel the presence of a spirit by making a Perception test. If the spirit is within the Sensitive's line of sight, he can attempt to see the spirit with another Perception test (obviously, the Difficulty Level will be higher). Perception tests can be used to hear the spirit's voice.

Séance: This Power does not come with a skill. However, if the Sensitive has any levels in the Séance Ritual, he can perform this ritual to summon a spirit. The number of gifts spent on the Power is equivalent to the number of spirits that can be summoned at one time. Keeping them present requires a great force of will. A Will test each minute will prevent the spirit from leaving. The ritual requires a minimum number of three people in order to summon a spirit.

The ritual is performed by having a group of people sit in a circle, with everyone holding hands. Everyone must concentrate on the spell. The more people you have in the seance, the greater are your chances of success. For every three people beyond the first three, you gain a +1 to your skill test to summon the spirit.

A Sensitive cannot force a spirit to speak or answer questions. A spirit's cooperation once summoned is purely voluntary.

Telekinesis

This is the ability to move objects by thinking about. Simply by concentrating on the object, the psychic can cause the object to move without the use of any physical force.

Most of the cases of telekinesis turned have turned out to be hoaxes. However, there are cases where cause of the object's motion could not be identified. The evidence in these cases strongly implies the use of some type of mental force, but are thus far not substantiated.

In most cases, only small, lightweight objects can be moved, but there have been rare cases where large objects have been moved in this manner.

Game Rule Implementation

A character can spend two or more gifts for the Telekinesis Power.

The range of a psychic's power depends on the number of gifts spent.

> Range = 10 feet X number of gifts spent

Manipulate Object: This Power comes with the Manipulate Object skill with a default level of Terrible. Each Gift you spend for this Power above two will add one free level to this skill.

Telepathy

Telepathy is the ability to communicate with another person through thought alone. There have been recorded cases of telepaths having full conversations with another person completely by thought. According to these reports, only the person initiating the communication needs to be a telepath.

Another reported use of telepathy is the ability to read the thoughts of another. Supposedly, the telepath is able to extract the surface thoughts of the victim without his knowledge. Powerful telepaths are said to be able to scan deeper into a person's mind and extract thoughts and memories that have been buried in his subconscious.

Game Rule Implementation

A character can spend two or more gifts for the Telepathy Power.

The range of a telepath's power depends on the number of gifts spent.

> *Range = 10 feet X number of gifts spent*

Telepathy Skill: This Power comes with the Telepathy skill with a default level of Terrible. Each Gift you spend for this Power above two will add one free level to this skill.

Ritual Magic

There are many forms of magic practiced in the world, each with their own differences based on culture and tradition. This report will only cover the form that I have personally investigated. Others surely exist and may be covered in future reports.

Ritual Magic is very much an art form. Magicians, or mages as they most often prefer, claim to use a force of energy that exists naturally in the world to perform their spells. This energy goes by many names depending on the magical tradition, but for convenience, I will choose the name "mana." The rituals are meant to help the mage weave or mold the mana into a form that will accomplish the desired task. The more difficult the spell, the more complex is the ritual.

The content of each ritual varies greatly from tradition to tradition, but virtually every one I studied includes a phase where they pool up all the mana that they need for the spell, a phase where they weave it into the form they want via spoken words, chants and other actions, and finally a phase to release it into the world.

Casting spells is a very dangerous. When you release the energy that you pooled up, there is no going back. The spell is cast and begins to take form. You may have one last chance to dismiss the energy as the spell is taking form, but that window of opportunity will disappear quickly. One mage explained it best. "Once you have gathered up the mana for the spell, it is there, and you must do something with it. If you release it as it is, it will simply disperse into the world harmlessly. But if you shape the mana through ritual, then its release will always have consequences because it now has form. If you are not totally correct with the performance of your ritual, the mana will take a form that is not quite what you desired, and the consequences will therefore be unpredictable."

I have managed to record the energy on film, and I could see the mana changing form as the rituals progressed. I have also seen the results of some rituals, both successful and unsuccessful, although I have not yet managed to gather sufficient evidence to verify its legitimacy.

Tools

The Celtic magical traditions that I studied employ many tools in their rituals. There are more tools that are used, but these are some of the more common:

Altar

A small table that other ritual components are stored and prepared on, and serves as a focal point in the ritual. Some are wooden, some are stone, but they do not have any required shape. As a matter of fact, one mage used a stone that was partially buried in the woods, and he would perform his rituals there.

Athame

This is a ceremonial knife. It is important to note here that none of the rituals that I witnessed involved any bloodshed. The athame was used mostly as a pointing device, for cutting strands of hair, stirring wine in a chalice, and for other harmless tasks. Sometimes a sword is used in place of the athame.

Book of Shadows

The book of shadows is what some mages refer to their book of rituals. Because of the extreme risks involved when performing rituals, mages are careful to write down the details of every ritual so that they can be performed perfectly every time.

Chalice

This is used for holding wine or juice that is blessed and drunk during the course of the ritual. It is sometimes used to hold other items, depending on the requirements of the spell.

Incense

This is burned usually to purify the circle in preparation for the casting of the spell.

Wand

This is used mainly for helping to direct the flow of mana and to help gather it up. Sometimes it is used in place of the athame.

FPI: The Show

The Paranormal

The Spirit World

Popular knowledge reserves the spirit world only for those who have died. Evidence shows, however, that there may be other denizens of that world that is only partly on this Earth. Spirits of the living have been reported to be seen walking among us in non-corporeal form. Angels have been seen in visions and demons have taken over the bodies of innocents. This section will introduce the reader to all of these manifestations in a scientific and objective light.

Poltergeists

Poltergeists are described as the cause of mysterious rappings, knockings and movement of objects in a house or other building. These occurrences are most often associated with prankster ghosts that have are merely trying to scare people away from their haunts. There are many theories as to the exact cause of these disturbances, from the spirits of dead people who are trying to communicate in the only way they can, to random magnetic forces. In virtually all cases, there have been no reports of any visions or apparitions associated with poltergeists. The spirits, if spirits they be, never show themselves visually, but merely resort to noises and hurled objects.

Most reports of hauntings turn out to be cases of poltergeists. Although these occurrences have been accurately verified, there has, as yet, never been any proof to back up the claim that they are caused by spirits.

Apparitions

The actual definition of the word "apparition" is "the act of appearing." However, modern culture has applied a more supernatural association with the word. An apparition is more commonly referred to as vision of ghostly figure. In most cases, the vision is of the ghost of someone who has died. There are reports of those who have seen the spirit of a living clairvoyant wandering outside his own body.

Incubi and Succubi

Many people have reported being raped or sexually abused by spirits. When a spirit is reported to have performed such acts, it is considered to be either an incubus or a succubus. An Incubus is a spirit that molests women, and a succubus molests men.

Shadow People

Not much is known about shadow people. They are spirits, like apparitions, but are more sinister in appearance and behavior.

The Colonel is *very* interested in all reports concerning shadow people. These beings closely resemble the creatures that he witnessed in Saudi Arabia, and he thinks they might be one and the same.

The following is an excerpt from one of the few reports that the FPI has collected concerning shadow people. It is the description of the beings given by a woman whose house they inhabit.

"They are all over the basement, hiding in the shadows, and are almost always seen only from the corner of your eyes. Whenever you look over at them, they scurry away, not giving you a good look at them. I did manage to get a quick look at them a few times, though.

"They are black. They look like squat, skinny people who are black as shadows and have no physical features, including eyes, mouth, ears, etc.

"Mostly, they just watch us. They don't talk, although sometimes my daughter says she hears whispering. We can sense them, though. We don't sense any evil from most of them, but some of them definitely do not like us. They don't seem to be able to do anything about us, though, and they have no affect on us except for making us keep all the lights on. When the house is dark, we feel very outnumbered."

Ghostly Phenomena

Ectoplasm

Ectoplasm is a term used most commonly to refer to any type of "spiritual energy", and are always reporting in the vicinity of a ghost sighting. This energy usually appears in photographs as blobs or balls of light. Scientific studies have been made to identify the blobs, but no definitive explanation has yet made.

There is, in rare cases, accounts of ectoplasm in solid form. This form of ectoplasm appears as a gooey substance similar to unhardened gelatin. There have been reports of this goo oozing from walls and even people near

FPI: The Show

where a ghost has been seen. So far, there has been no scientific analysis of the physical form of ectoplasm.

Orbs

This is merely a circular blob of ectoplasm. It is noteworthy for the fact that this is the most common, and indeed only consistent, form of ectoplasm. Many people speculate that orbs are spirits that have taken spherical shape.

Vortex

This is said to be the point of "break through point" or origin in this world of a paranormal activity. If a poltergeist is rapping on the walls, and a vortex has been monitored, it is most likely there that the poltergeist appeared. Vortices have been photographed and monitored.

Monitoring and Detection Devices

EMF Gauge

An EMF gauge measures the amount of electromagnetic charges in the atmosphere. It is commonly believed by ghost hunters that spirits and other such phenomena produce strong magnetic charges.

Electronic Voice Phenomena

Human voices always fall within the audio range of three hundred to three thousand Hertz. EVPs take the form of Extremely Low Frequency (ELF) voice recordings, and fall in within the range of one to three hundred Hertz.

To capture EVPs, the investigator would usually walk around the haunted site with an audio recorder and a sensitive microphone. He would ask questions or speak to the spirits, then pause to leave plenty of time for a response. It is nearly impossible to hear an EVP with the naked ear, so the investigator must wait until the recording is analyzed to hear any.

Analyzing the recording involves copying clips of the tape to a computer, then scanning the ELF range for sounds that could be human voices. Once a sound has been isolated, the section of the recording is amplified, and stretched to make it more audible.

Detection and study of Electronic Voice Phenomena is not an exacting science, but can produce quite convincing evidence of the existence of a spirit.

Demonic Possession

When a person is thought to be suffering from demonic possession, the person's behavior becomes completely taken over by the demon or devil. The entity can then completely dominate the victim.

The church was very proactive regarding demonic possession. Anyone who acted strangely or differently was immediately suspected. Today, the church is much more reasonable, although they do still investigate cases. The FPI has worked with the church on occasion to their mutual benefit.

Symptoms of Possession

A person who is supposedly suffering from demonic possession will have the following symptoms:

1. Superhuman strength.
2. Fits and convulsions (often, but not always).
3. Changes in personality.
4. Knowledge of the future and secret information.
5. Speaking in foreign tongues (a phenomenon called glossolalia).

Some other symptoms that are more extreme, but not always present are: terrible smells of sulfur or body odors, obscene or sexually lewd acts, rapid, life threatening weight loss, distended stomach, change of the voice to a low rasping, guttural sound, and even the appearance of writing on the body in the form of welts.

The FPI has not yet witnessed or reported on an actual case. Although some chapters have worked with the Catholic Church to investigate some cases, they have all so far turned out to be hoaxes or mistakes.

The Church's Relationship with the FPI

This is a shaky relationship at best. The Catholic Church feels that we should not involve ourselves with these cases, but since we will always investigate these cases, they have agreed to work with us as opposed to struggling against us. Although they rarely admit to it, the FPI has been a valuable resource to them.

Some priests have joined FPI chapters. In almost all cases, they have done so to ensure that our reports are accurate. However, it is our belief that they have their own agenda and will also try to make sure that we do not interfere too much in the church's affairs.

Exorcism

Contrary to popular belief, an exorcism is not meant to drive out a demon or devil, but merely to place the entity on an oath. Of course, this oath would forbid the entity from inhabiting the victim's body.

The church has not performed an exorcism in the presence of an FPI member and does not discuss its details. However, we do know that it is a long, drawn out ritual that can be quite involved, and is not always successful.

FPI: The Show

Strange Creatures

Throughout recorded history, there have been reports of bizarre creatures whose existence defies explanation. Many of these have eventually been explained, but there are still those that baffle scientists to this day. It is part of the FPI's charter to investigate these beings so that we may finally understand them.

The following sections describe what we know about some of the more well-known creatures.

Chupacabra

El Chupacabra is the most recent of the cryptids, or cryptozoological creatures. Also nicknamed the Goatsucker, it was supposedly responsible for a rash of exsanguinated farm animals in several small towns in Latin America. This happened in 1995, and had become such a problem that the mayor of Canovanas, Puerto Rico, sanctioned the use of paramilitary patrols to hunt down the creature.

In all cases, the animals it killed were completely drained of blood, often through tiny pin-prick holes.

Description

El Chupacabra was very bizarre-looking. It was said to be about four feet tall, a large, round head, lipless mouth and sharp fangs. Its red, lidless eyes were like large teardrops, and looked identical to the pop culture description of the "gray alien." Its body was quite skinny with clawed arms and webbed bat-like wings. Its muscular hind legs appeared designed for jumping, much like a kangaroo's. It was also reported to have a row of sharp spikes that ran from the top of its hairless head down its backbone. It was always described as bipedal.

Evidence

The only evidence of this creature comes from the corpses of a large number of animals that it had supposedly slaughtered, and the many sightings. No photographs, footprint castings, or other firm evidence has ever been found.

El Chupacabra sightings were pretty common during the year of 1995, with more than one hundred and fifty reported animal slayings. Since then, there have been few sightings and no confirmed animal slayings.

Some paranormal investigators think that the creature was extra-terrestrial in nature. Others think it was a government experiment gone wrong. There is no evidence to support either theory.

Jersey Devil

The Jersey Devil has been a local legend in New Jersey for as far back as 1735, when it was said that a cursed mother gave birth to a devil. There are many stories about how the devil came to be, and there are only two commonalities to the stories. One is that it takes place in New Jersey, near Burlington. The other is that the word "Leeds" is involved.

One of the stories claims that a Mrs. Shrouds of Leeds Point, who after having many children, stated that if she ever had another child, she wishes it would be a devil. Supposedly, she got her wish.

Another story of the devil's origin was that Mother Leeds in Burlington was a witch and was impregnated by The Devil.

Description

The Jersey Devil has been described many ways. The most popular description is given below:

It was about three and a half feet tall. Its hind legs, on which it stood, were like those of a crane. Its head was that of a collie dog, and it had the face of a horse. It had bat-like wings about two feet long each. Each of the two legs had horse's hooves. It walks on the two hind legs only, and its stubby front legs ended in paws.

Evidence

There is no real definitive proof that the Jersey Devil exists. Most evidence is in the form of eye witness accounts and tracks. There have also been found the mutilated bodies of animals, such as dogs and farm animals. None of the mutilations have been properly investigated, except for one, which was investigated by an FPI chapter in New Jersey.

"We came to investigate a sighting of the Jersey Devil in Burlington, NJ. Kevin Nathan had reported seeing a hairy animal walking on two legs take off and fly away from his back yard after hearing his dog barking and growling. When he went to the back yard, he found the dog mutilated.

"We took the remains to a local zoo, where an animal expert inspected it. After analyzing some saliva and fur traces that remained, he determined that it was from a wild cat. As it turned out, a leopard had escaped recently from the zoo. It was returned the following day."

Loch Ness Monster

On July 22, 1933, a couple was driving along Loch Ness Lakeshore Road when they had to stop short. A huge, black, long-necked creature was blocking the road. As they watched, the "prehistoric animal," as they called it, shambled across the road, slid through the underbrush and splashed into the Loch. This was the first known sighting of the mysterious creature known as the Loch Ness Monster.

Since then, there have been over three thousand recorded sightings, making "Nessie," as it has been nicknamed, the most popular cryptozoological phenomenon in history.

A good many of the sightings have turned out to be hoaxes. This is a fact. Most of the rest are merely reports from eye-witnesses, and cannot be proven. A handful of reports, however, have produced photographs, sonar images and other evidence that appear to be accurate.

The truth is that although many scientists have studied the Loch, there has yet been no evidence to conclude whether the creature exists or not.

What Is Nessie?

Most of the reports describe a creature with two humps, a tail, and a long, snakelike head. Other physical characteristics have been described, but these are the only ones that seem to be corroborated by the majority of sightings.

Some of the theories as to the creature's identity are walruses, long-necked seals, mats of plants, and giant eels. The following are two of the more popular theories:

Basilosaurus: This is an ancient species of meat-eating mammals, that are, in fact, the descendants of whales. They lived over forty-five million years ago during the Eocene period.

Plesiosaurus: Large sea reptiles with long flexible necks, flat bodies with four large flippers, and a long tail. This creature is the best fit for the reports given, but it is unlikely that this creature would have survived the massive environmental changes since the Jurassic period when it lived.

Sasquatch

Also known as Bigfoot, the Sasquatch is said to be a humanoid being that appears like a missing link between man and ape. It is described as being very tall, approximately 7' 10", and weigh anywhere from five hundred to one thousand pounds. They are covered completely with a course, black hair (not fur), and walk upright.

The Sasquatch has been reported all over North America, and most commonly in heavily forested and mountainous regions. The term "Sasquatch" is a derivative of a Native American term for the creature. There are over sixty different names for the Sasquatch throughout the many Native American tribes.

Although popular culture relates the Sasquatch to humans, it is very unlikely that there is any true relation. The creature does walk upright, but its inhuman gait suggests that it is a primate that has evolved down a different branch than humankind. Instead, if it exists at all, it is quite definitely a form of primate that is different from any known species.

Odor

Many of the close encounters have reported an awful, sickening stench. This may be similar to the stench that gorillas can produce in times of distress. Those who have sighted the Sasquatch have also reported a feeling of uneasiness prior to their encounter. It has been suggested, but not proven, that a pheromone may cause this effect.

Strength

They are reported to be exceedingly strong. They have been said to lift and hurl large rocks to scare off intruders, lifting the edge of campers, tipping over cars, throwing fifty gallon drums, etc.

Behavior

The Sasquatch almost always runs away from any contact with people. In the cases where it does not, it has attempted to scare the intruders off. There have been a few reports of the creature entering a camp at night and rummaging for food, or even attacking the campers. None of these aggressive accounts have been proven.

The Sasquatch are nocturnal creatures, and are therefore only rarely seen during the day. In most cases, they are silent. However, at night they have been known to exhibit a wide range of vocalizations. These range from whistles, moans, howls, grunts, hoots and very deep growls. The most disturbing sound, though, is a very chilling scream that rises over the course of several seconds from a low moan. This has never failed to fill those who hear it with terror.

Legitimacy

One team of FPI members encountered a Sasquatch in the forests of Washington State. As the credibility of the witnesses is not in question, it is considered likely that the Sasquatch does indeed exist. The members' chapter has made it their goal to study it in detail.

The following is an excerpt from their report:

"We were hiking through the deep woods in Snohomish County. We had recently crossed a stream and were climbing upwards towards some caves, where we were going to make camp. It was late in the afternoon and it was already starting to get dark.

"It was then that we heard it: a loud, low-pitched moan coming from the caves. Over the next few seconds, it rose in volume and pitch until it ended in the most terrifying scream I had ever heard. Our camera was out of film and we did not have any guns on hand. As we stood there deciding what to do, we suddenly heard a noise to our right, and heard a deep, throaty roar, much closer than

the scream was. At that point, our decision was quickly made. We turned and ran back to the way we came.

"The Sasquatch chased us, roaring and hooting. We glimpsed it several times as we ran. It was very large and black, and covered almost completely with black hair. It was not fur, but definitely hair. It ran in great strides that looked inhuman. It never locked its knees as it moved, which gave it a lazy appearance to its strides. Its arms swung in great arcs as it moved quickly through the trees. We thought it would catch us as we crossed the stream, but we managed to get away. We cannot be sure at what point the thing stopped chasing us, but we were definitely alone when we reached our truck three miles later.

"Apparently, we had inadvertently stumbled upon its lair. We regrouped, gathered weapons and cameras, and went back the next day. Nothing was there when we arrived, but we did find signs of recent habitation in the cave."

Thunderbird

Called the ba'a' by the Comanche, and chequah by the Potawatomi, the mysterious thunderbird is said to be a huge bird of prey, much like a condor. Its wingspan is said to be eighteen to twenty feet in length, making it the largest carnivorous flying animal still living today. Native Americans believed that the bird would create thunder by flapping its mighty wings, and shoot lightning from its eyes.

Evidence

There have been sightings of this animal even in modern times, but to date there have been no photographs, nor any remains or even fossils.

There have been reports that deer and even people have been carried away by thunderbirds. This would be a remarkable feat, as not even the Andean condor, with a wingspan of up to ten and a half feet does not have very strong claws.

Thylacine

The thylacine is not a mythical or legendary creature, but an actual animal that is now known to be extinct. It was commonly known as the Tasmanian Tiger, but the name was not accurate. A native of Australia and Tasmania, it was actually one of the last known carnivorous marsupial. It lived there from about 12,000 years ago until the last known thylacine died in captivity in 1936. Although hunting by man was one of the causes of its extinction, the greatest cause was the appearance of dingoes in Australia. Humans caused the Tasmanian thylacine population to disappear because the endangered carnivores were hunting farm animals. Bounties were placed on thylacine scalps, with the last one paid in 1909. Eventually, they received endangered status, but it was too late. Their numbers were already so low that there was little chance of them surviving.

The thylacine looked like a wolf with stripes. A male would grow to six feet in length, and weight around forty-five pounds. Its stripes began midway down its back, and continued to the end of its tail. They often hunted in pairs and were not fast. Its elongated jaws had a huge gape that could crush the skulls of its prey. They were primarily nocturnal, and were vicious predators. They showed no fear when hunted by men with dogs. When cornered, they would usually kill the first dog to get too close to it.

Sightings

Sightings of thylacine and their tracks began shortly after the last one died in captivity. They have continued to this day, although the sightings are not common. In the 1950's, there was a rash of sheep killings, where the tracks of the predators resembled thylacines. No thylacines were ever found, though.

Thus far, there is no conclusive evidence to suggest that thylacines still live, but of all cryptozoological creatures, these are the more likely.

Yeti

The yeti is described as being quite similar to its North American cousin, the sasquatch. It is found exclusively in the Himalayan mountain range wandering in its snowy reaches. Some sightings claim that it is all white; blending into the snow, while others say it is black. All sightings claim that it is very hairy and vaguely humanoid.

Evidence

The best, and most common, evidence found thus far are footprints. These are very similar to human prints, but are only about six to seven inches long by four inches wide at the broadest part of the foot. The heels of the prints end in a narrow point.

The creatures sightings are also fairly numerous, but very few photographs have been made that bear discernable features. There is currently no conclusive evidence of the yeti's existence, although the sheer number of similar sightings implies that something has been seen out there.

Extra-Terrestrials

Throughout all of recorded history, there have been reports and stories of beings from other worlds. Even the Bible makes references to them. The number of sightings has only increased in modern days, making this the most common of all paranormal phenomena. Not all FPI chapters focus on UFOs, but there has still been many sightings reported to the Head Office nonetheless. This section will attempt to summarize some of the more common data regarding Unidentified Flying Objects.

FPI: The Show

Close Encounters

Because of the frequency of reports, and the fact that government agencies have actively investigated them, UFO encounters have been classified into levels of severity. Any encounter, whether it is simply visual or intimate, is called a Close Encounter. There are five levels to a Close Encounter. Each level is described below.

1st Kind: This simply involves sighting a UFO. If you see something that you would consider a UFO, whether it is flashing lights, or a disc-shaped craft flying through the sky, then you had a Close Encounter of the this kind.

2nd Kind: This is for UFO sightings that are much more definite. For instance, if you see the craft close up and there is no doubt in your mind that you are seeing a craft from space, you just had a Close Encounter of this kind. Any interaction with the craft will also apply to this class of encounter.

3rd Kind: An alien was sighted. A UFO need not be involved, but if you see what you believe to be an extra-terrestrial, it is this type of encounter.

4th Kind: Actual contact with an extra-terrestrial being. This would include any kind of actual contact up to, but excluding, abduction.

5th Kind: Abduction by extra-terrestrial entities.

Unidentified Flying Objects

The number of UFO sightings in the world are too numerous to count. However, the vast majority of these sightings have very similar descriptions. Most of the sightings can be categorized into three groups of objects: Cigar-shaped objects, flying saucers, and grouped lights. The remainder are wide and varied and have never been qualified by photographs or videos. Descriptions of these common objects are given below.

Cigar-Shaped Objects

These are large objects that appear cylindrical, with tapered ends. In most cases, it is impossible to tell which end is the front and which is the back...aside from seeing the direction in which it is moving.

These objects, like most large UFOs, emit a low-pitched droning hum.

Flying Saucers

These are the most commonly known, although the other two are just as commonly reported. These take the form of flying discs. Some have a circular structure in the center of the top side of the object, and they almost all taper down to a fairly sharp edge. Some are said to spin as they fly, while others remain motionless. Most are reported to have lights on the underside of the object. They produce a similar hum to the cigar-shaped objects.

Grouped Lights

These are the most common type of object reported. It could be because it is most easily mistaken for natural or man-made phenomena. The Northern Lights, helicopters and other aircraft have all been mistaken for this type of UFO. Some of these have been reported to be accompanied by a hum, but not all.

Alien Races

Like the UFOs themselves, there have been countless descriptions of extra-terrestrials reported over the decades. However, only three descriptions have been widely reported.

Grays

These are by far the most commonly reported of all extra-terrestrials. They are also the most infamous, being the primary race involved in violent abductions and experimentation.

They are short, approximately three to five feet tall, with skinny, even bony bodies. Their heads are large at the cranium and taper down to a very small and often pointed chin. They have thin, lipless slits for mouths, and tiny, but humanoid noses. Their eyes are large, opaque, and black, with no lids or lashes. They are somewhat tear-shaped, lying sideways with the large ends close to the nose and the narrow ends wrapping around to the sides. They have no visible ears and no body hair at all.

The reports state that they either do not speak at all, or communicate telepathically. They are highly intelligent.

Humanoids

Also called Nordics, these extra-terrestrials look very much like exceptionally attractive humans. They often have a Nordic appearance, thus giving them their nickname. They are tall and fair of skin and hair. They are always reported to be friendly and kind. Some reports state that they speak like we do. Others claim they communicate telepathically.

These extra-terrestrials are mainly reported only in Europe.

Beasts

Reported primarily in South America, these aliens have had a variety of physical descriptions, but all of them are bestial. This includes large, insect-like beings, furry monsters, giant blobs, and the like. There have even been reports of a reptilian race of aliens.

Because the actual descriptions of these beings vary, and are accompanied by very little evidence, they are not

FPI: The Show

The Paranormal

as likely to be factual.

Crop Circles

Crop circles are unexplained designs that are imprinted on crops. Most of them are circular in shape, but some form more intricate patterns of circles with connecting lines. They mainly occur on corn or wheat crops, but have been known to be made in oats, grass, rape (canola), barley, trees and even snow.

The circles are created by bending the crops completely over in a swirling pattern either clockwise or counterclockwise. The circles are created in the span of one night, with no obvious means of creation.

Many witnesses claim to have seen bright flashes of light on the night that the circles were created, not unlike that of lightning. In addition, the damaged crops of many circles are often somewhat burned.

Some of the reported circles have been verified as hoaxes, but most have not been identified as such. The complexity of their creation makes it very difficult to perpetrate a hoax.

Creation Theories

Many theories exist as to the cause of crop circles. The following summarizes the most possible, although even some of these seem wild and unlikely:

Plasma Vortex: Some believe that a vortex of plasma could account for the circles. Although no one has offered a definitive answer as to the source of the plasma, the theory does show actual scientific merit when examining the evidence.

Ley-Lines: This is the belief that mystical energies like those that are said to be present at Stonehenge are responsible for crop circles.

Extra-Terrestrials: One of the most common theories is that they are created by UFOs or the aliens that control them.

Military Experiments: This implies that the military of a particular government is responsible for creating the circles. The only reasons suggested why the military might generate crop circles are the matter of conspiracy theories.

Project Blue Book

Project Blue Book is a program by the United States Air Force for the investigation of Unidentified Flying Objects. The project was active from 1948 until it was discontinued in 1969. According to reports filed with the Federal Bureau of Investigation, there were three reasons why the project was discontinued: none of the reports ever indicated a threat to the government, there has been no evidence to suggest that any technology was used beyond the government's own means, and finally, there was no evidence to suggest that any of the sightings were extra-terrestrial in origin.

Over the course of the two decades, thousands of reports were investigated. In every year there were reports that were never resolved, but the percentage of these unexplained incidents was low.

Men In Black

In 1953 a small civilian UFO group called the International Flying Saucer Bureau was suddenly dissolved. The final issue of the publication they printed had the ominous parting comment of "please be very cautious." One of the members of the IFSB later claimed in an interview that he was visited by three men in black suits and black fedoras and sunglasses. According to him, the three men threatened him to stop printing papers about flying saucers.

Since then, reports of Men in Black, or MiB as they are often called, have been almost as common as reports of UFOs themselves. So far, none of the reports have been substantiated.

Many theories abound concerning the identities of these Men in Black. Most say that they were sent by some government agency that has reason to keep UFO reports a secret. Others claim that they represent an agency outside of the government, but with government ties. Still others believe they are aliens from another world trying to ensure that the truth about them does not leak out.

The fact remains that there have been no evidence to support any of these theories. There have been no photographs of Men in Black. No recordings or any other evidence has been offered to prove their existence. At the time of this writing, no FPI member has reported meeting any Men in Black.

Roswell

In July of 1947, an unidentified aircraft crashed in the desert near Roswell, New Mexico. Air Force personnel arrived at the crash site shortly thereafter and cleaned up the debris, but witnesses claim that the craft was extra-terrestrial and that the Air Force recovered the wrecked vessel and two alien pilots.

The official report from the Air Force claims that the UFO was a balloon-borne research project code named MOGUL. The Air Force cleaned up the wreckage and issued a report.

What little the Colonel and his other contacts in the military could find is that there is more to the story than the Air Force is willing to state, but there is as yet no evidence to support the theory of a downed UFO. The Colonel does not believe that there is any connection between the incident in Roswell and the beings that he witnessed in Saudi Arabia.

The Big Dig

An FPI Episode

FPI: The Show

The Setting

The Big Dig

The Central Artery/Tunnel Project has been hotly disputed ever since construction began. Schedules have slipped and the project has exceeded its budget, not to mention the havoc the construction has caused the traffic in Boston, Massachusetts. However, the project, when completed, will greatly reduce the congestion of traffic in the city, which is why it is still underway today. The project has been nicknamed "The Big Dig" because of the sheer scale of the project, and the amount of time, money and effort that it requires.

This episode of FPI takes place in Boston when one of the tunnels is still under construction. Although the Big Dig itself is real, the particular tunnel used in this episode is not. The tunnel extends under Boston Harbor, and is currently unfinished. The mining is still underway approximately one half mile under the harbor.

Back Plot

It is October 26, 2003. Each of the past two nights now, a construction worker on the Big Dig tunnel project in Boston has disappeared under mysterious circumstances. Detective Robert Dunn has been assigned the case, and he is under a lot of pressure to get this matter resolved quickly so that the dig can continue. The project has been behind schedule for some time now, and the delay has caused quite a controversy. Those in power in the city government are anxious to get the project back on schedule, and this new development can severely mess with that schedule.

A bizarre creature has been trapped in an ancient cave that is currently buried under Boston Harbor. Once, the cave was accessible to the mainland, but the centuries have caused it to become submerged. An ancient tribe of primitive people who worshipped strange deities once used the cave. Evidence of their presence is scattered throughout it. The creature, the very creature that these ancient people had worshipped, is trapped in a network of underwater caves below the first cave. A well in the upper cave gives access to the caves below. During high tide, the well overflows and floods the cave, allowing the creature to come out to feed.

The tunneling of the Big Dig has disturbed this creature's home. The drilling of the hydraulic mining rigs causes enough vibrations to shake the walls and loosen dirt. The noise this causes is almost deafening to the creature. The creature wants the drilling stopped.

When the drainage tunnels were made for the highway tunnel, they came very close to breaking through to the cave. The vibrations of the drilling have recently broken a hole in the wall, allowing access to the old cave from one of these drainage tunnels.

In addition to wanting the drilling stopped, the creature also wants to feed and now has the opportunity to hunt prey that is much larger and more satisfying than the fish and small sea life that has been its diet.

For the past two nights, it has slipped into the highway tunnel and taken one worker as its prey. It always focuses on the drill operators, since they are the ones responsible for most of the noise and vibration. It will strike again tonight, but will not be quite as successful as usual.

The Cast

This episode was intended with a specific cast in mind. This cast includes Mike Malone, Christina Mariani, and Dr. David Walker.

Matt Hawkins can either play a supporting role or be played as a leading character by an actor. Matt's role in the episode is to add that chaotic element, by having the nosy reporter stir up trouble for the cast. With the right actor, he can be even more fun as a guest star!

There is a new leading character introduced as a guest star. His name is Detective Robert Dunn, a Boston homicide detective.

Of course, the actors can always use their own characters in place of the stock ones, but you should be sure that they will make sense in the plot. Also, if no one chooses to play Detective Dunn, you should run him as a supporting role.

Future Events

Almost every event that takes place during the course

A Word to the Wise

This is the demo of a game, and is therefore a work of fiction. Although the places in which the episode takes place are real, the characters, creatures and events are purely fictional. Any resemblance to real people and events are purely coincidental. No one who will be likely to take this game seriously should play it! This is a game of acting for entertainment, and that is all.

FPI: The Show

Detective Robert Dunn

Brawn: Good
Agility: Fair
Stamina: Fair
Luck: 3
Reasoning: Fair
Perception: Great
Will: Fair
Income: Fair

Skills: Area Knowledge (Good), Brawl (Good), Criminology (Fair), Dodge (Fair), Drive Car (Fair), Gather Information (Fair), Gun (Good), Interrogate (Fair), Notice (Good), Research (Good), Run (Good), Sense Motive (Fair), Shadow (Good), Stealth (Good), Surveillance (Fair).

Gifts: Keen Sense of Hearing (+1 to all hearing-based Notice tests).

Faults: Stubborn.

Props: Investigation kit (rubber gloves, fingerprinting tools, etc.), revolver, box of 50 rounds, speed loader, cell phone, notebook & pen, mini flashlight.

Robert Dunn is a tough cop. He grew up in the Boston area, and knows his way around town better than most people. He's also as stubborn as he is tough. When he makes a decision, there is no arguing with him, no matter how strong the opposing argument.

He has been with the department for 12 years, and has seen just about everything. He loves Boston, and loves being a cop there. He is a down-to-earth man who does not believe in the paranormal or anything weird like that. However, when faced with overwhelming evidence, he may be persuaded. In most cases, though, the most you could hope for is an admission that he has no idea what it is, but that it is probably explanable.

Dunn has had run-ins with the local chapter of the FPI, and is not overly fond of them. It's not that he dislikes them, it's that he distrusts them. Several times, he has caught them trespassing and nosing about crime scenes under the pretense of investigating ghosts or some such nonsense. They have never made more than the least of infractions, but it is enough to make Dunn cautious.

Christina Mariani: She is a marine biologist who does work for the Aquarium. He has consulted with her on several occasions regarding shark attacks and other cases involving sea life. She's young, beautiful and smart, which always makes it interesting dealing with her. But she really knows her stuff, and her enthusiasm can't be beat. She has gone with him on several occasions to inspect shark bites and the corpses of sharks to see if they were the culprits of attacks. She has no qualms about cutting open a shark and sifting through its stomach contents, which had just spilled out on the dock by her feet. Dunn always found that impressive about her. He knows that she works for the FPI, but that hasn't hurt their working relationship any.

Mike Malone: He's an ex-cop from New York that is now working as a private eye. He's tough and smart, and has got great cop instincts. If it weren't for his connection with that FPI group, Dunn would be more trusting of him. As it is, Malone has come damn close to crossing the line of the law while acting as a member of FPI. That has made Dunn cautious in his dealings with the man.

The Big Dig: Mike knows only what he has seen on the news and read in the paper. The Central Artery/Tunnel Project, or the Big Dig, as it is usually called, is a big project that is meant to relieve much of the traffic on the current highways that run through the city. The project includes the construction of large bridges, and the digging of several highway tunnels. A couple of these tunnels extend partly under Boston Harbor. The project has been in progress for many years, and is still years from completion. According to the news, the project is far behind schedule, and has greatly exceeded its budget. There have been people who have lobbied to have the project terminated, but at this point, it just doesn't make sense to stop.

Back plot: For the past two nights, workers have been disappearing from the unfinished William Turner Tunnel during the overnight shift. So far, none of them have been found and there are few clues. Dunn has been assigned to the case, and must spend tonight in the tunnel watching to see if anything happens.

of this episode will be completely based on the actions and decisions of the cast and the actors playing them, including the Director. However, there is the creature, and there are the workers. You may need to change their behavior somewhat to account for the events that the cast causes, but they both have specific plans, and will try to make them happen if possible.

The Creature: The creature is going to continue trying to take victims as long as it thinks it can get away with it. It will also try to stop the drilling. Eventually, it will realize that it cannot stop it, and will try to escape into the harbor. It likes to single out its prey, and it will flee if faced with a hard fight. Its forte is in stealth and ambush, and it will not risk a situation where it cannot use those tactics.

The Workers: They are under pressure to get back on schedule, and stay on schedule. The foreman on duty will always try to keep as much work going as possible. He can always find new workers to operate the drilling rigs, and any attempt to shut them down, even for a day, will meet with resistance. Detective Dunn can tape off the crime scenes and halt the use of any equipment involved in the case, but the foreman will protest and will report the problem to his superiors. Dunn may get overruled, but it would take a bit of time. In the meantime, work will continue around the crime scenes if at all possible.

The Scenes

Each scene is when each section of the story is acted out. In most cases, there will be one scene for each of the sets that are described in the demo.

The only scenes that can be described in this demo are the opening scenes. That is because the actors cannot affect what happens before these scenes begin. You have complete control over how the episode begins. However, once a scene begins, and the cast starts interacting in it, you lose full control over the story. The only way you can influence the story is by manipulating the supporting cast, the events, and the environment.

You must make up the rest of the scenes as you go along. To help you out, all of the sets, or locations, that are likely to be used in the scenes are described. These descriptions will help you run the scenes and keep the flow going.

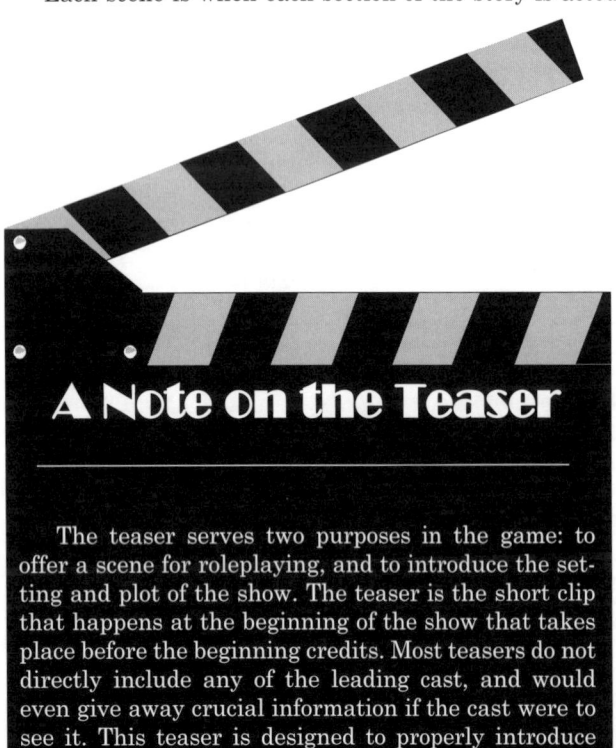

Where to Start?

The first scene that you should run is the Teaser. This will introduce the setting, plot and the character of Detective Dunn. He should be strongly encouraged to visit with Christina Mariani. If he chooses not to, you should find another way to get them involved, such as by having the foreman contact her. You can say that Christina is a close friend of Frank Barrows' family (see Supporting Cast at the end of this demo), and so he thinks of her right away.

The second scene should be Scene 1, where Christina and Mike Malone are introduced. From there, they may choose to perform or watch the autopsy, or go to the tunnel itself. There is a possibility that they will think of something unexpected, and you will have to roll with it.

The third scene should be Scene 2, where Hawkins is introduced. What he does and where he goes from there is completely up to him, but this will get him started.

The Facts of the Case

The following is a summary of the facts of the case. Detective Dunn has done an initial investigation into the disappearances, but has not come up with much. The first list summarizes all of the facts that Dunn has determined by the start of the episode. The rest have yet to be discovered.

What Detective Dunn Has Discovered
Two workers have disappeared. The first was two nights ago, and the other happened last night.
The only thing that the victims have in common is that they both operated the hydraulic miners, although each had operated a different one.
Both workers left items behind, which implies that either they meant to return shortly, or they were abducted.

A Note on the Teaser

The teaser serves two purposes in the game: to offer a scene for roleplaying, and to introduce the setting and plot of the show. The teaser is the short clip that happens at the beginning of the show that takes place before the beginning credits. Most teasers do not directly include any of the leading cast, and would even give away crucial information if the cast were to see it. This teaser is designed to properly introduce the mood and plot, while also allowing some good roleplaying for one of the characters.

FPI: The Show

Autopsy Results

Clue	Autopsy Result
Toxicology found a thin, clear chemical substance in the bloodstream. A sample has been sent to the lab for analysis.*	Good
Signs of stress on the skin and muscles of the neck and head indicate that the thing that was wrapped around the deceased's neck had held the subject tightly, and that it had supported the weight of his body.	Fair
The bite mark appears to have been caused by a human jaw.	Poor
Circular marks on the neck are consistent with the application of suction to the skin.	Always
There is a bite mark on the subject's left shoulder. It has taken a chunk of flesh from the victim's shoulder.	Always
The cause of death was a broken neck.	Always
There are many bruises on the body, indicating a fall from a high place.	Always

* The results should be given about an hour later, or during an appropriately theatrical moment. The neurotoxin maculotoxin was found in the deceased's bloodstream. Christina can identify that the Blue Ring Octopus uses that venom to capture its prey. A Good Nature Lore skill test will be enough to make that identification.

The Opening Scenes

Teaser: Excitement at the Big Dig

William Turner Tunnel

Boston, MA

October 26, 2003

2:16 AM

Detective Robert Dunn, you are standing outside, breathing in the brisk October air. The crisp sea air is refreshing after the stuffiness of the tunnels below. You've wasted the last two hours in the unfinished highway tunnel whose entrance you now stand by. Two construction workers have disappeared from the tunnel, and you have been assigned the job of finding out what happened to them. In one hand you hold a cigarette, and in the other a cup of coffee. You had taken a break from the claustrophobic chaos of the tunnel construction site to have a butt and a drink in the relative quiet of the tunnel entrance. The noise inside is deafening, and you are glad to take the heavy-duty ear mufflers off your head.

Suddenly, an electric car drives up, the throbbing hum betraying its approach. A worker climbs out of the driver's seat and runs to greet you. He looks anxious.

"Detective, Barrows needs you. He said it's an emergency."

Frank Barrows is the foreman on duty tonight, and is Dunn's primary contact.

The worker knows very little about the emergency. He had just driven up with a mining loader, when he saw workers leaving their rigs to rush toward one of the miners. When he left his own rig to see what the problem was, Barrows spotted him and sent him to get Dunn. The worker will insist that he come right away.

The unfinished tunnel is dank, musty, and dirty. Large floodlights illuminated the place, casting eerie shadows all around. The further they drive into the tunnel, the rougher and dirtier their surroundings become. Here, the walls are bare of tiles and are made up of dirt and concrete. Machines are busy digging, as they are round the clock. The mad rush for completion is hard felt in the bowels of the tunnel, and everyone is on edge. You feel you could cut the tension with a knife.

As you approach the end of the tunnel where the mining is underway, you can tell something is wrong. Although the noise of construction in this tight space is almost deafening, it is not nearly as loud as it had been only fifteen minutes ago when you left the tunnel. Several of the large construction vehicles are not running, and a crowd of people is huddled around one spot near one of the hydraulic miners.

As you approach, Barrows tells his men to make room. You can see the body of a worker lying in a heap on the ground. His hardhat is missing, and his face is twisted in an expression of pain and terror. The lifeless look in his eyes show that he is dead, and the strange circular marks on his neck tell you that this is no ordinary mining accident!

[CUT TO OPENING CREDITS]

End the scene here. This scene must be kept short and end on a climax for it to work. This is for two reasons:

1. This is the teaser, and as such, it always must be short and climactic. Also, the climax must properly introduce the plot.

2. This scene involves only one actor. By the time

FPI: The Show

The Big Dig

you reach this point, the other actors will be starting to get bored. You must switch scenes frequently when the cast is split up to keep them all focused and having fun.

Before switching scenes, have Dunn make one Notice skill test. This will serve as his initial investigation of the crime scene. Tell him that he has had the area around the body cordoned off, along with the miner that the victim had been operating.

The results of his Notice test will determine what clues he finds. The following table lists the clues that are found for each level that the test made. For instance, if he rolled a Good, then he will have found al the clues from Good down to Terrible.

You should remind Detective Dunn about how high profile the Big Dig is, and about the amount of pressure he's getting to resolve the case quickly and quietly.

Scene 2: A New Case

New England Aquarium
Marine Biology Lab
Boston, MA
October 26, 2003
9:00 AM

The specialized lab at New England Aquarium is where Christina Mariani does most of her work when she is not on location. It has long, heavy wooden tables with a variety of biology equipment. Two tables along one wall house computers. The printers are along an adjacent wall. The computers are connected to the university's network, and have Internet access.

Christina, Mike Malone, and Dr. David Walker are now huddled around one of the tables. A large dead fish is lying unceremoniously on it. Malone and Walker are both staring at fish with looks of both interest and disgust. The fish is pale and ugly, and it smells bad. A friend of Malone's had brought the fish to him, thinking it was a prehistoric specimen that had somehow escaped extinction. Malone had brought it to Christina to identify. Walker happened to be with her, so they are all now waiting for Christina.

Have Christina make a Nature Lore skill test. A result of Fair or better identifies the fish as a Coffinfish, a rare, bottom-dwelling fish. It is neither prehistoric nor thought to be extinct. In other words, it's nothing special. A result below Fair makes her find out that it is a bottom-dwelling fish, and makes her suspicious, but not positive, that it is not anything extraordinary.

At that moment, the door opens and a man enters. He's wearing a trench coat, is unshaven and looks quite tired. However, his manner is one that commands attention. He

Crime Scene Clues	
Clue	**Notice Result**
The deceased was found on the ground 13' to the left of his miner, which was still running.	Always
The deceased was not found until the other miner operator noticed that the victim's miner was running, but not digging.	Always
A clear, viscous goo is on the deceased's neck, shoulders and head.	Always
Marks like hickeys, about the size and shape of a quarter, exist at regular intervals around the neck.	Always
A clipboard with the deceased's work schedule is on a shelf to the right of the chair of his miner. A bag lunch is there as well.	Always
There are many footprints of workers around the body and his miner, but none appear out of the ordinary.	Poor
There is a bite mark on the deceased's left shoulder. A chunk of flesh has been bitten out.	Poor
The deceased's body was still warm, so the time of death was very recent.	Fair
The position of the body and the stress marks on the neck and shoulders make you think that the deceased was hanged by the neck above the ground, and then dropped some distance.	Good
Traces of the goo can be found on the arm of the miner rig, going like a trail all the way up its length.	Superb
Traces of the goo can be found on the floor of the miner's cockpit to the right of the chair.	Legendary*
Drops of goo extend in a line from the tip of the miner's arm to the door to the access tunnel.	Great**
* Reduced to Great after initial investigation	
** This should not be found during the initial investigation. It is a clue to bring out much later on. The person investigating must be in a position that can expose this clue.	

FPI: The Show

Detail Maps of Sets 3 - 6

NOTE: The map of Set 3 can be photocopied and handed out to the actors. However, you may wish to block out Set 4 until they reach that point.

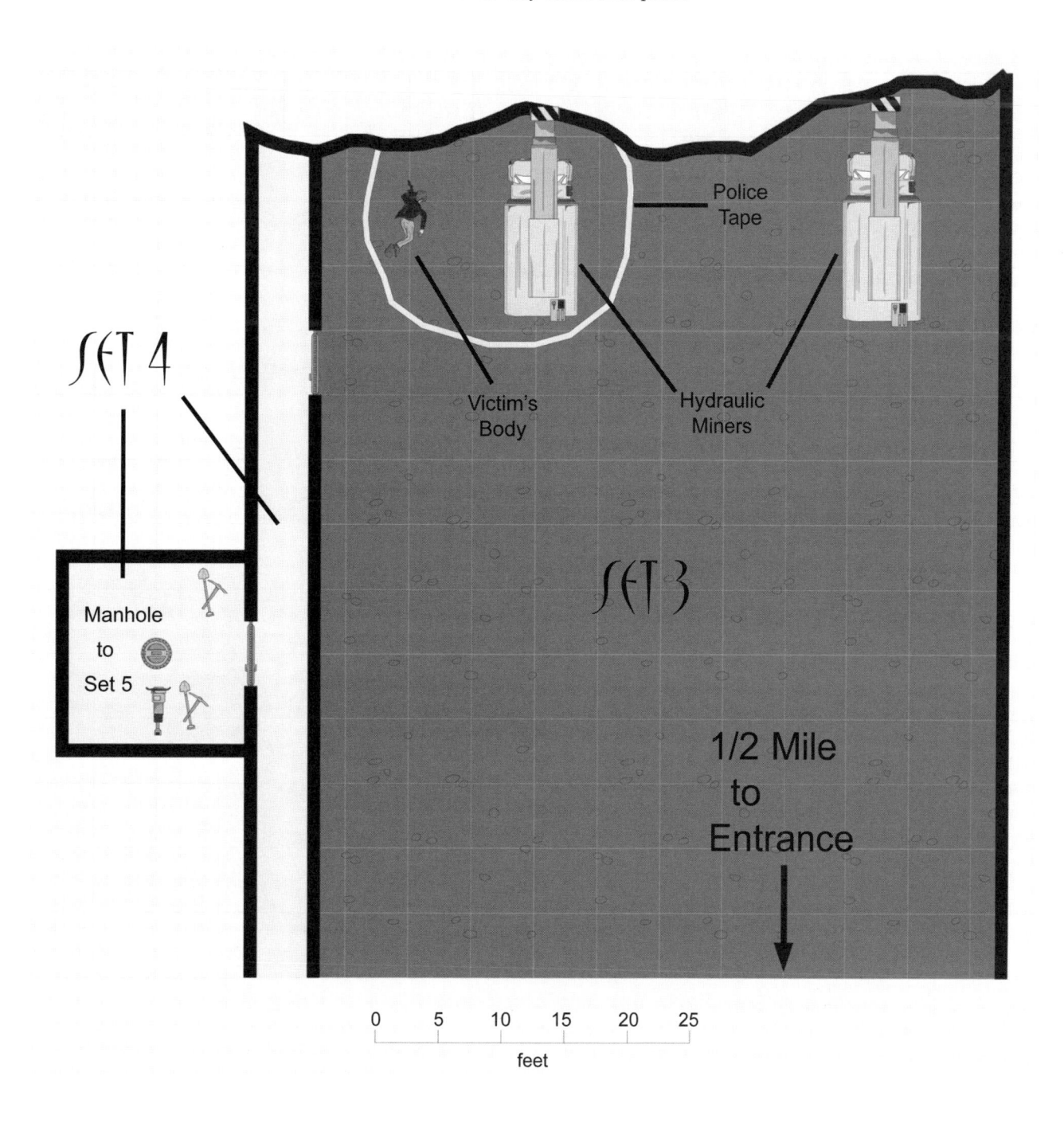

The Big Dig

- Police Tape
- Victim's Body
- Hydraulic Miners
- SET 4
- Manhole to Set 5
- SET 3
- 1/2 Mile to Entrance
- 0 5 10 15 20 25 feet

FPI: The Show

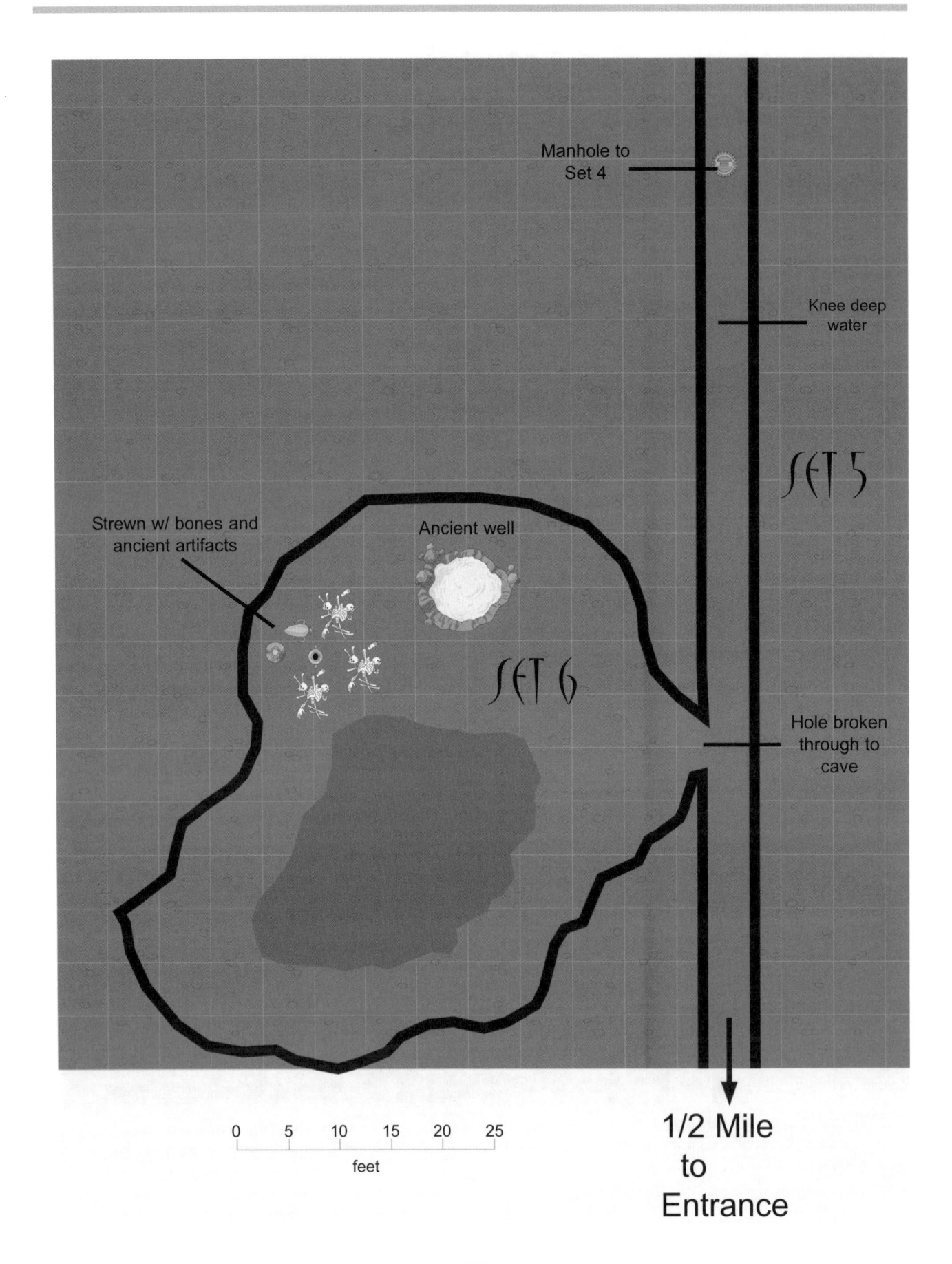

The Big Dig

- Manhole to Set 4
- Knee deep water
- SET 5
- Strewn w/ bones and ancient artifacts
- Ancient well
- SET 6
- Hole broken through to cave
- 1/2 Mile to Entrance

0 5 10 15 20 25
feet

FPI: The Show

is driven, and is obviously here on an important matter. Christina and Malone recognize him immediately as Detective Robert Dunn, of Boston PD's Robbery/Homicide division.

Scene 3: A Curious Stalker

New England Aquarium
Marine Biology Lab
Boston, MA
October 26, 2003
9:00 AM

Matt Hawkins, this morning, you have followed the Private Eye Mike Malone all around Boston. You weren't certain at the time, but you thought he was working on another of those FPI cases. So, you followed him to a wharf, where he spoke with a fisherman. The seaman gave him a large package and then Malone left, and went straight to the Aquarium. You're there now, hanging out by the side entrance, where employees enter, and where you saw Malone go in less than an hour ago. You feel sure now that he's on a case of the paranormal, since he went to one of Christina Mariani's haunts. Mariani is another member of that strange group of ghost hunters, and the fact that they're together cinches it.

You suddenly notice a car pull up and a familiar man in a tan trench coat gets out and enters the building through the side door. It is Detective Robert Dunn, from Robbery/Homicide. Things just got a bit more interesting!

Hawkins does not have access to the employee's sections of the Aquarium, and would have to pay to enter through the main entrance. Also, the Aquarium does not open for business until 10:00AM.

If he hangs out, he'll see the others leave when they complete their business at the Aquarium. It should be made obvious to Hawkins that he will need to get "in" with them and work closely with them. You can let Hawkins figure out how, or you can give him some hints to make sure he does. The game might not flow well if Hawkins remains separated.

The Sets

These are the locations where the scenes described in this demo take place. Once beyond the opening scenes, you cannot fully control the flow of the show. The actors have as much influence on the story as you do. Because of this, we cannot describe the scenes here in the demo. The best we can do is to describe the various sets that the scenes are liable to take place in, and to describe how the supporting cast is going to behave.

Set 1: Foreman's office

This is really just a trailer sitting above ground on the tunnel construction site. It has a desk, some filing cabinets, a drafting table, a small refrigerator, a couch and some chairs. All tabletops are covered in papers. On his desk is a newspaper that has a front-page article about the Big Dig's schedule issues.

Set 2: City Morgue

The body of Bob Harris, one of the workers who died, was sent to one of the many morgues located in Boston, where an autopsy is planned for that day. If the cast decides to watch or participate in the autopsy, you can adjust the time of the autopsy so that they will not miss it.

The examination room looks like any medical examination room. There are counters along the walls, all loaded with medical equipment. Near the center of the room sits a large metal examination table. A metal tray sits beside it, which is loaded with scalpels, clamps and other tools required for the autopsy. Mr. Harris' body is lying on the table, its vacant eyes staring at the lighted ceiling.

The doctor assigned to do the autopsy will agree to step down if Dr. Walker wants to do it.

The doctor must make an Autopsy skill test to complete the procedure. The result of the test will determine what he learns from it. Consult the table below to decide what is learned. The table below tells how many clues to hand out.

Unfinished tunnel

This is the site where the disappearances occurred. The tunnel is extremely wide, and will eventually house three lanes of traffic. Large floodlights on tall stands bathe the tunnel in an artificial glow. Several large construction trucks sit in position. One is designed to attach large slabs of tile on the tunnel walls. Another has a spiked ball device for digging and mining.

The workers are active in this tunnel twenty-four hours a day. The place is bustling and loud, very loud. Dozens of men and women wearing hard hats and heavy work clothes are busy operating the variety of machinery in the place.

Anyone entering the tunnel is required to wear a hard hat and goggles, and a member of the construction crew must accompany anyone who does not work here.

Crime Scene

This area is at the very end of the tunnel, where two large mining machines have been digging constantly since the project was started. Front loaders are waiting behind them to carry the dirt away.

One of the miners, the one on the left-hand side, is not running, while the other is. Police tape extends from the wall being mined to the right of the miner, and encircles the machine. The tape extends thirty feet to the left of the miner before connecting itself once again to the end of the tunnel. Two police officers in hardhats guard the area just outside of the tape. On the ground inside the tape, approximately thirteen feet to the left of the miner, the white outline of a human body has been marked on the ground.

Bob Callahan, the day shift foreman, is upset about the situation. He wants the area cleared and the miner working. They're behind schedule as it is, and this is only making matters worse. His superiors have already chewed him out, and he intends to dish out the same to the detective. However, as much as he will want to blow off steam, he wants the case solved and his men safe, so he will help.

Access Tunnel

Along the left hand wall of the tunnel, there are doors spaced evenly apart every quarter mile. These doors open onto a five-foot-wide passageway. This passageway was designed as an access passage for maintenance people. There are several storage rooms off the passage, their doors currently left unlocked. Each room is sparsely filled with various tools used by the tunnel workers.

One room in particular, the last one before reaching the unfinished end of the tunnel, has very little in it. There is a drainage manhole in the center of the floor. It is through this that the creature comes out into the tunnel. Anyone who is searching the room for clues will find traces of the creature's transparent goo on and near the manhole cover with a Notice skill test of Good or better. If the actor says he is specifically searching the manhole cover, he will notice the goo automatically.

Drainage Tunnel

This tunnel has no light and is short and narrow. It is only five feet high, so anyone in it must bend over. The manholes in the maintenance rooms above give access to this tunnel via a metal ladder down a circular chute. The tunnel is currently about knee deep in water.

This is not a sewer, but is simply drainage for any seawater that may get into the tunnel. Therefore, it is filled with very dirty seawater. The tunnel is new, as is everything here at the dig, but is still quite dirty. It runs straight in both directions. One way, toward the unfinished end of the tunnel, is cut short. The other goes quite a long way and eventually empties into Boston Harbor outside. It curves to the right about a quarter of a mile down from the entrance closest to the crime scene.

If you feel you need some action to keep things exciting, you can have the creature attack the lead person while in this tunnel. It will grab him by his legs and drag him away. It will remain in the water, and no one will get a good look at it. It will not kill the victim right away, but will bite him (see the creature's description to see how its venom works). Any attempt to shoot it will be at a -3 due to the darkness and water. If it was successfully dragging away a victim, the shooter will suffer an additional -1 to the attack roll. If the shot failed by 1, then the shot hit the creature's victim. The creature will take the captive back to the cave system. It will leave the victim paralyzed in the main cave and will then hide in ambush.

Cave System

In ancient days, these caves used to be on the surface, but they are now submerged. By luck, it had suffered a cave-in before it sank beneath the waves, and has managed to survive the centuries. It is still wet and musty, as the tide rises out of the well in the center of one cave chamber. A tribe of natives who appear to have worshipped beings very similar to the creature that is attacking the workers used to occupy these caves. Evidence of this is in crude paintings on the walls of the cave. Other artifacts can be found scattered throughout the cave system, mainly including stone tools and bones.

The tide has begun to come in and there is now about two feet of water on the floor. This will rise to about four feet within the next fifteen minutes. The well is nothing more than a circular hole in the ground that has a raised lip, and can only be seen if someone walks near it with a flashlight lighting the way.

If a cast member is attacked and dragged off, his body is left here in the main cave near the well, then dumped unceremoniously on a large rock, safe from the rising water. Such victims are alive, but although conscious, are so badly affected by the poison, that they can barely move their head or hands, and cannot utter more than a gurgle.

A Great First Aid skill test or Fair Diagnosis skill test will determine that the victim needs serious medical attention right away, and probably has about an hour to live.

The creature does not intend to leave its victim behind. It will try to single the cast out, so that it can attack one at a time. It is completely unaware of the existence of guns, and so is not concerned about anyone who is not in close range. It is intelligent, though, and will learn quickly once it has been wounded by a gunshot. At that point, it will take the defensive, and will probably try to retreat down into the well, dragging its victim in with it, if possible.

The creature uses its stealth and knowledge of the caves to its advantage. It singles out one victim at a time, and attacks, attempting to bite and then retreat. It figures that if it can paralyze everyone, it can always return to the corpses later.

The sound of drilling can be heard, and every now and then, it causes a rumbling that looses dirt and sometimes a few rocks. Anyone who makes at least a Fair Reasoning

FPI: The Show

test will be worried that the place might cave in soon. In fact, it will. The cave will eventually begin to collapse. Use this as a means of increasing the theatrical suspense of the scene. If they try to escape before then, the cave should begin to collapse as they do, to maintain the climax.

The mostly eaten corpses of two missing workers can be found on the floor of the cave.

The artifacts of the ancient tribe have little use here, except to give some clues as to what the thing might be and why it's there. Mostly, though, the artifacts are there to provide a seed for a future episode.

It is obvious that the drilling of the tunnel will destroy the creature's home. It will eventually realize this during the battle with the cast, and if the battle goes badly, it will flee. It will go down the well, and enter the harbor through the maze of passages down there.

If the battle is going badly for the cast, the collapse of the caves should become more imminent, and then the creature will break off and flee before its escape route can be blocked. This will allow the cast (or at least most of it) to survive.

If the battle is going badly for the creature, it will flee.

Anyone who jumps down the well will surely die. They will drop into a deep pool of seawater, but will have no means of escape. The exits would take a long time to find and are all completely under water. There are semi-dry tunnels down there, and survival would be possible for a time. However, with winter coming, death from hyperthermia would be inevitable. In addition, if the creature is there, it will hunt any survivors and it is not likely that any would last for long.

The Tag

Like the teaser, the tag is a short scene that has a special use. However, if the teaser is used to introduce the episode, the tag is used to end it. It provides a short, succinct wrap up of the events and allows closure.

You cannot really predict what will be in the tag, as it will be summarizing events that have not happened yet. So, once the climax has ended and you are ready to wrap things up, you can arrange a scene that brings the cast all together where they can discuss what has happened and perhaps to raise some questions that need to be answered in a future episode.

The following example is one way that the tag could have been roleplayed out. It should not be played out exactly like this, as the game should never be scripted, but it should give you a good idea of how the tag could go. In this example, the creature had not been killed, but had escaped into the well. However, they had managed to cut off part of a tentacle, which they had sent to the lab. The Director chose to have the results revealed during the tag.

The leading cast members are all sitting or standing around a park bench on a hill overlooking Boston Harbor. The harbor looks serene in the chill air, with the morning fog just starting to lift. To one side, the entrance to the tunnel site can be seen; the sound of drills and other equipment provides a muffled background.

Hawkins: So, the thing got away. {the others nod}. I suppose we'll never find it now.

Malone: Unless it strikes again. {Turns to Mariani}. Do you think it's trapped down there now?

Mariani: I doubt it. It's lived in there for a long time, and that means there must be a way for food to get in and out. It probably has a way out far down toward the bottom, but good luck trying to find it!

Dunn: {Shudders}. I don't think I'd want anyone to mess with it in it's own habitat.

Mariani: I don't think there's any worry of that. I doubt it liked all the attention it got. It's a solitary creature that prefers privacy. I think it will sneak away to a quieter haunt and leave us noisy humans alone.

Walker: You mean, "it's noisy relatives." {Waves a manila folder in the air}. I got the lab results back from the sample. It has both octopus and human DNA. There are no clues as to how it happened, but it's unmistakable. And what's more: it's very old; at least two hundred years old, and possibly older.

Mariani: I've never heard of any sea creature living nearly that long. Are you sure?

Walker: That's what the lab says.

Dunn: What about those artifacts?

Mariani: {shrugs} I think they're lost for good now, but I have no idea who they were from.

Malone: Well, at least it'll make a great report for the FPI.

Hawkins: Somehow, I don't think this case is closed...

Supporting Cast

Frank Barrows
(Big Dig Foreman)

Brawn: Good **Reasoning:** Great
Agility: Fair **Perception:** Good
Stamina: Good **Will:** Fair
Luck: 3 **Income:** Fair

Skills: Appraise (Fair), Area Knowledge (Good), Brawl (Fair), Climb (Good), Concentration (Good), Construction (Good), Demolitions (Good), Diplomacy (Good), Direction Sense (Good), First Aid (Fair), Notice (Fair), Sense Motive (Fair).

Gifts: Trustworthy.

Faults: Bossy.

FPI: The Show

Props: Hardhat with flashlight, work clothes, radio, cell phone, any normal mining gear.

Frank is a gruff and very down-to-earth man. He is accustomed to yelling, as he works with loud machinery on a daily basis. He is confident in his abilities and in those of his crew. He is a good leader, although rough in his manner. He'll have no qualms about calling someone an idiot if a mistake is made, but will also be as quick to deliver compliments and support. As gruff as he is, he still shows his men respect and expects the same from them.

He is under tremendous pressure to keep the work going and to get back on schedule. He knows all too well that the schedule is unrealistic, and that there is no way that the project will be completed in the time that the suits want, but he also knows there is no convincing them of it. He must keep everyone working around the clock and get the job done as quickly as he can. This case of the missing workers has really fouled things up. He cannot afford to keep one of his miners idle for even a few hours, much less a couple days! He'll see Hell for it for sure, and he's of a mind to share a little of that Hell with the detective that's causing the delay.

Frank takes his job seriously. Whenever he makes a promise regarding his work, he will do everything in his power to keep it.

He also feels the need to be in control of every situation. This is one reason why the intrusion of Dunn frustrates him so. He feels he is not in control of the situation, and it drives him mad.

Construction Worker

Brawn: Good **Reasoning:** Fair
Agility: Fair **Perception:** Good
Stamina: Good **Will:** Fair
Luck: 3 **Income:** Fair

Skills: Area Knowledge (Fair), Brawl (Fair), Climb (Good), Construction (Good), Demolitions (Fair), Direction Sense (Fair), Notice (Fair), Repair Device* (Good).

* Since this is for a generic worker, you can pick any one type of device, such as mechanical, electrical, etc.

Gifts: Obligation to do his job. (He will not willingly disobey the rules of his job or the instructions of his foreman. If someone tries to bribe or otherwise coerce him, the worker must make a Mediocre Will test to resist taking the bribe.)

This is really a template for all workers at the Big Dig. You can use this character for every worker you introduce in the episode. All the workers are tough and hard working. They all have great respect for the foreman, and will do anything he says. Anyone who publicly makes an enemy of the foreman will make an enemy of the workers, whether the foreman wants it or not.

The Creature

Brawn: Great **Reasoning:** Great
Agility: Good **Perception:** Good
Stamina: Good **Will:** Fair
Luck: 3

Skills: Bite (Fair), Climb (Great), Dodge (Fair), Grapple (Great), Intimidate (Great), Notice (Good), Stealth (Superb), Sting (Great), Swim (Superb).

Gifts: Venom (see below), Amphibious.

Faults: Needs water.

This creature is very old. For time out of mind, it has lived in the subterranean tunnels below Boston Harbor. Occasionally, it comes out into the harbor, feeding off the bottom and never coming near the surface. It is wary of humans, and has always avoided them. There was a time when a tribe of humans worshipped it, and dropped members of their kind down into the well as sacrifices for their continued well-being. It ate the morsels that they threw down, but cared nothing for the welfare of the tribe, or of anything but itself for that matter.

Suddenly, the peaceful silence of its life was disrupted. Loud noises and shaking roused it, and it was not happy. Eventually, a hole opened in the old tribe's cave, and the creature came out to see what was disturbing its world. It was humans. They were cutting a big hole in the ground, and this was causing the roof of its home to shake and rattle. It had to stop them. And it was hungry.

The creature attacks much like an octopus, by grappling its prey with its tentacles, and then poisoning it with its venom. When it bites its prey, the venom in its saliva enters the victim's bloodstream. The venom causes paralysis. The creature can then devour the victim not only while alive, but conscious as well! Because the venom affects the brain, it will try to bite the victim in the neck so that the venom does not have as far to travel.

The creature cannot remain away from seawater for more than an hour or it will begin to suffocate.

Anyone bitten must make a Stamina test. The result determines how many seconds it takes for the venom to paralyze its victim, as shown in this table:

Venom Effects Delay	
Test Result	Delay (secs)
Superb	45
Great	35
Good	25
Fair	15
Mediocre	10
Poor	5
Terrible	Immediate

It will drag its victim back to the cave, and will either devour it in the cave, or pull it down the well if necessary.

Haunted Holiday

An FPI Episode

FPI: The Show

Haunted Holiday

CONFIDENTIAL
FOR DIRECTOR'S EYES ONLY

FPI

"Haunted Holiday"

<u>TEASER</u>

FADE IN:

EXT. TSULOVA HOUSE - NIGHT 1975

The porch light is on, as are some inside the house. Two cars are parked in the driveway: a station wagon and a pickup truck. Voices can be heard from inside the house. It sounds like an argument between two adult men and several teenage boys. Shadows can be seen of people in the window to the FOYER. One shape swings something. It could be a baseball bat. A loud thud is heard, followed by screams. A fight breaks out, dimly seen in the shadows in the windows.

The FRONT DOOR opens with a burst. A six-year-old girl, SOFIA, in a white nightgown runs out. She runs down the stairs and across the yard toward the CAMERA. PULL BACK and PAN LEFT as Sofia begins to pass the CAMERA. One teenage boy, KEVIN, runs out of the house with a baseball bat as the CAMERA PANS AWAY. PAN TO follow Sofia as she runs past. She can now be seen running to WOODEN STAIRS that lead down a rocky cliff. The OCEAN can be seen dimly beyond the cliff. Sofia stops at the top of the stairs to look back. Kevin runs past the CAMERA, running toward the girl. Sofia turns and descends the steps out of view.

EXT. CLIFF STAIRS

A steep ROCKY CLIFF descends to a PRIVATE BEACH. Long strands of grass rise in ragged clumps from between the rocks. An old, weathered WOODEN STAIRCASE descends the cliff. The CAMERA ANGLES downward from the LEFT. Sofia is climbing down the stairs in a hurry; her white gown is billowing in the wind. She looks back at Kevin, who is now climbing down the stairs after her. He looks furious. She looks terrified, screams and turns to run down the stairs. She trips and falls on the steps, out of SIGHT. Kevin laughs maniacally, and runs to meet her. He begins pounding with the bat, swinging downwards. Sofia screams for a few hits, and then is quiet. Cursing, Kevin keeps hitting as we...

FADE OUT.

<u>END TEASER</u>

FPI: The Show

Stop Right Here!

This chapter is for the Director of the game only! If an actor reads this chapter, he will spoil the mystery and ruin the fun for himself. Any actor who reads this should not play this game, unless he decides to direct it.

The Director should read this chapter fully before running it. It is designed with the leading cast detailed in Chapter Ten in mind, but it is always recommended that the actors create their own characters.

Introduction

The cousin of an FPI member recently moved with his family into an old Victorian house in Maine. After they settled in, they discovered that the house is haunted. Concerned, he calls his cousin and invites him and his colleagues in the FPI to his place for a little vacation. The unwitting stars make the drive to Maine, unaware that there is more in store for them this weekend than fun and sun!

This episode describes Mike Malone as being the character whose cousin owns the house. It can actually be anyone in the cast. If no one chooses to play Mike, then you must pick someone else to be related to the Satlers.

Mystery Episodes

This episode is a mystery. This means that there is a mystery for the cast to solve. The majority of this episode is going to be freeform, where the cast must take the initiative to hunt for clues and get to the bottom of the mystery. It is up to you as Director to make sure that they do not flounder and lose focus. Make good use of the supporting cast, the ghosts, and other clues to help make sure they stay on track.

Because most of the action in the show is freeform, not many scenes are planned out. You will need to create scenes on the fly as the cast goes about their investigations.

Like all TV shows, this episode expects much dialogue between characters. This should be your primary means of keeping the show moving. The Brody kids, who are adults now, will be very nervous about the cast, especially when they start snooping around.

Chapter Structure

The rest of this chapter is broken into five primary sections:

The Stories

This tells you all of the backplot behind the episode. First, it describes the entire situation from the Satler family's perspective. Second, it describes what really happened to cause the hauntings that the Satler's recount. Thirdly, it explains what the ghosts are trying to do, and exactly why they are doing it the way they are.

The Cast

This describes each member of the supporting cast. Each character description will include all the details on how to play him. It will include his motivations, knowledge of events, and plans. It is very important that you become very familiar with each of these characters before you run the episode.

The Acts

This describes the flow of the episode in as much detail as can be. It will describe the goal of the act, and will list and describe each beat. In some cases, it will describe some scenes.

The Sets

This describes the details of every location included in the episode. Maps of important places will be included. Because you can never expect to predict what the cast will do or where they will go, you may need to create some sets on the fly. However, this section should give you most of what you will need.

How to Use this Chapter

Start by reading the stories. These will give you all the background you'll need to get started. After reading the stories, you will fully understand what the episode is about.

Next, read the cast through. Pay very close attention to the supporting cast, as you will be playing them. Again, the majority of this game should be spent with the supporting cast interacting with the leading cast.

Finally, browse through the acts. Make sure you understand all the beats for each act. The beats are the most important elements of the episode, so make sure they are covered in one way or another.

The Stories

The Satlers' Story

Mike Malone has been estranged from his cousin Jim Satler for a few years now. Jim does not believe in the paranormal, and feels that his cousin is wasting his life and talent chasing creatures that do not exist. He fears that Mike's obsession with the paranormal has irreparably damaged his career. Every time they talk, they argue about it.

FPI: The Show

Haunted Holiday

One day, Jim called unexpectedly and invited Mike to his new house in Maine. He sounded apologetic, and seemed to want to bury the hatchet. He also extended the invitation to some of his colleagues in the FPI. Mike thought that this was his chance to make good with his cousin, so he agreed.

Jim has an ulterior motive for inviting his cousin and friends to his house. He recently bought a beautiful Victorian house in a secluded little seacoast town in Maine. The problems started within a month after he and his family moved in.

It started with small things. Things began to disappear, and then found in odd places. At first, they assumed this was due to the chaos of unpacking. But it kept happening, and with things that they knew they put away. Then the noises began. First, there was the knocking on the walls. Then, there were voices at night. They were muffled and unintelligible, and almost sounded like the wind. However, the voices persisted, and could be heard even on the calmest of nights. Jim's wife Catherine swore she would wake up to the sound of someone whispering to her from beside her bed. As soon as she tried to focus on the voice, it would stop, and she never saw anything. As time went by, the voices got louder and more frequent. They could not understand a single word. In fact, it sounded like gibberish, but the more they heard it, the more they knew that it was a speaking voice. All of this time, Jim refused to believe in it. He stubbornly insisted that it was wind or mice, or even something normal and natural that he just can't explain.

Recently, though, the haunting took a more chilling turn. The family now began to see ghosts. Catherine has seen the ghost of an adult woman in a nightgown. She has long dark hair, and appears in her forties. She sees the apparition walking from room to room on the second floor, as if looking for something.

Jodie, their six-year-old daughter, has seen a young girl of about six run from the house. The ghostly girl would be standing in the foyer hiding by the post at the entrance to the family room. She would look frightened, and would be hugging a small teddy bear. Then, she would scream silently and run from the house, out the front door. She would run around the edge of the room, as though avoiding the center of the room. The door would not really open, and she would simply disappear through it.

Jim did not see anything at first, and was concerned that his family was just unnerved by the bizarre events. Then, one night while he was sitting in the family room watching television with his wife, he saw a man enter the room from the stairs. The man just stood there staring at them. Jim jumped up when he saw him, then froze. The man was not fully solid; Jim could see right through him. The man was dressed in pajamas and just stood there, with his arms hanging. He looked worried, and his mouth was moving, but Jim heard no sound. Jim could not believe his eyes. He tried talking to the ghost, but it seemed not to notice him. It just kept talking silently. Then, it turned and walked back upstairs. When Jim came out of his shock, he ran upstairs after it, but it was gone. He has seen the image twice since, but has never been able to follow it once it went upstairs.

After that, Jim realized that maybe he was wrong about the paranormal, and that he was too harsh on his cousin. Perhaps Mike and his colleagues from the Foundation for Paranormal Investigation might help. Of course, he couldn't just call him up and ask for help. He has too much pride for that. Instead, he would invite them over for a little holiday on their private beach. Hopefully, they will see the ghosts for themselves, and then offer to help.

The Real Story

During the mid-seventies, a rich elderly couple owned the house. They were rather reclusive, and did not go out much. They were retired and lived off their immense savings. Allan Brody, a local carpenter and handyman, has wanted that house all his life. Unfortunately, he is a drunk and a hothead, and has very few scruples. He decided to befriend the couple, and do work for them on their house in the hopes of convincing them to sell the house to him cheaply. This plan seemed to be working nicely. They liked him, and he made many renovations to the house free of charge.

Then, one day in 1994, the old couple died in a tragic car accident. Brody was called to the reading of the will, where he expected to get the house given to him. However, instead, he was awarded ten thousand dollars. He was furious. He cursed and he fumed, and then stormed out of the office.

For some reason, the house was not mentioned in the will. It was put up for auction. Brody tried his best to buy the house, but was outbid by a Russian family that had just moved into town. Again, Brody was furious. He felt that the house was rightly his, and that these foreigners have no business here.

The Tsulova family moved in and was very happy in the house. The family consisted of the mother and father, Dmitry and Natalia, two sons in their early teens, Anton and Roman. Finally, there was their five-year-old daughter Sofia. It was an old Victorian with quite a lot of charm. Their two boys attended the local middle school, and Sofia, went to kindergarten. They were a friendly and happy family, but were having trouble fitting in. There was a lot of prejudice among the locals, but eventually, people began to warm up to them. All, that is, except for the Brody's.

Brody's two sons, Kevin and Neal, were downright vicious to the two Tsulova boys. They would bully them every day after school. Anton and Roman were raised pacifists, so they did not fight back, until one fateful day in 1975. The two Russian boys decided to fight back and beat the Brody kids up, sending them running.

When Allan Brody heard about this, he was enraged. Drunk, he grabbed a baseball bat and he and his sons drove to the Tsulova house to settle the matter. It was late at night and the Tsulova's were preparing for bed. Brody forced his way into the foyer and began yelling and arguing with Dmitry. The boys all began arguing as well.

Suddenly, a fight broke out between the boys. Allan, drunk and enraged as he was, struck Anton in the back of the head with the baseball bat, killing him instantly. Sofia and her mother screamed and Dmitry leaped at Allan. There was a struggle, and Allan finally beat Dmitry to death with his bat. Kevin and Neal both strangled Roman.

Sofia bolted during the fight and ran out the front door before anyone could stop her. Her mother ran after her, but Allan caught her. He yelled to his sons to get the child, and Kevin ran off after her, grabbing his father's baseball bat as he did. Kevin caught Sofia on the steps that led down the cliff face to the private beach, and beat her to death.

Allan had calmed down by now, and was scared. He and his sons had brutally killed almost an entire family, and had no idea how to get away with it. He and Kevin tied up Natalia, and then thought up a plan. They decided that they would make it look like some kind of satanic ritual. They knew that the father and daughter were too badly beaten to do anything with, but the others were not. Allan buried Dmitry's body under the back steps. They drew a big pentagram in the center of the foyer with the victims' blood, and then arranged them on it. They finished it off by finding some incense and other Russian knickknacks that had an occult look to them, and placed them in the circle.

Allan figured that they could make it look like Dmitry had sacrificed his family to the Devil in some bizarre Russian ritual. None of the locals knew anything about Russians and their culture, and with the arms race, no one trusted them. If the local authorities thought that Dmitry had committed the murders, they would never look on the premises for more bodies.

They decided to drive the Tsulova's car off a nearby cliff into the ocean. At the last moment, they remembered Sofia, and dumped her body in it. Her teddy bear remained hidden among the rocks by the stairs.

Their plan worked like a charm. The police quickly concluded that Dmitry had committed the gruesome act, and that he and his daughter had fled in the car. They put a bulletin out for the car, but it remains under the water to this day.

The Brody's bought the house and moved in. They built a deck behind the house to help conceal the body. They were not there long before the ghosts began to haunt them. They were driven from their dream home. They never sold the house, so that the body would never be found. Years later, Allan went to jail on assault charges. His wife, who knew nothing about the incident, finally sold the house to the Satlers.

The Official Police Report

On October 5, 1975, the police were called to the Tsulova home at the request of Mr. David Brockman, the principle of the Carver Beach High School. The Tsulova children had not been to school for the past two days, and their teachers were concerned that something was wrong. A squad car was sent to the house where they found the door unlocked and the bodies of three people brutally murdered in strange and frightening circumstances. Detective Thomas Carter was assigned to the case.

The victims were identified as Natalia Tsulova, Anton Tsulova, and Roman Tsulova. Anton and Roman were teenagers, and Natalia was their mother.

The circumstances around the location and condition of their bodies are of special note. They were found in the foyer, where a large pentagram was drawn on the floor in human blood. The three bodies were laid out in a coffin position on three of the five points of the star. Candles had been placed at the tip of each point of the star, just above the victims' heads. They had burned down and were not lit when the police had arrived. An incense burner sat in the center of the circle. It had been lit, and its smell was still apparent in the room. These details suggest a ritual murder that is Satanic in origin.

The victims were killed in different ways. The two boys were bludgeoned to death. No murder weapon was found. Natalia had been strangled.

Both Dmitry Tsulova, the husband, and Sofia, their six-year-old daughter were not found. The Tsulovas' station wagon was missing, but everything else seemed in order. An APB was issued on the car, but it was never found. There were no witnesses.

All of the evidence points to conclusion that Dmitry Tsulova murdered his family in order to perform a bizarre satanic ritual.

FPI: The Show

Haunted Holiday

Jim Satler

Jim is a software engineer for a company in Portland. He is a realist. He does not believe in anything out of the ordinary. He sometimes works from home on his computer. He loves technology, but has always been in love with the Victorian era. He fell in love with the old Tsulova house as soon as he saw it. He is striving to have all the technology that he loves blend nicely into a Victorian setting. Thus, the house is decorated in a very Victorian way, with the computers and television cleverly hidden or disguised.

He is very shaken by the events that have taken place in his house. The concept of ghosts is so far outside of his conception of the world that he simply cannot deal with it. The ghosts terrify him, but he feels he must appear strong and fearless for his family. He will try to show that same strength with the cast, but it will not always work.

Jim will not want to admit the presence of the ghosts and will try to avoid discussing them. However, if pressed, he will eventually talk about it. He will try to make it sound like there must be a rational explanation for it, though, so he will not be the best person to get the story from.

Brawn: Good **Reasoning:** Good
Agility: Fair **Perception:** Fair
Stamina: Good **Will:** Fair

Luck: 3 **Income:** Fair

Skills: Area Knowledge Good, Computer Use Great, Concentration Fair, Software Engineering Great, Brawl Fair, Climb Good, Drive Car Fair, Run Good, Sail Mediocre.

Jodie Satler

Jodie is an adorable six-year-old girl. She is very happy and healthy, and always smiling and pleasant.

Since the hauntings began, she has been quieter. She spends much more time playing by herself in her room, mostly at night. At first, she complained about seeing the ghosts, and was afraid. Now she does not talk much about it, and no longer seems afraid.

In reality, she is the only one in the house who understands them at all. This is because Jodie is Sensitive. She has befriended the ghost of Sofia, and plays tea with her in her room at night. Sofia will only speak to her, and does so in English. Jodie has many of the answers to the mystery, but will not discuss them unless she is asked directly.

Jodie has learned much about Sofia. In this way, you would have Jodie keep the useful information a secret, and only bring it out if pressed.

Here is what Jodie knows:

1. Sofia lives here and Jodie's room is also Sofia's room.
2. Sofia is afraid of most boys.
3. Sofia likes tea parties.
4. Sofia went to kindergarten.
5. Sofia has a mommy, daddy, and two big brothers.

Brawn: Fair **Reasoning:** Fair
Agility: Great **Perception:** Good
Stamina: Fair **Will:** Fair

Luck: 3 **Scale:** -1 **Income:** Fair

Skills: Area Knowledge Mediocre, Computer Use Poor, Run Good, Uplift Spirits Great, Notice Superb, Climb Good, Swim Great, Escape Artist Good, Stealth Superb.

Fault: Child

Power: Sensitive

Catherine Satler

Catherine is a down to Earth and sensible. She has great common sense and is always calm. She takes almost everything in stride, and her warm smile brightens every room. She is the quintessential mother, keeping the house clean and orderly, and savory aromas always drift from the kitchen. Where Jim can be a little rough, Catherine is soft and inviting, able to make everyone feel at home.

Keeping her calm façade has been the toughest job of her life. The ghosts have her unnerved as well, and she is trying to act as though nothing is wrong. She will not avoid the subject, but she will not willingly bring it up. Her concern regarding it is always about the family. "I'm afraid of what it will do to Jodie."

Brawn: Fair **Reasoning:** Good
Agility: Fair **Perception:** Good
Stamina: Fair **Will:** Good

Luck: 3 **Income:** Fair

Skills: Area Knowledge Good, Computer Use Fair, Diplomacy Good, Appraise Good, Culinary Arts Superb, First Aid Good, Swim Good, Persuasion Good, Camaraderie Good.

Gifts: Always keeps her cool.

FPI: The Show

Allan Brody

Allan Brody is in prison about a half hour's drive away. He is a hothead, and will take almost any statement personally. He sees the negative aspects of everything. Although now sober, it is not by choice. The way to his heart is through alcohol.

If the cast mentions the Satler house, it will be the first time that he heard about the sale of the house to the Satlers. He will be very angry about the sale, and will act defensively regarding it. He will complain that his wife had no right doing it. If the subject of ghosts or anything out of the ordinary comes up about the house, he will act a little guilty, but will try to disguise it. A contested Sense Motive test will allow the cast to see through it. He will never confess.

He will not help his boys if they call him.

Brawn: Great
Agility: Fair
Stamina: Good
Luck: 3
Reasoning: Fair
Perception: Fair
Will: Fair
Income: Fair

Skills: Area Knowledge Great, Brawl Great, Run Great, Carpentry Great, Notice Fair, Repair Appliances Fair, Swim Good, Breaking & Entering Good, Stealth Good, Bluff Great, Intimidate Good.

Gift: High Pain Threshold

Faults: Drunk, Violent when enraged

Kevin Brody

Kevin is much like his father, except that he does not drink heavily. He took up his father's trade as carpenter, and works around town as a handyman. He is not married, and lives in an apartment in town.

Kevin is angry with his mother for selling the old Tsulova house. He has not spoken to her since. He makes no attempt to hide his displeasure of the sale of the house. Because of it, he does not like the Satler's, and will act hostile toward them. He is generally not needlessly violent, but he will be rude and unfriendly to them.

If he discovers that an investigation of the ghosts is underway, he will do what he can to put an end to it. He will first call his dad for help. When that avenue fails, he will decide to try to remove the evidence. He and Neil will drive a motorboat to the boathouse late that night. Neil will back the boat into the boathouse, and Kevin, in bathing suit with snorkel and goggles, will dive underwater and attach a rope with a hook to the bumper of the car. Neil will then try to pull the car out with the boat. The boat will have a spotlight that they will aim into the boathouse.

Kevin does not trust Neal to keep their secret. He may bully him to try to keep him silent.

Brawn: Great
Agility: Fair
Stamina: Good
Luck: 3
Reasoning: Fair
Perception: Fair
Will: Fair
Income: Fair

Skills: Area Knowledge Great, Brawl Great, Run Great, Carpentry Good, Notice Good, Seduction Fair, Swim Good, Breaking & Entering Good, Stealth Good, Bluff Great, Intimidate Good.

Gift: Attractive

Faults: Violent when enraged

Neal Brody

Neal has been emotionally scarred by the murders. The event caused him to grow apart from his father and brother, and he has not spoken much with them for years. He is rather weak-willed and emotional. He did not go to college, and has few useful skills. He has trouble keeping any job, and is currently working at a local video store. Unable to make ends meet, he has recently moved back in with his mother.

He feels guilty about what he, his father and brother did, and has been living with this guilt all these years. He resents them for the actions that ruined his life. Although he regrets it, and would like to see it resolved, he does not want to go to prison. He will try to keep quiet about the incident. Only if pressed hard will he talk, and only then, if he fears worse punishment.

If he finds out about the investigation, he will go to Kevin with the news. His brother will talk him into helping with the plan. He will be drunk when they go to the boathouse.

Brawn: Good
Agility: Fair
Stamina: Good
Luck: 3
Reasoning: Fair
Perception: Good
Will: Fair
Income: Fair

Skills: Area Knowledge Great, Brawl Good, Run Good, Hide Traces Good, Notice Fair, Haggle Fair, Swim Fair, Breaking & Entering Good, Sense Motive Great, Bluff Great.

Gift: None.

Faults: Defeated

FPI: The Show

Haunted Holiday

Karen Brody

She is a tough woman. Being Allan's wife is a real test to her endurance. She has had to grow tough to deal with his gruff exterior and his drinking problem. After the incident, the family fell apart. What made it harder was that Karen had no idea about the incident at the Tsulova place.

The trouble all started when they finally bought Allan's dream house. She was leery about moving into a house after such a brutal murder, but she knew that this was her husband's dream, so she went along with it. Soon after they moved in, they discovered that the house was haunted. Karen was from a simple local family, and fully believed in ghosts. It came as no surprise that the big old house was haunted.

The ghostly images that she saw were quite definitely of the Tsulovas. What surprised her was that she swore she saw Dmitry among the ghostly forms that haunted their nights. Also, the ghosts were quite vicious towards them. They literally seemed to be attacking them. They would break items in the house. Allan, Kevin and Neal all cut their feet on broken glass items that seemed to be placed intentionally for that purpose. When the ghosts would appear, they would appear just as they had died, and looked very angry. During the day, many bizarre things took happened. The house would ooze a horrid-smelling goo. Hundreds of flies or ants would swarm around certain spots in the house.

At night, they would have trouble sleeping. They would awaken to horrible sounds. They would hear harsh shouting, as though there were an argument happening in the foyer. When she would go down there, the shouting would disappear, and she would see nothing. But the sounds would return as soon as she left. The shouting would eventually turn to screams of terror and torment. Then, the thing that chilled Karen to the bone was that after the argument and the screams of torment, the ghosts would wander about the house, screaming in ravenous anger. Karen would hide under the covers in bed, shaking and whimpering until it finally stops.

They endured this for nearly a month before giving up and leaving the house. Karen wanted to see it right away, but Allan forbade it. Finally, after he was in prison, Karen sold it as quickly as she could. She never spoke to anyone about the ghosts.

If questioned about the house, she will tell everything she knows. She will explain why she sold it and everything. Of course, she has no idea who killed the Tsulovas.

Brawn: Fair **Reasoning:** Fair
Agility: Good **Perception:** Fair
Stamina: Good **Will:** Good
Luck: 3 **Income:** Fair

Skills: Area Knowledge Great, Run Good, Notice Fair, Culinary Arts Good, Swim Good, Persuasion Good, Sense Motive Great, Bluff Great.

Gift: Never forget a face

Detective Thomas Carter

He is a retired will be colorful. He has done a lot of thinking about the case over the years, and he is now thinking that he may have been wrong. There were things that just didn't make sense. Here are some points that he will make when talking to him:

1. Dmitry was a very well respected member of the community. Sure, he was a foreigner, but he always seemed like a good man and a good father.

2. Dmitry didn't take anything with him. If he and Sofia left, wouldn't they have taken clothes, toys and other personal items?

3. The murders were inconsistent. One was killed by blunt trauma to the back of the head, another was strangled, and the third was beaten to death by fists. This does not seem consistent for a ritual killing.

4. The car was never found, and there were no sightings at all of it.

5. There have been sightings of Sofia's ghost, but if she's dead, where's the body?

Brawn: Good **Reasoning:** Good
Agility: Fair **Perception:** Good
Stamina: Fair **Will:** Fair
Luck: 3 **Income:** Fair

Skills: Brawl Great, Criminology Great, Gun Great, Gather Information Great, Interrogate Good, Notice Great, Sense Motive Good.

Gifts: Trustworthy

202

FPI: The Show

Dmitry Tsulova

Dmitry is a ghost. He and the rest of his family are trapped in the house until his and Sofia's bodies have been found and put to rest.

He will actively try to make those who spend the night in the house find his the remains of his body. Unfortunately, his ability to do this is limited. He usually is seen walking into a room where someone is and trying to speak to him. The problem is that he has no voice. Anyone can try to read his lips, but it would be a Great task. Also, he will only speak Russian. If someone succeeds in reading his lips, he can recite it to Jelena, who can then translate.

If any of the Brody men enters the house, he will become active and violent. It is his intent, for as long as he exists in this house, to try to bring justice to the Brodys for what they did. He will torment them as much as he can, and try to show any others in the house that the Brody is responsible for the murders.

See the section Ghostly Powers for details on his abilities and limitations.

Brawn: Good **Reasoning:** Fair
Agility: Fair **Perception:** Fair
Stamina: Good **Will:** Good
Luck: 3 **Income:** Fair

Skills: Area Knowledge Great, Run Good, Notice Fair, Throw Great, Intimidate Superb.

Natalia Tsulova

Natalia is driven by two needs: finding her husband's body and having it put to rest, and seeing justice served against the Brodys. She will join Dmitry in exacting retribution whenever a Brody man enters the house.

Every night, she can be seen going from room to room searching for her child. If a Sensitive person, such as Jelena, sees her, she will turn and silently try to speak to her. Unfortunately, she cannot speak audibly, but anyone who can read lips may have a chance of catching words.

Her search for Sofia can extend outside to the yard. She has been seen several times by passersby.

Brawn: Good **Reasoning:** Fair
Agility: Fair **Perception:** Fair
Stamina: Good **Will:** Good
Luck: 3 **Income:** Fair

Skills: Area Knowledge Great, Run Good, Notice Fair, Throw Great, Intimidate Great.

Sofia Tsulova

Sofia will always try to show people to where her body is. Unfortunately, this will take a lot of energy, and she rarely manages to get beyond the point where she was killed on the stairs.

She has found a friend in Jodie. She can appear to her without much effort. This is because Jodie is Sensitive. Jodie lives in Sofia's old room, and they spend a lot of time there together. They have tea parties and talk about little girl things. She can speak with Jodie, but no one else.

Brawn: Fair **Reasoning:** Fair
Agility: Fair **Perception:** Fair
Stamina: Great **Will:** Good
Luck: 3 **Income:** Fair

Skills: Area Knowledge Great, Run Good, Notice Fair, Throw Great, Intimidate Great.

Anton & Roman Tsulova

These two do very little. They are responsible for moving misplacing items and other mischievous tricks. When they are seen, they are simply standing by a doorway just staring, sometimes together and sometimes separately. Sometimes they will appear as they had died, with their bloody wounds, and other times they will not.

You can choose to have them take a more active part, but that is up to you.

Brawn: Good **Reasoning:** Fair
Agility: Good **Perception:** Fair
Stamina: Good **Will:** Fair
Luck: 3 **Income:** Fair

Skills: Area Knowledge Great, Run Good, Notice Fair, Throw Great, Intimidate Superb.

FPI: The Show

Haunted Holiday

Townsfolk

The townsfolk tend to be very pleasant. Most of them know about the events of 1975, but only as reported by the police. Most believe the place is haunted, but mainly just from stories. A few people have trespassed on the property during the years that it had been abandoned. All of them claim to have seen ghosts. Their stories will be include the ghostly girl running to the wooden beach stairs, the boys standing in a dark corner staring, and the woman searching the yard for something.

Ghosts

The ghosts are the centerpiece of the episode, and it is therefore very important that you play them right. Obviously, the ghosts have all the answers to the mystery. However, they will not be able to give too much information to help the cast. Here are some guidelines for how to handle the ghosts in this episode.

Nightly Visits

The ghosts will rarely show themselves, and only then during certain times of the night with a specific behavior. Here is how each will behave normally each night:

Natalia: She will be seen late at night roaming the house, from room to room. She will look in closets, under beds, behind chairs, and any other place that might be able to hide a young child. She will make the rounds of the house and then fade. A Sensitive like Jelena might be able to talk to her. Unfortunately, her voice will not be heard, and they would have to rely on lip reading or pantomime. If someone thinks to make an ELF recording, her voice will be recorded there. She will speak in Russian, and will be pleading for information about the whereabouts of her daughter. She will be saying that she cannot find her and that she wants her back. Most of what she says will be unintelligible even to someone who speaks Russian. Only snatches of her dialogue will be recognizable.

Dmitry: He is seen less often. He will come into the living room if any one person is there late at night. He will stand at the doorway to the center hallway and talk to the person in the room. He will not show if more than one person is in the living room. Like Natalia, he cannot be heard except by ELF recording, and even that will be hard to interpret. He will speak in Russian and say, roughly translated, "Help me! Help me! I'm lost! Where am I?" He will stand there talking for some time, and then turn and walk slowly into the kitchen to stand at the door to the deck. He will stand there for a while staring out the door's window, and then fade.

Sofia: Sofia only appears for Jodie. She visits Jodie every night and plays tea with her. Jodie's parents do not interfere because they do not want to anger the ghost. This terrifies them, but they feel they have no other option. Sofia does not appear for anyone else. Cameras in Jodie's room will record Jodie playing with herself. If the camera, video or normal, has any infra-red, or other such filters, it will detect an aura where Sofia would be. ELF recordings will capture Sofia having little girl talk with Jodie in English. The voice will be hard to identify, and impossible to make out words because of Jodie's almost constant chatter.

Anton & Roman: They will never be visible, as their bodies were very badly mutilated. However, they will behave like poltergeists. Each night they will hide one or two small objects. They are all items that are commonly used, and they will be found in very odd places, making it clear that someone, or something, had put it there. ELF recordings may catch snatches of boyish playful talk, in English. No real clues to the mystery, except that they may refer to each other by their first names.

Voices

They cannot speak in normal volumes, but ELF recordings can pick them up. Jelena and Jodie can speak with them normally, if they use their Sensitive abilities. Jodie speaks with Sofia on a regular basis.

Séance

A séance can succeed in bringing one of the Tsulova's into view. The one performing the ritual will be able to ask it questions, and speak to it. However, the spirit will only live in the "moment of death." This means that the ghost will believe it is during the time of the murders, and anything it says would be in that context. The ghost will hear the questions, and will be trying to answer, though. For instance, if Jelena asks Natalia where Jodie is, she may answer, "Run, Sofia! Run outside! Run away!" as though she were yelling to have Sofia run away from their attackers. Of course, she was also telling Jelena that Sofia went outside. This will add a challenge and atmosphere to the séance.

The Sets

This section describes all of the locations featured in the episode. You may need to create new sets on the fly if the cast manages to stray from the expected areas. However, this will give you most of the sets that you will encounter.

Exterior Sets

Satler House

This is a large, old Victorian on a two-acre plot of land in Cutler Beach, Maine. The property is on the top of a steep hill, accessed by one dirt road that services five other households. The road is a dead-end, and is therefore rarely used. Over the years there has been talk about paving it, but the residents don't want it. Cars are forced to drive slowly on the unpaved road, and the residents prefer that. For these reasons, there is little traffic on the road, and any cars that go by are quite noticeable.

The yard is large and expansive. Catherine has set up a nice garden, and there are croquet hoops set up, as is a volleyball net. One edge of the yard, about a hundred feet from the house, is marked by a steep, rocky cliff that drops down to a private beach, which they own. There is an old, wooden staircase leading steeply down to the beach. The steps are in good condition, so the Satlers have left it alone, although they do mean to put up a railing. They have recently put up a white picket fence along the edge, to keep Jodie from falling.

The driveway is a five-hundred foot long dirt road that ends at a big circle in front of the house. Catherine has made a small garden with a birdbath and bench for sitting in the center of the circle. The circle is wide enough for cars to park.

The area is wooded, and the woods line two of the edges of their property. The ledge lines one edge, and the road lines the edge opposite the ledge.

Satler Private Beach

This beach is accessed by private beaches on both ends, and by the steep wooden staircase that leads down from the house. The beach is about sixty feet from the rocks to the water at high tide, and can extend to as far as ninety feet at low tide. The section of the beach that the Satlers own extends for a total of one-quarter of a mile, with the stairs descending to the center.

The beach is rocky and not very comfortable for about ten feet from the bottom of the cliff, but the rest is nice and sandy. The only reason why the house was affordable was that Karen Brody was desperate to sell the house.

Rocks from the cliff extend out to the water on one end. Built into this is a wooden boathouse. The water flows into it, so that a motorboat or sailboat can be docked there out of the weather. It is old and in disrepair. An old dirt road goes from this boathouse up to the road. It is very old and overgrown. Both the Satlers and their neighbors think that the boathouse does not belong to them, so it has been left abandoned. If this boathouse is mentioned to the Satlers, they will explain that they don't know who owns it. Jim might say, "You know, I guess it could belong to me. I'll have to look into it sometime."

When driving along the Satlers' dirt road, a Good Notice skill test will be needed to notice where the boathouse road meets this road. When walking, the Difficulty Level reduces to Poor.

The boathouse is painted gray and the paint is peeling very badly. Anyone who is paying any attention will notice it. The Satlers take it for granted, so they will not notice it.

Town of Cutler Beach

This is a nice New England beach town. It has a small, one mile public beach complete with a boardwalk that has plenty of restaurants, souvenir and nick-knack shops. The rest of the town has many residents, and most of the normal businesses. There is no industry in Cutler Beach, and its economy is designed mostly around fishing and tourism. There is a small fishing port, with wharfs and fishing boats.

Being a fishing town, Cutler Beach is known for their seafood restaurants, which are top notch. Even the cheapest places are very good. The town uses their fishing industry as their theme for the tourists. As a result, many of the restaurants and other shops sport lobster traps, nets and other fishing paraphernalia.

The town has most of the normal resources, including a library, town hall, fire station, police station, newspaper, etc. All of these places are small and poorly equipped. The library will have extensive local documents and books, as well as a nearly complete reference of the local newspaper.

Interior Sets

The Satler House

This is an old Victorian house, and the Satlers bought it because of its charm. They have decorated it the Victorian style as much as they could get away with.

The Satler House - First Floor

Hall: This is where all of the murders took place, and is the only place inside the house, except for Jodie's room, where Sofia will appear. About one-third of the Hall has been split into two small spaces. One is a brief entryway and the other is a coat closet. The rest of the Hall is open.

Like the rest of the house, the Hall is decorated in the Victorian style. There are framed prints of 1800's paintings, and a chandelier hanging from the ceiling that lights the hall. The chandelier looks like it would have candles, but uses electric lights.

Library: Most of the available wall space has bookshelves attached to them. The corner by the window and the Living Room has an armoire that opens out into a cleverly disguised computer desk. This computer is connected to the Internet. The books are a combination of novels, both old and new, and computer manuals that Jim uses when working at home. There are some children's books here as well.

Dining Room: This is a beautiful room. It has a bay window that overlooks the ocean, and has a fireplace in one corner. There is a nice hutch with some china and other knickknacks in it.

Kitchen: This is a nice large kitchen, and is the most

FPI: The Show

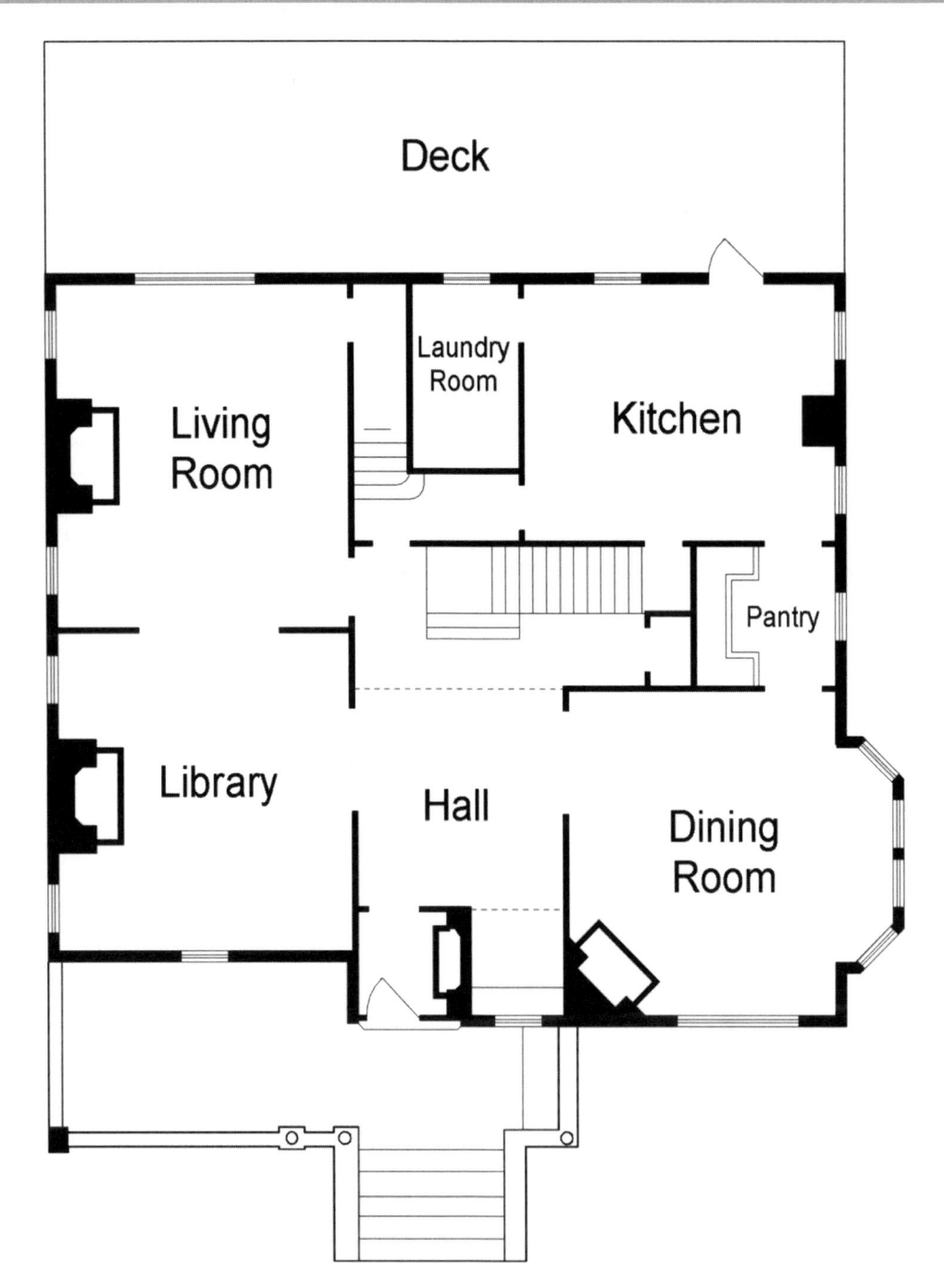

Haunted Holiday

modern looking of all the rooms in the house. It is very hard to conceal a modern stove, refrigerator, and other appliances. A small kitchen table is set up along the wall between the Laundry Room and the door to the deck.

Living Room: This room looks like the drawing room of an old English mansion, only on a smaller scale. The large fireplace has a roaring fire, and a decorated ottoman sits in front of the fireplace. A matching couch and love seat face each other on either side of the fireplace, so that an easy look to one side will give you a great view of the fire. A reclining chair beyond the couch and faces the fire. The rest of the room is decorated with end tables, paintings and other Victorian style fineries.

Pantry: This is loaded with all types of foodstuffs. It's essentially just a short hallway connecting the Kitchen to the Dining Room, but has plenty of shelves and cupboards for storing food.

Laundry Room: This was once the old pantry, but was converted into a Laundry Room. It has a washer and dryer, and a small table for folding clothes.

Deck: The deck is the newest edition, and appears to be around twenty years old. It is big and sturdy, with a latticework around below the deck to keep people and animals from going under. Normally, there would be a gate to give access to it, but that is strangely missing.

FPI: The Show

Dmitry's body is buried under here.

The Satler House - Second Floor

Master Bedroom: This is the biggest bedroom. It has a window overlooking the ocean, and a bay window overlooking the driveway. Like all the rooms, it has a fireplace. Between this room and Jodie's Room is a small hallway that sports two small linen closets. This supplies the upstairs with all of the sheets and bedspreads for the house.

Jodie's Bedroom: This room is bright and cheerful. It is filled with stuffed animals, games and other toys a six-year-old girl would have.

Guest Bedroom #1: This is the larger of the two guest bedrooms. Otherwise, it looks very similar to it. This room has two twin beds and three windows to give a great view of the yard and the distant dirt road. In addition, it has a comfortable chair, a bureau, and an end table.

Guest Bedroom #2: This room is smaller than the other guest room, but it has a great view of the ocean that the other room is lacking. It's nicely decorated, and has one twin bed, a comfortable chair, a bureau, and an end table.

Satler House - Attic

The attic is merely a crawlspace area with some room for storage. The Satlers have put several boxes of items up there, and they are all piled near the one trap door entrance located in the second floor ceiling in the main hallway.

Satler House - Basement

The basement is nothing more than a cement two-room basement. It is empty except for a furnace and some tools. It is only accessible via a bulkhead door on the outside of the house. There is nothing special about this room.

The Boathouse

The boathouse is big enough to house a medium-sized motor boat or sailboat. Its roof is fifteen feet above sea level at high tide, and nearly twenty feet at low tide. There is one door to the boathouse on one side, and a large garage-style door on the landward end, to allow a

FPI: The Show

trailer to back into the boathouse. The seaward end has a large opening that has no door. A dock-like walkway lines both of the long sides of the house, each one sporting several rusted metal ladders to give access to the boats during low tide. The boathouse is twenty-five feet wide by forty feet long. It is structurally sound, but is in dire need of maintenance. It smells musty, and there is much mold and mildew.

Anyone looking into the water with a light will see some color under the water. It will be dim, and hard to tell, but it will be there. One would have to dive down to identify it. This is, of course, the Tsulova's car, with Sofia's remains inside it. The roof of the car is ten feet under the water.

The Brody's figured that if they owned the house, they could easily prevent anyone from finding it. Besides, they intended to remove the evidence once everyone had forgotten about it. Unfortunately for them, they had never gotten around to it.

There are no boats currently docked here, but there are some equipment lying around, including old rope, rotted sails, empty fuel cans, and other miscellaneous gear.

Prison

Allan Brody is incarcerated in a prison about twenty miles inland from Cutler Beach. It is not a big prison, but otherwise appears normal. It is dark and dingy, and very cheerless. The receptionists are friendly, and although the rest of the staff is gruff, they are still helpful friendly enough.

No one likes Brody. He is a big mouth and complains a lot. He gives the guards as much trouble as he can without being punished. He is smart-mouthed and irritable. He has never mentioned the Tsulovas or the house. He may be a drunk and a murderer, but he is not stupid.

The staff will be as helpful as they can, but they really have little to tell, except to give them a good idea of Brody's personality.

Brody House

Karen and Neal Brody live in a small ranch on the outskirts of town. The yard is very small, and poorly maintained. Weeds run rampant and the grass is brown in spots. There is a small front porch with old wicker chairs on it. During the day or evening, Karen is likely to be sitting there with a drink. The house is in general disrepair, but is tidy. Neil is responsible for the few messes, which consist mostly of dirty clothes on the floors and furniture, and food left out on the counters. When visiting, Karen will busy herself by picking up these messes.

Town Businesses

All town businesses and offices are small and quaint. Their décor tries to give a professional feel with a homey New England charm. The people there are friendly and helpful, with heavy New England accents.

The Acts

The acts are where the story is played out. Like all TV shows, the flow of the episode has been planned out ahead of time. You should try to keep the actors focused on the beats of these acts. Of course, they are liable to stray somewhat from it, but if you keep the pace moving, they should stay pretty close on track. It is quite possible that they may skip some of the beats, or that they may play some out in the wrong order. That's okay. Just be careful, because many of the beats deliver clues that will help them solve the mystery.

The order of acts two and three can easily be swapped or even combined as though they were one big act. Although this may not be right for all shows, this episode will still work fine that way.

Act 1: A Haunted House

Beat 1: On their way to the Satlers, their van is stuck in the mud during a rain storm when they try to avoid hitting Mr. Powell. Powell points them to the Satlers' driveway.

Beat 2: The introduction to the Satler family, and settling down for bed.

Beat 3: Some of the cast see some ghosts.

Beat 4: At breakfast, the Satlers get shaken and scared when they can't find keys to their pickup.

Beat 5: They go to the private beach for a swim, and see the roof of the boathouse beyond the rock wall.

Beat 6: The Satlers finally confess about the ghosts.

Act 2: A Mystery

Beat 1: Interview townsfolk, and neighbors.

Beat 2: Research at the library to find out the history of the house.

Beat 3: Interview Karen Brody.

Beat 4: Interview the Detective Carter.

Act 3: Ghost Hunting

Beat 1: Hunting using EMF, monitors, motion sensors, etc.

Beat 2: Watching a tea party with Jodie and Sofia.

Beat 3: The Séance.

FPI: The Show

Act 4: Stealing the Evidence

Beat 1: Brody boys show up at boathouse with a boat to steal the submerged car.

Beat 2: Sofia appears to lead them to the beach stairs.

Beat 3: The Brodys try to pull the car out of the boathouse and into the deeper water.

Beat 4: A fight with the Brodys and hopefully their capture.

Beat 5: Finding Dmitry.

Tag

Tying loose ends and ending the episode.

Act 1: A Haunted House

The goal of this act is to set the mood and introduce the plot. It will focus on the house and the ghosts within. By the end of the act, the cast should realize that they have a mystery on their hands that must be solved in order to put the spirits to rest.

Beat 1

You can play this act out as a full scene. It should be the first scene of the episode.

> On their way to the Satlers, their van is stuck in the mud during a rain storm when they try to avoid hitting Mr. Powell. Powell points them to the Satlers' driveway.
>
> It is night and pouring rain. The cast has been driving in their van for almost the entire day, and it has been raining the whole time. It is now dark, and wet and miserable, and they are all tired and cramped from the drive.
>
> About a half hour ago, they drove through the center of Carver Beach, Maine, and are now in search of the Satler house, which is on the outskirts along the coast. They cannot see the coast, but are driving up a dirt road surrounded by woods. The van's headlights reflect off the pouring rain, making visibility almost nil.
>
> Suddenly, something bright yellow shoots across the road in front of the van, startling the driver.

Have the driver make a Drive Car skill test. If his test is successful, he will lose control of the van, and go off the road. Luckily, he misses the tree that he was heading for, and is now only stuck in the mud on the side of the road. If he fails the test, he hits the tree. No one is hurt, but the van is damaged and needs about one day's worth of repair work.

> The van has now stopped, and you are all recovering from the shock of the sudden development, when there's a knock on the front passenger window. An old weathered man in yellow rain slicker and matching rain hat is standing at the door, knocking on it. "You okay in there?" you can hear him asking through the closed window.

He will introduce himself as Charlie Powell, and is a fisherman that lives only three houses up the road on the left. He is very friendly and neighborly, and will help them try to get unstuck. All attempts will fail, and will leave anyone who tries soaked and covered with mud.

Mr. Powell will ask them where they are going. When told, he'll tell them that the Satlers' driveway is only about thirty feet up the road. He will point through the trees on the right side of the road, "See them lights over there? Well, those are the Satlers'. Couldn't a picked a better place to get stuck." He will then bid farewell, offer an invitation to come and visit, and then head off up the road, seeming right at home in the rain.

Beat 2

Jim and Catherine Satler will be waiting by the front door for them. They've been expecting them for a while now, and were wondering what happened. They will be glad to see them arrive. Jim will say that the weather is supposed to be great tomorrow, and will volunteer to help them free the van in the morning.

Catherine will find them clean, dry clothes to wear and will then show them to their rooms. There are two guest rooms that will be divided between the men and women of the cast. Jim will give them leave to make themselves at home, in case any of them would want to check out the library or rest in the living room. Then, the Satlers will wish them all a good night and go to bed.

Beat 3

What the cast sees that night depends on what they do. You should arrange things so that at least one of them sees Natalia making her rounds. If no one tries to stay awake, you could have one of them wake up at the right moment. Natalia will enter both bedrooms and make the rounds. One of the cast members may wake up with the sudden chill that the ghost creates as she silently searches for Sofia. Natalia will ignore them all, and simply continue with her search.

If Jelena tries to communicate with Natalia, the ghost will respond, and will speak urgently to her in Russina. Unfortunately, the sound of her voice will only come out as ELF, so no one will hear her. She will only be aware of Jelena. She will try to get Jelena to help her find her daughter.

Beat 4

At breakfast the next morning, Catherine will suggest going to the private beach for a swim or walk. Jim will volunteer to take his pickup truck to the van to help get it out of the mud. He will not be able to find the keys. He and Catherine will behave as though they are upset and scared about it. Pick one of the cast members to see the keys on top of the dining room hutch, just dangling over the edge.

They should all have no trouble rescuing the van. If it had hit the tree, it will need to be taken to the garage, and Jim will make the necessary arrangements. Otherwise, they will pull it out and get the van into the driveway within an hour.

Beat 5

Everyone swims from the dock at the bottom of the stairs. Catherine chooses a time when the tide is high, so that they cannot walk along the beach. The importance of this beat is to have the cast see the boathouse when describing the beach. This will get the boathouse in their minds when doing their investigation.

Beat 6

Catherine wants to talk about the ghosts. She will find a time when Jim is swimming with Jodie and will then tell at least one cast member the whole story. She will also explain how Jim feels about the situation, so that they will tread lightly.

Act 2: A Mystery

The goal of this act is to allow the cast to investigate the history of the house in order to find out who the Tsulovas were and how and why they died. Solving the case is vital to removing the ghosts.

NOTE: The Satlers know very little about the house's history. They know they bought it from Karen Brody for a very good price, but that is pretty much all they know.

Beat 1

The characters can go and talk to various townsfolk who might know about the history of the house. They now know Charlie Powell, so they can ask him. He will tell them about the Tsulovas, and their murder.

Beat 2

The library will have much more information and will be able to give them the official story of the Tsulova murders.

NOTE: A Fair Occult Knowledge skill test will make the character feel that the details of the satanic ritual just do not sound right. A Good skill test will make him realize that it is definitely not satanic. A Great or higher skill test will make the character suspect that it was a ruse made by someone who has no knowledge of the occult at all.

Beat 3

As her character sheet explains, she will tell them her whole story regarding the house. She knows nothing of her family's involvement, and will be angry if the cast accuses her husband or children.

Beat 4

He will give the same report as the official one, but will agree that there are holes in the story. He will explain his misgivings as described in his character sheet.

Act 3: Ghost Hunting

The goal of this act is to study the ghosts and their phenomena. This is where the FPI does its thing.

Beat 1

Jim will grudgingly allow them to set up cameras, sensors and other gear, and will partake in a séance, if invited. Here are some of the results:

— The motion sensors will not detect anything, except perhaps the moving of items during the night by Roman and Anton.

— The cameras on normal spectrum will not detect anything, but infrared will. Any time-lapse photography on a specific area will show an extremely vague and blurry image of a ghost if one passed by there.

— EMF will read high levels of activity in the foyer, and moderate elsewhere.

— ELF recordings created at night will capture various sounds as described in the appropriate beats and ghostly character descriptions.

Beat 2

Any attempt to spy on one of Jodie's tea parties will show that she is having tea with what appears to be an imaginary friend named Sofia. However, if any of the techniques used in Beat 1 are used, they will record higher levels. For hearing Sofia's voice, refer to Sofia's character description.

Beat 3

This one may only happen if someone plays Jelena or another Sensitive with the Séance ritual skill. As described in the Ghosts section above, a séance can be performed to cause one of the spirits to appear. That spirit will be able to speak with the one performing the ritu-

FPI: The Show

al, but only that person. Refer to both the Sensitive Power in Chapter Eleven: The Paranormal, and the Ghosts section above for details on how to conduct the séance.

Act 4: Stealing the Evidence

Beat 1

The Brody boys will plan to use a motorboat to pull the Tsulova's car that is submerged in the boathouse out into the deeper waters of the bay. They will show up late at night, at an appropriately theatrical moment. They will have one spotlight and perhaps one or two flashlights. They will shine the spotlight into the boathouse, and Neil will back the boat in as Kevin stands on the hood of the car, with water up to his waist, ready to attach a rope with a hook to the car's bumper. Once the motorboat has backed in enough, Kevin will need to dive underwater to do it. He has an underwater flashlight, bathing suit, goggles and snorkel for the task.

It is important that one of the cast members sees the light at the boathouse.

If the Brodys do not find out about the investigation, then they will not try this. It would be best if they do, however, because it will add a touch of action to the episode.

Beat 2

This can be optional if you need to coax the cast into going to the boathouse or to at least put them into a position for seeing the Brodys' light. This will always be at night, and preferably when the Brodys are making their late-night escapade.

Sofia can appear in the foyer and be seen to run in terror out the front door. She will run straight to the old staircase leading down the cliff to the beach. It would be best to say it is low tide, so that they can run along the beach. She will stop where she was killed, and start looking for her teddy. If anyone actively searches the area, he can make a Great Notice skill test to find the teddy. It will be hidden among the rocks and weeds beside the stairs.

At this vantage on the stairs, the light at the boathouse will be very obvious, and no Notice tests will be required.

Beat 3

This will not be an easy job for the Brodys for two reasons: the car is heavy, full of water, and sunken into the mud, and Neil is drunk. Eventually, they may succeed, but it will take at least an hour of fighting with it and the revving of the motorboat's engine can be heard at the house, with perhaps some Notice tests.

Beat 4

The Brodys will resist any attempt at capture. If surprised, Kevin will most likely dive into the water and try to swim away. Neil will immediately gun the engine and try to get away. This can go badly for them if Kevin is still holding the rope, or if it is attached to the car. Remember, Neil is drunk! He will try to flee with the boat even if you have a gun aimed at him.

Firing a gun or any other ranged weapon will suffer a -1 penalty due to the darkness.

Beat 5

Here are some clues regarding the whereabouts of Dmitry's body:

— The deck is a new addition put in by Allan Brody himself right after they bought the house.

— EMF levels will be great on and around the deck.

— Dmitry's ghost will go to the door to the deck and will stand there staring out the window.

— You can have the ghost that was summoned to the séance say things (within the context of its time of death) that can give them a clue to his location. After all, they can hear you and they know his location, but they cannot do anything about it directly.

Technically, if the car is recovered, the police will find Sofia's remains, as well as the baseball bat used to bludgeon Anton and Roman. This will be enough evidence to implicate Allan and his boys, especially if they are caught trying to remove the evidence. If the cast just seems unable to find it, you can always have them get a call from Jim at the end of the episode where he tells them that the police finally found Dmitry's remains.

The Tag

It is always a good idea to end the episode with a scene that summarizes the events, and adds closure. This could include any of the following events (or you can make up your own):

— A farewell conversation with the Satlers and all else involved.

— Seeing Sofia and Dmitry in an upstairs window waving to the cast as they drive off.

— One of the cast receives a call on his cellphone. It's another FPI member telling them about a new case (the next episode). This is nice because it will give the actors a teaser of the plot of the next episode.

— The cast could summarize the data they collected and what they learned from the investigation. Some of what they learned might not be objective enough to go into a report.

— Jelena hears Sofia say goodbye to her in her head.

Character Concept Questionnaire

1. What is your name? _____
2. How old are you? _____
3. What do you do for a living? _____
4. Where were you born? _____
5. Why did you choose that career path? _____
   _____
   _____
   _____

6. What is your key trait? _____
7. What was your family life like growing up? _____
   _____
   _____
   _____

8. Are you athletic or studious? Why/why not? _____
   _____
   _____
   _____
   _____

9. What physical marks do you have? _____
   _____
10. What are your strengths? _____
    _____
11. What are your weaknesses? _____
    _____
    _____
    _____

12. What is your favorite quote? _____
    _____
    _____
    _____

13. What is one event that best defines who you are: _____
    _____
    _____
    _____
    _____
    _____

Character Creation Cheat Sheet

Attributes
Brawn
Agility
Stamina
Reasoning
Perception
Will

Free Traits & Levels	
Attributes	3
Skills	30
Gifts	1
Faults	0
Powers	0*
*Will vary by genre	

Misc Default Values	
Luck	3
Scale	0
Income	Fair

All of these traits can be increased and decreased by taking gifts and faults.

Cost for Specific Skill Levels		
Desired Level	Non-Existent	Poor
Superb	7	5
Great	6	4
Good	5	3
Fair	4	2
Mediocre	3	1
Poor	2	0
Terrible	1	-1

Cost for Shifting Traits

1 attribute level = 3 skill levels

1 gift = 6 skill levels

1 gift = 2 attribute levels

Table 4-1: Gifts

Adrenaline Rush	Foreign Tech	Quick Reflexes*
Always Keep Your Cool	Grapevine (pick type)*	Rapid Reload
Ambidexterity	High Pain Threshold*	Refuge*
Animal Empathy	Increased Income*	Savoir-Faire
Artful Dodger	Inheritance *	Shot on the Run
Attractive*	Keen Sense (pick one)*	Single minded
Beautiful speaking voice	Lucky*	Skill Specialization
Blind-Fight	Never forget a feature (pick one)	Stunning Fist
Born to Money	No Identity	Sucker Punch*
Contact (pick one)*	Offensive Driver	Tough Hide*
Danger Sense*	Passionate (pick one)	Trustworthy
Defensive Driver	Patron (pick one person)	Two-Weapon Fighting
Diplomatic Immunity	Perfect Timing	Well-Traveled
Famous	Presumed Dead	
Favor (pick one person)	Quick Draw	

* These gifts can stack.

Table 4-2: Faults

Absent-Minded	Cursed	Hunted	Multiple Personality	Softhearted
Addiction	Decreased Income	Hunting	Obligation	Stubborn
Alienated	Defeated	Impulsive	Obsession	Submissive
Ambitious	Easily Distracted	Indecisive	Outlaw	Tunnel Vision
Amnesia	Enemy	Intolerant	Overconfident	Unlucky
Amorous Heartbreaker	Finicky	Lazy	Overly Talkative	Vain
Attention Hog	Foolish Bravery	Lecherous	Pacifist	Vendetta
Blunt & Tactless	Jinxed	Lost or Forbidden Love	Phobia	Violent when enraged
Bossy	Glutton	Low Pain Threshold	Practical Joker	Vow
Code of Behavior	Gossip	Machismo	Quick-Tempered	Worry Wart
Compulsive Behavior	Greedy	Manic-Depressive	Rivalry	Zealous behavior
Coward	Gullible	Melancholy	Secret Identity	
Curious	Handicap	Mistaken Identity	Socially awkward	

Table 3-1: Mental Skills

Skill	Default	Skill	Default	Skill	Default
Animal Care	NE	Engineering (pick a type)	NE	Profile	NE
Appraise	Poor	First Aid	Poor	Psychology	NE
Area Knowledge	Poor	Forgery	Poor	Read Lips	Poor
Autopsy	NE	Hypnosis	NE	Religion (pick one)	Poor
Business Sense	Poor	Interpret Language	NE	Repair Device (pick one)	Poor
Computer Use	NE	Knowledge (pick one)	Poor	Research	Poor
Concentrate	Poor	Language (pick one)	NE	Ritual (pick one)	NE
Cryptozoology	Poor	Nature Lore	Poor	Science (pick one)	NE
Culture (pick one)	Poor	Navigate	Poor	Streetsmarts	Poor
Decipher Script	NE	Notice	Poor	Surgery	NE
Demolitions	NE	Occult Knowledge	Poor	Surveillance	Poor
Diagnose	NE	Pantomime	Poor	Train Animal	NE
Direction Sense	Poor	Parapsychology	NE	Treat Injury	NE
Disable Device (pick one)	NE	Photography (pick type)	Poor	UFOlogy	Poor
Disguise	Poor	Primitive Tools	Poor	Write	Poor

Table 3-2: Physical Skills

Skill	Default	Skill	Default	Skill	Default
Acrobatics	Poor	Hide Traces	Poor	Shadow	Poor
Balance	Poor	Jump	Poor	Sleight of Hand	Poor
Brawl	Poor	Martial Art (pick one)	NE	Stealth	Poor
Breaking & Entering	Poor	Mimic Animal Noises	Poor	Swim	Poor
Climb	Poor	Pick Lock	Poor	Throw	Poor
Craft (pick type of item)	Poor	Pick Pocket	Poor	Track	Poor
Dodge	Poor	Pilot (pick craft)	NE	Weapon (pick one)	Poor
Drive (pick vehicle)	Poor	Ride Animal (pick one)	NE	Zero-G Maneuver	Poor
Escape Artist	Poor	Run	Poor		
Fish	Poor	Sail	Poor		

Table 3-3: Social Skills

Skill	Default	Skill	Default	Skill	Default
Bluff	Poor	Haggle	Poor	Perform	Poor
Camaraderie	Poor	Hold Your Liquor	Poor	Persuade	Poor
Diplomacy	Poor	Innuendo	Poor	Seduce	Poor
Etiquette	Poor	Interrogate	Poor	Sense Motive	Poor
Gamble	Poor	Intimidate	Poor	Tall Tales	Poor
Gather Information	Poor	Oratory	Poor	Uplift Spirits	Poor

Table 5-1: Standard of Living Resource Tickets

Income	Tickets	Description
Superb	10	Rich: owns more than one home, vehicles, lots of expensive items, etc.
Great	7	Upper middle-class: owns big house, multiple new cars, plenty of big items, etc.
Good	5	Middle-class: owns house or condo, new car, some big items, etc.
Fair	4	Lower middle-class: Rents a decent apartment or owns a small house or trailer, owns a used car, and a few big items.
Mediocre	3	Lower class: rents an apartment, owns an old car, and a couple big items.
Poor	2	Poor: rents a room, has no car, and has little to no big items.
Terrible	1	Homeless: owns only a handful of small items.

Name:

Profession _____

Birthplace _____

Sex _____ Age _____ Race _____

Height _____ Weight _____

Eyes _____ Hair _____

Luck _____ Scale _____ EP _____

Income _____

Attributes

Brawn _____

Agility _____

Stamina _____

Reasoning _____

Perception _____

Will _____

NP

Character Concept (Personality & Background)

Skills

Skill	Level	Skill	Level
_____	_____	_____	_____
_____	_____	_____	_____
_____	_____	_____	_____
_____	_____	_____	_____
_____	_____	_____	_____
_____	_____	_____	_____
_____	_____	_____	_____
_____	_____	_____	_____
_____	_____	_____	_____
_____	_____	_____	_____
_____	_____	_____	_____

Result Levels & Trait Costs

Num.	Level	EP Cost (Skills)
+3	Superb	8
+2	Great	4
+1	Good	2
+0	Fair	1
-1	Mediocre	1
-2	Poor (Skill Default)	1
-3	Terrible	1

Damage = RD + OF - DF

 RD = Relative Degree

 OF = Offensive Factor

  (or Weapon Strength)

 DF = Defensive Factor

Wounds

1, 2	3, 4	5, 6	7, 8	9+
Scratch	**Light Wound**	**Severe Wound**	**Incapacitated**	**Near Death**
○ ○ ○	○	○	○	○

Shows & Episodes

Show: _____

Episodes:
_____
_____
_____
_____
_____
_____
_____
_____
_____
_____
_____
_____
_____
_____

Props

Resource Tickets: _____
_____
_____
_____
_____
_____
_____
_____
_____
_____
_____
_____
_____

Gifts

_____
_____
_____
_____
_____
_____
_____

Faults

_____
_____
_____
_____
_____
_____
_____

Powers

_____
_____
_____
_____
_____
_____
_____
_____

Weapons & Armor

Weapon	Strength	Weapon	Strength
_____	_____	_____	_____
_____	_____	_____	_____
_____	_____	_____	_____
_____	_____	_____	_____
_____	_____	_____	_____

Armor	Modifier	Armor	Modifier
_____	_____	_____	_____
_____	_____	_____	_____

Name:

Brawn _____ Agility _____ Stamina _____ Reasoning _____
Perception _____ Will _____ Luck _____ Scale _____

Skill	Level	Skill	Level	Skill	Level
_____	_____	_____	_____	_____	_____
_____	_____	_____	_____	_____	_____
_____	_____	_____	_____	_____	_____

Gifts _____

Faults _____

Name:

Brawn _____ Agility _____ Stamina _____ Reasoning _____
Perception _____ Will _____ Luck _____ Scale _____

Skill	Level	Skill	Level	Skill	Level
_____	_____	_____	_____	_____	_____
_____	_____	_____	_____	_____	_____
_____	_____	_____	_____	_____	_____

Gifts _____

Faults _____

Name:

Brawn _____ Agility _____ Stamina _____ Reasoning _____
Perception _____ Will _____ Luck _____ Scale _____

Skill	Level	Skill	Level	Skill	Level
_____	_____	_____	_____	_____	_____
_____	_____	_____	_____	_____	_____
_____	_____	_____	_____	_____	_____

Gifts _____

Faults _____

Name:

Brawn _____ Agility _____ Stamina _____ Reasoning _____
Perception _____ Will _____ Luck _____ Scale _____

Skill	Level	Skill	Level	Skill	Level
_____	_____	_____	_____	_____	_____
_____	_____	_____	_____	_____	_____
_____	_____	_____	_____	_____	_____

Gifts _____

Faults _____

CARNIVORE GAMES

FOR FREE GOODIES AND UP TO THE MINUTE NEWS ON UPCOMING PRODUCTS, VISIT

WWW.CARNIVOREGAMES.COM

LOOK FOR THESE TYPES OF PRODUCTS ON THE WEB SITE:

Check out Carnivore on the web!

Shows

These are complete "campaing" settings with at least one fully defined show storyline and an episode guide of season one.

Genres

These take one genre of television and focus on it, going into detail on how they are made. It explains how you can make your own Now Playing shows within the genre. This comes with one small show defined to give you something to have fun with.

Episodes

These are the actual adventures that you can play. Make your own or buy a premade one. It's your choice!

Index

A

Absent-Minded 52
Acceleration 104
Acrobatics 28
Act 144, 147
Acting 118
Action 136
Acts 130
Addiction 53
Adding Skills 27
Adrenaline Rush 47
Advancing Characters 24
Adventure 136
Agility 16
Alien Races 181
Alienated 53
All-Out Attack 98
All-Out Defense 98
Always Keep Your Cool 47
Ambidexterity 47
Ambitious 53
Ammo 68
Amnesia 53
Amorous Heartbreaker 54
Animal Care 28
Animal Empathy 47
Animals 23
Apparitions 176
Appraise 28
Area Knowledge 28
Armor 75, 102
Artful Dodger 47, 137
Assault Rifle 68
Associated Skills 22
Attack Roll 97
Attacks, Simultaneous 97
Attention Hog 54
Attractive 47
Attributes 16, 18, 92
Automatic Death 101
Automatic Success 91
Autopsy 29
Availability of Powers 22
Axe 71

B

Balance 29
Bazooka 68
Beasts 23
Beat 144, 149
Beat, Season 112
Beautiful Speaking Voice 47
Bicycle 76
Blast Level 99
Blast Radius 99
Blind, Fighting 98
Blind-Fight 47
Bluff 30
Blunt and Tactless 54
Bossy 54
Bow 68
Brawl 30
Brawn 16
Breaking & Entering 30
Bruise 102
Bursts 98
Business Sense 30

C

C-4 73
Called Shots 98
Camaraderie 30
Camel 81
Cameo 152
Campaigns 145
Canoe 76
Car, Compact 77
Cartoons 142
Cast 5, 9, 134
Leadin 9
Leading 134
Supporting 134
Cast, Supporting 112, 123, 152
Cat 82
Chain Mail 75
Changing Skills 28
Character Concept 14
Characters, creating 18
Characters, Supporting 118
Choosing Skills 26
Chupacabra 178
Clairvoyance 172
Claymore Mine 73
Climb 30
Close Encounters 181
Club 71
Cobra 82
Code of Behavior 54
Combat 94
Melee 95
Non-lethal 101
Rounds 95
Combat Powers 22
Combat, Large Ship 132
Compulsive Behavior 54
Computer Use 30
Concealable Vest 75
Concealment, Item 94
Concentration 30, 107
Contact 47
Cop Shows 137
Courtroom Drama 138
Coverage Level 102
Coward 54
Craft 31
Creature Hunt 141
Crime Drama 138
Critical Failures 91
Critical Successes 91
Crocodile 83
Crop Circles 182
Crossbow 68
Cryptozoology 31
Culture 31
Curious 55
Cursed 55

D

Dagger 71
Damage 100
Damage Capacity 100
Damage Reduction 102
Danger Sense 48
Dart Pistol 69
Dart Rifle 69
Daytime Dramas 139
Daze 102
Death 100
Decipher Script 31
Decreased Income 55
Default Level 19, 26
Defeated 55
Defensive Driver 48
Defensive Factor 100
Deleting Skills 28
Demolitions 31
Demonic Possession 177
Derringer 69
Diagnosis 31, 103
Difficulty Level 90
Diplomacy 31
Diplomatic Immunity 48
Directing 110
Directing, Challenges of 121
Direction Sense 32
Disable Device 32
Disguise 32
Divination 108
Dodge 32
Dog 84
Dramas 138
Drive 33
Dynamite 74

E

Easily Distracted 55
Ectoplasm 176
Electro Magnetic Frequency 160
Electronic Voice Phenomena 160, 177
Elephant 84
EMF. See Electro Magnetic Frequency
EMF Gauge 177
Empathy 172
Enemy 55
Engineering 33
Episode 5, 144
Episodic Drama 128
Escape Artist 33
Etiquette 33
EVP. See Electronic Voice Phenomena
Exorcism 177
Experience Points 24
Experienced Characters 20
Explosives 73, 99
Using Barriers 100
Extra-Terrestrials 180

F

Failures, Spectacular 92
Falcon 84
Famous 48
Fatigue 102
Faults 17
Faults, determining 19
Favor 48
Fear 94
Finicky 55
First Aid 33
Fish 33
Foolish Bravery 55
Forbidden Love 58
Foreign Tech 48
Forgery 33
Formats 128
Formats, Episode 146
Fortune Tellers 173
Foundation for Paranormal Investigation 156
Chapters 158
FPI. See Foundation for Paranormal Investigation
Free Levels 18
Fudge Cards 90
Fudge Dice 90
Fullsize Sedan 77

G

Gambling 33
Game System 5
Game Systems, Converting 108
Gather Information 34
Genre 135
Ghost Hunting 160
Ghosts 176
Gifts 17, 46
Gifts, determining 19
Glutton 56
Gossip 56
Grapevine 49
Greedy 56
Grenades 74
Grizzly Bear 85
Gullible 56
Guns 98

H

Haggle 34
Handicap 57
Handle Mana Skill 106
Handling 105
Hatchet 72
Healing 103
Detailed 103
Simple 103
Hide Traces 34
High Pain Threshold 49
High Tech Devices 132
Hold Your Liquor 34
Holdout Pistol 69
Horse 85
Hunted 57
Hunting 57
Hurt 102
Hypnosis 34

I

Impulsive 57
Incapacitated 101
Income 64
Increased Income 50
Incubi 176
Indecisive 57
Inheritance 50
Initiative 95
Injury 100
Innuendo 34
Interpret Language 35
Interrogation 36
Intimidate 36
Intolerant 57

J

Jersey Devil 178
Jet Fighter 77
Jinxed 57
Jump 36
Jury-Rigging 39

K

Keen Sense 50
Kevlar Vest 75
Knockout 102
Knowledge 36

L

Language 36
Large Ships 132
Laser Pistol 69
Lazy 58
Leather Armor 76
Lecherous 58
Legendary Attributes 18
Legendary Traits 18
Levitate Object 108
Light Wound 101
Lion 85
Literature 36
Loch Ness Monster 178
Lost or Forbidden Love 58
Low Pain Threshold 58
Luck 19, 92, 137
Luck Points 120
Luck Rolls 94
Lucky 20, 50

M

Mace Spray 72
Machete 72
Machine Gun 70
Heavy 70
Machine Pistol 70
Machismo 58
Magic 106
Magical Aptitude Power 106
Magnum Revolver 71
Mana 106, 107
Manic-Depressive 58
Martial Art 36
Martial Arts 136
Medical Drama 139
Melancholy 58
Melee Combat. See Melee
Men In Black. See Unidentified Flying Objects
Mental Skills 28
Meta Gifts 46
Meta Skills 27
Metagaming 123
Midsize Sedan 78
Mimic Animal Noises 37
Miniseries 9
Mistaken Identity 59
MK-ULTRA 172
Modern Day Thriller 141
Modifiers, Situation 90
Monsters 23
Motorboat 78
Motorcycle 78
Multiple Combatants 97
Multiple Personality 59
Murder Mystery 140
Musket 70
Muzzle Loader Pistol 70
Mysteries 140

N

Nature Lore 37
Navigation 37
Near Death 101
Never Forget a Feature 50
No Identity 50
Non-Human Races 22
Notice 37
Nunchaku 72

O

Obligation 59
Obsession 60
Occult Knowledge 37
Occult Thriller 140
Offensive Driver 50
Offensive Factor 100
Oratory 37
Orbs 177
Outlaw 60
Overconfident 60
Overly Talkative 60

P

Pacifist 60
Pantomime 37
Paranormal 172
Parapsychology 37
Passionate 50
Patron 51
Perception 16
Perfect Timing 51
Perform 38
Persuasion 38
Phobia 60
Photography 38
Pick Lock 38
Pick Pocket 38
Pickup Truck 79
Pilot 38, 146
Plate Mail 76
Poltergeists 176
Power Gaming 111, 120
Powers 17, 22, 131
Practical Joker 61
Precognition 173
Presumed Dead 51
Primitive Tools 38
Profile 38
Project Blue Book 182
Psychic Powers 172
Psychokinesis 173
Psychology 39
Purchasing A Power 22

Q

Quick Draw 51
Quick Reflexes 51
Quick-Tempered 61

R

Race Car 80
Range 68
Rapid Reload 51
Rapier 72
Read Lips 39
Reality Shows 128
Reasoning 16
Referee 110
Refuge 51
Relationship Wheel 135
Relative Degree 91, 100
Religions 39
Repair Device 39
Research 40
Revolver 71
Ride Animal 40
Rifle 71
Riot Armor 76
Ritual 40
Ritual Magic 175
Ritual Skill 106
Rivalry 61
Rolls, Secret 91
Romance 139
Roswell 182
Run 40
Running, Shooting while 98

S

Sail 40
Sailboat 81
Sasquatch 179
Savoir-Faire 51
Scale 20
Scale Multipliers 20
Scene 115, 117, 144, 149
Scene, Preparing 112
Science Fiction 141
Scratch 101
Season 9, 145
Season Finale 146
Season Opener 146
Secret Identity 61
Seduction 40
Semi-Auto Pistol 71
Sense Motive 42
Sensitive 174
Serial 9, 129
Series 6
Session, Ending 124
Session, Preparing for 110
Set 152
Setting Elements 130
Severe Wound 101
Shadow 42
Shadow People 176
Shields 97
Shifting Levels 18
Shot on the Run 51
Shotgun 71
Show 5
Single Minded 61
Single-Engine Airplane 80
Situation Comedy 128, 139
Skill Specialization 51
Skills 16, 92
Untrained 92
Skills, determining 19
Sleight of Hand 42
Smilodon 86
Soap Operas. See Daytime Dramas
Socially Awkward 61
Soft-Hearted 61
Speed 105
Spells 107
Spells, Casting 106
Spin-Off 129
Spirit World 176
Sports Car 80
Stacking Gifts 46
Staff 72
Stamina 16
Standard of Living 64
Stealth 42
Storyteller 110
Streetsmarts 42
Stubborn 62
Stun 102
Stun Gun 71
Sub-Machine Gun 71
Submissive 62
Succubi 176
Sucker Punch 52
Superhero 137
Superpowers 137
Suppressive Fire 99
Surgery 43, 104
Surprise 95
Surveillance 43
Swim 43
Sword 72

T

Tag 131, 145
Tall Tales 43
Tasks, Performing 90
Teaser 131, 144
Technology 131
Telekinesis 174
Telepathy 174
Tests 90
Opposed 91
Unopposed 91
Thrillers 140
Throw 43
Thunderbird 180
Thylacine 180
Tough Hide 52
Track 43
Trailer Truck 80
Train Animal 43
Trait Levels 17
Traits 19
Treat Injury 44
Trustworthy 52
TV Movie 128
Twin-Engine Airplane 81
Two-Weapon Fighting 52

U

UFO. See Unidentified Flying Objects
UFOlogy 44
Unidentified Flying Objects 181
Unlucky 62
Uplift Spirits 44

V

Vain 62
Vehicle 131
Vehicles 76, 104
Velociraptor 86
Vendetta 62
Violent When Enraged 62
Vortex 177

W

Weapon 44
Weapon Strength 68
Weapons 67, 132
Creating 67
Weapons, Drawing 97
Weapons, Loading 97
Well-Traveled 52
Westerns 137
Whip 73
Will 16
Wire Fu 137
Worry Wart 62
Wound Levels 101
Wounds 101
Write 44

Y

Yeti 180

Z

Zealot 62
Zero-G Maneuver 44
Zoo 81